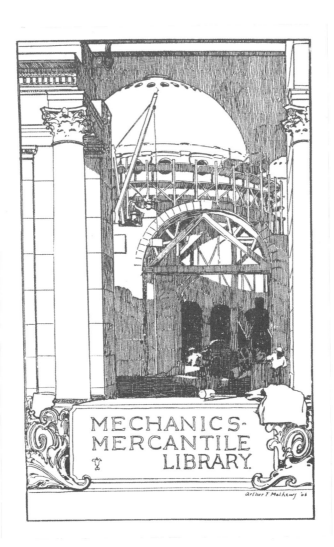

Soldiers and Slaves

SOLDIERS AND SLAVES

*American POWs Trapped by
the Nazis' Final Gamble*

ROGER COHEN

Alfred A. Knopf  New York 2005

THIS IS A BORZOI BOOK
PUBLISHED BY ALFRED A. KNOPF

A portion previously appeared in *The New York Times Magazine*.

Library of Congress Cataloging-in-Publication Data

Cohen, Roger.
Soldiers and slaves:
American POWs trapped by the Nazis' final gamble / Roger Cohen.—1st ed.
p.   cm.
Includes bibliographical references and index.
ISBN 0-375-41410-X (alk. paper)
1. Berga (Concentration camp) 2. World War, 1939–1945—Prisoners and prisons, German.
3. World War, 1939–1945—Concentration camps—Germany—Berga.
4. World War, 1939–1945—Conscript labor—Germany—Berga.
5. Death marches—Germany. 6. Prisoners of war—United States—Biography.
7. Prisoners of war—Germany—Biography. I. Title.
D805.5.B46C63 2005
940.54'7243'0943184—dc22   2004057691

Manufactured in the United States of America
First Edition

To Bertram Cohen
and to the memory of Charles Guggenheim

*Pain and love—the whole of life, in short—cannot
be looked on as a disease just because they make us suffer.*

—Italo Svevo, *The Conscience of Zeno*

CONTENTS

CHAPTER ONE: The Devil Quotes Scripture 3

CHAPTER TWO: Sucker Punch 18

CHAPTER THREE: The Obedience of Corpses 40

CHAPTER FOUR: The Selection 67

CHAPTER FIVE: Prayer Book and Sword 93

CHAPTER SIX: Walking Shadows 125

CHAPTER SEVEN: Weasels in a Hole 159

CHAPTER EIGHT: The Dying Weeks 186

CHAPTER NINE: Orders from Nowhere 217

Epilogue 250

Notes 271

The Berga Prisoners 285

Acknowledgments 291

Index 293

SOLDIERS AND SLAVES

The Devil Quotes Scripture

A HEAVILY PADLOCKED steel door, topped by a barred vent, swings open, and from the depths of the tunnel a current of cold air is released into the summer haze. All is quiet. The White Elster River flows lazily, flies hovering at its eddying surface. On the far bank, visible through the trees, lies the small eastern German town of Berga. The tranquillity seems real. But it is an illusion.

Germany must be seen in space and in time. To see what is there, it is necessary to see what is hidden. At this spot, the tunnel extends about 150 feet into the tree-covered hillside. Water drips, some of it close by, some deep in the bluff. A few boulders and scattered rocks lie around small pools of water. The shaft, with its jagged walls of black slate, is still and damp.

But beyond the peace lies something else. The sound wells from the depths of the tunnel, advancing across the years. A sound of rending and blasting, of screeching and booming, of screams and pandemonium fills this confined space. The tunnel, perhaps twenty feet high and fifteen feet wide, is peopled now with bedraggled men, their faces blackened with dust, drilling and shoveling and heaving and loading as explosions turn the air into a lacerating gale of fine shards. The fragments penetrate the unprotected mouths of American and European prisoners of the Nazis, cutting their throats, devouring their lungs, weakening them day by day.

The Americans are young, most of them no more than twenty years old, from Ohio and Virginia, New York and California. They have been sucked into a place they cannot comprehend. It is March 1945, the war is almost over, but these GIs are dying at a rate unknown among American prisoners of war elsewhere in Europe. Each day they are herded into the tunnels. They have scarcely been fed, they have no protective clothing, and their cuts are infected, but still they must hold the heavy pneumatic drills against the rock face and bore a hole sufficiently large for the German engineers to insert dynamite.

When the explosion comes, they are pushed back deep into the tunnels. They must pick up the rocks, some of them large and unwieldy, and load them onto small carts that run on a narrow-gauge railroad track. They have no gloves. Their hands are a mess of scratches and wounds. They push the carts down to the river and empty them. If they slow down for a moment, they are beaten by the guards.

One of the Americans is Sanford M. Lubinsky of Lima, Ohio, captured by the Germans at the Battle of the Bulge and brought here because he has been identified as a Jew. Lubinsky, a private in the 28th Infantry Division, has to maneuver the drill. But sometimes his strength gives out: "My arms were coming down slowly. And so it happened that when that SS guy came through inspecting with his whip and his stick, hateful, strutting in, at that time my arms gave way and that drill came falling down. Oh, was he mad! 'You damned Jew,' the SS guard said."

The SS man grabs a shovel. He hits Lubinsky in the back, crushing part of it. He kicks him when he goes down, then takes out his whip. Lubinsky curses the German; he is now beyond caring about his fate. "I didn't care. I thought I was going anyway. The heck with him. What kept me going, I guess, was a fighting hate. I wanted to get out of there. I was going to get out somehow and kill those dirty sons of bitches."

Every afternoon when the sun shines, four or five old women gather on a bench in the main square of Berga. The town is quiet today, too quiet. A flag flaps. Children's voices carry from distant gardens of roses and sunflowers. An air of abandonment pervades the neighborhood. The plasterwork of the town hall is crumbling. The textile factory that once produced kit for the doped and indomitable East German Olympic team is a ghostly sprawl. A new clock scarcely uplifts a redbrick train station that has not been refurbished in decades.

In the west of Germany, after World War II, the past was quickly swept away. All the putrescent ruins of war were removed to make way for shopping centers and slabs of abstract art and homes with geranium-filled window boxes, places so anodyne, so lulled by prosperity, they speak only of a placid existence and the rewards of striving. But the east of Germany is another land. Its postwar Communist rulers could not afford to neuter history with new construction. German pain and the secrets that produced it lie closer to the surface.

Even in summer a brisk breeze may descend from the hills that cradle and conceal this somnolent town, so the women, white-haired but disarmingly vigorous, wear pale cardigans. In their bags they have cushions that they carefully place on the bench when they arrive and carefully fold away upon leaving. Habits such as this are comforting: for them, German twentieth-century life proved unpredictable. The square is also frequented, at times, by spiky-haired punks with folding aluminum scooters, but most of Berga's youth have departed to seek work in the West. Politics here is increasingly the painstaking politics of managing pensioners.

Before Germany was unified in 1990, the men of this region worked in nearby uranium mines that provided raw material for the Soviet nuclear industry; the women worked for the textile plant. Three shifts a day kept people busy around the clock. But both industries, deprived of their markets, collapsed soon after unification, leaving a pall of gloom that the promise of capitalism has scarcely lifted.

The older people here, like these women, lived under a dictatorship, Nazi or Communist, from Hitler's rise to power in 1933 to the fall of the Berlin Wall in 1989. The compliant habits of mind of more than a half century are not easily overcome. The charm of this new Germany of elbowing consumers, Turkish-owned kebab joints, Thrilling Drilling body-piercing stores, and widespread unemployment tends to elude them.

For the old women, the story of Berga is principally about work—its presence or absence. Now many people are idle. But there used to be jobs in the town, even before the war, when the textile factory was in private hands and more than a thousand people worked there. At the time, the business belonged to a family named Englander—Jews, the women note in passing, who disappeared from Berga around the time of World War II. An unhappy thing, the war. But say what you like, one woman remarks, Hitler took people off the streets and put them to work. A generation of Germans had money in their pockets for the first time. They wanted to enjoy it, they wanted to live.

It seemed possible for a time. At first Hitler's war consisted principally of the inebriation of victory, but then came the slow encroachment of a defeat never admitted by the Führer. "Victory or Siberia" said some of the last slogans as Russian and American forces closed in on Berga: desperate bravado. It was in this latter phase, in the final spasm of Nazi rule, as things fell apart, that the war visited Berga in a particular way, one that would mark these women who were witnesses.

The first indication of unusual stirrings came in the late summer of 1944, with the arrival of SS administrative staff led by Lieutenant Willy Hack, who requisitioned the central Ratskeller Hotel as headquarters. Engineers, mining experts, and land surveyors came to Berga, too, inspecting the hills on the far side of the Elster—their topography, their rock formation, their potential to conceal a production facility in a planned underground complex of tunnels and chambers. With the onset of a bitter winter, the rumbling thunder of dynamite charges detonating in the hills could be heard as tunnels were bored.

Such a flurry of activity had been unknown in the town before then; naturally it aroused curiosity. But asking questions—the old women sigh—was dangerous. The notorious Buchenwald camp was less than sixty miles away, and ending up there was easy enough. Still, in so intimate a town, it was impossible to overlook the construction of a concentration camp, on the site of part of the textile factory, between the Elster and its tributary, the Mühlgraben.

The first prisoners destined to work in the tunnels arrived in Berga on November 12, 1944, pitiful, emaciated creatures in striped, pajama-like uniforms, their faces hollow, eyes haunted, movements halting. The women learned later that most of them were European Jews dispatched from Buchenwald. The appearance of these frail figures, aged between thirteen and sixty and barely alive, was shocking. Some of the prisoners stuck newspapers in their pants for warmth. Others put papers around their necks. As a slave-labor force brought to Berga to dig tunnels into the hills, these men left much to be desired because they were so weakened. Still, their number grew to more than one thousand by the end of 1944.

In the vast complex of Nazi camps, the great sprawling labyrinth of detention and death, Berga, code name "Schwalbe 5," amounted to a detail. It was dwarfed by the Buchenwald camp, which held 84,500 prisoners at its Weimar complex by the fall of 1944. The Berga camp did not appear on most World War II maps; its activities were secret and its existence little known. After the war Berga was subsumed into the Soviet-controlled part of Germany, and nobody asked too many questions about its ephemeral little hell. But the camp lived on in these old women's minds, a discomfiting memory shoved aside, awakened only occasionally, perhaps by a wartime photograph of a lighted swastika in the main square of Berga glowing among trees heavy with snow.

A memory, as these women like to describe it now, of helplessness. "*Man muss alles mitmachen*"—"One must participate in everything." The prisoners were behind barbed wire or cordoned off by guards and dogs as they marched. It was impossible to talk to them, let alone help them. When shifts changed they could be seen crossing the Elster, trudging slowly out toward the tunnels being mined in the hills. If ever they passed nearby, the prisoners would put their hands to their mouths, a silent shriek for food. When they could, they would pick from the streets oats intended for the horses or a discarded piece of potato peel or an eggshell. Some local women, like Marie Scheffel, would spill buckets of oats as the prisoners passed. But that sort of impetuous gesture—the women shake their heads—could get you in trouble with the Nazi authorities.

The explosions punctuated the night as the seventeen tunnels were mined. Hundreds of the prisoners died during the brief existence of the Berga camp. The dead, often enough, could be seen as they were trundled through town on wheelbarrows, half covered with pieces of cloth, a frail limb, already stiff, protruding here or there. Better not to look too closely: war makes you mute in the end.

Most of the corpses were dumped in a mass grave in the woods on the other side of town, a place still known as the Jewish cemetery. The old women do not know if all the dead were Jews; the place simply took, and kept, that name. But when asked, they say they do know that many Americans GIs were among the imprisoned at Berga and among those who died here.

In fact, Berga's little secret is that it was perhaps the most intense killing field for American prisoners of war in Europe. To this little town, Jewish American soldiers, U.S. POWs deemed to resemble Jews, so-called troublemakers, and GIs unlucky enough to be picked at random were sent by the Nazis soon after their capture, most of them at the Battle of the Bulge, which began on December 16, 1944. Arriving here on February 13, 1945, three months after that first trainload of starving prisoners from Buchenwald, many of these

Americans, too, were worked to death in the last months of World War II.

Stronger on arrival than the European Jewish captives sent from Buchenwald, the Americans were appalled by the pajama-clad concentration-camp prisoners they saw, so disembodied did they seem, so unseeing, so skeletal. Some Americans said they could hear the bones of these prisoners rattling. But the GIs, too, quickly learned the inexorable arithmetic of Nazi *Vernichtung durch Arbeit*—destruction through work. When day after day the outlay of energy exceeds that consumed, the body wastes away. In the end, survival comes down to calories; calories and, in some measure, the mysteries of the mind.

So it was that beside the gently flowing Elster, as virtually nowhere else in Europe, the fate of captured GIs and persecuted European Jewry intersected, middle America and Mitteleuropa briefly joined in a dance of death. Here, as nowhere else, American Jews understood the fate of European Jews under Hitler. For a period of fifty-two days at Berga—from February 13 to April 5, 1945—and during a death march southward lasting more than two weeks after that, the lot of hundreds of American GIs and hundreds of Jewish survivors of Auschwitz and Buchenwald largely coincided.

To almost all Americans, the Holocaust was an idea that only coalesced after 1945, when the Nazi crime against European Jewry could be seen in its full proportions. But to this group of 350 American soldiers brought to Berga in Hitler's last months, the crime was an immediate, agonizing reality, even if they could not grasp its scope. Of those 350 men, more than 20 percent would die in a little over two months, an attrition rate unknown among American prisoners of war elsewhere on the European continent.

These American soldiers selected for extinction did not know they were part of a last-ditch Nazi effort to offset relentless Allied bombing of German fuel facilities by building underground synthetic-fuel production centers, one of the most important of which was to be at Berga.

On May 30, 1944, in an attempt to stabilize fuel production, Hitler appointed Edmund Geilenberg as *Generalkommissar für die Sofortmassnahme*, or general commissar for immediate measures, at the Reich Ministry for Armament and War Production. Geilenberg's most urgent task was the reconstruction of fuel-production factories destroyed by bombing. By June 22, 1944, German production of airplane fuel had fallen to 632 tons daily, compared with 5,645 tons on May 1. Hitler's order called for "unrelenting energy" in the pursuit of recovered production.

Geilenberg, who had earlier been the manager of a steel factory and head of a special commission for ammunition, presented his program for the decentralization and underground production of synthetic fuel—the so-called *Mineralölsicherungsplan*—on August 1. It was a hugely ambitious project, given the Nazis' plight on both the western and the eastern front by this stage of the war.

The plan called for numerous underground facilities, many with the code name Schwalbe ("swallow"), and gave the highest priority to Schwalbe 5, Berga, where jet-fighter fuel was to be produced. The tunnels were to converge on a central production facility housed in a vast underground chamber. October 1, 1945, was set as the completion date, with the last of eight Schwalbe facilities to be operational by July 1, 1946.

Hitler gave the order for thousands of concentration-camp prisoners to be used in pursuit of this fantastical plan and gave the SS the central role in the selection and exploitation of the prisoners and in the organization of construction. The SS had "full authority" to seek workers for the Geilenberg program in every concentration camp. The contractors for the project at Berga included several mining companies from the region; a firm called Brabag Zeitz was chosen to handle the future fuel production. But the SS was in charge of building the underground Berga facility and finding the workforce to do it.

A problem, as events at Berga would show, was that by late 1944 concentration-camp prisoners were in such a pitiful state that they could scarcely work. The vast Nazi death factory in Poland, doing its murderous business at camps including Sobibor and Treblinka, had largely shut down by this time. Indeed, in the latter part of 1944, only Auschwitz was still operating at full capacity.

By November, Heinrich Himmler, the head of the SS, had decided that the "Jewish question" was essentially solved. The evacuation and destruction of Auschwitz began well before Soviet troops reached the camp on January 27, 1945. The result was that, with the Polish killing centers gone, former Auschwitz prisoners, many of them Hungarian Jews, were dumped into concentration camps in the Reich. Tens of thousands of Jews poured into Buchenwald alone between May 1944 and March 1945. Often they had survived death marches to get there. Some were then moved yet again, to Berga. Their skeletal state helps explain why the SS turned to American GIs to get the job done in the Berga tunnels.

Because speed was of the essence in mining the tunnels that would converge on Berga's central underground production area, Lieutenant Hack, the SS commander, was impatient with the quality of the European Jewish prisoners sent from Buchenwald in November 1944. So shriveled were they, so incapable of productive effort, that Hack busied himself sending many of them back to Buchenwald and demanding replacements.

Before doing so, according to one witness at his postwar trial, Hack would sometimes amuse himself by setting his dog on the prisoners or beating and kicking them. It was in the same spirit that he greeted the Americans who arrived soon afterward, prisoners of war destined to become his slaves.

Hack was thirty-two years old when he came to Berga in 1944. He was born in the southern German town of Reutlingen, near Stuttgart, on March 26, 1912, and had studied building engineering at a technical school in Stuttgart before joining the SS on March 1, 1934. By 1943, after being injured on the eastern front, he was in charge of a major construction project for the SS in the central German town of Ellrich. It was from there he was transferred to Berga to direct the tunnel project.

Ups and downs had marked Hack's SS career. Soon after joining, he applied for a marriage permit but did not receive approval from the SS Race and Settlements Department. He married anyway, on July 20, 1935, causing consternation and an increasingly testy correspondence.

On October 19, 1937, Hack wrote to the Race and Settlements Department, again demanding his marriage permit. His irascible, impatient nature, widely noted at Berga, was already apparent. The letter, with several passages underlined, says: "I do not understand why such a small affair can cause so many problems. I was married three years ago and already have a two-year-old son. If a belated permit should nevertheless be denied me, then I ask to be immediately removed from the SS."

The reply, on October 29, was brusque. "Since you married on July 20, 1935, without receiving permission from the SS Race and Settlements Department, we do not see why your present application should receive any preferential treatment. Your last letter indicates that in spite of four and a half years of belonging to the SS, you still lack any understanding of the duties of the SS Race and Settlements Department in general and for the importance of *blood cleanliness* in particular, the checking of which is the duty of this department."

Apparently Hack was able, in the end, to satisfy his superiors of his family's "blood cleanliness," that is, the absence from their blood of any Jewish trace. The Berga job was far too important to go to any official about whom suspicions of racial impurity lingered. For it involved putting those whose blood the Nazis deemed less than pure to work in relentless fashion.

Edward Gorinac, from Port Huron, Michigan, a private in the 110th Infantry Regiment, was part of the pandemonium in the tunnels. He had been captured at the Battle of the Bulge on December 18, 1944, and, in the company of the other Americans, had arrived at Berga on February 13, 1945, a young man of thirty-two from the Midwest in reasonably robust health. By March 22, just over a month later, he was dead. Until March 19 Gorinac kept a diary, which was recovered by a fellow American prisoner and eventually sent to his family. The diary captures the Americans' gradual descent into an abyss at Berga they could not at first comprehend.

Like the whole group of 350 GIs, Gorinac had first been held at the Stalag IX-B prisoner-of-war camp at Bad Orb, near Frankfurt. He quickly perceived that, hard as conditions at Bad Orb were, Berga represented another level of horror, one exactly equivalent to that being endured by the European "Jews and political prisoners." This entry in his diary reflects the shocked realization of one American soldier that he has become part of a process without a name that later became known as the Holocaust.

Gorinac was not Jewish. He evidently had no idea why he was marched out of Bad Orb on February 8, 1945, and put into a boxcar for transport to Berga. Eight days later, on February 16, he began work in the tunnels, as he recorded in his diary:

> **February 16, 1945:** We were called at 4:30 a.m. Started to work digging out a tunnel. We had to shovel stone. The dust is bad. We work eight hours, 6 till 2. We have no dinners and only a

cup of coffee and what bread we can save from supper, which isn't very much.

February 17: We were called 10 minutes to 4. Worked in same tunnel. The fellows are too weak even to walk out there.

February 18: Called at 4 a.m. We have to work today (Sunday). Won't even let us go to church.

February 19: I had cup of tea and about one-and-a-half slices bread, on which I have to work until 2 p.m. Start at 6 a.m., work till 2 p.m. Seen Jerry officer hit Jew with a stick.

February 20: Was put on the afternoon shift. I will start work at 2 p.m. and work till 10 p.m. On this shift the night foreman is a bastard. They hit Young with a shovel and others with rubber hose. Oh yes I got hit above right eye.

February 21: Had coffee with milk in it. This place is worse than Bad Orb. They treat us as slaves. We are even on slave rations like [European] Jews and political prisoners. And to think how we treat their prisoners. Here we do not even have cards or letters to write home. Nothing on Red Cross packages. We are not represented by the Red Cross.

February 22: Heard our armies crossed the Rhine. Russians have Berlin. The bosses are beating hell out of our GIs. It's really a shame to be treated this way. Some of the fellows have to be helped to the mines. Couple bad cases of pneumonia.

February 23: Still on afternoon shift. Have a terrible cold. Hope I can keep from catching pneumonia. The fellows are getting weaker every day. Right now I am nothing but skin and bones and so are the rest. Every day at least five fellows faint. The bosses on the job sure beat hell out of us. One boss even carries a hose to beat us with. To think I married into a German family.

February 24: We had the best soup since we came here, it was potatoes, carrots, turnip and a few noodles. Today at work, Nagel, I and three others were knocked off the scaffold. I hurt my leg and knee. I was told to go back to the barracks by our medic. On way our foreman met us and made us go back to work. He even kicked Nagel. For supper we had two spoonfuls of sugar.

As he grew weaker, but was still forced to work on the drill for eight hours, Gorinac remained observant. He saw his fellow GIs reduced to "fighting a lot about chow." On February 27 he noted: "Last night we had a new boss and he hit me across the back because I couldn't understand he wanted a board." On March 1 he wrote of "daily beatings," and the next day, for the first time, he gave a name to the place he was imprisoned: "Still at the Slave Camp at Berga (Elster)."

By March 10, 1945, less than four weeks after his arrival, Gorinac scarcely had the strength to write. The entries become grimmer, more laconic.

> **March 10 to March 12:** Rogers died today. We are getting skinnier every day.
> **March 13:** Fred from Lansing died today. I was moved to Barracks No. 2. The infection is getting worse.
> **March 14–15.** Nothing new. Still working on 2 to 10:45 shift. We were cut on our bread. Now it's 5 men to a loaf instead of four.
> **March 16.** I have an awful sore throat. Tried to stay from work but was driven out.
> **March 17:** Another man died today which makes three.
> **March 18:** I was sent to barracks 6 which is used as a hospital with my sore throat (strep).
> **March 19:** Still in barracks 6. Throat is sore as hell. Another man was brought in this morning. He died hour later. Making it 4.

That is the last entry. On March 20 four American medics imprisoned at Berga, in the company of two guards, were ordered to take several acutely ill prisoners, including Gorinac, to a hospital attached to Stalag IX-C, a prisoner-of-war camp about thirty miles to the northwest. This is one of the very rare instances of the Germans allowing American prisoners at Berga to be taken to a hospital.

But for at least two of them, Gorinac and Private George Snyder, the gesture came too late. Gorinac died on the train, Snyder soon after arrival. The cause of Gorinac's death was given by the Germans as diphtheria. All the American medics could say with certainty was that he could no longer breathe; the slate dust, the relentless work, the filth, the cold, and hunger had destroyed him. In short, and in short order, he had been worked to death.

The German government reported Gorinac's death to the United

States government through the International Red Cross. For no other American's death at Berga is there evidence of such information, required by the Geneva Conventions, being provided. But it proved of little help or solace to the Gorinac family, which spent the next several years trying to establish the whereabouts of his body and the circumstances of his death. Their travails are a reflection of the scant attention events at Berga received from U.S. authorities after the war, when those who had been there were encouraged, or even obliged by signed oaths, to remain silent about their experience. The postwar world was one of new political realities.

Today the Berga prison in which the Americans were held captive is a miserable, derelict place. When they emerged on February 13, 1945, from their packed boxcars after a five-day journey across Germany from Stalag IX-B, the Americans marched up a hill on the south side of Berga, past the textile factory that once belonged to the Englander family.

Their little camp, about a mile from town, consisted of four one-story barracks filled with triple-decked bunks; each barracks was equipped with a single latrine (one cold-water tap and a wooden bucket) and a single potbellied stove. Between the barracks was a slit trench where the men could relieve themselves during the day; at night, when the barracks were locked, they used the bucket. The 350 soldiers were crammed into the barracks, scarcely fed, taunted by their guards, and often made to stand at attention outside for many hours as they were counted and recounted.

On the way up from the barracks to the tunnels, some of the Americans went past the Berga concentration camp holding the mainly Jewish European prisoners from Buchenwald, many of whom had survived Auschwitz. Private Sidney Lipson of Boston, a rifleman with the 28th Infantry Division who had been captured at the Battle of the Bulge, recalled the scene this way: "They were right up against the fence, holding the wires, looking at us as we came in. Quiet. Didn't say a word. Just looked gaunt, beat up, skinny. I mean, hollow-looking eyes. In other words they could see right through you. They didn't see you. How else can you describe it? They were an entity that really wasn't an entity. They just weren't. They were standing. They were looking at you. But they just weren't . . . I remember thinking: Is that going to be us? I knew I had been singled out for transport to Berga because I was a Jew, but I don't believe I put it together with the Jews of Europe."

From the outset the Americans worked in the tunnels, just as these European concentration-camp prisoners did. Within days of arrival, their physical condition began to deteriorate, providing an answer to Lipson's question: *Is that going to be us?*

Before the American prisoners arrived, the collection of buildings that housed them was used in the 1930s as a camp for young Nazi volunteers, workers brought there to build roads. Then, after World War II, the refurbished site became, in the words of Sabine Richter, a Berga municipal employee, "a holiday camp for young Pioneers," the youth of East Germany who were sent every summer to camps such as this one to imbibe country air and acquire Communist convictions. When the Berlin Wall fell and East Germany collapsed in 1989, ethnic Germans from Russia were invited back to a united Germany and the refugees, many of them boasting "German blood" but unable to speak a word of German, were housed here on their arrival.

Little vestige of this tumultuous history remains. One of the wooden structures in which the American soldiers were held is intact, flanked by gray concrete buildings put up during the 1945–1989 Communist period. Weeds grow waist-high on the gravel. Among them a few wild roses persist. Rusting flagpoles bear no flags.

Almost overgrown with juniper bushes, a memorial stone is visible, inscribed to the memory of Ernst Thälmann, the prewar German socialist leader imprisoned and killed by the Nazis at Buchenwald. Every government chooses its heroes: Thälmann was selected by Communist East Germany as a symbol of leftist opposition to Hitler. At the southern end of the little complex, hidden behind long grass, is an empty swimming pool once used by the youthful East German Pioneers, its bottom filled with weeds. Inside the buildings, just visible through dirt-spattered glass, are strewn buckets, clothes, mops, pipes, tires, worn-out mattresses, and other bric-a-brac.

Lubinsky, Gorinac, Lipson, and the countless others who suffered or died at this spot are not honored here. What has triumphed is chaos, as if the whirlwind of German twentieth-century history has blown aside any attempt at ordered consideration.

The abandonment is complete. Time passes. Old women, like those on the central Berga square, forget precisely what they have seen. Whole countries, like East Germany, disappear from the map.

Files get lost. Events churn, turning and turning like the modern windmill turbines on the hills around Berga. Memory can be a cheap umbrella held up to the gusts of time: it can bend, twist, crumple, and it can even disintegrate.

A nation of perpetrators can gradually become a nation of victims, wondering how their forebears could inflict on them the pain of living with what Hitler's Germany did, wondering why the ethnic Germans who were persecuted and evicted from homes across central Europe after World War II have no memorials dedicated to them. Young Germans, let it be stated, bear no guilt. But inevitably, they are conscious of guilt, that of their forebears.

That guilt, those crimes, still weigh on Joe Littell of the 106th Infantry Division, a former Berga prisoner who is stuck with his memory of the place. What haunts him is an old dilemma: "How can all those trim little houses that many of us have seen, with their quaint window boxes filled with cheery bright flowers, have been the homes of human beings who gave the world such grisly new perspectives on the outer reaches of malignity?"

Stephen Spender, the British poet, visiting Germany at war's end in 1945, was struck by the same paradox as he gazed at houses that remained intact near the northern German town of Lubeck. "The houses," he wrote,

> look as if you could eat them, they are all so sweet, so icing-colored and creamful, striped with beams which look like bars of chocolate. Often they have written on them, like Happy Wishes, good thoughts charmingly lettered, painted round the outside walls under the eaves or carved on the eaves. These *Sprichwörter* are characteristic of German seriousness, German piety, German good intentions, German self-congratulation, the desire to label every environment with a few inches of thought sliced out of the Bible or the Poets of the Classics, the desire at the same time to reduce thought to a common denomination of banality, the desire, at the worst, of the devil to quote scripture.

German good intentions and German proverbs are also evident in the small Berga museum. No reference to the camp is made in it, but the story of the Englanders, the Jewish textile entrepreneurs who did not come back after World War II, is told, at least in part:

how Ernst Englander started the silk business in 1899, how there were more than four hundred automatic sewing machines functioning by the next year, how he gave money to the town to build a hospital that was never completed.

Illustrating the now defunct local production, a silk towel is on display with the embroidered figure of a happy *Hausfrau* mouthing the words "*Ordnung erfreut*"—"Order is pleasing."

But there was no order, pleasing or otherwise, on that hill in Berga where Americans were imprisoned. To gaze at the neglected mess is to find the puzzle of Germany as intractable as ever. In the space of just over six decades, these buildings had housed Nazi volunteers, starving American prisoners of war, Communist youth, and Volga German refugees. These events amounted to an encapsulation of German turmoil. Yet at the end of all this upheaval lay only dereliction, advancing weeds, things scattered helter-skelter. No doubt the little complex would soon be reduced to rubble. Before that happened, and the wind or the river took everything, it seemed necessary to sift through the debris stained with American blood.

CHAPTER TWO

Sucker Punch

WITHIN DAYS, the gruesome became commonplace. Private William J. Shapiro would watch from a distance as shells slammed into foxholes and know, before he got there, what to expect: body parts all over the place, intestines spilled, blood seeping into the earth. He would look for movement, signaling life. Without it, or a sound, however faint, there was no point hanging around. To do so was to invite being hit by the next round. In combat he had learned quickly that the most important thing was to keep moving no matter what.

As a frontline medic with the 28th Infantry Division, Shapiro, aged nineteen, had to look out for the living. It was not his job to tag the mounting American dead—more than eleven thousand of them in Normandy within four weeks of D-day, June 6, 1944. But life could be hard to discern in the carnage. Chest wounds were often invisible because the blood did not always soak through uniforms, with the result that the injury was betrayed only by gasping. Morphine was the standard treatment. Shapiro carried the drug in tiny needle-tipped aluminum tubes. After giving the injection, he would tag the injured soldier to ensure that another dose was not administered too soon by somebody back at the battalion aid station. If a GI was hit in a limb, Shapiro would give the shot and apply a tourniquet. Then word was sent with a rifleman or runner for the litter bearers to come and collect the wounded and the dead. Triage was done back at the aid station by the medical officer, but Shapiro could not help doing his own. He found that he involuntarily distinguished those who would survive from those who would not. Death did not advance unannounced; it clouded the eyes before occupying them entirely, a sudden blankness.

As for his own mortality, in combat Shapiro scarcely gave it a thought. Through the French hedgerows, he would follow fifty yards behind the riflemen of his platoon. If one was hit and shouted, "Medic!" he would rush forward to see what had happened. That movement, into a position where a fellow soldier had just been hit by shrapnel or a bullet, became automatic.

Shapiro, through a mysterious process, was subsumed into his unit. An unspoken pact existed: the riflemen protected him until they no longer could, whereupon he tried to save them. His individuality, his life itself, had ceased to have much meaning. All that was left was what had to be done: provide relief where possible.

The fear that haunted him on arrival in Normandy and preceded battle evaporated, and the rules of his existence became simple: shoot or be shot, tag the injured and move on, feel nothing because in feeling may lie hesitation. What the GIs had been taught in the United States seemed almost quaint, a bloodless imitation of battle where you took aim from more than a hundred yards. Here men were cut down by shots fired from ten feet away. You watched them die, in detail, the blood seeping from the mouth, arms thrown back, eyes shocked, then expressionless. You got very cold after a while.

A few GIs could not take it. They saw a lead scout or two killed and they cracked, crawled back to the rear on their stomachs, eyes wild, muttering that they had to get out, get back, get home. You lived with that for the rest of your life. Perhaps it was better to die. But not slowly. One young soldier, hit in the chest, cried for his mother all night long. Sometimes, under fire, there was nothing that could be done to move the injured.

Names became a blur, as indistinguishable as the icy forests through which the GIs sometimes trudged and fought. Dark forests always seemed to be waiting, to be pregnant with malevolence. What they bestowed was death. It seemed to Shapiro that death was easy to come by. The difficult thing was staying alive. At night, on patrol in the forest, it was so dark that the only way not to get lost was to cling to the ammunition belt of the soldier in front: the blind leading the blind.

Shapiro would be introduced to first sergeants and lieutenants, and in the first battle thereafter they would be wounded or killed and others would come in as replacements. That was how it was. Lives amounted to names noted then deleted in the master sergeant's roster and were no more commented on than a change in the weather.

One name, however, he did remember: Norbert Schramm. A Pole from Chicago, Schramm was a fellow medic. After their unit left France, they went out together one day in November 1944 to pick up the injured in the fifty-square-mile Hürtgen Forest, which straddles the Belgian-German border. The Battle of Hürtgen Forest was an appalling one. German artillery slashed the trees, it was impossible to see, and Shapiro's division took 6,184 casualties before the battle was won in late November. A German bombardment began. Shapiro took cover, losing sight of Schramm and the other medics, and in the snow he quickly got lost, blinded by the whiteness, deafened by the insistent shelling. Only much later, when he found a communication wire and followed it back, was Shapiro able to make his way to the battalion aid station, where he was told that Schramm had been shot in the head and killed instantly. That one death, alone among the tens of thousands, marked Shapiro. It resisted deletion. But he suppressed his pain, buried it deep inside himself, in order to go forward, in order not to stop. It was useless to reason. He dealt not with why but with how. His father had told him: "If you do a job, do it right."

There had been little respite for Shapiro since he was drafted in September 1943, at the age of eighteen. He received basic military instruction at Camp Grant, Illinois, before being sent to Walter Reed General Hospital in Washington, D.C., where he trained as a surgical technician from December 1943 to May 1944. At Camp Grant Shapiro had found himself the butt of occasional anti-Semitic comments from a corporal with a marked southern accent. This came as a shock to Shapiro, who had grown up in the overwhelmingly Jewish Pelham Parkway neighborhood of the Bronx.

His father, Jacob, had come to the United States in 1903 from the Minsk area of what is now Belarus, part of the great wave of Jewish immigrants fleeing hardship, exclusion, or persecution in Europe. He found employment in Manhattan as a garment worker, married, and had five sons. Shapiro was the last of them, born in 1925, late enough for his first clear memories to be of the Great Depression. His father lost his job, the older boys were sent out to find whatever employment they could, the evening meal often dwindled to potatoes, and Shapiro himself was put to work at the age of twelve.

Whatever pay he received for toiling in a drugstore, with the exception of tips for delivering prescriptions, was given to his mother, who used the money in part to provide the family's weekly indulgence, a chicken that she contrived to cut into seven "quarters." In ways such as this, ingenuity filled the gaps left by scarcity. The Shapiros pushed their sons to look beyond their two-room Bronx apartment and educate themselves. Assimilation and advancement were bywords. Their Jewish identity was lightly worn; visits to synagogue on High Holy Days were secondary to the immigrant quest to become integrated Americans. In his father's corner of Europe, Judaism had been synonymous with danger. Rather than Jews who lived in America, the Shapiros sought to be Americans who happened to be Jewish.

The past had a name—Europe—and they wanted to put it behind them. Like most American Jews, Shapiro had little awareness of the mass murder of European Jews, even when he was drafted. This despite the fact that in the previous year, 1942, an estimated 2.7 million Jews had been killed by the Nazis as the apparatus of the Final Solution became fully operational.

He had heard about concentration camps, but only as places of indiscriminate atrocities; the very notion of a systematic attempt to annihilate the Jews of Europe was unthinkable to him. In the prewar years, reporting of the anti-Semitic rampages of the Nazis, including *Kristallnacht* in November 1938, had been intense: these acts were immediately verifiable, as was the Jewish suffering. But once the war started, American newspapers published little about the Holocaust—indeed, the word had no meaning in this context—because the reports of it were fragmentary and hard to verify, and because their appetite to uncover the story was limited. Indeed, the coverage became insignificant as the horror grew larger and the conflict wider.

So wide, in fact, that by 1943 the Pacific war, with its clearly identifiable onset in the Japanese attack on Pearl Harbor, was for many Americans of much more immediate interest than the fighting in Europe. As for Shapiro, he had heard nothing from his family to link himself to the beleaguered European Jews. Indeed, the four decades since his father's arrival in the United States had served precisely to establish a separation from Jewish European life that amounted to a form of amnesia, one shared by many Jewish American families bent on assimilation.

"I wasn't a Jew when I went to war," Shapiro said. "I was an American soldier." Like other Jewish GIs, he wore the *H* dog tag, for "Hebrew," around his neck. But this, to Shapiro, was worn in the same spirit as Catholics wore a *C* and Protestants a *P.* Religions were equally respected, appropriate ministrations to the dead or injured important.

Shapiro sailed for Europe from New York harbor on June 16, 1944. It was harder than he had imagined to say good-bye to his family and his girlfriend, Betty. He landed at Liverpool in early July. Shortly afterward, he was assigned to the 110th Infantry Regiment as a combat medic. Shapiro's landing in Normandy at Omaha Beach later that month, on July 24, coincided with an intense bombardment by Eighth Air Force B-17s of the area around Saint-Lô, about fifteen miles inland. The ground shook as he burrowed into a foxhole. Fear gripped Shapiro then, for this was the beginning of his indoctrination in war. His education proceeded rapidly. As his unit worked its way through Normandy, Shapiro's fear subsided in pace with his own absorption into the labyrinth of conflict. He stopped asking questions. He injected morphine; he applied tourniquets; he tagged people.

There could even be pleasant surprises. On August 25 Shapiro's unit was transported by truck to Versailles. Three days later, he found himself bivouacked in the Bois de Boulogne beneath the leafy plane trees with orders to shave and clean up for the victorious Allied march through Paris the next day. The summer air was sweet, roses bloomed, people cheered. But the joy of that moment was to prove ephemeral; Shapiro would soon be advancing eastward, and would suffer the persecution his father had escaped.

At the age of seventy-nine, six decades after he was feted as a young soldier in Paris, Dr. William J. Shapiro is a measured man. Methodical by nature, disciplined in what he eats, he keeps his affairs ordered, his body trim. His airy house, built upon his retirement from a career as an obstetrician, is set beside a Florida golf course, and every now and again a ball comes through a screen. But there are few other disturbances or surprises. He and his wife, Betty, live in one of the gated "communities" that fan out across the flatness of Florida. The streets are quiet and secure. In the garages, electric golf carts flank sport utility vehicles with Global Positioning Systems.

The old strive to stay active. At dawn and at dusk, when the heat is not so overwhelming, slim figures may be seen trundling in their golf carts through the streets bordered by lawns of prickly Bermuda grass, blue plumbago bushes, and hibiscus trees. The very old, in wheelchairs, are accompanied by black nurses. They look timorous, these almost diaphanous Jews; their mouths are pinched, their skin waxy, their bones brittle. The journey has been long to this air-conditioned existence beneath the palms and beside the fairways: from the tenements of New York to these plush bungalows, from chicken soup to seared salmon with arugula, from the struggle to make it to the difficulty of spending it. Here, at last, beneath a cloudless sky, all is in order.

But Dr. Shapiro has been having nightmares. They are predictable enough. He is running, he is trapped, he is being pursued. Orders are being barked at him. When he awakens, his wife asks him: "Are the Nazis still chasing you?" They try to laugh about it. It has been a long time, after all. But for much of that time, the memory was repressed. Dr. Shapiro did not want to think about the experiences of Private Shapiro. He did not want to tell the story because to tell it, he would have to relive it.

He was an American GI who was captured by the Germans and had a hard time of it, but that was not a big deal, or so he told himself, and so he told his children when they asked, which they stopped doing after a while because they knew the questions would be met with evasion or silence. To get on with life meant to move forward, and that was what he had done after the end of the war. It was possible to push a season in hell so far back it seemed not to have existed. But then a car door slams and it sounds like a rifle shot and you already have one knee on the ground, moving by instinct. The bitter season's harvest is perennial, after all. It returns now, and Shapiro tries, but fails, to stifle a sob.

The atmosphere is suddenly more brittle in this high-ceilinged Florida room. The ceiling fans still turn, smoked salmon and herring are still arrayed on the table, and, beyond the screens, the sprinklers on the golf course still glint in the sunlight. But Germany is now present, casting its shadow, and the doctor's eyes have filled with tears.

Six decades on, many Germans clamor for closure on the Holocaust, a final accounting, a resolution. If they do not say "Enough," they think it. They bite their lips to stop the word from coming out; they know that if they raise their chins even an inch, someone will push them down again. But is it not reasonable to demand this *Schlussstrich*, this closure, now that the Nazi perpetrators are already dead or will be soon? It may seem reasonable, but memory is not linear and reason has little purchase on it. The crimes of the Germans have taken a tortuous course through the psyches of survivors and their descendants. As Primo Levi observed, "A person who has been wounded tends to block out the memory so as not to renew the pain." But in this moment, the pain inhabits even this Florida bungalow.

They were young Americans, most of them eighteen or nineteen, many of them promising students recruited under the Army Specialized Training Program. Established in 1942, the ASTP was the largest education program in the nation's history, sending more than 200,000 young men who were deemed gifted to colleges to study engineering, science, languages, and other courses. Most of those recruited expected to become officers or to be assigned to technical units, but the war changed that. Pressure for replacements in Europe became so intense that most ended up as infantrymen. In general, they had little preparation for war.

By 1944, when most of these young soldiers went to Europe, the word from the generals was that the conflict was going America's way. Although the progress across France to the Siegfried line and Germany was hard, it was steady. For the GIs, there seemed little reason to question that the advance toward Berlin and the Nazi surrender would be uninterrupted.

But Hitler, gambler to the last, had decided on a last roll of the dice, an attempt, against all odds, to reverse the situation on the western front with a decisive thrust. To this end, he rapidly amassed more than 1.3 million troops by mid-December 1944, in preparation for what became known as the Battle of the Bulge. It was a fight that, over the course of a little more than a month, would result in the death, injury, or capture of 81,000 American soldiers before the German advance was repulsed and reversed. The toll on the 28th and 106th Infantry Divisions was devastating. Some of the GIs involved had been in combat in Europe no more than two months.

Sonny Fox, a member, like Shapiro, of the 28th Infantry Division, had arrived at the front in October, after "chasing the war" eastward through France. The chase was swift now that the coastal cliffs and inland hedgerows no longer presented any obstacle, and he wondered at the sacrifice of those before him who had secured such formidable terrain. By December, he was patrolling close to the Our

River between Luxembourg and Germany. It had been quiet at the front—"We were still licking our wounds after the Hürtgen Forest"—so the sound of artillery shells shrieking overhead early one morning came as a surprise.

"It was 5:20 a.m. on December 16, 1944, and I ran out of the farmhouse we were in to where we had our slit trenches, a few yards away," Fox recalled. "And I asked them how long this had been going on. They said about twenty minutes. So I ran back to the house to get the rest of my squad out and into their positions. We sat and waited, and pretty soon the assault started."

Benefiting from surprise and superior numbers, the Germans cut through the American lines to the north and south of Fox's outpost near Hosingen, Luxembourg, eventually driving more than thirty miles westward. But he knew little or nothing of this at the time. As an infantryman, he dealt with what was in front of him. Nothing much else existed.

In the afternoon, Fox heard tanks coming down the road from behind him; he was not sure if they were German or American. "They turned out to be ours," Fox said, "and I thought we had beaten them off, but the captain said no, the Germans were behind us and the fighting was going on well behind our lines."

Fox was ordered to hold his position with his squad—eleven men and himself. A ranger squad and two tanks were sent to his position just outside Hosingen. "Here's a skinny Jewish kid from Brooklyn, and I was now in charge of two tanks, a ranger squad, and my squad," Fox said. "I felt like I had an army. And I was deploying my tanks and I was deploying my troops and having a great time thinking we were in good shape."

They were not. The next day, about midmorning, two German Tiger tanks appeared about four hundred yards away. Fox was standing in front of one of the two American Shermans when the Germans opened fire. A shell struck the turret of the tank behind him, but fortunately it hit at enough of an angle to ricochet and explode about a hundred yards away. Concluding that they were outgunned, the American tank drivers immediately took off, with Fox in hot pursuit yelling, "Come back, come back!"

Nobody heard him, of course. For Fox, this ended what he calls "the shortest tank battle of World War II."

Marooned without his tanks, Fox sent a message to the command in Hosingen saying he would withdraw by evening if he did not hear word to the contrary. There was no response. Fox pulled back. By the middle of the next morning, December 18, no more than four houses in the middle of Hosingen were still in American hands and ammunition was running low. The captain decided that they should come out with their hands up. Two captured Germans were sent out to deliver the message of American capitulation.

Fox and the other men walked out, arms raised, into an uncertain captivity. Some attached pieces of white sheet to the ends of their guns as a sign of surrender. The Germans rounded them up in a staging area on the outskirts of town; a machine gun facing them suggested their end might be immediate. But after a few hours the GIs, in steadily growing numbers, were marshaled into a long line and ordered to start moving down the road toward Germany, past the farmhouse that Fox had occupied, past several German corpses that prompted in Fox an impulse—restrained—to boast of his squad's prowess, past German officers congratulating one another on their victory. It was the start of a three-day march to Gerolstein, Germany.

There was nothing heroic about capture. Numbed and stunned, drained by three days of almost sleepless combat, Fox felt very little. That he was a Jew in the hands of the Nazis and so perhaps in special danger scarcely occurred to him. Captivity was like a serious injury whose full extent takes time to reveal itself. He was relieved at not being summarily shot; he was cold in this bitter European winter; he was bone tired. His nerves, it seemed, had gone dead on him. Germans jeered at him and the other prisoners as they passed through villages; he hardly noticed. Through the dull fog of exhaustion a vague sense of shame at having surrendered and a nagging disquiet at the uncertainty of his fate percolated, but dimly. War is lived day by day just like the rest of life, frequently in drudgery and despondency, rather than in the stirring emotion and swift action with which it is often depicted.

The first night, already in Germany, the GIs slept in a church, where they were allowed to slide into pews, sitting, heads slumped, on the straight-backed benches. It was freezing. A hayloft provided shelter on the second night, and the prisoners were allowed to sleep for three hours. The next day they arrived at the railhead. Fox was handed a shovel and told to clean out the manure from the boxcars that were to be used to transport the American soldiers to prison camp. This job completed, the GIs were herded onto the train, as many as seventy-five men to a car, enough to ensure that they could not all lie down at the same time, even in the fetal position. The cars were then locked.

The American prisoners were each given a can of headcheese, their first real nourishment in days. "I had never eaten headcheese before," Fox said. "I have never eaten headcheese since. And if you ask me what headcheese is, I'm not sure I could tell you. But we had it and we ate it. That was it."

As the sealed boxcars lurched out of the station, Fox, like his fellow captives, had scant notion of the myriad doomed loads already transported across Europe in this way by the Nazis. All they knew was the darkness, the cold, and the occasional flicker of ever scarcer and more coveted cigarettes.

Edwin Cornell of Rochester, New York, was also in the vicinity of Hosingen in mid-December 1944. After instruction under the Army Specialized Training Program at Fort Benning, Georgia, he had been destined for medical school. But destiny was a particularly fickle thing in 1944. His plans, like those of countless others, were abruptly put on hold as the demands of the war against Hitler intensified. The program folded, and he was sent to the 86th Division in Louisiana, and from there on to Europe as a replacement. He, too, joined the 28th Infantry Division, survived the haunting combat of the Hürtgen Forest, and moved on to Luxembourg.

On December 16 Cornell, like Fox, was in a farmhouse a few miles outside of town. He remembers searchlights illuminating the initial thrust of the German attack. His platoon had two machine gunners; they took care of the first wave of the Nazi offensive, and Cornell watched the German soldiers falling one after the other, forms keeling over like bowling pins. After that came a lull, and it seemed the short battle had been won.

But the next day the German attack resumed in earnest, accompanied now by mortar fire, and the fifteen GIs in the house, cut off from the rest of their outfit, were running out of ammunition. The sergeant in charge called them together and declared the situation hopeless. There were only two courses: certain death or surrender.

They chose the latter, walking from the house behind a soldier with a piece of white cloth attached to his gun, and were lined up on the road. But one GI refused to give up, firing shots in the direction of the Germans and the newly taken American prisoners, hollering

"Cowards!" at the other members of the platoon. It took some time to capture the holdout; he was severely beaten by the Germans. "It's a wonder they didn't kill us all because of this one guy," Cornell said.

Shortly after he was captured, Cornell began to worry about being Jewish. He had been raised in a middle-class family, the son of an insurance agent. His father was religious, his mother not, and as a child he attended an Orthodox temple. Like most other Jewish GIs, he had heard only vague accounts of the Nazi persecution of European Jewry. But even these accounts seemed to him to warrant concern. Cornell's immediate awareness of a specific danger appears to set him apart from most, but not all, other American Jews taken prisoner.

When he went to war, Cornell took with him a small Hebrew Bible that he carried in his breast pocket. He would look at it from time to time, in brief moments of respite, and he felt it gave him a connection to his childhood, his family, and God. Such links were not easy to establish in the mayhem of a war that came upon these young men suddenly. As he now began the march toward Germany, a prisoner of war, Cornell found his thoughts turning with growing insistence to this Bible, which had become disquieting evidence of his Jewish identity, a source of danger rather than comfort.

On the second day of the march, the prisoners were allowed to rest for a moment by the side of the road. Cornell noticed that the soil at this spot was soft. "I thought to myself, I've got to get rid of this Bible; it's evidence of my being a Jew," he said. He dug a small hole, surreptitiously removed the Bible from his pocket, kissed its cover, said a prayer, and buried it in the dirt of Germany.

Soon afterward Cornell was locked into a boxcar and transported across Germany to an unknown destination. Crammed against other American soldiers, he overheard a group of four discussing the fact that they were Jews and might be vulnerable. Cornell remained silent.

"I did not say anything to them because my feeling was, the less people knew about what I am, the better," he recalled. "I knew I was in enemy territory. But the conversation got me thinking about what it must have been like to be a Jew in Germany at that time."

Gerald Daub of the 397th Regiment of the 100th Infantry Division happened to know a lot about the fate of German Jews. Born and raised in Brooklyn, he was of German Jewish descent, and the family had friends and relatives in Germany. Unlike the Jews of Poland and other European states that fell under Nazi control, German Jews had several years to observe the growing ruthlessness of Hitler's assault on them. For years after the Nazi ascension to power in 1933, it remained possible for German Jews to escape, albeit with growing difficulty, and a majority of the prewar population of just over 500,000 did. Among them was a young man named Siegfried Kahn, a friend of the Daubs, who was able to obtain an American visa through the family's efforts on his behalf.

Kahn told Daub of the portrayal of the Jews as vermin draining the lifeblood of the Germans, infecting them with moral and physical disease. Daub heard of Heinrich Himmler's definition of the Jews as "bacteria," and that the Nazis uniformly viewed the Jews as criminal and parasitic. Kahn described the progressive exclusion of the Jews from German society, the assault on their businesses, the quashing of their rights as citizens. What Kahn did not know, and Daub only discovered later, was that all this was but a prelude to Hitler's ultimate design: the physical elimination of the Jews through the organization of an industrial-scale system of gas chambers and crematoria designed to bring, for the first time, the efficiency of the assembly line to the business of murder.

Daub became a soldier in 1943 under the Army Specialized Training Program, studying in Charleston, South Carolina, before being assigned to the 100th Infantry Division at Fort Bragg. The division was filled with eighteen- and nineteen-year-olds like himself whose studies had been interrupted and whose knowledge of war was slight. He remained in Fayetteville, North Carolina, for a few months, then sailed on the USS *George Washington* for Europe, through the Strait of Gibraltar to a landing in southern France, near Marseilles. A rifleman—the first scout of the second squad of the first platoon of F Company—Daub moved up the Rhone Valley before seeing combat near Épinal, where he was injured by a rifle shot. By early January 1945, he had recovered and was in Alsace-Lorraine, in the town of Remling, as it came under German attack.

Most of the division's armor had pushed on northward the previous month to reinforce the American lines at the Battle of the Bulge, so Daub's unit found itself vulnerable to German tanks. Attacking at night to avoid Allied bombing, the German 17th SS Panzer Grenadier Division encircled the American position on January 8, 1945.

"I don't know exactly what time of night it was when a German tank appeared with a squad of infantry around it," Daub said. "The flares went off, and there was machine-gun fire and bullets whizzing up and down the street, and I was at the window of the house with a buddy named Howard Hunter and we were firing at the tank and the infantrymen. Eventually, they rumbled the tank up to our window and put their 88-millimeter cannon right in the window. It was at that point that we decided it was time to leave the house because they were about to blow it up."

Daub and Hunter took off, jumping over a retaining wall to find themselves in the midst of a squad of German soldiers. Hunter, moving swiftly, smashed his rifle butt into the first German they encountered, and they dashed into an adjacent house. Their intention was to get out one of the windows and move as fast as possible to the American command post in the center of town, but they found all the windows boarded up and sealed.

The Germans followed them in. Daub and Hunter could hear their footsteps advancing. They flipped the kitchen table on its side and just had time to duck behind it before the Germans opened the door and tossed in a hand grenade. Fortunately it was a concussion grenade that momentarily stunned the two men but did no greater damage.

Hunter suggested to Daub that they surrender.

"Not me, Howard," Daub replied. "I'm Jewish. I'm not going to surrender to them."

A few minutes later there were more footsteps and the two Americans heard a machine pistol being cocked at the door. Daub began to reconsider his decision. "I said to Howard, I don't think this is a good situation. Perhaps you are right. Perhaps discretion is the better part of valor."

With that, Daub and Hunter threw down their guns and walked slowly out. The Germans grabbed them and dragged them up onto a tank.

Daub was worried. While recovering from an injury in the station hospital at Épinal, he had heard about the December 17, 1944, Malmédy massacre, when, on the second day of the Battle of the Bulge, about 150 GIs from the 7th Armored Division were captured and rounded up in a field. The Nazis opened fire on them, killing about eighty on the spot—an instance of organized murder of prisoners of war that remained unique in its scale during the Ardennes battle. Word of the killing spread very fast, with three immediate results: a number of SS troopers who surrendered were shot by American forces, some GIs considering surrender thought better of it, and those who did surrender and knew of Malmédy had new cause for alarm, especially if, like Daub, they were Jewish.

The day after they were captured, Daub and Hunter were placed on the front of a tank with a severely wounded German soldier and told to try to keep the man comfortable. The soldier screamed as the tank's movement jolted him. When the soldier suddenly went quiet, Daub's first thought was that the German had died and he and Hunter would now be shot. Instead, the Germans stopped the tank, handed the two Americans a shovel, and told them to bury the dead man.

The ground was frozen hard as concrete. The best Daub and Hunter could do was to scrape out a shallow trench in the snow. But the German tank commander declared this adequate. They rolled the dead man into the furrow and covered him with snow; German dead were clearly too numerous by this stage of the war to merit much ceremony. Then the American prisoners were hauled back onto the tank and taken across the nearby German border to a village where the panzer division was headquartered. Daub was struck by how young many of the German soldiers jeering at him appeared. They looked no more than sixteen. The Nazi war effort was plainly stretched to the limit.

The next day, after a night spent in a barn, Daub was summoned to be interrogated by an SS officer. The interrogation took place in a small room, where the officer stood behind a desk on which lay several American magazines, including a copy of *Reader's Digest.* The first thing the officer did was to reach into his holster, take out his revolver, and place it on the desk.

With that, the officer asked what company Daub was in and the name of his captain. Daub replied that he was only required to give his name, rank, and serial number. The SS man said he already knew that Daub's unit had landed near Marseilles. Daub said he knew virtually nothing because he had only just arrived in Europe. The German accused Daub of lying.

"State your religion," the officer said.

Daub had hidden his dog tags, with the *H* for Hebrew.

"I am required to state my name, rank, and serial number, and that is all I will do," Daub replied.

"You're Jewish!" the officer shouted at him.

"I am not," Daub said, to his subsequent shame and regret. "My family is of German heritage. My father's father was from somewhere near Frankfurt, and they were Lutheran."

The SS officer ordered Daub to take his pants down. Daub argued that the exercise was pointless. "I am circumcised," he said. "And so are most American soldiers. So I don't think that you will learn what my religion is by having me remove my pants."

After some hesitation, the German officer asked a few more questions and dismissed Daub. Within a few days, Daub was locked into a crowded boxcar full of other American prisoners trundling across Germany to an unknown destination. Other Americans had preceded him, but he knew nothing of their fate. Still, he had already learned that his religion—or what the Nazis called his race—was of interest to his captors.

In 1997, not long before his death, John W. Reifenrath, who had served in the 106th Infantry Division, wrote down his memories of captivity in a thirty-page document entitled *An American Slave in Nazi Germany*. A sober chronicler, Reifenrath observed: "The things that I recall may well differ from what others recall. Not everyone had exactly the same experiences or saw the same events in the same manner. Also our memories can be flawed." For all his caveats, Reifenrath is notable for his scrupulous observation of detail, drawn in part from letters he wrote to his family from a hospital bed in England immediately after his liberation in 1945, and which his family had saved.

Why Reifenrath, who was Catholic, was taken to the concentration camp in Berga is not clear. It seems that after the Germans identified as many Jews as possible, they filled the quota for the labor detail at Berga with prisoners they regarded as troublemakers and others simply grabbed at random. Reifenrath was captured in the Ardennes on December 19, 1944, during the Battle of the Bulge. His description of his capture illustrates the already drained and exhausted state of many American soldiers at the outset of the one hundred days of captivity that would land them in the world of Holocaust victims.

"December 18, 1944, dawned foggy and dreary," Reifenrath wrote.

Our communications phone lines were not secure and messages were sent by runners to the various areas. We got word in the light machine section about 8.00 a.m. that we were to pull off the ridge that we were on and that our company was to fight a rearguard action.

We had three machine gun emplacements and the sergeant put me out at the far machine gun on guard in the fog. He said he wanted someone out there he could count on. I think he must have appealed to my ego because he didn't know how scared I was. That was the longest and loneliest time that I had experienced so far in my Army life. The fog was so thick that at times I could see no more than three feet, beyond which everything was gray white. The muffled silence played on my nerves.

An order came to move out. Reifenrath's unit was told to take only combat packs because they would be traveling fast; a patrol was left behind to blow up the bunkers. But the envisaged rearguard action was never fought, because, as he discovered later, the unit had already been cut off far behind American lines.

After heavy German shelling, on the afternoon of December 19, the remnants of Reifenrath's company surrendered. As he knelt before a group of German soldiers, Reifenrath, wondering if he would be summarily shot, opted to eat his ration's chocolate bar before it was too late.

But soon he was marched away to join other American prisoners being held at a church with a low fence around it and a graveyard. It was snowing. Because of his fear of an asthma attack, Reifenrath had abandoned his heavy overcoat and overshoes. He was dressed in shorts, T-shirt, long johns, wool pants and shirt, wool sweater, a field jacket, and helmet and helmet liner. Without blankets, he was cold and his sleep was fitful.

His account continues:

On the 20th we were lined up in a column and marched with other prisoners joining us. We were on a road that was in rolling open country. I remember passing an American tank with a dead soldier hanging halfway out. We passed a dead American every now and then. Some were without shoes. They probably had been taken by a German soldier because they were better than his. As we marched through the open country as far as I could see ahead and behind was the column of prisoners. We were marched all day without food or water. At one rest we were at the edge of a field of turnips. I dug up several, put some in my pocket and peeled and ate one.

A day later they were in Gerolstein, which had already been largely destroyed by Allied bombing. At a stone bridge over a stream, a German filmed the long line of American prisoners as they trudged along a path bulldozed through the rubble: evidence of a German victory even in defeat. All around, in the very soul of Europe, there was only chaos and disintegration.

"Civilians were watching us," Reifenrath observed, "and if looks could kill, we would all have been dead."

He and other survivors of his company were loaded into boxcars meant for eight horses and locked in. It was in this confinement, under Allied bombing, that Reifenrath and the others would spend Christmas 1944.

For Shapiro, the best of times came between mid-November and mid-December 1944. He had been transported southward by truck from the Hürtgen Forest and was billeted, like Fox, in a hamlet in Luxembourg, close to the front line at the Our River. His temporary home, a one-story farmhouse, was an improvement on the timber-covered foxholes of the Hürtgen; Shapiro slept snugly next to the stove. Barns and stacks of grain dotted the hills, and it was just possible, in the lull, to imagine that all was at peace.

The nearest town, Clervaux, where the battalion aid station was located, conjured up a fairy-tale Europe: steeples, castles, and timbered buildings on narrow streets, and cafés that Shapiro would frequent before enjoying a hot shower. He tended to the sick, but the work was not too arduous. Europe was dying, the age of American domination was dawning, and this American, for a moment at least, was happy.

On Thanksgiving Day the mess sergeant delivered a fine meal to the farmhouse that everyone, including the farmer and his wife, washed down with apple brandy. It seemed reasonable, in that moment, to give thanks for the fact that the worst was over.

But that was before the Germans' December surprise. Shapiro

had first encountered the so-called screaming meemies in the Hürt-gen Forest—multiple-launched rockets whose screeching sound earned them their name. Now, in the early morning of December 16, they rained down on his position. Shapiro saw a very bright flash of light in front and to the right of him, followed by an explosion. That was the last he remembered.

He woke up, head aching, ears ringing, vision blurred, at the aid station in Clervaux. No bones were broken and he had no cuts; the detonation of the German shell had merely knocked him out. Shapiro lay there watching fellow medics carrying wounded men on litters. It seemed quiet outside. But by evening, German machine-gun fire was audible, drawing closer to the railroad station where the makeshift American hospital was. Shapiro heard somebody say they were sur-rounded by SS troops and must surrender.

"I was groggy," he recalled, "but I also heard someone say, 'If you're a Jewish GI, throw your dog tags away because there are SS troops here.' "

Shapiro, obeying without thinking, threw his dog tags marked with the *H* for Hebrew into a potbellied stove in the middle of the room. He had never paid much attention to the dog tags and even now did not associate destroying them with a sense that being Jewish put him at risk of death in Hitler's Europe. He walked out of the aid station with his hands above his head and heard, for the first time, what would become a familiar German order to move out: "*Raus! Raus!*" To his amazement, he also heard some German soldiers say-ing, "Hands up, Chicago gangsters!"

The Germans searched him. They took a gold ring he had been given by his brother for his bar mitzvah, his medical supply packs, his cigarettes (part of a small package distributed by the Red Cross), his helmet with the Red Cross insignia, and the combination eating implement distributed by the army. Shapiro was left, however, with his Red Cross armbands and an International Red Cross card that was now his only identification.

The next morning Shapiro joined the column of captives trudg-ing into Germany. At times they had to walk in ditches beside the road to allow German troops to move forward to the front. These troops appeared in pitiable condition. They advanced in comman-deered vehicles of every sort, including wood-powered trucks and horse-drawn wagons, with artillery pieces being towed by horses. The German soldiers looked disarmingly young. Bicycles were stacked on all the vehicles, apparently with the idea that they would be used should retreat become necessary. This German army that had surprised and humiliated the fresher American forces was ragged and shabby.

For the first time, hunger and thirst afflicted Shapiro. His goal was to try not to think about food or drink, but a growling stomach soon made that impossible. He imagined meals his mother would cook back in the Bronx; with those thoughts came the pained realization that his parents would soon be informed that he was missing in action. He gazed at the bombed-out rubble of Gerolstein and, as the prisoners were congregated in large groups, heard the threatening German shepherds barking at him. As he was piled into a boxcar, his head still pounding, Shapiro listened to other men moaning from injury or exhaustion. Some shouted at one another as they maneuvered for the best position in the boxcar.

They use the straw in the boxcars for toilet paper until it runs out. Then they use letters from home. For the several hundred captured Americans being transported in the days before Christmas 1944, it is an introduction to the extremes to which they can be driven. Now they smear excrement on the words of their loved ones. Soon they will reach into latrines to retrieve potato peels, they will learn to steal from the living and from the dead, spurred by the urge to survive. They will live with the shame of it for the rest of their lives, unable even to acknowledge that shame, or the silence it imposes, for decades.

The air grows putrid inside the boxcars as men urinate against the walls or defecate into two boxes near the middle of the car. Some use their helmets. When the helmets are filled with excrement, somebody with a little strength tries to reach up to one of the two narrow openings at either end of the car to empty them.

A few of the men speak German. They plead with the guards to open the doors for a moment to air the cars. The request is refused. The train rattles into the unknown as men fight over nothing, maneuver for an inch or two of additional space. Some crouch, some stand, some lie down.

Several of the GIs are wounded. They have shrapnel in their legs, and there has been no time to tend to the wounds. The march to Gerolstein has weakened them. Their moaning, the clattering of the

U.S. Soldiers' Odyssey

DENMARK

Baltic Sea

North Sea

Hamburg

Bremen

Elbe

NETHERLANDS

Berlin

Oder

GERMANY

Rhine

Transport in boxcars of the
350 American prisoners to Berga,
arriving February 13, 1945.

Transport on foot
to Gerolstein, arriving
December 21, 1944.

STALAG IX-A
Ziederhain

STALAG IX-C
Bad Sulza

Leipzig

Elbe

Dresden

BUCHENWALD
Weimar

STALAG IX-B
Bad Orb

Berga

Elster

BELGIUM

Gerolstein

Frankfurt

Prague

Clervaux

Main

Manetin

LUXEMBOURG

Demmelsdorf

CZECHOSLOVAKIA
Bohemia and Moravia
annexed by
Nazi Germany in
1939

Nuremberg

Cham

Battle of the Bulge
German counteroffensive
through the Ardennes,
beginning December 16, 1944.
Many American soldiers were
captured in the Clervaux area.

Rhine

Transport in
boxcars to Bad Orb,
arriving December 26, 1944.

A group of 169 American prisoners
is liberated north of Cham on April 23, 1945.

Danube

Munich

FRANCE
Occupied by
Nazi Germany in
1940

Inn

AUSTRIA
Annexed by
Nazi Germany in
1938

LIECHTENSTEIN

SWITZERLAND

ITALY

Geneva

0   Kilometers   100

0   Miles   100

train, voices raised in altercation, conversation about the absent pleasures of sex and food: the din is almost constant. Nearly everyone has frostbite. Feet swell and ache, toes are full of open sores, shoes are removed and prove impossible to put back on.

There is almost no food. The headcheese is soon gone. The Germans provide part of a loaf of bread one day, a little water another. Some men try to drink their own urine. They find that they cannot. Thirst is worse than hunger, more insistent. Out of the one window at the back, they can see the snow. If they could get out for a moment and grab some snow and eat it . . . But the Germans will not let them out, even for a minute. The train lurches forward, then stops for long periods on railroad sidings.

Allied bombing runs are frequent. American commanders are intent on preventing the Germans from resupplying the front at the Battle of the Bulge. The concussive power of the two-thousand-pound bombs is terrifying. Rails curl into the air like twisted wire; refineries explode in sheets of flame. When veterans of the Normandy campaign cry, you know you are in hell.

Soldiers who can speak German, like Private Stephen J. Schweitzer of the 106th Infantry Division, ask that the prisoners be allowed into shelters during the bombing. The requests are refused; the GIs remain locked in the cars as their guards take refuge. At one stop Schweitzer sees the bodies of eight American soldiers killed in the bombardment being taken out of the car in front of his. At another stop a German civilian responds to cries from the cars by bringing water, but a guard knocks the water out of his hands.

On Christmas Eve the train is in the railroad yards at Limburg, about 175 miles from Frankfurt, when a ferocious bombardment by British Lancasters begins. The bombs seem to lift the boxcars several feet off the ground, suspend them there a moment, and then drop them with a crash. Stomachs are pushed in and pulled right out. In the lulls the soldiers hear people singing Christmas carols.

Men bang on the doors, clamor to be let out. Sirens wail, bombs whistle. Prayers are heard. Some GIs want no more than a quick end, anything but a stomach wound or a lost limb, anything but this confinement beneath Allied bombs. A few men do find a way out of one of the cars, only to be killed by the next bomb.

Shapiro looks at his frozen hands. The mark left by the gold ring the Nazis stole is still visible. But it is fading, like everything in his life that preceded this moment. At night, in the car, it is pitch-black.

Lubinsky of the 28th Infantry Division has a dream in which he is eating snow, but the more he eats, the thirstier he gets. Philip Glaessner of the 106th Division, another prisoner, thinks to himself that only three things will help him survive: hate, love, and hope, in that order.

Christmas Day in the boxcars: some recite the rosary, or the Lord's Prayer. For a few the prayers are answered in the form of British Red Cross boxes, one for every five men—British food after British bombs. At last, on December 26, the train arrives at its destination and the doors of the cattle cars are pushed open to reveal Bad Orb, about thirty-five miles east of Frankfurt. The Americans fall in the snow and put fistfuls of it in their mouths.

Just outside town, in the woods on the hills, is a camp called Stalag IX-B, a collection of one-story barracks surrounded by barbed wire. It is a prisoner-of-war camp, but for 350 of the American prisoners, it is also preparation for a slave camp farther east.

CHAPTER THREE

The Obedience of Corpses

THUNDER ROSE from Budapest's Erzsebet Boulevard. Thrust from the reverie of listening to a Chopin polonaise during a music lesson, drawn by mingled fascination and fear, Mordecai Hauer rushed to the window and found himself gazing down on a German mechanized division. Tanks, gleaming motorcycles, and helmeted soldiers in high boots with pistols across their chests advanced through the street, a menacing procession that scattered the citizens of the Hungarian capital in helter-skelter flight. The mood was one of sullen dismay. It was March 19, 1944, and the deafening display of these occupying forces marked the close of Hungary's long dalliance with Hitler's Germany.

In the end no Hungarian proclamation of fealty to Hitler, no contribution of soldiers to the Nazi campaign on the eastern front, no further enactment of anti-Semitic legislation penalizing its large Jewish middle class could save Hungary from the German conquest endured years earlier by much of the rest of Europe. Hitler, battered but still belligerent, had grown impatient with Hungary's prevarications. The country, a neighbor since the occupation of Austria six years earlier, was still home to more than 700,000 Jews. Their very existence, five years into the war, amounted to an affront to a Nazi regime daily drawing closer to what Hitler had once called "the annihilation of the Jewish race in Europe." By the end of 1943, more than 4.3 million European Jews had been killed by the Germans.

Hauer himself knew little of this slaughter, despite the fact that much of it was taking place no more than 250 miles to the north, at Auschwitz. Hungary had believed itself secure in its Axis alliance. Many of its Jews were lulled, although not all were ignorant of the Nazi death camps in Poland. The broad windows from which Hauer gazed were those of the Jewish Theological Seminary and Teachers' Institute, a respected rabbinical center of learning where Talmudic studies were accompanied by instruction in the range of subjects needed to pass the Hungarian *Matura*, or high school final exams. Throughout the war, the institute had thrived. Hauer, aged eighteen, was a good student; only a weakness in mathematics and a dreamy disposition prevented him from making the very top tier. Just months from his exams, he had no more expected the war to intrude on his life than had the countless young American GIs pulled from their studies in 1943 and 1944 to prepare to fight in Europe.

A thoughtful young man, carelessly handsome with his pale eyes and gentle gaze, Hauer had been raised by a doting mother and a domineering father in the town of Goncz in northeastern Hungary before coming to Budapest to study. He was patriotic. "Much like the German Jews, we were proud of our country," he said. "I used to write poems about my love for Hungary."

But, for all his ardor, Hauer was not entirely assimilated into Hungary's hierarchical, largely Catholic society. Rather, he hovered between a strong sense of his Jewish identity and the desire for integration. The great great-grandson of a learned chief rabbi of Bohemia and Moravia named Mordecai Binet, the son of a prosperous merchant with a large general store, Hauer came from a family whose Orthodox Jewish inclinations remained strong even as it sought and secured social advancement.

Before Passover, the sprawling house behind the family store was still thoroughly cleaned, each item of clothing taken into the large garden and checked to ensure not a crumb remained in a pocket. The local synagogue was refurbished in 1932 with substantial help and prodding from the Hauer family. Hauer's beautiful mother, Camilla, kept her hair short so that she could easily wear a wig on Jewish High Holidays. At the same time, his father, David, pursued the expansion of his store (selling everything from nails to gasoline), contributed to civic projects like the construction of the first municipal swimming pool (while insisting, against resistance, that Jews be allowed to swim in it), and pushed his three sons and one daughter to acquire the best education available (so scattering them around Hungary).

When the war began, more than half of Hungary's physicians and close to half of its lawyers were Jews. Like many members of the country's Jewish middle class, the Hauers saw no limit to their ascendancy, far less any danger, even as the pro-Nazi Hungarian authorities began passing laws that barred Jews from state service, limited their participation in the very professions at which they excelled, and denied them the right to acquire real estate.

These measures, steadily tightened between 1938 and 1942, were disturbing, and Hitler's rhetoric menacing. But Hungary, eleven years after Hitler's rise to power, remained an island of relative safety for Jews in Europe. An alliance with Germany had enabled the country to recover some of the vast swathes of land taken from it under the Treaty of Trianon after World War I. These were arguments invoked by many Hungarian Jews to comfort themselves—until the very moment the German army appeared in the streets of Budapest, with Adolf Eichmann and his now experienced staff of bureaucrats and killers not far behind.

Gazing at those Nazi troops, Hauer's music teacher, an old man by the name of Erdos, shook his head. Then he turned for the last time to his thirty-six pupils. He said that he had planned to analyze the polonaise. But now, he continued, he could think only of Chopin's life and homeland: the composer's native Poland swallowed by Germany and Russia, his exile, his premature death. "How symbolic," said Erdos, "that I was playing his composition when the Germans that Chopin so hated roared into our city."

With that, the professor gathered up his things, left the room, and gently closed the door behind him, only for it to burst open again as the dean of the institute, breathless and flushed, rushed in with an announcement: everyone was to return home at once. Those, like Hauer, who came from the provinces were to take the first available train, if it was still possible to do so. Rumors already abounded that the Germans or quisling elements of the Hungarian gendarmerie had taken over the railway stations.

More than half of the several hundred students at the institute came from outside Budapest. Their dilemma was acute. One student, Martin Braun, joked that, thanks to the Germans, he would face no final exam and might become a rich businessman rather than an impoverished teacher. But any hilarity was short-lived. Within half an hour of the Germans' arrival in Budapest, the old center of Jewish learning was empty.

The instructions to return home were well meant. But as Eichmann, a primary Nazi overseer of Jewish deportation and murder throughout Europe, went to work over the next four months, the only tenuous sanctuary for Hungarian Jews would lie in Budapest itself. Very soon the countryside would be *Judenrein*, free of Jews, as deportations proceeded at a furious pace. Hauer, however, could not know that his journey home was also a journey toward greater danger, one that would end, almost a year later, in the Berga concentration camp.

Goncz was a pretty town set in undulating countryside and laid out on the banks of the Patak River, where in summer children swam and in winter they skated. Its main road was partially paved, its nearby spa renowned for its curative waters. Lumber and farm produce were plentiful. An odd mixture of folk, from an aloof count representing Hungary's beleaguered but unyielding aristocracy to a community of Gypsies, contrived to coexist there.

About forty of the families, or 5 percent of the population, were Jewish, a ratio consistent with that in all of Hungary. The majority was Catholic, but a Protestant community also thrived. Each of the three religious groups had its own elementary school and house of worship. Tolerance, if not exactly harmony, prevailed; the Jews still thought it wiser to keep to themselves.

The chief of the gendarmerie knew that he could extract the favors and loans he wanted from David Hauer, the owner of the main general-goods store, but he also knew that he could not with impunity close down the Jew's business. Most people who needed medical attention turned, however reluctantly, to the two Jewish physicians, Grossman and the curt but brilliant Rona. Modernity and quasi-feudal backwardness, parvenus and aristocrats, hucksters and hunters, found an accommodation with each other, but not without engendering little resentments that could be fanned. Here, in the torpor of the provinces, Mordecai Hauer had passed his childhood quietly enough—but not without violence that marked him—until he was sent to study in the capital at the age of fifteen.

Hauer's father was an imposing man, given to tailored suits and fine shoes, a man whose gray eyes could harden in anger to steeliness, particularly when he was disappointed by his son's lack of business acumen. In the store, the young Hauer was sometimes inclined, when confronted by a poor client, to put a little extra grain on the scales, a natural gesture of charity, or so he thought. His father saw things otherwise. He beat him roundly for such foolishness. David, who was head of the town's Jewish community, was equally intolerant of his son's dreamy lapses in synagogue or at Passover dinners. Then, the failure to answer questions correctly was sometimes met with a slap across the face. His mother's tears and entreaties could not change his father's ways.

For his mother, Camilla, Hauer felt a love without reserve. When he was about ten days old, he had fallen mysteriously ill, refusing to eat for several days. Drs. Grossman and Rona were called, but each pronounced the case hopeless. In despair, Camilla recalled a small, white linen bag given to her on her wedding day by her mother. It contained crystal candy blessed by Camilla's grandfather and said to have miraculous healing powers.

She took a little of the candy, dissolved it in boiling water, allowed the syrup to cool, and gave some to the baby, who quickly responded. For Camilla, her son's recovery was proof of God's existence. For Hauer, the story was evidence of his mother's powers and helped explain the mystical bond between them. To him she was life itself, generous and impulsive, loving and delicate. As for the God invoked so often by his father, He seemed stern and remote, dividing as often as He healed. Fearful of his father, Hauer often kept his thoughts to himself.

He had one secret he would certainly never divulge. Margit, the family maid, had arrived at the Hauer household in 1940, after her husband and infant son were run over and killed by a vehicle as they brought produce to market in Goncz. She was a simple and hardworking young woman, responsive to Camilla's many demands. For months after the accident, Hauer would hear Margit whimpering in the room beside his. One night he ventured into the room to try to calm her. He took her hand in his and held her head in his lap. To his embarrassment, Hauer now became aroused by the warm touch of the maid's skin. Flushed and breathless, Margit embraced him. So was he initiated, at the age of fourteen, into the pleasures of sex.

Their relationship continued throughout Hauer's adolescence, although Law XV of the following year, 1941, prohibited marriages and extramarital sexual relations between Jews and non-Jews. Like other such anti-Semitic laws, it long seemed that it could be safely ignored.

Hauer's nature was sensual, and he was drawn to beauty. Whatever form this beauty took, it exerted a spell on him that was hard for his more practical father to understand. Sometimes he would climb the hill toward the spa, drawn by the magnificent oaks, the wildflowers, and the cool breezes. Sprawled in the soft grass, he would gaze at the shimmering, tremulous leaves against the summer sky with its shifting clouds. At times he felt an exultation that was overwhelming, a pleasurable convulsion of his whole being, a lightness as insubstantial as the cumulus clouds above him, and was moved to write poetry in the notebook he always carried.

Music could also transport Hauer. None was more moving to him as a child than that played on the accordion by his little neighbor Andras. Already in his late twenties, Andras was so small that no woman would look at him. Night after night he would sit on a wooden bench in front of his house playing sad tunes of unrequited longing. It seemed he was the village idiot, but Andras was no fool, merely a gentle soul bereft of social graces inhabiting a stunted body. He never drank and seldom spoke. Sometimes he would let Hauer touch the black-and-white buttons of the instrument he adored, a privilege granted to nobody else. Most people kept their distance from Andras because he was different. Sometimes his strangeness could even provoke anger.

One evening, as Hauer sat beside Andras on the bench, a passing gendarme tripped over Andras's feet. The policeman, furious, grabbed his rifle and drove its butt into Andras's face. A colleague seized the accordion and smashed it over the young man's head. As the policemen pummeled his friend, Hauer looked on, too terrified to speak, even when they dragged Andras off to jail.

Hauer picked up the broken accordion and rushed home to tell his father, who quickly secured Andras's release and had him tended to by Dr. Grossman. The next morning, Hauer wanted to skip school in order to spend the day with Andras, but his father would not allow that; nor was he permitted to miss the religious school that followed. So it was evening by the time Hauer found his friend and, by the light of a faint oil lamp, saw the missing teeth, the flattened nose, the purplish skin, the eyes reduced to slits by swelling. "Andras," he said. "I brought your accordion."

Hauer had to bend down close to his friend's lips to hear the reply. "I'll be better when the night is over. I'll have no pain. You go home now. It's late, and I feel a storm coming."

The next morning Hauer awoke to the screams of Margit. She had found Andras hanging from an apple tree, dead. Hauer ran out of the house into the garden next door, where he saw his friend hanging from a low branch. Andras was dressed in his Sunday suit, and the tips of his shiny boots just touched the ground soaked by the storm he had foreseen. Across his chest hung the smashed accordion, by his side an overturned milking stool.

The three legs of that little stool pointing to the sky cut through Hauer like daggers. Here, it seemed, innocence and violence had come together in intolerable juxtaposition. So this was what Andras had meant when he said he would feel no pain by night's end. Margit sobbed as the gendarmes cut the diminutive body from the tree and, with a white cloth, covered Andras's pummeled head. Even in a small town, the placid, ordered surface of things could be illusory.

On his way to the station the morning after German troops occupied Budapest, Hauer saw, ouside the National Theater, banners reading HUNGARY FOR HUNGARIANS and JEWS TO PALESTINE. The placards were being paraded by a group of students wearing the armbands of Hungary's anti-Semitic, Magyar nationalist Arrow Cross movement. They chanted the name of Ferenc Szálasi, the founder of the movement and a man whose hatred for Jews was boundless. It did not take long, Hauer reflected, for the vermin to crawl out of the woodwork once the poison was introduced. He was frightened; his world seemed suddenly fragile.

Fortunately, he did not have to buy a train ticket because his mother had just sent him one in anticipation of a journey home for Passover. So he was able to go at once to the train, taking a seat in the front car. The train to Miskolc, the largest town near Goncz, was due to depart at 7:45. But the minutes ticked by and the train stood motionless as a commotion erupted outside.

An elderly man looked out. "They are looking for Jews," he declared. "Thank God. They should all be sent to Palestine."

As a young boy, Hauer had been told by Rabbi Shloime Seltzer of Goncz that he must learn his prayers by heart because he might want to pray on occasions when he had no access to a prayer book. Now he found himself involuntarily mumbling the first of King David's psalms: "Happy is the man that hath not walked in the counsel of the wicked..." A young woman beside him leaned over and said, "It seems they are combing the whole train." But Hauer scarcely heard her.

Two policemen and a German soldier entered the car and demanded identification papers. Their progress toward Hauer appeared inexorable until one of them yelled: "Moses Marcus! How did you get into the station? Don't you know that Jews are not supposed to be on the train?"

The terrified young man in question protested that he was merely in transit through Budapest, but the police would hear nothing of it. A scuffle ensued as the police dragged him from an aisle seat opposite Hauer. The German soldier, apparently satisfied by this capture, took a last look at the fair-haired Hauer and the blond young woman beside him, then turned and left. A moment later a piercing whistle sounded and the wheels began clattering reassuringly over the track.

Hauer, who had spent most of the previous night gathering his things and saying good-bye to friends, drifted into a deep sleep. When he awoke, blinded by sunlight, he could not find the small suitcase that had been perched on his lap. As he began looking for it, the pretty young woman beside the window turned to him with a smile. "It fell," she said, "and I took the liberty of placing it on the luggage rack." Hauer thanked her.

They drifted into conversation. She, too, was going to Miskolc and then on to Goncz. Her name was Ilona; she was the daughter of the local judge. This judge, a self-important man, had earned some renown in the Hauer family by taking extensive credit in the store and then making his anti-Semitic views clear at any opportunity. Perhaps, Hauer mused to himself, the judge would be in his element with the Nazis now ensconced in Hungary.

Ilona was a beauty, cherry-lipped, pale-necked, blue-eyed, fine-boned. A violent attraction stirred between them as the train clattered rhythmically onward. The wind came through the open window in unseasonably warm gusts. Hauer smelled the earth, felt the budding of things all around him. They wanted each other, but they talked, of course, of the issues of the moment. No, she felt no hatred toward Jews. Yes, Hitler would fall soon, the Americans were advancing, the Russians, too, and all would be well. They could meet then in Budapest, go for strolls along the river, eat ices and chocolate. Everything seemed attainable. One world was coming to an end and another was not yet born. In a sense, even as menace crowded in, new possibilities came within reach. Taboos fell away and postponing pleasure seemed senseless. A Jewish man, a Christian girl, but how, Hauer wondered now, did they look to others on the train? Like brother and sister? Or young lovers? He was certain they did not look like a student of the Talmud and the daughter of an anti-Semite. As the train rocked, their fingertips and calves would touch from time to time, and Hauer felt his whole being riveted at that fleeting point of contact. Danger, like power, was arousing, he noted.

Ilona talked of her father. He was not what he appeared, she insisted. To hide his humble origins in Slovakia, he had changed his name to one of thorough Hungarian pedigree. The son of an itinerant tailor, he had moved to Hungary and done brilliantly at law school, finishing at the top of his class. But the justice ministry discovered his background, and a distinguished career in one of the most class-conscious of European capitals eluded him. Frustrated, he settled for the county judgeship in Goncz. "That is why he drinks," Ilona said. "That is also why status matters so much to him and why he can be so narrow-minded and prejudiced."

People are not what they seem, Hauer mused to himself, not this judge with his anti-Jewish bile, not even perhaps his own neighbors. Could it be that the whole country he had grown up in was some vast illusion? This question troubled him. He was an optimist; he tended to be gullible. His frankness attracted people, it could even inspire them, but it also made him vulnerable. Still, he did not want to protect himself with some adopted cynicism, especially not now, with Ilona beside him.

The train pulled into Miskolc, where, to Hauer's relief, no further police checks were imposed. With a five-hour wait for the connection to Goncz, he and Ilona decided to go to a park, where they sat on a bench, drank in the March sun, and ate cookies prepared by Hauer's landlady in Budapest.

"How old are you?" Ilona asked.

"I was eighteen in January. And you?"

"Eighteen today."

She was going home to a birthday party to be given by the judge. All the Christian notables of Goncz would be there. Perhaps even the count would appear, along with the priest, the pharmacist, the postmaster, the game warden, officers of the military garrison, top county officials, and assorted other representatives of the local gentry. Hauer felt their momentarily elided worlds diverging. He could no more appear at such a gathering, especially in Hungary's changed circumstances, than attend a church service or hunt elk with the country's countless courtiers, snobs undeterred by the fact that the king's court had long since disappeared.

Frustrated, on an impulse, to deny the unbridgeable distance that Hauer felt opening up, he clasped Ilona's hand. She moved closer—as if in defiance of all that was closing in around them, as if in mockery of Hitler, Hungarian bigotry, and every stifling small-town stigma—and placed her head on his shoulder. Their hearts thumped, their fingers trembled, their kiss, when it came, lingered hungrily. But within hours, as they walked out of the Goncz station to meet their families, they had to pretend they did not know each other and that their declarations of love were no more than the soon-to-be-forgotten folly of an early-spring day late in a long war.

Hauer's unexpected arrival home provoked alarm. Camilla, the driving force in the family at moments of crisis, immediately decided to collect her youngest son, eleven-year-old Emerich, who was studying at a renowned Hebrew boarding school in Nagyvárad. She insisted that she go herself, despite her husband's protests, and left her family with the fatalistic words: "Remember this, there is no luck, or misfortune, only the will of Almighty God." After two days, she returned safely.

The Hauer family was now reunited for a last time as Passover approached. Life assumed an almost normal rhythm. Hauer was struck by how different they all were: young Emerich, musical, moody, and brilliant; the exuberant, athletic Benji, four years Hauer's junior, who loved action more than words; solemn, beautiful Edith, aged sixteen, who studied at home with a private tutor because her parents were protective. In addition, of course, there was Margit, who, after Hauer's absence of several months, made little secret of her desire for him. But his obsession with Ilona left him as cold to her advances as he was indifferent to the forces closing in on the family.

The young couple managed to meet once, for a few minutes, and the tryst only reinforced their longing for each other. Ilona wrote a letter, which Hauer reread often: "I know you must be thinking the same way as I do: life is cruel because we can't be together. Still, I ask you not to lose heart, even though it may take some time until we meet again. I feel sure that it won't be long before you return to your school in Budapest—perhaps as soon as Passover vacation is over. Then we shall be together every blessed day. But no matter how long I'll be waiting for you always."

Hauer wanted to believe the words in the letter. He tore off a corner of the paper, wrote the words "I love you," and entrusted the note, unsigned, to a friend of Ilona's, who delivered it. But soon Ilona was gone, back to Budapest. Just a day later, the old town crier passed through Goncz announcing that, under decree number 1240/1944, all Jews were to wear a yellow Star of David over their garments from the next day onward. The prospect of being back in Budapest, after Passover or at all, receded.

A dark mood of frustration descended on Hauer. Tensions rose between him and his father. On the first night of Passover, he refused a great honor: to conduct a special service in the synagogue, a privilege normally accorded to David as president of the Goncz Jewish community. David then asked his son to assist him in conducting the service, but Hauer again demurred, unable to shake his mood. They walked home in silence. The seder, a normally joyous occasion, began. At the point when the ten plagues were recited, each member of the family dipped his right little finger in a cup of wine and shook off a drop, one for each of the plagues. It was a moment the children had always enjoyed, sometimes licking rather than shaking their fingers.

"Children," David said with abrupt earnestness, "can anyone tell me the real reason for what appears to be the wasting of ten delicious drops of wine?"

There was silence around the table. As the oldest and most educated of the children, Hauer was expected to respond.

"Would my firstborn kindly give the answer to the question?" David insisted, his voice growing icy and his eyes assuming the steely hue that his children had learned to fear.

Benji and Emerich started babbling all kinds of answers, trying to protect their strangely withdrawn brother.

"Quiet!" David shouted. "Stop trying to cover for him! I am addressing my learned son who sits in the place of honor to my right."

At last, Hauer spoke: "I don't know the answer, Father. I am sorry if I disappoint you."

David could no longer contain himself. "You are a liar! You are an impudent, shameless liar!" He rose, moving swiftly, and slapped Hauer twice across the face, once with each hand. Hauer fell to the floor, knocking his head hard against the foot of the table. His nose and mouth began to bleed.

Camilla, pale, her eyes gleaming, rose from the far end of the table. "You murderer!" she screamed at her husband. "You killer! What do you want from this boy?"

The two younger boys started to cry. Only Edith had the presence of mind to run to the kitchen and alert Margit, who brought a damp towel with which she lovingly dabbed Hauer's face. "It's nothing, Mrs. Hauer," she said. "The young master will be all right in a minute."

Hauer got up and walked unsteadily to the kitchen behind his mother and Margit. His head ached; he had a large swelling behind his right ear. Margit took a knife with a wide blade and pressed its cold surface to the swelling.

Thoughts of revenge filled his head, a desire even to strike his father. But a defiant pride outweighed these feelings, and he returned to the table to chant the Haggadah with the rest of the family. The ancient, lilting sound was comforting. But he felt many troubling things around the table, as if the fear and foreboding and emotion of the past few weeks had suddenly concentrated themselves in this gathering and exploded in violence.

It was strange, he thought later, that such anger could erupt within the family but was never directed at the Hauers' German tormentors, even as the Jews of Goncz and hundreds of thousands of others were led, compliant and almost uncomplaining, to their deaths that year. Strange, too, that his family could argue over the riddles and wisdom of a holy book, as Jews had for generations, rather than look around themselves and decide that the time had come to set aside the word and take up the sword.

On the last night of Passover, Hauer had a vivid dream. He was traveling by train to meet Ilona, full of happiness at the thought of seeing her. The train halted at Hatvan, the last station before Budapest, a stop famous for its chocolate cart, a gleaming, glass-topped mahogany thing with shiny chrome spokes on its thin rubber wheels. "Fresh and famous from our own factory!" a girl cried. "Buy chocolate and candies at bargain prices."

Hauer immediately recognized Ilona's voice. He jumped down from the train to see the girl pushing the magic cart away from him toward the front of the train. "Ilona!" he cried again and again, pursuing her. At last he grabbed her from behind and swung her around. "Can't you hear me?"

A startled, unfamiliar face confronted him. Hauer apologized and made his way back to the car, which had been full of passengers but was now empty, its chatter replaced by an eerie silence. He looked out the window; nobody was to be seen there, either. Everyone had vanished, as had the cart. The train did not move. A pregnant stillness, like that before a storm, inhabited the little station.

There was knocking at the door of his compartment. "Let us in, let us in!" a man shouted. The door shook. Hauer wanted to say that the door was open, but from his parched throat no sound would emerge. The door handle moved back and forth, faster and faster, as if unhinged. Still, nobody entered. At that moment, filled with panic, he awoke—to hear real knocking on the front door of his house.

"Mr. Hauer, open up! I am an officer of the gendarmerie, and we must talk right now."

Gathering himself, moving quietly to the door of his room, Hauer saw his father admit a gendarme named Juhasz, well known to the family as a decent sort, and another, unfamiliar man. What, David demanded, was this disturbance about? Juhasz spoke: "We have received telegraphic orders from our national headquarters in Budapest to collect every Jew in Goncz, adults as well as children, by nine o'clock in the morning."

"But what is this about? What have we done?"

"We don't know, Mr. Hauer. We have nothing against you. As far as we are concerned, you have done nothing wrong. But we did receive orders from Budapest, and we can't disobey them, whether we like them or not."

The gendarme had an idea, one that would perhaps make this disruption more palatable to the forty Jewish families of Goncz. Rather than police going door-to-door, a procedure certain to be alarming, might not David Hauer, as head of the community, go now and explain to each family that they must attend this gathering, but they need not worry, for it would surely be no more than a question of a few hours at most?

Out of concern for the Jews, the gendarme continued, his chief had already made arrangements for this concentration of Jews to take place not at the Goncz courthouse, as the authorities in Budapest had ordered, but at the Catholic school, whose pupils were still on Easter vacation. The school would be more comfortable, and, after all, the courthouse was for common criminals. One more thing—the gendarme said he had almost forgotten this—every Jew was to bring clothes because if, by some chance, the stay at the school was to last more than a few hours, say one or even two days, a change of clothing would be useful.

"But why all this? What have we done? What will happen to us?" Hauer was surprised to note that his father's voice, usually one of such authority, was weak and imploring.

"Look, Mr. Hauer, we cannot ask questions of clarification because it may appear we are hesitating to carry out the order. But don't take this too hard. Nobody is going to get hurt. The world is not coming to an end."

The gendarme paused for a moment before adding: "Remember, there is no mention from Budapest of the need to bring any food. That is surely a good sign. Because if the stay was to be a long one, you would obviously need food."

"I hope you are right. In any event, please tell your chief that the Jewish community is grateful for the considerate implementation of the orders from Budapest. We hope to show our gratitude one day. You can report to him that every Jew will be at the school in the morning. We are law-abiding citizens."

The Hauers were just that, even after Hungary's laws began to discriminate against Jews. They did not believe, could not grasp in time, even at this late stage in the war with so much of the Nazi genocide already accomplished, that everything could be torn up overnight, pistols pointed to the heads of loyal citizens of Hungary, muddy peasants' boots applied to their pale, intelligent faces. They lived in civilized European society, after all, not some Chicago slaughterhouse. Never, perhaps, did the phrase "blind obedience" find a more apt application: the Hauers and hundreds of thousands of other Hungarian Jews were blind. They had become characters moving about on a theater set, reciting lines, even remembering them well, but quite at a loss as to what the play was about, even when their own blood was splattered on the props. Adolf Eichmann, who knew the sinister plot by heart at this point and could direct it without consulting any notes, had another phrase for his own zeal for orders: *Kadavergehorsam,* or "the obedience of corpses." The obedience of corpses! Obedience all around fed the crematoria with Jewish bodies and filled the air of southern Poland, year after year, summer and winter, with the acrid-sweet stench of burning flesh.

But Poland was far away and, as the gendarme Juhasz had put it, the world was surely not coming to an end. So, at eight-thirty the next morning, the Hauers arrived at the Catholic school, the first of the two hundred Jews in Goncz to assemble there. They had eaten a quick breakfast and gone to a morning service at the synagogue. A gendarme stood at the gate, checking off names.

By nine o'clock, only three Jews were missing: the village idiot, Lucius, who slept in haystacks and was therefore hard to locate, and the retired county medical officer, Kardos, and his wife, who did not consider themselves Jews because they had converted to Christianity. Between the wars, tens of thousands of Hungarian Jews had accepted baptism, and many had entered mixed marriages. But, under Hungary's anti-Semitic laws, Jewishness was now defined by the religion of grandparents rather than confessional status. His list, the gendarme insisted, was incomplete.

The hours passed. Children discovered the playground. Their squeals of delight echoed around the school as if this were just another break from class. Parents met inside and talked in worried tones. As for Hauer, he gathered with his contemporaries—Ferko Hamburger, Tibi Fried, Bela Kornweitz, Lasci Weissman, Jeno Reiss—boys with whom he had grown up, and tried to assess their situation.

Some had dire forecasts because, they said, at root the Christians of Goncz hated the Jews, hated them for saving money, for not drinking, for educating their children, for moving up in the world. Now, with the Nazis in Hungary, every frustration could be vented; all that the Jews had patiently amassed would be taken. But others were more optimistic. The war was nearing its end, they argued; the Germans were reeling, and with patience the whole misunderstanding, or whatever this was, would be peacefully resolved. Had the Russians not already emerged triumphant over the Nazis at Leningrad and Stalingrad? "We are in the dark," said Reiss. "So what? Sooner or later, the light comes on. And even if the darkness lasts, people's eyes can get used to darkness and they are a little more careful not to trip on anything."

Darkness was one thing, however, hunger another. By the early afternoon people were hungry. One young woman, Lea Wertheim, was eight months pregnant; she needed food. Older folk were faint. As head of the community, David Hauer felt he had to confront the authorities, now represented in the school director's office by a gendarme named Barcsai.

The official was apologetic. Food had not been mentioned in

either of two cables from Budapest. But, he announced casually, it was now known that the Jews would have to spend the night at the school, so clearly there was a need for food. Barcsai promised to cable for clarification. Then, in a conspiratorial whisper, he told David Hauer that he would allow him to leave the school for an hour in order to gather provisions.

This mission was fruitful, although David had to endure a hissed taunt—"They'll cut you up like watermelon"—from one passerby. With Margit and the Hauers' neighbors setting an example, numerous Christian families brought packages of food to the school. Although nervous, the gendarme allowed their distribution. Soon everyone had eaten and the mood in the school brightened.

But not for long. In the midafternoon, an Interior Ministry official arrived from Budapest, accompanied by the local chief of the gendarmerie. Hauer watched his father introduce himself as the president of the Jewish community, only to be insulted by the official: "You ought to know better than to stand before me with your hat on, damn you! We are in Hungary, not in Galicia!"

David apologized—that deferential tone of voice was evident again—and removed his hat. Then he disappeared with the officials for a half hour, emerging with an announcement that the authorities wanted to inspect everyone's possessions. Privately, he told his family that the Budapest official believed the Jews had "large amounts of gold and diamonds" and wanted this jewelry for himself because "the Jews are leeches that suck the blood of other people."

Each family proceeded into the director's office, where all their jewelry, other than what they were wearing, was taken. The Budapest official ranted because he found the booty insufficient; he was convinced that much had been hidden. The Hauers had in fact entrusted their most valuable possessions to a beloved neighbor, the carpenter Misha Kruly, before reporting to the school. But it seemed to Hauer that no amount of gold would have satisfied this bigot from Budapest with his conviction that Jews had plundered the wealth of Hungary.

As night descended, people stretched out on the floors of the school with their clothes on. Exhausted, most of them slept. In a matter of hours their lives had changed—almost none of them would ever return to live in their homes—but after the interrupted sleep of the previous night, they were too tired to think or talk, much less act. For the first time since he came home, Hauer found that thoughts of Ilona receded; he could not focus on her. He saw his father lying awake and was filled with a sense of humiliation on behalf of this proud, prickly patriarch sprawled between little desks on a classroom floor.

Then, in the dark, Hauer heard his father's voice repeating questions from the previous night. "What for? What are they going to do with us?" Gazing into the gloom, he was able to make out the familiar form of the town priest, Father Laczko, who was suggesting that the Hauers hide in the church rectory. "No. As president of the Jewish community, I could not possibly run away."

The priest said he had expected that reply, but he knew for a fact, having heard it from the chief of the gendarmerie, that the Jews would be transferred out of Goncz that morning on the five a.m. train to Kassa, a larger provincial town in the northeast. (Kassa is now Kosice, in southern Slovakia.) "I am sure this exile will not last more than a few days, but still I am worried," the priest said.

The churchman had a further offer. He noted that many Christians despised Jews as the killers of Christ but said that he believed Jews and Christians were brothers in God. "Our Lord Jesus was of the Jewish faith," Father Laczko said. "He lived by the commands of the Holy Torah." No subsequent religious divergence between Christians and Jews should obscure that fact. He had therefore come to suggest that the Torahs be removed from the Goncz synagogue, which might be desecrated in the absence of the Jews, and placed for safekeeping inside the church.

So, accompanied by a Christian clergyman who negotiated his temporary absence from the school, David Hauer's last conflicted act in Goncz was to make his way into a dark and silent synagogue, remove the six sacred Torahs from their exquisite velvet drapes, steal along the left bank of the Patak, enter an equally dark and silent church, kiss the Torahs one by one, and place them behind metal doors in a closet in an arched chamber near the altar. As he later told his son, he thought he would be back within a week to reclaim them.

The women and children were put on horse-drawn carts; the men walked. They moved in the dark, a ghostly procession toward the station of the town they had grown up in. On the way, old Kardos and his wife, the converts to Christianity, were picked up, their protests summarily dismissed. Crazy Lucius was never found. The train with its cowed load left on time, carrying Jewish life out of Goncz. It was never to be revived.

In Kassa, they were herded into a Jewish ghetto surrounded by the gendarmerie. Each Goncz family was assigned to the home of local Jews, the Hauers to the Schreibers, wealthy textile merchants. Other Jewish families from nearby towns were also lodged in the crowded house. Every morning and evening, the men went to a packed synagogue to pray and to exchange hearsay: the Russians were at the Hungarian border; Hitler had been assassinated; the Americans would soon land in northern France. The Jews placed their trust in God.

After three weeks a government decree appeared on posters all over town. It ordered all Jews to assemble the next day at a large brick factory on the outskirts of Kassa. Food, clothes, and blankets should be brought. No exceptions to this order were permitted: the sick, invalids, and decorated war heroes should also present themselves. Hauer noted the menacing tone of these instructions, all semblance of civility now gone. But obedience still seemed the only reasonable course, for even this latest command must have a logic behind it, and a reasonable outcome was in everyone's interest.

The vast area of the brick factory, bisected by a highway, was surrounded by a six-foot barbed-wire fence. Inside were a series of "barracks"—corrugated-iron roofs held up by poles where bricks fresh from the kiln were generally stored. Now the bricks would be replaced by human beings. There were no walls to these structures; a deep red dust covered the ground. Thousands of Jews lined up at the gate to be assigned to these temporary abodes.

The Hauers were assigned to barracks 8. David Hauer, in his capacity as president of the community, organized its occupants into three neat rows with a blanket surrounded by packages demarcating each "bed." The spring nights were still chilly; people pressed against one another for warmth. Food was brought by Jews accorded passes out of the brick factory for that purpose, but because the Jewish stores had been closed down, none of it was kosher. Rabbis, citing the Talmudic instruction that "the preservation of life takes precedence over all other considerations," said it was now permissible to eat anything. Hauer, in some awe, watched his father eat cured ham.

Everyone adapted. There was communion, even some happiness, in hardship. The starry nights could be beautiful. In barracks 12, a boy who played the accordion reminded Hauer of Andras. He would go there to listen to Hungarian and Hebrew songs. Teenagers danced and flirted. Hauer's eye was caught by a tall, slender girl named Sharon Becker, from the nearby town of Encs, whom he had known slightly through his family. He talked of Ilona. She talked of her passion for painting and of her love, a young man serving somewhere on the Russian front. But this talk barely masked their growing attraction to each other. Life had an urgent quality. Only the here and now mattered.

During the third week in the brick factory, it was announced that a senior German officer would come to conduct an inspection. Hauer, from a position near the gate, watched a military limousine arrive. Two German officers and a civilian emerged and were greeted by the head of the factory. A few minutes later one of the officers stepped out onto the roof of the main administrative building. Through the public-address system, he introduced himself as SS-*Obersturmbann-führer* (Lieutenant Colonel) Adolf Eichmann.

"This name, which I heard clearly, meant nothing to me," Hauer said. "I knew nothing of the concentration camps and the killing. Call me naïve, but that is the way it was. I still believed that Hungary had enough influence with the Nazis to ensure that its Jews were treated with decency."

In an unpublished memoir, he recorded the words of Eichmann, as he remembered hearing them, in German, that day in late April 1944:

> *I am Adolf Eichmann and I bring an important message to you. I know that you must be wondering what this concentration means and why it had to be done to begin with. I will explain. The eastern front is nearing the borders of Hungary. You are intelligent enough to understand that we don't anticipate that Jews would aid the joint German-Hungarian war effort. We know that in certain areas, the Jews have given signals in the night to Anglo-American bombers. You can hardly blame us for taking measures to prevent precisely such things, and this is the reason for your concentration. Here you cannot possibly collaborate with the enemy.*
>
> *Now the head of the brick factory tells me that this place is not fit for people to live in, and I can see it myself. There are no proper sanitary facilities, no adequate food supplies and no possibility for useful employment. I have therefore decided to empty this*

place. I shall make arrangements to transfer you to the spacious prisoner-of-war camp in Kenyermezo. We have everything there for your convenience. Depending on the availability of trains, the transfer will commence in two or three days. The tracks reach into the factory, so you won't have to walk at all, and the whole operation will be effected swiftly.

There might be some amongst you who will spread rumors to the effect that those who arrive at the new camp first will receive better housing and jobs. I give you my word that this is not so, and I caution you against rushing the trains. We like to work judiciously and with meticulous care. We prepared housing and jobs for all of you. It is my personal hope that this big operation gets completed without harm to anyone, and therefore we must work in orderly fashion. The loudspeakers will call you to the loading zone, which is on the other side of the factory, barracks by barracks. Don't come before you hear the number of your barracks called. If you try, we will take you last. You must cooperate with us until the successful completion of the war. This is all I have to say. Thank you for hearing me out. Heil Hitler!

It was a masterful piece of plausible deception. Was it not true that if the war was going badly for Germany, it had every reason to detain Jews to ensure they did not help the Allied effort? Did this Eichmann not look and speak like an officer and a gentleman? How hard would it be, after the past few weeks, to wait a further month or two in another Hungarian camp? These were the arguments that Hauer heard, and he himself subscribed to them. In addition, some of the Jews at the brick factory had received postcards supposedly sent from relatives at Kenyermezo, northwest of Budapest. The cards, an apparent German ruse designed to dampen any alarm among the Jews in Kassa, spoke of the charms of the place. Eichmann's mention of Kenyermezo seemed to confirm that it had been chosen as the concentration point for all Hungarian Jews. In fact, however, that point was not in the heart of Hungary but Auschwitz-Birkenau in southern Poland.

Eichmann had been hard at work in Hungary for several weeks by the time he made the visit to Kassa that Mordecai Hauer witnessed. Prior to invading the country on March 18, 1944, Hitler had admonished Admiral Miklós Horthy, the Hungarian leader, for not having "introduced the steps necessary to settle the Jewish question." This question Eichmann and his *Sondereinsatzkommando* (special operations unit) took it upon themselves to resolve, with zeal.

The situation appears to have held a particular allure for Eichmann. Nowhere else in continental Europe did such a high concentration of Jews remain. At no other time did he have such a wide range of sinister talent available to bring to bear on the issue, because elsewhere the Jews had already been deported and murdered. Nazi experts in the handling of Jewish deportation were idle and eager. They were brought to Budapest from Slovakia, Greece, France, Bulgaria, Yugoslavia, and Austria. From Berlin, Eichmann summoned his legal expert, among others. Despite the colossal scale of the task, everything went "like a dream," Eichmann later enthused.

The deportation took place at an unprecedented pace. In less than two months, 434,351 Jews, packed in cattle cars, were delivered by train from Hungary to Auschwitz. When Rudolf Höss, the Auschwitz commander, was informed of Eichmann's plans for Hungarian Jews, he ordered the construction of a new branch line of the railway to bring the cars with their doomed loads closer to the crematoria. The number of people manning the gas chambers was quadrupled in order to deal with the killing of between 6,000 and 12,000 people a day.

This, late in the war, with much already known to the Allies of the systematic extermination of Jews, amounted to a crime on a singular scale. It was also an extraordinary bureaucratic and logistical effort at a time when the Nazi apparatus was stretched on every front by the toll of a war that had turned against Germany. Indeed, in 1944 Eichmann, at the direction of Heinrich Himmler, engaged in discussions with a representative of the Hungarian Zionist movement on a curious proposal: the sparing of one million Jewish lives in exchange for ten thousand trucks to be provided to the Nazis by the Allies. The negotiations went nowhere. But they did suggest that even as the killing intensified, so did German desperation.

The German difficulties were not overwhelming enough to save lives, however. If 350 American soldiers, many selected on the basis of their Jewishness or their resemblance to Jews, ended up in the Berga concentration camp less than one hundred days before the suicide of Hitler, and Mordecai Hauer, a young Hungarian Jew, ended up there beside them, it was precisely because, even at the end of the war—with everything falling apart, the center no longer holding, the Russians and the Americans closing in from east and west, the SS scrambling to cover up the evidence of the genocide—even then, with the apparatus of totalitarian terror in partial dissolution, enough Germans were ready to go on obeying enough orders enough of the time for the killing to continue. The appeal of obedience is a central German conundrum.

One German physician, Peter Bamm, who witnessed the killing of Jews in mobile gas vans on the eastern front, did toy with the idea of protest. But he rejected it. Later he wrote of the slaughter: "We knew this. We did nothing. Anyone who had seriously protested or done anything against the killing unit would have been arrested within twenty-four hours and would have disappeared. It belongs among the refinements of totalitarian governments in our century that they don't permit their opponents to die a great, dramatic martyr's death for their convictions. A good many of us might have accepted such a death. The totalitarian state lets its opponents disappear in silent anonymity. It is certain that anyone who had dared to suffer death rather than silently tolerate the crime would have sacrificed his life in vain. This is not to say that such a sacrifice would have been morally meaningless. It would only have been practically useless."

Acting out of fear or opportunism, convenience or anger, the overwhelming majority of Germans sided with complicity, active or passive. If they had a conscience, they declined to listen to it. They declined to disobey.

Among the Jews herded together at Kassa, Mordecai Hauer observed, "the question of disobedience did not even enter anyone's mind; people were not going to change their law-abiding habits when the defeat of Germany was so near." But on the same day that Eichmann spoke, one young man did try to urge the Jews to resist. He spoke to a gathering of young people, including Hauer, in barracks 12.

"I come to you with an urgent message of warning," the tall, narrow-faced young man said. "I must be brief because there is no time to waste. In these past weeks, you-have been lulled into a false sense of security. The clever speech you just heard from the Nazi, Eichmann, was full of deception and lies, designed to dispel your fears about the future. I warn you that at this very moment, Jews are being deported from other ghettos in the country. They are being taken probably to Germany, or possibly to occupied Poland, where death or slave labor awaits them. The liquidation of this factory is imminent. The camp at Kenyermezo is a fiction, but your parents would never listen to me. They are set in their ways and, as always, cling to the faith that God will take care of everything."

The man, a member of Hungary's small Zionist movement, made an offer. He had twenty temporary passes to leave the factory. The twenty volunteers would be met by a truck that afternoon that would take them to a nearby town. From there, they would proceed by train and "within a few days you will be on your way to our beloved Israel." Forged documents in the man's possession would ensure there were no problems. "Those who have Zion in their hearts," he concluded, "will take the chance on freedom instead of sure slavery or death."

Hauer was shaken by the speech. He was sitting next to Sharon Becker, the young woman from Encs, and took her hand. "The man is right," she said. "This will end in tragedy."

"Why don't you join the twenty volunteers then?"

"My parents would never understand. They would be broken-hearted if I left. But what about you? Go, Mordecai, you are a man who could do a lot in Israel. Hurry, there is no time to lose."

Hauer did not move. He had been impressed by the speech but still believed in a positive outcome and still considered Zionists to be dangerous fanatics. In Budapest, early in the war, he had attended a Zionist youth meeting. The boys and girls wore uniforms, acted as if they were soldiers, and spoke of murdering British Mandate forces in Palestine. The talk made Hauer uneasy, and besides, he loved Hungary.

"Look," said Hauer. "Hitler has been yelling about a Jew-free Europe for years, and Horthy has protected us. We will not be harmed."

"But we are now under German occupation," Sharon said. "Perhaps Eichmann did lie and we will all be killed."

"No," Hauer replied. "Time is running out for the Germans. The war will soon be over. Everything will return to normal."

"I would like to believe you. I would like to show you my paintings back home. But I don't believe you will ever see them. Nor will I."

That night an announcement blared around the brick factory: "Attention! Attention! Tomorrow morning you will be transferred to Kenyermezo, which is good news. Unfortunately there is a shortage of passenger trains, and therefore you will have to travel the few hours in cattle cars. Go early to bed and get a good rest and be warned: a false rumor appears to have been spread saying that you will be taken out of the country. This is a Zionist lie. They are the ones who take Jews out of the country, not us. Do not listen to them, and do not try to escape from the factory. From now on, anyone who approaches the fence will be shot without warning by the gendarmes on patrol."

With each announcement, the tone grew steadily harsher. Anxiety increased among the Jews, but they could not be shaken from their credulity. Hauer walked with Sharon to the edge of the camp. It was a beautiful night, full of the smell of spring and wildflowers that always reminded him of the hill leading to the spa near Goncz. They resumed their earlier discussion.

"Despite what we just heard, you have to believe that tomorrow will be better," Hauer said. "That you will be home and you will be painting."

"Let's not think about tomorrow," Sharon said. "I believe the Germans are more dangerous now because they are cornered rats. They are desperate and panicky. For us, tomorrow may never come, or if it does, it will not be like today."

She moved closer. They kissed breathlessly and the world was blotted out. The touch of their bodies brought release. Through their passion, their words of love, the force of their physical bond, life was affirmed and encroaching death repulsed. Under normal circumstances, they knew, this could not have happened. But this pleasure, however ephemeral, was what remained to them. They savored it until they were spent, all fear now gone.

For a long time, they were silent, gazing at the stars. At last Hauer said: "You know, Sharon, according to Jewish law, we are now man and wife."

She laughed. "Don't let your imagination run away with you."

"But it's true. The Talmud states that a marriage is valid when performed by a contract, a ring, or through physical communion."

"Then I am now your wife. And the ceremony was wonderful!"

The bodies were found on a cement platform beside the administration building where Eichmann had spoken. Three teenage girls had been shot in the chest as they tried to get through the fence around the brick-factory ghetto. Their naked breasts were torn to pieces. Hauer had heard the shots ring out as he made his way back to his barracks after parting from Sharon. But he had not imagined this.

How relentlessly the menace had intensified. Hauer thought back to the first visit of the gendarme in Goncz. A few hours, he had said, and the Jews would almost certainly be back home. More than a month had now passed, and still they had not seen their houses again. Now, as they were about to board another train, this first unbelievable violence had been inflicted on them. Eichmann's encouragement to board the train had been subtle. This was encouragement of another kind.

Hauer had said good-bye to Sharon, whose barracks, number 12, was loaded separately. They had promised each other everything. Now he found himself with his family being pushed and shoved into a boxcar. At last, the sliding doors shut, enclosing about one hundred Jews inside, with just a narrow opening for air.

When the train moved, it quickly became apparent that it was heading north, toward the Slovakian border, rather than southwest as promised. Soon after, a man from Goncz named Frankfurter noticed words scrawled on a wall with a crayon: "You are going to Auschwitz!" This name was known to Frankfurter, who announced that they were destined for a camp in Poland or Germany and were doomed. People began to scream and beat the sides of the car.

A few, including Hauer, tried to calm them. They were still in Hungary. What did they know of Auschwitz anyway? Perhaps the train would soon change direction. But it did not. After some time the train did rattle to a halt, the sliding doors opened, and a German SS man appeared. He announced that the Jews were no longer on Hungarian territory and would now be guarded by the Waffen-SS. Addressing the Jews as "dogs," he demanded that they hand over all their jewelry. With that, he left, saying he would be back to collect it soon.

David Hauer tried to organize the collection of everything that remained after the first confiscation in Goncz, but old Mrs. Kardos, the wife of the doctor who had converted to Christianity, refused to give up a gold necklace, hiding it beneath her fur coat.

When the SS man returned, he seemed satisfied at first with the jewels he was handed. But then he began to search the wagon. Reaching Mrs. Kardos, he screamed: "You dirty bitch, take off that

Mordecai Hauer's Odyssey

Baltic Sea

GERMANY

EAST PRUSSIA

Gdansk

Elbe

GERMANY

Oder

Berlin

Vistula

Poznan

POLAND
Occupied by Nazi Germany

Warsaw

BUCHENWALD
Hauer's father dies here in late 1944.

Hauer arrives in Berga in February 1945.

• Lodz

May 7, 1945
Hauer is liberated in Manetin.

AUSCHWITZ
Hauer's mother and youngest
brother die here in the summer
and late fall of 1944, respectively.

Dresden

Neisse

Wroclaw

Hauer and his family held
here in a brick factory in
April 1944.

• Berga

Elster

• Manetin

• Prague

Oder

• Kraków

BOHEMIA
Annexed by Nazi Germany in 1939

JAWISCHOWITZ

• Cham

MORAVIA

CZECHOSLOVAKIA

SLOVAKIA
German Protectorate

Kassa

April 1945
Hauer is forced onto a death
march from Berga to Manetin.

Danube

Vienna

Goncz

Miskolc

• Munich

Inn

AUSTRIA
Annexed by Nazi Germany in 1938

• Kenyermezo

Annexed by
Hungary in 1938

Budapest

*Lake
Balaton*

Hauer flees the Hungarian capital
on March 20, 1944, and arrives in
Goncz that day.

0 — Kilometers — 100

0 — Miles — 100

YUGOSLAVIA

HUNGARY

coat! It's just the right size for my wife." She protested that she was cold.

Ignoring pleas from Kardos, the German tore off the coat and saw the exposed necklace. "So, the woman is cold!" he shouted. "Well, I have the best medicine."

He drew his revolver and shot the old lady three times between the eyes. Then he ripped the choker from her neck.

The train jolted into movement again. The Jews journeyed on in terrified silence. Soon after, there were cries from one corner of the car. A baby was delivered to Lea Wertheim, the beautiful young wife of the Goncz butcher. That night Hauer had a confused erotic dream about Ilona and Sharon and awoke to find the girl who had been next to him, whom he did not know, making love to him. He tried feebly to resist. "I love you," the young woman murmured. "You are my first." The Germans, it was clear now, wanted to make animals of them. The Jews, their limbs intertwined, lives unraveled, longings unutterable, clattered through the night, a corpse and a newborn baby in their midst.

CHAPTER FOUR

The Selection

T HE SPA TOWN of Bad Orb, a place far enough from the front lines to be intact, was a quaint labyrinth of cobblestone streets and gabled, cream-colored homes: thoroughly gemütlich. As in many German towns, the church, the timbered town hall, and the adjacent inns blended harmoniously to proclaim a cozy, comforting haven for the industrious and the faithful. But the American soldiers' destination was not the town itself.

As they spilled from the cattle cars where they had been confined for five days, their feet frozen, their stomachs empty, the GIs captured at the Battle of the Bulge were assembled in line and marched out into the surrounding wooded hills. It was cold, and Joe Littell was limping. He had suffered a shrapnel wound just before his capture a week earlier, on December 19. A medic had removed the shrapnel, but the long forced march to the rail yard at Gerolstein, where the soldiers had been herded into the boxcars, had aggravated the injury. Once or twice he had blacked out as he walked through the heavy snow. What kept Littell going then was the physical assistance of his companions, the certain knowledge that to stop was to die, and words from somewhere that kept running through his head: Get up, be courageous, do what you have to do.

The Germans of Bad Orb stared at the Americans. In towns closer to the front, most of the civilian population had been evacuated, but here everyone seemed to be out on the street. Littell, aged twenty, gazed at these expressionless burghers. They did not throw stones, they did not jeer; they looked, if anything, more curious than contemptuous. He knew the Germans well enough, having spent some of his youth in the country, but that was before they became the enemy. Now Littell found himself unable to fathom these onlookers.

He had become enraged in the boxcar. As a German speaker, Littell had personally pleaded with guards on more than one occasion to provide sanitary facilities, or at least let the prisoners out to relieve themselves during the long stops. His appeals were met with disdain. Because he had some experience of the treatment of German prisoners of war in the United States, this was doubly infuriating. Shortly after he was drafted in 1943 and received basic training at Fort Devens, in Massachusetts, Littell had been selected on the basis of his language skills to interrogate German prisoners captured in North Africa. From what he saw, Germans were always handled with respect on their way to prison camps in the Midwest, where food was plentiful and conditions satisfactory.

The son of a Christian missionary in China who later became the bishop of Honolulu, Littell had spent much of his youth overseas. On breaks from China, the family would spend time in France and Germany. Most recently, in 1939, Littell, then fourteen, had been an exchange student at a German school in Prussia. He graduated from the equivalent of junior high school that July, at an elaborate ceremony where his pressed brown uniform was adorned with swastika armbands, every remark began with a brisk *"Heil Hitler,"* and the diploma he was handed was signed by Heinrich Himmler.

Littell, a bewildered teenager battered with questions as to whether President Franklin Delano Roosevelt was really a Jew named Rosenfeld, was still in Germany when the Nazis invaded Poland on September 1, 1939. This prompted Britain and France to declare war and, less conspicuously, his own hasty departure through Switzerland. Now, back in Germany as a prisoner and staring at the red-and-black swastikas adorning Bad Orb, he saw the destructive power of the forces he had often experienced as no more than strange theater when he was a schoolboy five years earlier.

Out of the town, up the snow-covered hills the American prisoners trudged, weary and disoriented. Some had overcoats, others only their combat fatigues. Littell, along with fourteen thousand soldiers of the 106th Infantry Divison, had left the United States for Europe in October 1944, one of the "youngest, greenest bunch of peach-fuzzed draftees ever to set sail," as he later put it. He had only been brought up to the front line in the Ardennes on December 11, 1944, five days before the German offensive that ignited the Battle of the Bulge.

The Germans, he had been told prior to that battle, were on the run. Yet, as he gazed through his rifle sight, what he saw were German infantrymen coming straight at him. One that he cut down in the Ardennes, no more than a hundred feet away, and later examined prone in the snow, could not have been more than sixteen years old. Like Daub of the 100th Infantry Division, Littell, scarcely a veteran himself, was struck by the youth of the German soldiers. But however desperate its conscription methods, Hitler's army kept advancing; the surrender of Littell's unit followed almost immediately.

"I never thought I'd be in combat so soon, never thought I'd be fighting so soon, never thought I'd be captured so soon," Littell said. "Many of my comrades felt the same way."

As Littell struggled to digest the rapid chain of events, he was surprised by the sight of a familiar building on the road out of Bad Orb. During the summer of 1939 he had spent some time with his older sister, Nancy, who was studying German literature at Heidelberg University. There, she aroused the interest of a German major in the medical corps, Fritz Esser.

They dated and became engaged in August, a month before the war broke out. Esser would bring Nancy, then twenty-one, and her little brother to Bad Orb, where he was the director of a sanitarium housed in the redbrick building Littell now saw. This coincidence was so extraordinary that Littell refrained from telling his fellow GIs. He knew they would tell him he was hallucinating.

But he was not. Esser, a Nazi, had been a diligent suitor. The appearance of the building stirred clear memories of nights watching his sister and the German officer dancing to Viennese waltzes at the Red Ox Inn in Bad Orb, or strolling on the banks of the Neckar River in Heidelberg. They were in love, or so it seemed. When war broke out, Nancy lingered, unsure what to do. It took several weeks for Esser's behavior to convince her that her future did not lie in being a *Hausfrau* in Hitler's Germany.

Her decision was formed when Esser defended Nazi policy toward the Jews and tried to explain that he needed documentation proving Nancy was of Aryan stock because, without it, his Nazi superiors would not allow him to marry her. She said that her father was a bishop, she a Christian, but balked at the notion of furnishing proof.

Esser insisted: You have dark hair and you do not have the long, tapering fingers of the Aryan. Suspicions might arise unless she could produce proof that her bloodline was free of any Jewish taint. He begged for her understanding. But her sympathy had its limits. She left for Honolulu and six months later was married to an American Marine officer.

What, Littell wondered now, had become of Esser, who had always treated him well? Perhaps the German was also a prisoner. Nothing was knowable beyond this long line of bedraggled men walking slowly up through the towering snow-dusted pines, passing civilians and horse-drawn carts. The wretchedness of the humanity on the road contrasted with the hush and majesty of the dark woods.

At last, the Americans arrived at a vast, dismal expanse of one-story wooden barracks, divided by parade areas and surrounded by a barbed-wire fence and guard towers. One of a constellation of prisoner-of-war camps in Germany, where conditions had grown steadily worse, Stalag IX-B was ill equipped for a massive influx of new prisoners. When the Americans arrived, it already housed large numbers of Russian prisoners, some there since 1941. The Russians, viewed as *Untermenschen,* or subhuman creatures, by Hitler, were so mistreated that more than fourteen hundred died at the camp of cold, hunger, and untreated illness.

Conditions for everyone were bad. On January 24, less than a month after the arrival of the first American prisoners, Werner Buchmuller, a Red Cross official from the Swiss legation in Berlin, visited the prison camp to inspect conditions. His report was alarming. The camp housed 2,803 American privates and 1,263 American noncommissioned officers living in sixteen barracks. It was "totally unprepared" for the reception of these Americans, with the result that "about 1,500 of the men had to sleep crowded on the bare floor in barracks in which many windows were missing." At the time of the visit, 1,300 were still sleeping on the floor in virtually unheated rooms. With no "stock of Red Cross food whatsoever," German rations were "scarcely sufficient," and were often being eaten out of "steel helmets in place of eating bowls." In short, the situation was "untenable."

When Buchmuller protested, the German camp commander, Colonel Karl-Heinz Sieber, "claimed that this is only a transit camp and that the prisoners would be transferred at the earliest possible opportunity," the report said. Of this claim Buchmuller was skeptical, given Germany's military plight.

His skepticism proved well-founded. Shortly after the war, the military intelligence service of the United States War Department compiled a final report on the camp, dated November 1, 1945. Based on the questioning of former prisoners and reports received by the State Department, it said that after a first group of 985 American prisoners arrived on December 26, 1944, the number of Americans incarcerated at Stalag IX-B rose steadily to a peak of 4,070 on January 25, 1945. That day a large group of noncommissioned officers was transferred to Stalag IX-A in Ziegenhain, but even at the time the camp was liberated, on April 1, 1945, more than 3,000 Americans were still there.

"From 290 to 500 prisoners of war were jammed into barracks of the usual one-story wood and tarpaper types, divided into two sections with a washroom in the middle," the report said. "Washroom facilities consisted of one cold water tap and one latrine hole emptying into an adjacent cesspool which had to be shoveled out every few days. Each half of the barracks contained a stove. Throughout the winter the fuel ration was two armloads of wood per stove per day, providing heat for only one hour a day. Bunks, when there were bunks, were triple-deckers arranged in groups of four. Three barracks were completely bare of bunks and two others had only half the number needed with the result that 1,500 men were sleeping on the floors."

The barracks were "infested with bedbugs, fleas, lice and other vermin." They were in a state of total disrepair: roofs leaked, windows were broken, lighting was "unsatisfactory or lacking completely." Some barracks floors were covered with straw, "which prisoners used in lieu of toilet paper."

Littell, after brief questioning by a Wehrmacht officer, duly took his place in one of these barracks. His initial judgment was that conditions were terrible but perhaps survivable, at least in the short term. What he did not know was that Esser's curious obsessions about the purity of Nancy's blood were representative of Nazi ideas that would affect the camp in ways that Buchmuller, the Red Cross official, failed to report.

As was discovered after the war, German prisoner-of-war regulations stipulated that "Jewish prisoners of war are to be separated from other prisoners of war in Stalags." Another regulation said: "For reasons of race hygiene, prisoners of war are not acceptable as blood donors for members of the German community, since the possibility of a prisoner of war of Jewish origin being used as a donor cannot be excluded with certainty."

Many of the Jews among the Americans were scarcely aware of the special danger they faced. In a letter sent from the camp, dated January 18, 1945, Shapiro wrote to his parents that he was a prisoner of war and "as best as could be expected." He would be able to receive packages, he explained, and requested that the following be sent from his home in the Bronx: "Graham crackers, jams, Kraft Velveeta cheese, dehydrated soups, powdered milk, pancake flour, dried fruits, cans of salmon, sardines, tuna, meat, a bottle of vitamin tablets, packages of hot chocolate, pipe tobacco, Milky Ways, Hersheys, gum, all dehydrated food is good."

In fact, no packages or letters were ever received by the prisoners at Stalag IX-B. Food became an obsession. Shapiro's particular fantasy was a pastry to which he used to treat himself with the tips he received from delivering prescriptions when he worked in the Bronx drugstore: a round sponge cake, known as a charlotte russe, topped with swirls of whipped cream and a Maraschino cherry, a cake that over periods of hours, Shapiro found, he could conjure up the sensation of eating, licking the cream slowly until his mouth encountered the agreeable soft resistance of the cake itself, which in turn broke into buttery pieces that he allowed to crumble against his teeth.

The reality encountered after such reveries was bleak: watery soup with forlorn pieces of turnip or potato floating in it, a slice of bread, so little to drink that the prisoners ate snow. According to the War Department report of 1945, rations provided by the Germans consisted of 30 grams of horse meat, 300 grams of bread, and 550 grams of potatoes, supplemented by "soup made from putrid greens" and tea. It was not unknown to see a horse's head floating in a huge vat of soup.

The quest for food was intricate. Cigarettes, won in the endless games of craps or extracted from a German guard in exchange for a wristwatch, could be bartered for extra bread rations or even occasionally a piece of sausage. Idleness intensified the fantasies about food (favorite recipes were laboriously recited). But it also tended to put off starvation. For apart from chores like cleaning out latrine trenches or carrying logs, the American prisoners were not made to work. If the input of calories was minimal—probably no more than one thousand calories a day—the output was also limited.

On his arrival at the camp, Shapiro had been questioned for five minutes by a German officer who spoke fluent English. As required, he gave his name, rank, and serial number, 42040855. In exchange, he received a prisoner-of-war number—25053—a blanket, and a small metal pot for his soup. His obviously Jewish name appeared to elicit no particular interest at this stage. Asked what he did, Shapiro said he was a medic. He was required to empty his pockets, revealing a Red Cross card and a package containing four cigarettes. These he was allowed to keep.

Arriving in his assigned barracks, Shapiro found a long room full of triple-decker bunks. The latrine consisted of a hole in the floor at one end; a piercing cold cut through his blanket and overcoat. The barracks soon filled up, mainly with privates from Shapiro's own 28th Division and from the 106th Division.

"I began to notice that many of the people coming were Jews," Shapiro recalled. Among them was Morton Goldstein of the 106th, a garrulous young man who often led the craps games, and Bernard Vogel, also of the 106th. Neither would survive the slave-labor camp at Berga.

Accounts differ of how Jews were concentrated and segregated at the camp. In sworn testimony given to the War Crimes Branch at Fort Dix, New Jersey, on September 7, 1945, "in the matter of the discrimination against and segregation of American prisoners of war of Jewish faith at Stalag IX-B"—an official investigation that went nowhere—Arthur J. Homer gave the following account of the manner in which Jewish GIs were separated from others. A private in the 707th Tank Battalion attached to the 28th Division, Homer arrived at the prison camp on December 26, 1944, the same day as Littell and Shapiro.

"On or about January 3, 1945," Homer said, "while being processed as a prisoner of war at Stalag IX-B, I was given a personal history questionnaire to fill out. This questionnaire, besides asking for home address, parents' names, previous employment and so forth, included a questionnaire on religious faith. This same questionnaire was distributed to all prisoners of war in the American compound."

Homer, who was not among the 350 prisoners eventually selected to go to the slave-labor camp at Berga, went on to say that the ranking American officer in the camp at the time suggested that "no harm would be done if we answered the questions as directed." Homer continued: "Soon after these questionnaires had been answered and collected by the German camp authorities, prisoners of war who had stated they were of the Jewish faith were segregated in barracks number 32 in the American compound."

A short time thereafter, Private Johann Kasten of the 106th Infantry Division, the "man of confidence," or elected leader of the American prisoners of war, was "told by the Germans to advise us that any Jewish American prisoner of war who had not indicated his faith on the questionnaire should report to Barracks 32 on threat of punishment at a later date if his Jewish faith were discovered," Homer testified.

This sworn testimony was provided just seven months after the events in question. In testimony given to the War Crimes Branch at Aberdeen Proving Ground, Maryland, two weeks earlier, on August 22, another American serviceman, Philip Glaessner, also imprisoned at Stalag IX-B until he was transferred to Stalag IX-A on January 25, 1945, gave a broadly similar account.

"The Germans requested and intimidated the American prisoners of war with threats of beating and denial of food to complete what they referred to as a Red Cross card," he said. "On this card information such as father's name, mother's name, place of birth, date of birth, civilian employment, Army organization, religion, etc., was requested. When these cards had been filled out the German authorities insisted on the segregation of American prisoners of war who had indicated they were Jewish. This insistence continued even after protest was made by the American leader, Pvt. Kasten. . . . As a result of the segregation, approximately 300 American prisoners of war were separated and were shipped to work in a slate mine on the Elba [sic] River."

These, however, are only two of several accounts, differing in significant details, of how the Germans identified Jewish prisoners. Shapiro, for example, recalls no such written questionnaire. The prisoners had no calendars, they were hungry, they were often sick, and in general they tried to suppress their memories after the war, often succeeding for decades. So it is not surprising that their memories do not always coincide.

What is not disputed by anyone is that this segregation took place. Nor can there be any doubt that it formed the basis of the group dispatched to work and die at Berga. As Glaessner put it to the war-crimes investigators, the soldiers singled out and sent eastward were made up of "those who had indicated that they were Jewish and those who the Germans considered as troublemakers."

Among the "troublemakers" identified by the Germans and dispatched to Berga was Private Kasten, the elected leader of the American prisoners. Nothing incensed the Germans quite as much as the haughty defiance of this German American.

Tall and insouciant, the American army private bearing the name of Johann Carl Friedrich Kasten was born in Hawaii in 1916, the son of a businessman who had emigrated from the northern German city of Bremen. The Kastens were a well-to-do family with important connections in Wisconsin, where relatives ran the First Wisconsin National Bank. From Hawaii, Johann moved with his family to Milwaukee, before attending the University of Wisconsin. "When I finished college," Kasten recalled, "I retired."

Part of his education had involved a visit with his two brothers to Hitler's Germany in 1936. Kasten was supposed to study German at the University of Heidelberg, but he was never a man inclined to do what he was told. Instead, he set off by bicycle and traveled the length and breadth of Germany for two years, getting himself arrested at one point near the Siegfried line for taking photographs close to military installations, introducing himself at another to Adolf Hitler.

Kasten was in a youth hostel in Bavaria at the time. Hitler had come to dedicate the establishment as the Adolf Hitler Youth Hostel. After the Führer finished his speech, Kasten approached him and shook hands. "So you are a German American student," Kasten recalled Hitler saying. "Very interesting." To Kasten, Hitler appeared "crazy from the start."

During the trip, the young man became fluent in German, which did not prove of immediate use on Kasten's early "retirement," in that he chose to return to his roots in Hawaii, in search of good times, before roaming the south seas. In Samoa in 1941 he managed to get himself appointed a "high chief" for various benevolent acts, many involving the extraction of Samoans from jail. That was before he contracted pneumonia on the island and was told he had no hope of recovery. Incensed by this pessimistic view, he recovered, the first of several brushes with death.

The next followed soon after when a ship he was on "in the fringes of the Pacific War" was torpedoed by the Japanese. Kasten found himself on a life raft for four days eating nothing but raw fish. As in other situations, he decided to apply "sheer will" to the challenge of survival. This paid off when a ship came by and picked him up.

Although raised a Lutheran, Kasten had never believed in God or His power to deliver anybody from trouble. "I'm an atheist," Kasten, eighty-seven and married to his fourth wife, said with some gusto. His last appearance in church was on March 21, 1931, at the age of fifteen, when he was confirmed in Milwaukee. Several weeks later, alarmed by Kasten's failure to appear for services, the pastor came by to see what had happened. "My son," the pastor said, "I haven't seen you in church. Why is that?"

"First, I am not your son," Kasten replied. "Second, you won't see me in church, now or ever."

Having recovered from his Pacific escapades, Kasten decided to join his country's war in a more conventional fashion. In 1943, at the age of twenty-seven, he went to Fort Sheridan, north of Chicago, and volunteered. He joined the Transportation Corps, drawn by the fact that it was headquartered in New Orleans—Kasten never could abide the cold. An attempt was made there to transfer him to a teacher's job in an officers' candidate school. No thank you, said Kasten; he had joined the army not to teach but to fight.

He sailed for Liverpool, where he was put to work handling the arrival and distribution of supplies. But to his disgust he noted that some goods were being rolled off on sidings and sold on the black market. This was not the sort of war he sought, either. Kasten, accompanied by the closest friend he had made in basic training, a diminutive Polish American from New Jersey named John Kupchinski, volunteered for the infantry. Most people thought they were mad.

Infantry training was at Tidworth Barracks, near Southampton, where Kasten proved to be the best marksman in his company. Then came the Normandy landing on the great exposed sweep of Omaha Beach, where Kasten scrambled ashore into the German shooting gallery and lost more than half his buddies. Fortunately, Kupchinski also survived, the big German American and the little Polish American side by side in the aftermath of D-day. By December 1944, Kasten had fought his way across France with the 106th and was in the Vosges when his company was overrun by the Germans at the Battle of the Bulge. The first night of the fighting, Kupchinski took three bullets that left him paralyzed.

The survivors were marched away by the Germans as prisoners of war. This was not to Kasten's liking. In the confusion of the night, he did a U-turn and walked away, his first escape. Eventually he made his way back to company headquarters, where he found the American commander hiding in a potato cellar.

"Do you speak German?" the commander asked.

When Kasten said he did, the commander asked him to stick around so that he could do the talking when they were captured.

"Well," Kasten replied, "that's not what I'm here for. I'm getting out."

He went upstairs just as the Germans came through the front door; he would have shot at them, but too many surrendering GIs were in the way. Kasten and a first sergeant got out a window and took off across a field to battalion headquarters in Clervaux, the town where Shapiro had woken up in the aid station on December 16. A castle housed the headquarters. There Kasten reported the bad news: "My entire gang has been marched away."

Ordered, at last, to fight, Kasten took up a position in a tower with his rifle perched on the windowsill, where, looking out, he saw the Germans moving across a cemetery toward the castle. Shots would take chips off the headstones, which made things easier, because he could then zero in on the adjacent German troops, killing several—some revenge for Kupchinski, at last.

German blood flowed in him, but he was an American fighting a war he deemed just. He felt not a qualm, not even a slight wavering of allegiance. But when he tried later to explain all this to his father, it was not easy, for Kasten's father could never accept that the country in which he was born could become what it did under Hitler. Telegrams sent to his father were tossed away partly read, he later discovered. What they related was too much for the old man.

Until he ran out of ammunition, Kasten kept shooting. There were sixty-two Americans stranded in the castle at the end. Only when the food ran out after two days did they surrender. Their first night in captivity was spent digging graves for the German soldiers they had shot, hard work because, to Kasten's considerable satisfaction, they had shot a lot of them.

Kasten was marched into Germany in the procession of GIs, loaded into a boxcar, and taken to Stalag IX-B. Soon after his arrival, an election of sorts took place. Each barracks had to select a leader; those leaders then chose an overall leader: Kasten. He became, in this capacity, the principal go-between in negotiations with the Germans. His two chief assistants, also chosen for their language abilities, were Littell and Ernst Sinner of New York, whose mother was a German Jewish immigrant.

Conditions were so bad that a few soldiers gave up. One day, the two chaplains came to tell Kasten that a GI was convinced he had been "forsaken by God" and wanted to die. As an atheist, Kasten had little notion how to deal with the situation. As camp leader, however, he had an obligation.

There was a faraway look to the young soldier's eye, a blankness, an absence that Kasten was to come to know well as death's annunciation. "If you don't have the will to live for yourself, at least live for your family," Kasten admonished him, brandishing a photograph of the soldier's relatives. But a few days later the young man was dead. Without the will to live there was little to be done.

For the living Kasten worked hard, helped by Littell and Sinner. His first achievement was to persuade the German authorities, after much acrimonious discussion, to delouse the prisoners. They were allowed to take showers and given a special chemical treatment; their clothes were also cleansed.

"Those were five minutes of joy," Littell said. "Show me a man who has lice falling off him, and I'll show you a happy man."

The happiness was short-lived. The German decision to delouse the Americans appears to have been prompted in part by the imminent arrival of the Red Cross delegation. In the days before January 24, when the Red Cross appeared, patches were also put on windows. The Germans placed buckets of coal next to the stoves and told the American prisoners not to touch them. Kasten, as the chief representative of the prisoners, was chosen to speak to the Red Cross officials but warned by the German commanders that he should be circumspect.

Kasten recalled the events of that day in this way: "So the Red Cross fellows arrived, three of them, and sat down, and I said I presume what we have to say will be held in confidence. Oh, of course. Of course, in confidence, so I talked openly for over two hours with these fellows, told them everything, gave the names of men who had died, the problems with the negligible food we had, everything. When we had finished talking, what did they do? They took me down to the German commandant's office and recited everything I had told them."

The Red Cross report, which reached the American embassy in Bern, Switzerland, and was forwarded from there to the State Department on February 15, confirms that Kasten was interviewed. It cites him as the man of confidence and says he had listed several complaints. Among them was the fact that "upon being captured, many men were forced to give up certain articles of clothing, such as articles not being worn at the time, including blankets and overshoes, as well as personal belongings."

The commandant was furious that Kasten had given such a frank description of the squalid conditions. The next day, January 25, the American noncommissioned officers were transferred out of the camp to Stalag IX-A.

Around the same time, shortly after the Red Cross meeting, Kasten was summoned to a small conference room on the second floor of one of the administrative buildings. A group of six or seven German officers were seated around a table. In front of the one vacant seat a loaf of bread had been placed, clearly an inducement to cooperate with whatever was to come.

"We want the names of all the Jews in the American sector of the camp," one of the officers said.

Kasten, who is adamant that this was the first demand of this kind made on him and the first time he heard anything suggesting that the Germans might be determined to segregate the Jews, pushed the loaf of bread back to the middle of the table. "We don't differentiate by religion," he said. "We are all Americans."

This defiance prompted a couple of German officers to rise. They grabbed Kasten and threw him down the stairs. "I lay there for a while because I didn't know if I had broken anything. I hesitated to stand up, but finally I got on my feet, bruised but able to move. I went back and called the barracks leaders together and told them to tell all the men that nobody was to admit he was Jewish."

Littell's account corroborates this one. He, too, has no recollection of any German request prior to this time for the Jews to be separated. Informed by Kasten of what had just happened, Littell said he went to the barracks leaders and warned them there would be repercussions, but insisted that "nobody under any circumstance is to admit to being Jewish, nobody."

Within a day, American prisoners were ordered out of their bar-

racks onto a parade ground, where a dozen German guards stood
with fixed bayonets. Littell's recollection is that about 500 prisoners
were assembled. From the accounts of other prisoners, it appears that
the Germans had already concentrated a number of Jews in one barracks. It seems they now sought to complete this process, by securing
the numbers requested, in anticipation of dispatching a group to
work in a slave-labor camp.

The German commandant stepped up on a platform in front of
the assembled soldiers and said, "*Alle Juden, einen Schritt vor-
wärts*"—"All Jews, one step forward."

Nobody moved. The commandant stepped down, grabbed a rifle
from one of the guards, and, in the words of Kasten, "took it like
Babe Ruth with a full swing and clobbered me across the chest and I
flew about fifteen feet backwards." Littell's recollection is similar:
"He went over to Kasten and hit the back of his neck with a blow you
couldn't believe. Hans got up again. [The commandant] struck his
back."

As he lay on the ground, Kasten saw two or three German officers going down the ranks of American prisoners, picking out those
they believed "looked Jewish." Littell, who as a barracks leader was
standing in front of the assembled troops, saw the same thing. Of
course, this method of selection was completely arbitrary.

No record has been found of any German order or request to send a
group of Americans, selected on the basis of their Jewishness or
resemblance to Jews, to the slave-labor camp at Berga. But it is
known that the SS had "full authority" to seek workers for the
Schwalbe program in German prison camps. At his postwar trial,
Hauptmann (Captain) Ludwig Merz, the German officer in overall
charge of the Americans at Berga, testified that he first heard about
the planned arrival of a work detail consisting of Americans in January 1945 (the emaciated Europeans had arrived in November 1944).
The information was conveyed to him, he said, in a phone call from
the headquarters of his unit, *Landesschutz* (National Guard Battalion) 621. This battalion, whose mission was to guard prisoners of war,
had its headquarters at Bad Sulza, about thirty miles northwest of
Berga, where there was another prisoner-of-war camp, Stalag IX-C.
The fate of prisoners in Stalags IX-A, IX-B, and IX-C was coordi-
nated by the same German officials.

Merz testified that he had no direct contact with Stalag IX-B, where the American prisoners were initially held. But it was certainly known to his superiors that conditions of terrible overcrowding existed at that camp once the Americans started pouring in on December 26. With the authorities at Berga, under SS Lieutenant Willy Hack, pressing for more and better manpower to work in the tunnels, this camp would have been a natural place for the Germans to seek for reinforcements. German prisoner-of-war regulations discovered after the war said that Jewish prisoners may be "grouped in closed units for work outside the camp." In short, it was natural enough for the Nazis to try to gather Jews, even American Jews, for work-to-death assignments.

The 350 Americans dispatched in boxcars to Berga from Stalag IX-B departed on February 8, 1945, arriving five days later. If Merz's testimony that he was informed in January of the plan is accurate, it suggests that German preparation for this transfer had gone on for more than a week, at a minimum. The parade-ground selection of additional prisoners in late January, described by Kasten and Littell, appears consistent with this planning and organization.

It seems equally clear, however, that many of the Jews, like Shapiro, had already been concentrated before late January in a barracks separated from the others. Why Kasten and Littell were unaware of this is unclear. One factor may have been the vastness of the camp, another that very few people wanted to talk about the issue. Given Kasten's forthright character, it seems unquestionable that he would have told the Red Cross delegate of any segregation, had he known about it.

Yet many Jewish prisoners date their segregation in a separate barracks to about mid-January. The selection process often confronted them with acute moral dilemmas as they wrestled with the question of their identity and their obligations. Some saw no choice but to join other Jews in a separate barracks. Others concealed their identity and resisted German pressure. All felt fear in varying degrees.

Private Sydney L. Goodman was captured in Luxembourg on December 17, 1944, and transported to Stalag IX-B. On the back of a series of photographs of his then one-year-old daughter, Karen, Goodman, twenty-seven, kept a rudimentary diary. Photographs of Karen on the front porch and asleep in the front seat of the car were a strange accompaniment to a chronicle of suffering. They also provided a powerful incentive to go on living.

Goodman wrote on January 2, 1945: "The fuel situation is desperate. Not enough heat to warm the stove, let alone the room. Nothing to do and life is down to one of its lowest ebbs for me. All I think of is home and food. I wonder if Grace [his wife] knows anything?"

He scrawled this entry on January 14: "Sunday. Protestant and Catholic services this morning. I listen in because it's religious and I miss our own service. I have a New Testament and I don't think it's harmful to pray with it even though it's not my own religion. There isn't a Jewish chaplain or even a Jewish officer here. Thought of home today and I couldn't keep from crying."

Four days later, on January 18, Goodman described the segregation of Jewish prisoners like himself. "Thursday. All Jewish boys to be separated tonight into where the officers formerly lived. Very cold. I wonder what the future holds in store for us?"

In 1985, at the age of sixty-eight, Goodman recalled in a newspaper interview what happened then: "An American officer came in and told us it was the policy of the German government to segregate the Jewish soldiers from the rest. He asked all Jewish soldiers to identify themselves. Only a few did. He said he didn't want to frighten us, but said, 'If some of you guys are Jewish and they find out about it, dire things could happen.' A little later, he came back with a list of names that sounded Jewish, and we were all moved to another barracks and locked in." From there, Goodman was dispatched to Berga.

Morton Brooks (then Morton Brimberg), who arrived at Stalag IX-B two or three weeks after the first batch of American prisoners, also recalls an American officer playing a role in identifying him as a Jew to the Germans. A soldier with Company C of the 242nd Infantry, Brooks had landed in southern France in October 1944 and come up through Lyon to the Strasbourg area. There he was captured by German forces in early January.

Like others, he pondered what to do with his *H* dog tags, deciding eventually that as an American soldier he could not be vulnerable to persecution as a Jew, but without a dog tag he might be shot as a spy. On arrival at the prison camp in what was probably the second or third week of January, Brooks said he was questioned by an American who insisted that, under German orders, he had to register not only name, rank, and serial number, but also religion.

"I tried to say no," Brooks said. "But when he asked me a second time, I said I'm a Jew."

A day or two later, Brooks said, he was summoned and moved to a barracks "already known as the Jewish barracks." There he met Shapiro and Daniel Steckler, among others, who were also to go to Berga. By his estimate, there were about 80 people in this barracks. That was approximately the number of Jews at the top of the list of the 350 American soldiers sent to Berga.

Gerald Daub recalled that about two weeks after his arrival at Stalag IX-B in early January he was told by his barracks leader that the Germans wanted to separate the Jews from other prisoners at the camp but that these efforts should be resisted. At a roll call the next morning, none of the Jews identified themselves. The barracks leader, clearly under increasing pressure from the Germans, then instructed the Jews that they would have to turn themselves in the next day. "I was very uncomfortable with that," Daub recalled. "My barracks leader said I would have to step forward. I knew that he knew that I was Jewish. It was apparent to me that I was to volunteer to be separated. The next morning we did step forward, and we were gathered up and marched to a separate barracks."

Sonny Fox also dates the selection process to the middle of January 1945. He said that about three weeks after he arrived at Stalag IX-B—or around January 18, the date noted by Goodman—the Germans read out a list of names of Jewish prisoners. To his surprise, his own name had not been included.

"That's a moral crisis for a nineteen-year-old," he recalled. "Do I remain mute, or do I say, Take me? Finally I rationalized that if I was going to help them at all, it would be easier to help them from the outside than the inside."

Fox stayed where he was as other Jews were led away to the "Jewish barracks." He was shocked that night to hear the American soldiers left behind in his barracks making anti-Semitic jokes. "It was one of those moments where you think about the distance between who we profess we are as a people and who we really are as individuals in the society," he said.

Eventually, Fox was one of the noncommissioned officers transferred to Ziegenhain on January 25. He heard of the fate of those dispatched to Berga only after the war had ended.

Edwin Cornell, also of the 28th Division, the man who buried his Hebrew Bible before being pushed into a boxcar, went through a similar moral crisis when the Germans started to round up the Jews. His memory of the selection is similar to Fox's. About two weeks after his arrival at the camp, he remembers, an order was delivered that all Jews were to report to a certain barracks.

"My first thought was, Who in hell, why in hell, how in hell do they have to do this to me or any other Jew?" Cornell said. "We are American soldiers. We are fighting for our country. It's entirely against the Geneva Convention."

Cornell had a buddy, Fred Roys, in whom he confided that he didn't know how to respond. Roys told Cornell he would be a fool to give himself up; he offered to take his dog tags and hide them. Cornell was persuaded but had the impression that "the majority" of Jewish GIs complied. "If your name was Greenberg or Goldberg or Cohen or something like that, what chance did you have?" Cornell said.

So began what Cornell called a "period of guilt." The place where the Jews were housed was, he said, "outside the periphery of the camp, a separate barracks." One day, soon after he had decided to hide his identity, he went for a walk around the camp and "saw these fellows in this separate barracks and it just made me sick."

Cornell agonized: "I thought to myself, maybe I should have gone with them. I think it's a natural reaction. I couldn't stand it. It just made me sick to my stomach. It was more than I thought I could bear. I mean, these are my brothers really."

Cornell never told Roys in any detail how the situation had affected him. But when they went for walks that would take them close to the "proscribed area" where the Jews were held, Cornell would opt for a shortcut to avoid being discomfited. The pressure to identify himself continued.

From time to time, Cornell said, German officers would come through the barracks and declare that they knew "there are more Jews in this camp than are identifying themselves." The Germans warned that anyone caught hiding his identity would be dealt with severely. "I can't tell you the stress I was under during that period," Cornell recalled.

Once, when the prisoners were allowed out of their barracks to get exercise, they passed a place where potatoes were being unloaded from a truck. A bag of potatoes broke. The Americans, Cornell among them, ran up to try to grab a few. "One of the fellows who knew me from combat looked at me and said, 'Hey, Cornell, you

know you act like some damn Jew the way you grab those potatoes.' "
Cornell was paralyzed, speechless. He had not told anyone but Roys
that he was Jewish. The comment cut to the heart of his unease.

The fear was most acute for Cornell when, on January 27, American GIs killed two German guards in the kitchen when they were surprised stealing food. Along with the other men in his barracks, Cornell was called in and ordered to present his dog tags, which Roys had handed back to him, for inspection. But it soon became clear that the Germans were looking for bloodstains—murder clues—rather than Jews. The next day everyone was hauled out onto the parade ground and made to stand there until those responsible were identified.

Stephen J. Schweitzer of the 106th Infantry Division, who was later sent to Berga, recorded the scene in testimony given to war-crimes investigators soon after the war ended. A few of the Americans had their overcoats on, he said, but most of the prisoners assembled were wearing no more than field jackets. "I made a note in my diary that the temperature was one and a half degrees below zero. We were made to stand on top of a hill where the wind was blowing strongly." After some time, "men were dropping from the cold until one hundred laid on the ground. There were thirty-five hundred of us standing in the cold for six hours when someone turned in the boy who was identified as the one who assaulted the guard."

Another American prisoner, John Griffin, remembered the scene this way: "They dragged us all out in the snow there for hours, while the machine guns were on us. And they said we would stay there until they found out who did the killing. They finally did get the two GIs. They went through all the barracks and found their bloody clothes. Then they took them out and that was the last we saw of them."

Griffin, unlike Cornell, was dispatched to Berga. To this day he doesn't know why. "I think I was just one of the unfortunate ones," he said. "Because I wasn't Jewish. I sure to hell didn't think I looked Jewish. In my view, they got the Jews, then they got other guys with what they thought were Jewish-sounding names, and then just filled the quota with anybody they grabbed and I was one they grabbed. They had to grab somebody. I was in line and they called my number."

Donald Hildenbrand of the 100th Infantry Division also had his number called and went to Berga, for no reason he could identify. "It seemed to me they just took people at random," he said. "Any other theory is just baloney."

In his vacillation, Cornell sought moral justification for his decision. He reasoned that he should take care of himself so long as the pursuit of his own well-being did not harm anyone else. Nobody, not a soul, had been affected by what he had done and therefore he could not be criticized for it. After the war, he heard that somebody had once suggested that because Cornell did not go to Berga, another prisoner had to go in his place. This he found deeply offensive.

Talk was cheap. Like Shapiro, Cornell had known the hell of the Hürtgen Forest in November 1944. He lived in foxholes, cutting down limbs of trees to protect and hide himself. The shelling was relentless. One day, a shell slammed into a tree near his position. He heard cries of pain from an adjacent foxhole. Cornell and his buddies crawled over and dragged the two injured men to the nearest medical station, saving their lives.

For a long time he never spoke about this. Everyone did such things. There was no need to recite his war record, action by action.

Like Cornell, Ernest Kinoy of the 106th Division hesitated when the order came for the Jews to identify themselves. He had thrown away his dog tags when he was captured because "I was politically aware to the point where I was not about to register with the Germans as Jewish." Faced with the order, he tried initially to hide his identity. But he found himself unable to live with his conscience.

"After a number of days," he said, "I decided that I really could not live with myself pretending otherwise. I knew a number of people who were down there in the barracks. I went and turned myself in. Basically, it was an ethical decision, that I really didn't feel that I could separate, get away with something that other people could not. There are all kinds of subtle things involved in a decision as to what your identity is or is not. Of course, the possibility of the Germans doing something was apparent, because you don't segregate without something in mind."

Jack Goldstein of the 28th Infantry Division also felt that he had to comply. He had declared his religion as "Pennsylvania Dutch" when he was questioned on arrival at the camp, but when he saw other Jews outside his barracks he felt an obligation to follow them.

"In front of all the other fellows, I couldn't say I wasn't Jewish when they all knew I was," Goldstein said. "I felt it was not right for me not to say. I didn't want to show that I was yellow or something like that, that I was afraid. I saw the other Jewish fellows stepping forward, so I had to step forward."

But David Barlow of the 110th Infantry, 28th Division, concealed his identity. He recalls hearing an order for all Jews to step forward and the terror the order inspired in him as a twenty-year-old Jew. But he has no recollection of seeing Kasten and believes this attempt to organize the segregation of Jews was made in mid-January, well before he, as a noncommissioned officer, was transferred to Ziegenhain in late January. "I figured in the end that there was no reason to expose myself as a Jew," said Barlow, who had hidden his dog tags in his boots when he was captured. "I cannot tell you whether this was straight fear or an intellectual exercise. A little of both perhaps, but mostly fear."

Peter Iosso, a Christian, was sent to Berga. His view is that the Germans "made an effort to get every Jewish American soldier on the work detail. The rest of us who were not Jews were there, I think, for two reasons. One, to fill out the complement, to complete the number required. Two, some of us may have gotten into trouble with other American soldiers or the German guards."

Iosso places himself in the latter category. He had noticed that one American prisoner acted as a middleman for GIs seeking to barter watches or rings or pens or any other item of value for cigarettes or food. Iosso believed the American go-between was lying and profiting from the system. He would tell GIs he could deliver twelve cigarettes when in fact he received a packet of twenty from the Germans. Then he pocketed the difference. With these extra cigarettes, he was eventually able to accumulate watches and other valuables himself.

"I pointed all this out to the man and he did not like it, asked what business it was of mine," Iosso said. "And he may have said to the Germans, Look, this Iosso, he's a troublemaker."

Peter Iosso was number 88 on the German list of prisoners sent to Berga on February 8. Joe Littell was number 92. John Griffin was number 315. The last name on the list was that of Kasten. None of these men was a Jew. But defiance or simple ill fortune placed them, in German eyes, at the level of Jews. They were therefore deemed fit for inclusion on a list of men whom the Nazi authorities, in their last months in power, considered appropriate fodder for a production system based on working human beings to death.

It seems unlikely that the precise procedure followed by the German authorities in selecting the 350 Americans who went to Berga will ever be known. The immediate postwar inquiry that might have come to a determination was abandoned, and no real effort was made in the succeeding years by any branch of the American government or by the army to establish who went to Berga or why.

The November 1, 1945, War Department report on Stalag IX-B, so complete in other respects, said, without further comment, that when the elected leader of the American prisoners "refused to single out Jews for segregation, a German officer selected those American prisoners whom he thought were Jews and put them in a separate barracks."

It also noted, without elaboration, that "on February 8, 1945, 350 of the physically fit prisoners were sent to a work detachment in the Leipzig area." What the official American report failed to take into account was the considerable overlap between these segregated American Jews and the "work detachment," which was in fact a group of men sent not to the Leipzig area but to the Berga concentration camp, more than forty miles away.

In this official atmosphere of inattention, vagueness, and even obfuscation, the prisoners involved tended not to talk about the event, with the result that when they tried to record it, often a half century later, memories had faded, details had gotten blurred.

What can be gleaned from the various accounts of events at Stalag IX-B in the first thirty-nine days of 1945 is that the Germans set out first to identify the Jewish American prisoners and then to pressure them to come forward. It seems that this pressure was steadily increased through January, culminating with the violent beating of Kasten when it was perceived that he was being uncooperative. From more than one account, it appears that some American officers cooperated to some degree with the German efforts, or at least did not resist them. The growing German pressure certainly reflected a conviction that some Jews, like Cornell and Barlow, were hiding; it also indicated that there was prodding from above to provide the numbers demanded for work in the Berga mines.

Once the noncommissioned officers among the American prisoners had departed on January 25, it is likely that the German officers felt less constrained in their actions, which they knew to be in flagrant violation of the Third Geneva Convention of 1929. This convention, revised and amplified in 1949, stated that "prisoners of war must at all times be humanely treated" and "at all times protected, particularly against acts of violence." It continued: "No physical or mental torture, nor any other form of coercion, may be inflicted on prisoners to secure from them information of any kind whatever. Prisoners of war who refuse to answer may not be threatened, insulted or exposed to unpleasant or disadvantageous treatment of any kind." The convention also stipulated that the prisoners should be detained in conditions "as favorable" as those provided to forces of the "Detaining Power"— in this case, the Germans.

In the end, at least 23 percent of those sent to Berga from Stalag IX-B were Jews. At the time, Jews accounted for about 3 percent of the American armed forces. The German efforts to identify Jews were not unsuccessful.

The German list, discovered after the war, begins with seventy-seven names that are conspicuously Jewish. These men—including Shapiro, Lubinsky, Lipson, Kinoy, Daub, Steckler—appear to have been gathered in the so-called Jewish barracks. Several of them recall this barracks being "emptied" when the transfer to Berga took place.

Soon after the Nazi capitulation, Edward Charles Mayer of the 106th Infantry Division gave testimony to war-crimes investigators from the Judge Advocate General's Department "in the matter of the segregation of Jewish prisoners of war at Stalag IX-B." Responding to questioning on May 24, 1945, he said, "About January 15, 1945, at Stalag IX-B, the Germans told us that all Jewish prisoners of war had to go to a special barracks, which had a fence around it." Such testimony abounded, but the investigation of this "segregation" never led to any prosecution of the Germans responsible.

Writing on June 15, 1946, in response to an investigation by the Vogel family into how their son, Bernard, came to be selected for transport to his death at Berga, Arthur A. Boucher, a prisoner at Stalag IX-B, said: "I was working in the American personnel office which had been set up to establish a little law and order. We received the travel orders for the 350 men and the Germans insisted that all men of the Jewish faith be placed on the orders. We could do nothing but comply. As I recall there were about eighty of these men."

A few other Jewish names are scattered through the list. The majority of the other prisoners sent to Berga appear to have been rounded up at the last moment, some only a day or two before they were on their way. Hildenbrand said he did not even know there were any Jewish prisoners in the group.

Far weaker than when they arrived just a few weeks earlier, the 350 Americans marched back down the road to Bad Orb, guarded by German soldiers with dogs. Several boxcars awaited them. Quickly they were forced into the freezing containers—the second time in six or seven weeks that these Americans prisoners had been treated as cattle. There were about fifty prisoners to a boxcar, packed in, with standing room only, like milk cartons in a refrigerator. Kasten, Littell, and Sinner, as German speakers, were ordered to help in this process; after they did, they were told they were part of it.

"Just as the men had been placed in the cars, the commandant came out and said, 'Kasten, Littell, and Sinner, you're going, too,' " Littell said. "Well, of course he wanted Kasten to go because he hated him, and he didn't like me much, either."

Littell had walked back past the redbrick building he associated with his prewar life in Germany. Before his abrupt departure from Stalag IX-B, he had managed to satisfy one point of curiosity. He asked a German civilian worker at the camp if he had ever heard of Fritz Esser, his sister's former suitor, who had been the director of the sanitarium housed in that building. At first the man did not react, but, when pressed, he said that, yes, he recalled Esser; he was killed in November 1942, on the eastern front at Stalingrad. Littell felt a pang of affection for a man who had almost become part of his family.

But all that, the romance and the Germany he had loved as an adolescent, was gone now. It was freezing and crowded in the boxcars. Once again, the prisoners were not allowed out to relieve themselves despite Littell's protests and the long stops during a five-day journey eastward.

These Americans, like Hauer and the Jews from Goncz, had no idea of the fate toward which they were being herded. In the Jewish barracks at Bad Orb, an attempt had been made to organize Friday-night services. But as Ernest Kinoy recalled, being American Jews, they "didn't particularly know the services."

Because conditions were so bad at Stalag IX-B, it was possible to believe that things might be better wherever they were headed. Nonetheless, foreboding filled the boxcars rattling across Germany in the dying throes of its lost war. "Some of the people were from families of European Jewish immigrants," Kinoy said. "And this was taking them back to what they got out from. And so it had to be alarming in that sense."

The prison camp of Stalag IX-B stretched over an area of about eighty-five acres, set in the middle of a beautiful pine forest. Before World War II, children came here, to a holiday camp. Today the place has returned to its original function: children's bright backpacks, caps, and cuddly toys fill the rebuilt wooden barracks where American prisoners once languished. On one child's T-shirt, tossed on a bed, are written the words BORN IN THE USA.

Good intentions abound. But the shadow of the past, as in much of Germany, is not far away. In one corner of the camp, hidden behind a fence, is a cemetery for Germans who died here after being evicted from countries farther east at the end of the war. Under one cross of pinkish granite lies Theresia Kummen from Hungary. Next to her lies Edeltraut Hubel. Millions of ethnic Germans were thrown out of the countries in which they had lived, often for centuries, as rage against what Hitler had perpetrated played itself out after the Nazi defeat. A few ended their days here.

Deeper in the woods is a monument to the 1,430 Russians who died at the camp. The names of only 356 of them are known. "These were not nameless heroes," says an inscription. "They had their names, their stories, their desires, their hopes. The pain of the last was not smaller than the pain of the first whose name is remembered."

Countless dead of other nationalities at Stalag IX-B, including the Americans, have no monument to their names.

Europe's soil, nowhere more so than in Germany, is steeped in the blood of war and forced migration. The knowledge of this suffering lies, like a dull pain, beneath the bright surface of modern prosperity; people carry this knowledge even if, increasingly, they had no direct experience of the bloodshed. The German burden in this respect is particularly heavy. Pampered modern life, so determinedly and patiently built, cannot quite overlay the destruction from which it emerged, just as the radiant backpacks scattered through these barracks cannot quite offset the pain that suffused these buildings.

The tension between the placidity of Germany today and the violence of its past, the need to remember and the desire to forget, produces many thoughtful, if troubled, people.

One of them, Joachim Winter, presides over the children's camp on the former site of Stalag IX-B. His father, a soldier in Hitler's Wehrmacht, was long imprisoned after being captured on the Russian front; at least he came home, whereas millions did not. A generation of postwar Germans grew up fatherless in what amounted to a kind of vast, bleak Freudian experiment.

Winter's goal, he says, is to give the children who come here "inner freedom." His approach is based on a rejection of what he himself was taught by his father. "I grew up in a world where obedience was the most important thing," he said. "*Befehl ist Befehl*—an order is an order. But when you obey, of course, obey blindly, your responsibility is diminished. On the other hand, when you do things from your own conviction, your responsibility is engaged. I want to make children self-responsible. That to me is the most important thing."

Surveying the old barracks, Winter—a modern German, a product of the pain of German memory, a well-meaning man—added: "You have to come to your own discipline through the right to disobey."

His words linger in the bright air of what is left of a prison camp where obedience to the last, even in the face of defeat, sent dozens of Americans in boxcars across Germany to their deaths.

CHAPTER FIVE

Prayer Book and Sword

T HE DOORS WERE thrown open to the smell of burning flesh. Mordecai Hauer gazed out into the dazzling light: spirals of barbed wire, fences, smoke, skeletal figures scurrying this way and that. A German voice boomed over a loudspeaker, ordering the Jews to leave the train, set aside their belongings, and line up five abreast, women to one side, men to the other. Hauer jumped down onto the ramp of the Auschwitz-Birkenau camp.

He could not take his eyes off the cadaverous men in the striped uniforms of prisoners—members, as he later learned, of the Jewish work parties, or *Sonderkommandos*. Their task was to ensure that the boxcars were emptied. "*Raus! Raus!*" they yelled, ordering the laggards out. But some of the Hungarian Jews, just weeks after their arrest in Goncz, were too weak or terrified to move. "Who are you?" Hauer asked one of the *Sonderkommando* members. There was no reply. The silent man moved through the wagon, almost tripping over the corpse of Mrs. Kardos. "This one is lucky," he muttered.

They had arrived in a place where the dead provoked the envy of the living. The camp reeked of death, proclaimed its proximity from the first instant, trafficked in it as everyday currency. Death resided in the features of the living, hummed through the electric fences, was borne on the cloying air. Hauer shuddered. He turned to see Lea Wertheim clutching her newborn baby. An SS man tore the infant from her arms, and, before anyone could move, smashed the little thing against the side of the boxcar. Pieces of flesh stuck to the car like leftovers on the side of a pot. The German tossed the corpse into the wagon where it landed on top of abandoned possessions—a limp, oversized doll. The soldier shouted, over the prostrate young woman's screams, that he was doing her a favor. It would take some time for

93

Hauer to begin to grasp the crazed logic of this infanticide: all women with babies were sent directly to the gas chambers.

Hauer pushed his way through the crowd to embrace his mother. As ever, Camilla seemed indestructible to him because the love in her was more powerful than any other force. What tenderness he had known as a child came from her. She had the generosity of the strong. Her face was smeared with the grime of the journey and the tears provoked by introduction to this inferno, where, it seemed, all knowledge was useless because the rules of existence, of survival itself, had changed. But still she was beautiful. From a young age, he had noticed the looks that men gave her in the store—the small compliments, the hands lingering as change was accepted, the whispered invitations, the glances at her full hips. To all this she responded artfully. To rebuff the flattery was perhaps to lose good business for the family. The men kept coming back, spending their money, staying too long in the store, looking for a little sign, hoping in vain.

Now she was as practical as ever. "Go, darling," she said. "Your father looks sick and needs your attention. Take care of Benji and Emerich, too. I will look after Edith, and soon we will be reunited."

Whatever his mother said, Hauer believed. Everything in his world had shifted, save that. He moved back to his pale father's side, linked one arm in his, the other in that of his younger brother Benji. Little Emerich stood to Benji's left, flanked by another man. His father was silent. Stripped of his dignity, David Hauer had already begun to crumple. He looked hollow, as if humiliation had sucked the substance from him. Ahead of them were other rows of men and boys, lined up in fives as instructed, waiting to file past a table where a group of SS officers stood. In the distance, square smokestacks were dimly visible, belching flames and smoke. That this was a crematorium Hauer did not yet know. To him it resembled a chemical factory.

A German officer who introduced himself as Dr. Josef Mengele took up a microphone, and in his memoir Hauer recalled Mengele's words:

> *We will now process this transport, and we will work fast. All of you will file past this table. I will indicate with my hand whether the person before me goes to the right or left behind the table. Whichever side you go, you must regroup five abreast, as you are now. Those who go to the right will be working. Those too young*

*or too old to work will go to the left. All of you will take showers
and be disinfected. You will receive fresh clothes and be assigned
to your blocks. The workers and the nonworkers will be separated
for a few days, but then all families will be reunited.*

The women moved forward first. Camilla was flanked by Edith
and by Bertha, an old woman from Goncz who was too weak to stand
unsupported. When they reached the table, Mengele's gloved hand
motioned Camilla and Edith to the right. But Bertha, judged too old
to work, was sent to the left and collapsed.

Camilla, moved by Bertha's pleading, said in her broken German: "Please, let me take care of this woman, who needs me." A
German officer promptly bundled Camilla to the left. "Fool," he
commented. Edith disappeared in the other direction. Hauer tried to
make out his mother's plodding progress beside the old woman, but
the floodlights blinded him, obscuring the ground beyond them, and
she was quickly lost in the gloom, lost forever.

Hauer shuffled forward with the male members of his family.
Mengele scarcely hesitated, sending him, his father, and Benji to the
right. But Emerich, eleven, was motioned to the left with a wave of
the white-gloved hand. He pretended not to understand and followed his father. An SS man grabbed the little boy and hauled him
before Mengele, who said: *Why don't you want to go to the left? Don't
you prefer playing with your mother to working with your father?*

Emerich replied that he would rather work. Perhaps it was his
perfect German, perhaps his fine features, perhaps just a whim that
led Mengele to allow Emerich to follow Hauer into the depths of the
camp.

Surrounded by SS men, the Jews moved fast, spurred by the beating of those moving slowly. The acrid stench of burning flesh and
hair hung in the air. They found themselves close to the edge of a
large pit. Corpses were piled side by side—hundreds, perhaps thousands of them, it seemed to Hauer, enough anyway to make of the
human forms a ghastly, almost abstract geometry of entangled limbs.
Wood had been placed between the layers of bodies. Prisoners in
striped uniforms were pouring gasoline into this mass grave. How
had all these people been killed? Why? Questions crowded in on
Hauer, who had not yet grasped that he had moved into a terrain
outside that of rational inquiry. Here, at the epicenter of the Nazis'
Endlösung, or Final Solution, words were just so much wasted

energy. Only later did he come to understand the silence of the *Son-derkommando* members. Like everything else in this place, such silence had one overriding motive: survival.

They advanced into a large building, where a barking German voice over a loudspeaker ordered them to undress and toss their clothes onto a pile, keeping only shoes, suspenders, or belts. In the middle of the room was a mountain of hair, piled as if in preparation for a pyre. Theirs was now added to it as two prisoners shaved the newcomers. Numbers were then tattooed onto their lower left arms. Hauer was A9092, his father A9091, Benji A9093, and Emerich A9094.

Stripped now of names, of hair, of identity itself, the Jews were ordered into a second large room with showerheads attached to the ceiling. The door was closed behind them, and another order came telling them they had three minutes to shower. A moment later, hissing slightly, the showers came to life. Onto these prisoners, deemed fit to work until they could work no longer, the perforated nozzles spilled warm water.

After delousing in a bluish pool, the Jews were given striped uniforms and marched past fences of electrified barbed wire to a long, wooden building filled with rows of bunks. There were no mattresses on them: people could be seen sleeping, two to a bed, on the bare boards. Hauer looked at his wrist to see what time it was, but there was only a white spot where his watch used to be. That blankness, like the mark left by a stolen ring, seemed to him to express the loss of his former life, its disappearance into a void. Time had framed the decisions that shaped his life; here, in a world framed by barked orders, it seemed to have scant meaning. Higher up his arm was the tattooed number. He had seen cattle branded in Goncz. The value now placed on his life by his captors was clear.

The block leader, or *Blockältester*, whom they had just met, a tall man in striped uniform, was talking. Evidently, he was a Polish Jew and had been here for some time. "While we from Poland have been rotting for years in various concentration camps, you were living a good life back in Hungary," the man said in Yiddish. "I feel no sympathy or pity for you. My wife and children were killed even before I was brought here. You'll be sent out to work, and wherever you are sent you will work hard. As for those who find they can't work, they will be dead sooner or later."

Instructions in the routine of the camp followed this bleak summation. Wake at six in the morning, run to the washroom, line up by six-thirty for roll call, known as the *Appell*. Two meals: breakfast, consisting of coffee and a small piece of bread, immediately after the *Appell*, and at noon a lunch of watery soup. Anyone found outside the block after seven in the evening faced possible death at the hands of the SS. "But even if you don't get caught by the SS," the block leader said, "you'll get a beating from me and my assistants that you won't ever forget."

So, Hauer thought, there were, after all, some affinities here with the world outside. Whatever the degree of misery and humiliation in which they all resided, hierarchies were still formed, status craved, privileges of rank clung to, needless cruelties inflicted. This Polish Jew had lost his family to the Germans, but his anger at the Hungarian Jews for being spared the hell of Auschwitz until mid-1944 seemed almost to outweigh this loss. He had clawed his way to a position within the camp, one that might even save his life, or so he evidently thought, and he displayed all the zeal of a recent convert. That the German system he now served placed the value of his life at zero seemed scarcely to matter, so long as the value placed on the lives of those he controlled was less than zero. Even among the damned, it seemed, it was possible to foment division, handing out trivial titles or insignia—a red triangle on the jacket rather than the customary yellow one—that had all the real value of medals pinned to the breasts of scarecrows. If it was Hitler's policy to make animals of the Jews—and Hauer now understood at last that this was indeed the case—it was also part of his design to encourage the animals to devour one another.

Some chose a quick way out. On his first morning in the camp, as he ran to the washroom with his father, Hauer saw several bodies hanging from the electric fences. Perhaps they had died trying to escape, but Hauer thought it more likely that they had opted for suicide. He briefly toyed with the idea himself but was driven, as he would be for a long time, by the conviction that he must survive for the sake of his mother, who was indestructible. She had also instructed him to take care of his father, and David Hauer showed every sign of weakening fast.

Just how fast soon became evident. On the second day in the camp, an SS man assembled everyone in Hauer's block for inspection. He then divided them into three groups, splitting the Hauer family. Benji was placed in one work detail, Emerich in another, Hauer and his father in a third. As Benji and then Emerich departed, with feeble waves and wan smiles, David Hauer turned from his sons and ran toward the electric fence and its jolting release.

Hauer set off in frantic pursuit and caught his father before he could electrocute himself. That night he bound his father's wrist to his own with a leather belt to ensure that the attempt at suicide, which had brought a beating from the block leader, would not be repeated. He gazed at his sleeping father, so recently a proud and prosperous man possessing an authority as brisk as his temper. His mouth was open, his face unshaven, his breath foul, his breathing fitful. "Camilla," he murmured in his sleep. "Camilla, my darling wife . . ."

Hauer and his father left Auschwitz-Birkenau after three days. They marched out in a column of about a thousand men, five abreast once again, flanked by SS guards. Before their dazed eyes the gray labyrinth of death unfolded: inmates pushing two-wheeled carts full of corpses, the crematoria, the pit once filled with bodies. As they emerged onto a tree-lined highway, with the early-summer sun glinting through the pale green leaves, it was the gradual change in air that struck Hauer most forcefully. A shroud had been lifted. Gone was the bitter, emetic stench of death, its place taken by a fresh breeze that made his skin tingle.

They passed through simple villages of thatched homes that were not unlike Goncz. Some people just stared; a few children threw stones at them. The nearest thing to an expression of sympathy that Hauer saw was the sign of the cross made by an old Polish woman, but when he looked more closely he thought she was blind. As the march stretched into a second hour, the SS went to work, beating those who could not keep up. When the prisoners were ordered to halt at the approach of a military vehicle, the pause came as a relief to all.

A German officer emerged from the car. He introduced himself as the commander of the camp, Jawischowitz, where the prisoners would now work. "You are just a few minutes from the camp," he said. "You will have no problems so long as you work well. If you do not, we will have to treat you as saboteurs, and you know the punishment for saboteurs in wartime. Work, eat, and sleep; work, eat, and sleep. This routine will ensure your survival. Now, right face! Forward march!"

Jawischowitz, which appeared around the next bend, looked almost pastoral compared with Auschwitz-Birkenau. The barracks, set out around a large quadrangle, were painted light green; in front of them flower beds had been planted and carefully tended. An electrified barbed-wire fence and four guard towers made clear that those housed here were prisoners, but no crematoria loomed, no deathly smell lingered. About three thousand prisoners inhabited the camp, marshaled by SS guards whose living quarters were adjacent to the gate. On an arch above the gate were inscribed the words ARBEIT MACHT FREI—"Work sets you free." Hauer, ever the optimist, breathed deeply, smelled the surrounding pine trees, and felt comforted.

In fact, the pretty geraniums and tantalizing maxim made up a lie. The twee and the terrible, tulips and torture, could coexist in Hitler's Germany, reflections of the divided German soul. The business of this camp was work and death, the one leading inexorably to the other. That was its sole function, its sole logic. The process was held in place by violence, sometimes in plain view, sometimes no more than a shadow, but always present. Survival required vigilance, discipline, and, as always, the absence of bad luck.

The newly arrived inmates were assembled on the *Appellplatz* and separated into three roughly equal groups. Each would work a different shift. The arduous nature of the labor soon became apparent when a group of prisoners arrived, their striped uniforms and faces blackened with what could only be coal dust. Hauer, to his consternation, was separated from his father, whose will to live still seemed fragile. He was taken to a block, number 8, that by now looked familiar: long lines of three-decked bunks. But at least the place was clean; at least there were blankets, neatly folded, on each bed; and at least the block leader, when he spoke, showed a greater humanity than his counterpart at Auschwitz-Birkenau.

He was a Christian Pole named Janek, and he described himself as a political prisoner, captured three years earlier and held for his socialist beliefs. Somewhere, he still had a wife and two children—or so he believed—but he tried not to think of them too much. "Thinking about them constantly will not help them, nor will it do any good to me." Any distraction, in short, was a distraction from the business of survival. He would treat everyone with dignity but demanded dignified conduct in return. German policy, Janek said, was simple: destroy the humanity of the prisoner. Against this, the best defense was the preservation of self-respect.

"It is the only thing you still possess," he insisted. "Hunger does terrible things to people, and you won't get enough food. The temptation to steal food will be strong, but you must resist it. Remember, when you steal a piece of bread from your comrade, you steal his very life. You also lower yourself to the level of a beast."

Hauer admired the rigor, physical and intellectual, of this young man. His group had been chosen for the night shift, the toughest of the three. He would be awoken at six in the evening, be inspected on the *Appellplatz* at eight, depart for the mines at eight-thirty, and begin his underground shift at ten. At six in the morning he would emerge from the mine; he'd return to the camp by eight, and receive his daily ration of bread and coffee at eight-thirty. He should be in bed by nine and expect to be wakened at one in the afternoon for soup. Then there was more sleep, until the six o'clock summons to work.

That night, the last before he began his new nocturnal existence, Hauer felt an overwhelming loneliness. For the first time, he was separated from every member of his family. The brief euphoria brought on by the fresh air had evaporated, replaced by fears for his father and mother. His former life—Ilona, Sharon, the family store, studies in Budapest—lay shattered. Perhaps Sharon had been right: there would be no tomorrow for them. Through habit, he began to recite his prayers and, seeing a man about his age on the bed to his left, said good night to him in Hungarian.

"I am not a Magyar," the man retorted in Yiddish. "Go back to your useless prayers."

Hauer was shocked by this hostility. Again it seemed that the Jews, even as they faced the same fate, were divided against one another.

Over the past few weeks, as his life had been transformed, Hauer had become increasingly divided within himself. On one side, and ascendant in this internal struggle, loomed the young Zionist who had appeared in the Kassa brick factory with his exhortation to cast aside the old parental conviction that God will take care of everything. The Zionist had warned Hauer that Eichmann's promise of a gentle existence was a lie. He had told the Jews that death or slave labor awaited them in Poland. He had urged them to abandon a fatalistic faith in an all-powerful God for a willful faith in the struggle to build the Jewish state of Israel. In all of this, the secular Zionist seemed vindicated, for how could the smashing to death of Lea Wertheim's baby be compatible with the belief that the Jews were the chosen people of God? Perhaps his prayers were indeed useless.

On the other side, however, stood all the weight of his upbringing, of his mother and father, of the religious devotion and learning that had been the cornerstone of his family's values over centuries. His mother's words came back to him: "Remember this, there is no luck, or misfortune, only the will of Almighty God." His father's repeated advice resonated, despite all the horror that seemed irreconcilable with any but the most perverse divine will: "God gave you lips and a tongue so that you can praise Him."

Swayed by the evidence of mass murder that no God could countenance, but susceptible still to the belief that nothing happens without God's will, Hauer struggled for bearings that would guide him. In prayer lay comfort. But in action lay salvation. Were the two, Hauer wondered, as irreconcilable as they seemed?

At Jawischowitz this dilemma soon confronted him with a particular immediacy. On his first morning in the camp, he became aware of a whispering. It stemmed from the bed beneath his own, and its source was almost invisible: a man wrapped from head to foot in a blanket. Listening more closely, Hauer was able to distinguish the sounds of a Hebrew prayer. He lifted the blanket slightly to find himself staring at the pale, ascetic face of a religious Jew whose beard clearly had been shaved on arrival at Auschwitz. In his delicate hands he held a small prayer book, somehow preserved from destruction at German hands. "I am sorry to interrupt you," Hauer said. The man put one finger to his lips, indicating the need for silence, and continued with his prayers.

A few minutes later, this devout Jew introduced himself as Reb Yankele, the spiritual leader of a small Hassidic congregation in northeastern Hungary. Asked how he had managed to preserve the prayer book, Yankele said merely that he had done so with the help of God. Faith, in all its enviable simplicity, shone from the man's eyes. Yankele offered to lend Hauer the book, an offer Hauer hesitatingly accepted, without giving voice to his doubts. Opening the book, he began to pray: "Thank you eternal living King who mercifully returns my soul unto me. Great is Thy trust . . ." But his thoughts strayed; the central doctrine of Jewish faith—a single omnipotent God—no longer convinced him.

In the bunk adjacent to his, such nagging skepticism found fierce support. The man who had dismissed Hauer's prayers as "useless" was an eighteen-year-old Polish Jew named Israel Katz, whose parents had been killed by the Nazis. Before his death, Katz's father had said he would disown his son if he joined the Zionists in the kibbutzim of Palestine: only the Messiah's coming could open the way for the return to Zion.

"My parents died, shot to death by the Germans, with the name of God on their lips," Katz told Hauer. "A lot of good God did them. Do you know how many millions have now died at the hands of the Nazis, all victims of a belief in God and Jewish tradition? But not me! I will not die like a lamb, as my parents did. God is a figment of our imagination, and I shit on Him!"

Hauer was shaken. The convictions of both men were ardent; they seemed to permit no common ground. Not even a shared enemy as implacable as the Germans could bring these two Jews closer. His position in a bed between them seemed apt in that Hauer vacillated between the two extremes, of religion on one side and resistance on the other. During the first moonlit march to the mine, he found himself reciting evening prayers and finding comfort in the familiar sound. But at the same time, he realized that their content meant little to him. The prayers were no more than a consoling echo, a dumb mnemonic, words tumbling through habit from the mouth of a lost and lonely young man.

The steel cabin dropped with vertiginous speed. It whined and whistled as it descended, stirring a vicious draft. Hauer felt his stomach plunge; his legs seemed to fall from the rest of his body, and his eardrums felt close to bursting. He would have collapsed but there was no room. The thirty other people packed into the elevator held him up. The ride ended with a jolt, the door opened, and Hauer found himself in the bowels of the Hermann Göring Werke mine, facing a German engineer with an iron-tipped cane in one hand and a whip in the other.

He and four other prisoners, including Israel Katz, were assigned to a stocky, middle-aged foreman, a Pole named Kowalsky, who was a farmer but had been forced by the Germans to work in the mine. They rode in V-shaped wagons behind a small locomotive down a tunnel lit by dirty electric bulbs hanging from crossbeams. At stops along the way, other prisoners got off and disappeared into smaller branch tunnels. It was dark, dusty, and damp, but, Hauer mused, he had known worse and longer train rides.

Hauer's tunnel was a new one, about fifteen feet long, descending sharply. Kowalsky explained that, according to German engineers, there was a rich seam of coal about 150 feet below the level where they now stood. Their task was to dig a three-hundred-foot-long tunnel, in steep descent, to reach this coal. It was dangerous work, especially after blasting, when chunks of rock had to be removed before the ceiling could be secured with beams. But they had to push ahead fast.

Kowalsky had no love for the Germans. But he was a realist. "If you don't make this tunnel fast enough to please the Germans, there will be trouble," he said. "You saw the German boss, and I can tell you he and his assistants are beasts. I've seen many Jews beaten or shot to death right here in the mine."

The pumps—delivering fresh air to the miners, compressed air to the pneumatic drills, and seepage water to the surface—pounded. Explosions ripped through the confined space, sending black dust everywhere. Within a few hours, Hauer's hands were thick with blisters and his muscles ached. He could scarcely force himself to rise after the single fifteen-minute break at two in the morning. By the end of the shift, he had been introduced to a new kind of exhaustion and hunger that made his body shriek in protest. But still he had to trudge back more than five miles to the camp, counting his paces, praying, reciting verses learned in childhood—anything to distract himself from the repeated, life-sapping infliction of injury that was now his lot.

Back at the camp, after receiving coffee and a piece of bread, Hauer thought of his father. The previous day, he had located him in block 12 and had learned that he was working the afternoon shift. The one time of day when they might see each other was the morning. But there were risks. Already Hauer had noticed that any deviation from the strict work-to-death routine set by the Germans could incur vicious punishment. The assistant to Janek, his block leader, was a brutal Polish Jew named Mathis, who seemed less than happy if he had not broken a nose or knocked out a couple of teeth by mid-morning in response to some trivial transgression like failing to make a bed impeccably, or folding a blanket less than perfectly, or reaching for a larger piece of bread. The SS guards seemed to live to beat prisoners. Hauer had seen them, grunting with pleasure, pound the buttocks of a group of prisoners who, in search of scraps, had hoisted themselves onto the rims of large cooking vessels left outside the kitchen and were reaching into the bottom of them. He had taken to heart Janek's admonition that self-respect was the best defense for a prisoner. But that could not mean mere compliance with the letter of a barbarous order; a measure of defiance was needed, enough anyway to ensure that he saw his father.

Hauer found him in his barracks. They ate together, with some other Hungarian Jews from Kassa, blessing the bread before eating, reciting another prayer when the bread was finished. David Hauer had just awoken, fresher than his exhausted son, but he was largely silent, refusing to be drawn into any conversation about a future in which he evidently had no faith. Hauer felt that he was engaged in a constant battle to stop his father from slipping away from him, but the task had a Sisyphean quality. Nudged forward, cajoled into living, his father nevertheless slid back.

When he returned to his barracks, Hauer found the other prisoners already in bed. Mathis immediately demanded to know where he had been. "You know very well that you are here to work," he said. "And if you don't sleep, how can you work?"

Hauer mouthed something about seeing his father, but his protests were interrupted by a vicious blow to the throat that knocked him to the floor, breathless. Fortunately, Janek entered at that moment, heading off further blows with an admonition to Mathis.

By such violence, and by lack of food, were they worn down. As the days grew longer and the weather warmer through July and August, there were moments of brightness and companionship. At breakfast gatherings with his father, Hauer began a ritual of going through favorite recipes of Camilla's—goulash paprika, gefilte fish, roast meats. In this way a hunk of bread, like Shapiro's cherry-topped charlotte russe cake, was transformed into a feast. Hauer's long conversations with the devout Yankele and the radical Katz did not resolve his doubts, but they did bring pleasure and cement friendships with both men. These, however, were brief sunny interludes in an endless season of menace. The fact soon became irrefutable that Jawischowitz was an extermination camp, as relentless in its devouring of human flesh as Auschwitz-Birkenau, of which it was merely a satellite. The slaughter was more drawn out, but slaughter it was.

Every Sunday a general inspection took place on the *Appellplatz.*

Prisoners stood in line, block by block, and the *Lagerführer,* or camp commander, looked into the eyes of every one of them. What he looked for there was resignation and absence, signs that the prisoner had given up and was of no more use to the Reich. Such a prisoner earned a fatal designation: *Muselmann.*

"Common to all Lagers was the term *Muselmann,* 'Muslim,' given to the irreversibly exhausted, worn out prisoner close to death," wrote Primo Levi. "Two explanations for [the term] have been advanced, neither very convincing: fatalism, and the head bandages that could resemble a turban. It is mirrored exactly, even in its cynical irony, by the Russian term *dokodjaga,* literally 'come to an end,' 'concluded.' " A *Muselmann* would be pulled from the line.

Hauer watched as these prisoners were loaded into the back of a black van, never to be seen again. None resisted; some had to be helped into the vehicle. They were taken, as Mathis delighted in informing him, directly to the gas at Auschwitz. It seemed to make no sense to kill people in this way; after all, treated in another manner, they might have been made to work longer. But they were not people to their captors. They were scum to be eradicated after each usable calorie had been spent.

David Hauer's closest friend at the camp was Samuel Schreiber, the textile merchant with whom the Hauers had initially stayed in Kassa. One summer day Schreiber gave up. He refused to eat his bread. When he spoke, it seemed he was talking to himself. He muttered about not having been a good enough Jew. "My children are grown up, thank God," he said. "They don't need me even if they live through this, and I am sure my wife is dead."

At the next inspection he was designated a *Muselmann,* removed from the line, and, a little later, bundled into the black vehicle. His son, Baruch, tried to run after him. Hauer had to restrain him in the same way he had restrained his father once at the electric fence. "No," he said. "You are the only son, and it is your duty to stay alive and say Kaddish for your father."

After Schreiber's removal, David Hauer's morale deteriorated still further. He was silent; he refused to make up favorite recipes; he insisted that his wife, too, was dead. Hauer battled to revive his father's spirits but to little avail. Then, a few days later, Hauer's block, number 8, incurred its first victims—brothers named Bloch.

They were a gentle pair, well educated, given to saying "please" and "thank you" at every opportunity. Small and delicate, the brothers looked as if they had been raised to listen to chamber music rather than electric drills. When the bread they sometimes hid in their mattresses was stolen, both cried. Their susceptible temperaments earned them the disdain of Mathis, who took every opportunity to humiliate the pair. As the weeks went by, the brothers' strength, but not their touching love for each other, ebbed. Now, Hauer watched from a window as the older brother helped the younger into the back of the black van that would take them to the gas chamber. It was parked near one of those pretty flower beds with its abundant blooms. The air was heavy with the scent of summer blossoms. Butterflies fluttered here and there. The van swept away.

The brothers' disappearance shook Hauer. He looked up, as he had so often at the hill beside Goncz, at the passing clouds in a blue sky, but the unchanging beauty of nature could not console him now. Then he heard the whispered chant of Reb Yankele, praying for the Bloch brothers.

Yankele looked up at Hauer. "Have faith," he said. "We are being tested, and some of us are weak. But God will avenge us."

This was too much for Katz, who was standing nearby. "Don't talk to me about God and tradition!" he shouted. "The Bloch boys died because they were weak and stupid. All you religious fools know is the teachings that, for two thousand years, taught us to be moral and ethical and gentle. Can't you see what it has done to us? We have become a bunch of bench-warming Talmudic scholars, bookworms, too soft and too cowardly to be masters of our fate. Tradition and faith made us easy prey, my mother and father included."

"You are desecrating the memory of your parents," Hauer shot back. "And the Bloch boys, too."

"Desecrating my parents? They were blind fanatics like your friend Yankele, and they paid for it."

Yankele approached. "I understand your bitterness, Israel," he said to Katz. "You are still young, and you have suffered enough for a lifetime. But you are terribly wrong in turning against the Creator, blessed be His Name. How can you call those who believe in Him stupid and cowardly? Have you not studied our history?"

"So why does God not save us now?" Katz shouted. "Why does He not do something while at least a few of us are still alive?"

"Did you ever read the Book of Job?" Yankele asked. "You must be patient. We are the descendants of Jacob, not of Esau. We live by the book, not by the sword. We are commanded to live by the ethical and moral precepts of the Torah."

"And will the Torah prevent the Nazis from killing you and me?"

"Just as it was not our will that we came into this world," Yankele said, "so it is not for us to know or decide when and how we must die. And if, God forbid, it is our lot to die at the hands of the Nazis, how do you know that life is better than death?"

At this moment, Mathis appeared, in his usual foul temper. "We need extra hands to peel potatoes!" he yelled. "If you have to argue, do it while you're doing something useful."

Hauer found his father sitting on his bunk coughing violently. In his hand was a cigarette, a rare commodity in the camp. Very occasionally cigarettes were handed out to prisoners for exceptional work in the mine; they could then be traded for bread. But his father, whose lungs were not strong, had no business with a cigarette. He seemed to be choking on the smoke.

"Where did you get that?" Hauer shouted. "Tell me at once. Don't you see what smoking does to you? You know that Mother was always against it."

His father did not respond. He lay back on his bed, breathing hard. His eyes were open but showed no sign of life. To Hauer, there was still hope that his family would one day be reconstituted, if not in Goncz, elsewhere. His mother was alive; he was sure of it and would find her. Edith, too. As for Emerich, he had appeared one day at the camp, along with other children, and been placed in a new *Kinderblock*, adjacent to block 8. The children were put to work aboveground at the mine, removing pieces of stone scattered amid the chunks of coal moving along a conveyor belt. It was wonderful for Hauer to know that Emerich was alive and to have him close. Soon after Emerich's arrival, a note miraculously reached the Hauers from Benji, confirming that he, too, had survived and was working at a mine. Yet this good news seemed to have little effect on David Hauer, who appeared ready to smoke himself to death in front of his children.

Although he had trouble admitting it to himself, Hauer was angered by his father's attitude. His sense of filial duty was strong, but the facts were painful. This man in his forties had been so sure of himself, so ready in Goncz to criticize his son for intellectual or moral weakness, yet he had given up so easily, or so it often seemed, relinquishing that essential self-respect demanded by Janek and seeming to declare through his abandonment the unpardonable conviction that his beautiful wife was dead. Camilla should not be betrayed in this way. Hauer thought back to the stinging blow inflicted on him by his father at the Passover meal just a few months earlier in Goncz and to the anguished cries of his mother. The fear his father had inspired then was real. It stemmed from his unquestioned authority, within the family and in the community. Yet now he seemed a pathetic figure. Was it possible, Hauer wondered, that his father blamed himself for what had happened to such a degree that he was left with no will to live? Or perhaps his father was simply a more rational man than he, one who had concluded from the evidence that, before such a sentence of slow death, all resistance was futile. Perhaps the answer was simpler yet. Camilla had always, in reality, been the pillar of the couple. Without her, his father had crumpled.

"Don't you want to see Mother again?" Hauer asked.

"I do, oh God, I do. So much that I cannot stand it anymore," his father replied. "I am no good without her. If she were here, everything would be different. But I fear that she is dead. What is my life worth without her?"

"Father, we will find Mother again. You have to believe that."

His father was silent once more. After much questioning, Hauer learned from others in block 12 that his father had been trading his bread for cigarettes. There could be no clearer declaration that David Hauer wished to hasten his designation as a *Muselmann.* More alarming, a couple of prisoners told Hauer that his father had done so little work of late in the mine that the foreman had reported him to the Germans. This, Hauer knew, was a certain prelude to a sentence of death.

"This has to stop," he told his father. "You must eat. You must believe in our survival." But even as he spoke, he knew his words carried little authority.

That night, at the mine, Hauer was flat on his back in a narrow section of the tunnel when a terrible rumbling sound enveloped him. "Push your ax against the ceiling!" Kowalsky screamed.

Hauer did so, then he felt a lacerating blow to his head and was knocked unconscious. When he came to, the top of his head was bandaged and the fourth finger on his right hand was in a splint. His first thought was not that he had survived. It was that he might now be selected by the Germans as unfit to live any longer. He could not accept that; his duty was to look after his father and find his mother. Pained, he pulled himself into a sitting position, drawing a reprimand from a young Polish nurse. "Lie down. You have a broken finger and may have a broken skull."

"But if I am not strong enough to work, I will be selected as a *Muselmann.*"

"I think you still have the will to live," the nurse said. "When they brought you in, you looked more dead than alive. And now look at you! Please, sleep."

Hauer relented, on condition that she wake him in time to walk back to the camp with other members of his shift. The five-mile march was more agonizing than ever. Each step sent a shooting pain through his head. He learned that one man had died in the accident, but Kowalsky had survived. At the camp, Hauer was put in the infirmary, where conditions were the best he had known: clean sheets, better food, and no wake-up call. But he could not relax. Fears for his father gnawed at him. He persuaded the doctor to discharge him after a couple of days.

That night, on the march to the mine, Hauer felt his religious faith returning. Had he not been spared? Was it not God's will that he live? No mere rational equation could explain why the full force of the tunnel's collapse had not come to bear on him. He prayed with more than usual fervor, not to pass the time, as had been the case, but to proclaim anew his belief. His father's advice came back to him: always pray out loud because enunciating the words drowns out everything else, while silent prayer is an invitation to distracting thoughts.

"What are you mumbling?" an SS man asked sharply.

"I am praying, sir," Hauer said. "I always do on the march."

"But I never heard you before."

"Because, before tonight, I always prayed silently."

"I understand. You are grateful to be alive. I know something of you, Hauer."

"How do you know my name?" Hauer was astonished—and afraid.

"I have been watching you. I like your guts. It was a friend of mine who brought your brother's letter to you. My name is Edmund Weber."

"Why are you telling me this?"

"Because," Weber said, his voice dropping, "I have something important to say. I used to be a teacher in a small German town, and I am only in the SS because the mayor forced me to join. It was that or God knows what. I am not like the other SS. Most of them are scum, fed on lies, avenging lives of frustration. I know now that we have lost not only the war but the respect of the world. I am ashamed of being a German and of this uniform." With that, he pressed a large piece of bread into Hauer's hand.

The declaration was so extraordinary that Hauer was speechless. At last, he said, "Thank you. I, too, had thought of becoming a teacher."

"You will be yet, and I hope you will recall that not every German is a Nazi."

This was not the first kindness Hauer had received from a German. At the camp the highest-ranking prisoner was an aristocratic German named Wurffel around whom many rumors swirled, including the suggestion that he had been a cabinet member during the Weimar years. It was through Wurffel that the commandant generally communicated with the block leaders and the Kapos. Wurffel seemed a considerate man. What chinks there were in the discipline of the camp appeared to stem from him.

He was lodged in spacious quarters next to those of the SS guards and was addressed, even by the camp commandant, as "Herr Wurffel." This towering, silver-haired German, with mild blue eyes and a florid complexion, appeared tolerant of the networks, the ties of friendship and family, that could offset in a limited way the harshness of camp life. Wurffel had, for example, taken Hauer's little brother Emerich under his wing, employing the boy to play the violin, sing, and do odd jobs as a way of extricating him from the arduous work at the mine.

As he marched on, Hauer took in the full impact of Weber's words. Hitler was losing the war he had started. He was also losing some of the men apparently most committed to him. He was *losing*, even if the machinery of torture and death still functioned. All Hauer had to do then in order to *win* was to outlast a beleaguered enemy. Not for a long time had he felt so lucid. He and other prisoners existed in a fog. They were told nothing, did not even know what day it was. Their minds weakened. They were susceptible. Now Weber's words had lifted the fog, revealing new possibilities. Even his father would see this, surely.

Further encouragement came that night in the mine. Kowalsky had been concerned about him. It would be too stupid to die now, he told Hauer. The Russians were closing in; the war would soon be over. Soviet forces were no more than thirty miles away, to the north. As evidence, the Pole produced from his pocket a German-language newspaper dated September 14, 1944, that he had found in the nearby village where he lived. A report in it spoke of "minor skirmishes in the Katowice area." It was not much, but it was something. Kowalsky made Hauer swear not to mention the newspaper to anyone. "If the Germans find out," he said, "they will hang me."

The next evening, heavy rain pounded on the window near Hauer's bunk. It was Saturday, the one night of the week he had off. Outside, he could see sheets of rain falling against the white glare of the lights beamed at the camp's barbed-wire perimeter. He hated that constant light. Even the blackness of night was denied them.

His father should be returning from his afternoon shift at about this time. They would inspect him by this light before he was allowed to sleep. The Germans never relented. Yes, they were losing, but they had not lost. Hauer's thoughts grew somber. He could not outlast them. Nothing would change. But then something did.

The beams were extinguished and the camp plunged into darkness—a power cut caused by the storm, he thought sleepily. A fleeting notion that he might escape flickered through his mind; the fences would not be electrified. Then he heard Katz's urgent whisper. "Can you hear it?"

"What? The rain. Of course I can."

"No, not the rain. Listen harder. Airplanes, bombers."

Straining now, Hauer could hear it: the steady drone of high-flying aircraft. "I hear them," he said. "But they could be German."

"If they were German, why do you think the SS have ordered the lights to be put out?" Katz retorted. "They are scared."

Hauer could not contain himself. Despite his vow to Kowalsky, he told Katz what he had learned in the mine from the newspaper clipping. The Russians, it seemed, were near, an offensive looming at Katowice.

Katz seemed transfixed. He had always spoken of action; Hauer's news now seemed to provide a catalyst.

"I was born in Katowice," Katz said. "I know the whole region, and my Polish is perfect. I will get through the fence somehow. Then I'll bring the Russians here and I will personally kill every SS man. You've heard the SS telling us over and over that no matter who wins the war they will have time to massacre us before it is over. Well, that is what I want to prevent. I will ensure the camp is liberated before the SS can make good on their threat."

Hauer admired his friend but lacked his passionate conviction. He was more of a fatalist. He valued judgment as much as courage. Perhaps if he had seen his parents shot, he might feel differently. But his parents were alive, he believed that. "You must be careful, Israel," Hauer said. "After all this is over, we Jews will need your conviction and energy."

There was no reply.

The next morning, a Sunday, Hauer's father appeared in block 8, looking weaker than ever. He fell to the ground and had to be forced to eat. This was the day of selections, when those of no further use to the Germans received their death sentence. Hauer was terrified that his father would be among them. He wanted to watch over him, encourage him with word of the Russians' approach. But an unexpected announcement calling for the night shift to line up on the *Appellplatz* drew him away. The *Lagerführer* himself would address them.

The German commandant was in a foul mood. There has been an air raid, he said. The camp might be bombed by the enemy. "But you'd better pray that it won't be, because you will be the casualties. The SS will be in shelters that you are going to build right now. And do not make the mistake of trying to escape during a blackout. The current in the fences and the gate is never off."

They were put to work to the left of the main gate, digging a seventy-foot-long, seven-foot-deep trench that would serve as an air-raid shelter for the SS. In the midst of the digging, Hauer heard the whistle summoning prisoners to the weekly inspection. He could do nothing. The *Appellplatz* was not visible from where he worked. He dug feverishly, hoping to stop thinking by working himself into a pit of pain. His arms ached; sweat filled his eyes. Dig, don't think, he murmured; dig, don't think.

At last the trench was completed. The commandant ordered the prisoners to lay planks across it and shovel the dirt on top. As he heaved the soil onto the planks, Hauer heard a second whistle marking the end of the *Appellplatz* inspection. Soon after, he was allowed to go.

In block 12, his father was nowhere to be seen. "I am sorry," the block leader said. Hauer rushed to the *Appellplatz*. The black van was not there yet. Perhaps it had already left. Or perhaps his father would be in the room next to the infirmary where the *Muselmann* group was gathered each week before being removed to their deaths. An SS guard was at the door. But he did not react as Hauer peered in through an open window. His father was sitting on a bench smoking a cigarette.

"Father!" he shouted. "You promised not to smoke." It was, in the circumstances, an absurd thing to say, like criticizing somebody's choice of a last meal before an execution. But Hauer was half crazed. He was exhausted, his body had withered to perhaps half its weight on arrival at Auschwitz, and for months now he had felt his own survival to be bound to his father's.

"Son, don't be angry with your father. I did not sell my bread. I exchanged my shoes for the cigarettes. They are of no use to me any longer, so why should I not smoke and enjoy my last few hours?"

"Father, you cannot—"

"This is the way God wants it, sweet child. You cannot be angry with Him. And I want you to know that I love you all . . ."

Hauer did not hear his father's last words. He was running to his barracks, looking for Janek, the block leader. "Save my father, please," he said, dropping to his knees. But Janek said he could do nothing for a man who was not in block 8. In desperation, Hauer thought of Wurffel.

The German listened to Hauer's agonized plea as Emerich looked on. He went straight to the point. "Does your father have a craft?"

Saying he was a merchant would not help. Hauer thought quickly. His father would sometimes repair the broken windows at the store and frame pictures. "He is a glazier," Hauer said. "With the winter coming, surely you could use him."

Wurffel hurried off to see the commandant. When he returned, his beaming face left no doubt as to the outcome. His intervention had saved David Hauer, who would now work as the camp's glazier. But there was one condition: Hauer's father, who was brought immediately to Wurffel's quarters, had to be strong enough by the following Sunday to pass the inspection. Hauer embraced his father, who sobbed but said nothing. Was it shame he saw on his father's face? Or regret? He could not say, but there was no sign of satisfaction.

As he walked back slowly to his block, Hauer thought about Weber and Wurffel, two Germans who had helped him. Even after all he had suffered at their hands, he had difficulty feeling hatred for the German people as a whole. His belief in justice and in peace made it impossible for him to espouse an indiscriminate revenge, immense as the German crimes were and the resultant suffering of the Jews. He thought of the words Yankele had uttered to him a few days earlier: "The Torah does not set us apart from other people forever. On the contrary, for it is written that the Law shall spread from Zion, meaning that God wants the good of all people. Everything and everyone in the universe is His concern. Yes, you are a son of chosen people. But only if you try hard to approximate to the divine image, if you serve as a living example to your fellow men. We must have unshakable faith that as God's plan unfolds, we will find that He has prepared the healing cure before He allowed this terrible plague to strike us."

The healing cure... The words echoed in Hauer's mind. What might that be, after all this was over? He believed in conciliation and the spreading outward to all people of goodness. But then he again heard Katz's fanatical words: *"I will personally kill every SS man."* Of one thing Hauer was sure as he considered Yankele and Katz: their fight was over nothing less than the future of the Jews, if there was to be one.

Accompanied by an SS man, Katz walked into the infirmary, his face white, his left hand wrapped in a blood-soaked bandage. The doctor unwound the bandage to reveal two fingers smashed to a bloody mess. The fingers, what was left of them, had to be amputated immediately. After the operation, Katz slept.

When he awoke, he told Hauer that, a few minutes before the end of his shift, he had deliberately placed his hand at the impact point of two wagons loaded with coal. Now he was assured of at least a one-week stay in the infirmary. During that time there would be an air raid. "That," he said with a smile, "is when I will make my move to escape in the darkness."

Hauer himself was in the infirmary after being beaten to the point of death by the SS. He had done extra cleaning work for Janek to earn bread for his father, which he hid in his straw mattress, where it was discovered by Mathis and an SS man, who accused Hauer of stealing. The SS strapped him to a table. Several Germans were playing cards.

"Get it over with, Franz. I'm holding the best hand I've had all day," one of them said. "What did he do, anyway?"

"Mathis says he stole two rations of bread."

"Then he deserves it, but make it fast."

The SS man looked at Hauer: "You get twenty lashes. You count each one of them out loud. If you forget the count, we start over. Clear?"

The German brought the whip down on him with an awful force. "One," Hauer groaned. At five, he passed out. A pail of cold water poured over his head brought him around.

"All right, you dirty Jew, let's see how your memory is. How many is that?"

"Five, sir."

"Smart kid. Keep counting."

At ten, Hauer fainted again, was doused again, and was asked the count. "Thirteen," he ventured.

"Missed by three," said Franz. "We start over."

His life was saved only by the intervention of Wurffel, who had apparently been alerted by Janek after a confrontation with Mathis. All Hauer could remember were angry voices and, much later, awakening in the infirmary, where he had spent several days before Katz's arrival. The most gratifying day of the week had been Sunday, when he had watched from the window as his father, fed and rested, survived the *Muselmann* selection.

Now he was worried about Katz. Any disappearance from the infirmary, which was small, would be discovered immediately. The commandant had said the fence remained electrified even in a blackout. Hauer's guess was that the German was not bluffing. Even if Katz escaped, he would be instantly recognizable in his prisoner's clothes. All of this he told his friend.

But Katz was not to be deterred. "Don't worry," he whispered. "I have a plan. At the side of each block, including the infirmary, there is a barrel filled with sand. You must have seen them. When the blackout comes, I will climb out the window, empty the nearest barrel, push out its bottom, shove it between the wires, and squeeze through. The wood will protect me against the electricity. Then, as soon as I get to the village of Jawischowitz, I will steal some civilian clothes. I just need another day or two here to get my strength back, and I'm going."

Hauer listened. His friend seemed blind to the risks. "The war is almost over," he said. "Why get yourself killed now?"

"Don't you see what's going on around us?" Katz's voice had assumed the venomous hiss that Hauer had come to know well. "Jews are standing in the *Appellplatz* like sheep in a slaughterhouse. A German butcher is making decisions about their life and death. Enough! If I have to die, I want to die fighting, not like a dumb animal."

Katz looked intently at Hauer. "My friend," he continued, "you are either the world's greatest optimist or you are as naïve as a newborn baby. I love you as a brother, and it would be nice if all the world were like you. But it is not. The Germans are vicious, mad dogs. When the Russians come, the Nazis will make you dig the biggest trench you have ever seen, and then they will line up every one of you and mow you down with machine guns. I've seen it done in my hometown."

This young man, Hauer knew, had emerged alive from a trench full of the dead, including his own parents. He had escaped by night into the forest, where he was later captured by the Germans and brought to Auschwitz. The rage in him was understandable. His plan was wild: to direct the Russians to the camp, have them bomb the newly dug SS shelter and parachute into the camp, freeing everyone. Hauer felt overwhelmed by his friend's burning certainties.

"Isn't it worth the risk?" Katz asked, his eyes flaming. "Is it not my duty as a Jew? Speak now."

"I . . . if only I were sure you will not be captured. What if something goes wrong? And I don't believe the Germans will kill us. They know us. We have worked for them for months. They will be afraid to kill us now that they know the war is lost."

Hauer listened to himself. The words were sincere but delivered without real conviction. He remembered all the earlier arguments he had made based on a lingering belief in German humanity or goodwill: the Jews would not be deported, they would not go to Auschwitz, they would not be slaughtered. In all of this, he had been wrong. Still, it was also true that Wurffel and Weber existed. Perhaps they counted for little on the other side of the scale. But in his mind they could not be discounted completely.

"Don't worry, my friend," Katz said. "I won't die. But if I do, it will be for the best cause I know of, for my people, Israel. I have not forgotten what Yankele told me—that life is not necessarily better than death. In this one thing I agree with him. A noble death is better than a miserable life and a lot better than a miserable death."

"But—"

"There are no *buts* to discuss," Katz concluded. "Know only one thing, my Magyar friend. If I should die, it will be because the Polish Christians refused to help me, even so close to the end of the war. Then you and other idealists like you may finally understand that there is only one place for Jews: *Eretz Yisrael.*"

Two days later Hauer returned from the mine in heavy rain to find the *Appellplatz* filled with prisoners and SS guards. He knew the reason immediately. His exhausted group was lined up with the rest of the prisoners, who were already drenched. The commandant was striding back and forth while the SS searched every building. Prisoners began to collapse, dropping to their knees in rain that was quickly turning to snow, the first of the winter. Hauer's spine felt like glass about to shatter; his eyes were swollen, his fingers numb. Prisoners, perhaps a dozen of them, were dying in front of him. The commandant vowed that nobody would be dismissed until Israel Katz was found and punished.

Two SS men came running across the courtyard to report that they had found an empty sand barrel stuck between the wires of the fence behind the infirmary. The commandant ordered a search party to be sent out immediately. He also ordered all the barrels burned. "This criminal Jew will be captured within twenty-four hours and will hang right here in the *Appellplatz* for all of you Jews to see," he declared. With that, the prisoners were at last allowed to disperse to their barracks.

Winter set in with heavy snowstorms. The march back to the camp from the mine became a daily nightmare. Hauer and the other members of the night shift stumbled and crawled through blinding snow. If he had survived this long, it was only because the weather had been mild. Perhaps Katz had been right to take the risk. With each passing day, Hauer's hopes for his friend, and his pride in what Katz had done, grew.

Then, two weeks and one day after the escape, Hauer returned to the mine one morning to find the *Appellplatz* filled once again with prisoners. He hoped that there had been a second escape. But the commandant announced that Katz had been captured and would be brought back to the camp to hang the following Sunday.

On Saturday night, Hauer watched the SS erecting a gallows in the center of the *Appellplatz*. He felt an icy hand on his heart. An image of his childhood friend Andras hanging from the apple tree in Goncz flashed through his mind, the three legs of the upturned milking stool pointing to the sky and the tips of Andras's shiny boots just touching the moist soil. In the distance he heard the church bells of the village. A hastily prepared wooden staircase was brought out from the carpentry shop and placed next to the gallows.

At ten o'clock on Sunday morning, the whistle blew. Snow was falling. Everyone was required to attend the hanging. The prisoners stood for half an hour in the freezing Silesian air before a military vehicle came through the gate and halted near the gallows. Out of the rear door stepped an SS officer. He was followed by Katz, gaunt, bearded, straight-backed. The young Pole looked serene. He had no shoes and no socks, his striped jacket was torn, and his hands were tied behind his back, but his expression declared his unconcern and, ultimately, his freedom. His steps were steady as he walked to the gallows, flanked by two German officers, who tried to assist him up the four stairs, but Katz shook them off. He ascended alone.

Katz stood there, an eighteen-year-old man who, as Yankele once said, had already endured the trials of a lifetime. Hauer trembled; Katz was motionless. An SS officer read out the accusation against Katz: escape, theft of food, the knifing of a Polish farmer and two Germans who arrested him. The unanimous verdict: death by hanging.

"Israel Katz! Did you hear the charges and the verdict?"

Katz replied in Yiddish that he had.

An SS officer produced a short, white rope from his coat pocket and turned to the camp commandant. After a brief discussion, the commandant said: "I want a volunteer to perform the execution." No prisoner moved. "I want a volunteer, and he will receive an extra ration of bread for a month." Still there was no response. Hauer was terrified that nobody would volunteer and he would be pulled from the line. What would he do then? He could not tear his eyes from his friend: the rib cage bulging through the torn jacket, the light beard, the absence of anger in his gaze. It was difficult, in that moment, not to see Katz as a messiah.

At last, somebody stepped forward: the block leader of his father's barracks, a German called Hans, who had been a convicted murderer before the Nazis sent him here. The rope, with a steel ring at one end and a noose at the other, was handed to him. He walked up the four steps, attached the ring to the hook on the gallows, and turned around, as if to ask whether to proceed. The commandant nodded.

Hans tried to get the noose around Katz's neck, but the rope was too short, descending only to eye level. The German became red with embarrassment. The commandant stepped forward to the foot of the gallows. "*Kopf hoch!*" he ordered—"Head high." Katz obeyed at once, raising himself on his toes and stretching his neck until the noose could be slipped under his chin. The German jumped down from the platform and awaited the order.

"Pull away the plank!"

Hauer had been thinking all along that he would close his eyes because he would not be able to bear to see his friend's struggle with death. But Katz's calm was an exhortation to be a witness. His strength demanded that Hauer be attentive to it, record it, absorb it, live with it, through the years. To shut his eyes, Hauer knew, would be an act of cowardice. Katz had made clear to him why, with his eyes open, he chose a noble death over a miserable life; he had also stated what that death should signify. It was now, Hauer felt, up to him to protect the lesson, the meaning, of this man's eighteen years on earth.

He watched without flinching. Katz, in a clear, strong voice, spoke his last words: "*Am Yisrael Chai*"—"The people of Israel shall live." His parting cry echoed around the square. He did not struggle. His feet stayed together. Katz would not give the Germans the satisfaction of seeing him writhe. The only movement was that of his head, which slowly tilted forward and to the right.

Yankele, who was standing next to Hauer, leaned forward and whispered: "*Boruch Dayon Emes*"—"Blessed be the Eternal Judge."

Still, the prisoners stood there. The SS officer who had arrived with Katz ordered that the body be left on the gallows for the rest of the day. The commandant proceeded to conduct the weekly *Muselmann* inspection. Never before had Hauer seen so many prisoners taken away to the gas. He counted forty-seven. At least seventeen others had collapsed before or during the hanging. They, too, were carted away. But Hauer's father, a little stronger since he quit the mine, remained.

The camp commandant addressed those still standing: "The next time a prisoner tries to escape from this camp, one hundred of you will be executed. I must also warn you that I am aware of the Jewish custom of gathering ten people to conduct a memorial service when somebody dies. I am determined to prevent this from happening. I have given orders to the guards that anyone attempting to conduct such a service for this dead, misguided Jew will be shot on sight. You are now dismissed."

From his window, Hauer could see the body of his friend. The snow was quickly turning him into a hanging snowman. He could not shake from his mind the life that had shone so vigorously from Katz's eyes. He felt all his doubts of the past months coalescing to form a great weight in his soul. He should have tried harder to prevent the folly of Katz's escape. Or perhaps, rather, he should have tried to go with him. They would surely have had more chance together. Tears welled up.

Through his sobs, the voice of Yankele reached him. "Do not cry. The tears will do no good, and Israel would not want you to be sad. I know how much you loved him, but you cannot contest God's will. Israel had to die because he would not have died if God had wanted it otherwise. He died with peaceful courage, and I pray for the same courage when my time comes, for death is surely no worse than life."

"But why would God want Israel to die?" Hauer retorted. "You said yourself that God will save His people. I do not know anyone more worthy of life than Israel. What did he do to deserve such a death?"

Yankele put his arm around Hauer. "Now you are beginning to sound like Israel, God rest his soul. Your questions are beginning to sound like accusations. You are not searching to know but expressing your anger. The most important thing to remember is this: nothing happens in this world, not even the falling of a leaf from a tree, without God's will. Perhaps we cannot always understand that will, but we must not be angry. To be angry is to be guilty of the sin of pride. You must have faith that God creates even when He seems to destroy."

"I am sorry," said Hauer. "My faith is shaken."

"Try to think of all this in a different way," Yankele said. "Israel has now reached the happy shores for which we are all destined. If he did not cry, what right do we have to cry? No, we must not be bitter. We must praise the Lord, so that Israel's soul may partake of heavenly bliss."

Perhaps, Hauer thought, the young rabbi was right. Perhaps death was better than starvation, slave labor, lice, and cold. But, grief-stricken and weak, he found it impossible to order his thoughts. Slowly, he drifted into sleep.

When he awoke, it was to the sound of Yankele's voice once again. "Come," he said. "It is time to pray for Israel. We need a minyan, and I want you to recite Kaddish for your friend." Yankele began to search the block for the eight additional Jewish males required to constitute the quorum of ten.

After Hauer's beating, Janek had relieved Mathis of his duties. So they were freer to talk and organize within the block. Still, it took some time to find the minyan.

"Let's go," said Yankele, and headed for the door.

Everyone was surprised—and afraid. Yankele evidently wanted to conduct the service on the *Appellplatz*, in front of the body. One prisoner spoke out, suggesting that the prayer be conducted inside the block. The risk of being killed by the SS was too great.

"A shame and an outrage!" Yankele exclaimed. His eyes shone with the fervor Hauer had long associated with Katz. "A Jew dies as a martyr, and you do not even have the courage to pay a final tribute to him. God's command is more important than that of a camp commandant."

He strode out onto the freezing square. It was dusk; perhaps the SS would not see them. Hauer followed, as did three others. But five stayed back, reluctant to move. Hauer turned to them. "The SS will be playing cards by now. If they see us, we will have time to run away before they reach the gallows." Still they did not move. Hauer felt anger rising in him. "He died for us," he said, "and you are scared even to show a little appreciation."

Now the five followed and gathered in front of the snow-covered corpse. Yankele began to chant. Hauer wanted the rabbi to complete the prayer quickly so that he could begin the Kaddish. Like the other prisoners, he kept looking toward the gate. Suddenly, he saw two SS men walking toward the gallows.

He ran. They all ran, except Yankele, who continued his prayer,

apparently oblivious. The SS men walked; they had clearly come out
not because they had seen the gathering but to remove the body from
the gallows. It was almost dark, and the snow continued to fall.
Hauer watched from a nearby latrine as they dumped the body into
the snow, no more than a few feet from Yankele, whom they now saw.

"Look," one SS man exclaimed. "This idiot is praying."

"Dirty Jew," said the other. "Get lost, before I shoot you."

Yankele continued to pray.

"Stubborn bastard. I will count to three. You hear me, you dirty
Jew? At three, I will pull the trigger. *Eins... zwei... drei...*"

The shot rang out.

Hauer fell to the floor of the latrine. For what seemed a long
time, he was unable to move. It was dark now, except for the glow of
the snow and the beam of the light on the camp's perimeter. He
edged out into the middle of the *Appellplatz*. The two bodies lay
there, Yankele's right arm across the shoulder of Katz, their heads
close together. Hauer kissed the snowy heads. He washed his hands
and face in the snow and began to utter the Mourner's Kaddish: "*Yis-
gadal v'yiskadash sh'mei rabboh...*"

Hauer had struggled so long to reconcile the opposed beliefs of
his two friends. Now that struggle seemed foolish. Their lesson, in
the end, was a shared one: that of courage, the courage to believe in
what is right, against the world, if necessary. It was this courage that
the German nation had lacked so conspicuously. The force of such
courage, it seemed to Hauer, had no limit, on the icy square where he
now stood or in any time or place he could imagine. It was the only
insurance against collective surrender to evil. Without it, human life
had no value. Without it, the beasts were free to rampage where they
would.

As the weeks of November 1944 passed, Hauer withdrew into silence.
When Weber attempted to give him more bread, he pushed it away.
When his father and Emerich came to see him, he would not talk to
them. Every day prisoners died. His own will to live had gone. A
courageous death, he now thought, could be an example. Katz and
Yankele were at peace.

It took a rapid sequence of explosions to break his mood. They
came in early December, as he trudged back one day from the mine.
The sound of heavy artillery shells was unmistakable. At last, he

thought, the Russians. After breakfast, a truck appeared in the main square. Emerich rushed in to see him. The children, he said, were being evacuated. Hauer asked where they were going; Emerich said Wurffel had assured him he would be safe. As the truck moved away, his little brother waved to him. It was the last time he ever saw him.

The explosions continued intermittently over the next two weeks. Then, returning again from the night shift, Hauer saw flames. He remembered Katz's warning: the Germans would kill everyone before they fled. He thought the barracks were on fire with everyone in them. But when he reached the gate, he saw the SS burning all the papers and files from the camp, trying to erase every trace of their deeds. At his block, Janek spoke: the Russians were a few miles away, the day shifts at the mine had been canceled. The camp was to be evacuated within the next several hours. Everyone should try to sleep and bring a blanket when they were ordered to move.

Hauer went to block 8 and found his father. When the call to move came, they lined up together in the snow. The commandant spoke, for the last time: "As you see, the camp is being evacuated. Our destination is Buchenwald, several hundred miles away in Germany. There are no trucks. But you will not have to walk more than about thirty-five miles, to a railroad station. There, we hope to catch a train. But in the snow the walk will be difficult. Some of you may be too weak. I offer a second option. You may stay behind in the infirmary, where your fates will be in the hands of the Russians, who are ruthless. Those who wish to stay with the sick in the infirmary, go now. You have two minutes to make up your minds."

The offer sounded good. Liberation by the Russians could be no more than a few hours away. But Hauer had not lived the last months for nothing. He remembered Eichmann's seductive lies at Kassa. He would march to Buchenwald rather than go to the infirmary.

"Then I will stay without you," his father said. "I cannot move."

With the help of another prisoner, Hauer was able to restrain his father. But at least two hundred prisoners did step forward and were taken to the infirmary. Hauer saw them being pushed in. Then the door was locked.

Those who had opted to go to Buchenwald were lined up, five abreast, as ever. The Germans had their habits. Each man was given a loaf of bread, the equivalent of four days' rations. The column started to move. But no sooner had they reached the highway than the Germans gave an order for the prisoners to pause. Hauer expected one of the endless counts. He looked back at the camp and saw SS men crossing the *Appellplatz*, holding tanks of gasoline and automatic weapons. Screams and cries began to issue from the infirmary.

The building erupted in flames. Prisoners smashed windows; some jumped. The SS cut them down before they hit the ground. The burning walls soon collapsed, trapping everyone inside. The SS stood for some time, with guns poised, watching to be sure that nobody survived, thorough to the last.

Above the gate, Hauer read the words he had seen on entering Jawischowitz: ARBEIT MACHT FREI. He turned away. Ahead of him lay the snow and an icy road that, for him, would end not in Buchenwald but beyond it, in the small German town of Berga an der Elster.

CHAPTER SIX

Walking Shadows

THE BLUFF ON the far side of the Elster River was reached by a narrow bridge. As Sanford M. Lubinsky of the 28th Infantry Division approached for the first time, flanked by a dozen German guards with fixed bayonets and dogs, he saw the ominous black mouths of seventeen shafts in the hill and emaciated men in striped prisoners' uniforms milling around beside them. This was clearly where he would be put to work.

Lubinsky had reached Berga on February 13, 1945, along with the other 349 American prisoners of war selected by the Germans for transport eastward from Stalag IX-B. On arrival, he was marched up a hill to a collection of four barracks surrounded by a barbed-wire fence just over a mile from the little town. The barracks closest to the gate was for the more than eighty Jewish GIs, including Lubinsky and Shapiro.

Lubinsky was lodged in a room about the size of a two-car garage, filled with the familiar three-tiered bunks. The soldiers slept two to a bunk, which was uncomfortable but provided some warmth. Helmets served as receptacles for what food there was, wooden buckets as receptacles for excrement during the night, when they were locked in. The buckets were emptied at daybreak into an outdoor slit-trench latrine, whose stench, even in winter, pervaded the Americans' little prison camp.

The arrival of the Americans coincided to the day with the ferocious Allied bombing of Dresden, which left tens of thousands of Germans dead, including the wife and daughters of one of the Berga guards. The bombardment of the city, about fifty miles to the east, lit up the night sky to the extent that some of the American prisoners thought it was dawn. The bombs hardly disposed the Germans to indulge their new charges.

The Americans were put to work on February 15. They were divided into two work shifts, one from six in the morning until two in the afternoon, the other from two until ten at night. The Jews, Lubinsky among them, were in the second shift. The Germans lined them up in the little *Appellplatz* between the barracks and counted and recounted them. The guards were older men, many of them in their fifties, some with injuries that prevented them from serving at the front. They were mostly from the Volkssturm, or Civilian Guard, and Lubinsky wondered at first if they were simply incompetent. But it did not take him long to realize that the endless counts were just another form of humiliation.

Lubinsky now saw for the first time that out of the tunnels came little rail lines, which extended about a hundred feet down to the Elster. Pajama-clad prisoners were guiding V-shaped carts loaded with rocks down the tracks, swiveling them at the bank and dumping the stone into the water. Whoever these ghostlike people were, they seemed to move in slow motion.

The month of February was particularly cold in Berga. Lubinsky soon found himself freezing in the damp tunnels. Certain crews had stoves, but not his. Water dripped down the jagged black rock, and sometimes, when his mouth was caked with slate dust, Lubinsky cupped his hands and drank it. He remembered the pills the army had given him to disinfect river water. But that was in the time before. Such niceties would not keep him alive now. The regulations he had once lived by seemed almost quaint. Now he was living on hate, the hate he felt for his German tormentors. Here only hate would keep him alive, keep him placing one foot in front of the other. He did not want to be buried so far from home, get tossed in some anonymous pit; he did not want to give the Germans that satisfaction or any other.

Back home in Ohio, Lubinsky had worked briefly in a steel mill, dangerous work, high up on the light steam lines, with dust clouds spewing from the coal-fired ovens. But he had never known anything like the hell of the tunnel to which he was now assigned. The Germans and the bedraggled workers slaving for them were 150 feet into the bluff, in a damp shaft. Lubinsky—at five feet eight inches the smallest man in his infantry unit—was made to work a heavy drill.

He had to bore straight, so the dynamite charges could be properly inserted, but the dust was so thick that he could scarcely see the man next to him. No fan or ventilation system dispelled the black fog. If he paused or slackened in his work, the guards were relentless: a fist to the side of his head, a shovel swatted across his backside, a rifle butt driven into the back of his neck, a kick in the kidneys. The Germans, whatever they were building, wanted it completed fast.

Lubinsky had to fight the feeling of being reduced to nothing, because that was tantamount to surrender. But his body had its own rules. It did not take long for him to begin to feel the slate particles accumulating in his lungs and his strength ebbing with the inevitability of a tide.

The drill was about four feet long; he reckoned it weighed close to a hundred pounds. Lubinsky had to bore about five feet into the rock. He tried to banish any thoughts and keep the drill steady. Leave it, blank it, block it, he told himself, as he had before, during the advance through the fields of northern France, when orders were given to take a ridge or a village, often for no apparent reason, and the only way to go forward with buddies falling to the left and right of you was not to think, not to yield to the temptation to say Kaddish for yourself.

It took a long time to bore five feet in. When the work was done, one of the German bosses placed charges and connected a length of wire to the dynamite. The Americans were ordered back, but not very far; when the explosion came, shards often lacerated Lubinsky and the other prisoners, who had to load the rock onto the little carts. They had no helmets; working with their bare hands, they cut themselves. The smallest nick festered. It was brutal work in any circumstances. With little food, it amounted to a death sentence.

"The drill was taking away my will, taking away every ounce of any strength that I had left," Lubinsky said. "For me to hold the drill up with my arms and keep it in there and keep it steady to go in pretty straight—all that was weighing on me, weighing me down. My arms were giving out. There was nothing there, the muscles were gone. Everything's gone. You know you don't have any muscles left, you don't have any meat on your arms or on you. My legs were giving out, and I was going down and down."

Lubinsky had already known plenty of humiliation in his short life. Perhaps that helped him now. In his hometown of Lima, a railroad junction between Toledo and Columbus, there were a lot of German immigrants and a lot of Irish, but the Jewish community

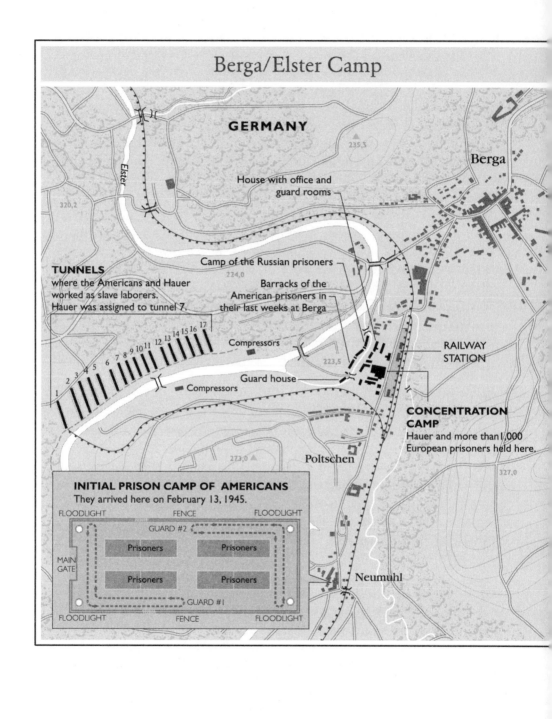

Berga/Elster Camp

GERMANY

Elster

235,5

320,2

Berga

House with office and
guard rooms

224,0

Camp of the Russian prisoners

TUNNELS
where the Americans and Hauer
worked as slave laborers.
Hauer was assigned to tunnel 7.

Barracks of the
American prisoners in
their last weeks at Berga

1 2 3 4 5 6 7 8 9 10 11 12 13 14 15 16 17

Compressors

223,5

Guard house

Compressors

RAILWAY
STATION

**CONCENTRATION
CAMP**
Hauer and more than 1,000
European prisoners held here.

273,0

Poltschen

327,0

INITIAL PRISON CAMP OF AMERICANS
They arrived here on February 13, 1945.

FLOODLIGHT   FENCE   FLOODLIGHT

GUARD #2

MAIN
GATE

| Prisoners | Prisoners |
| Prisoners | Prisoners |

GUARD #1

FLOODLIGHT   FENCE   FLOODLIGHT

Neumuhl

consisted of no more than a dozen families served by a small synagogue. At school he was often taunted—"Germans to one side, Irish on the other side, and the Jew with no side," as he put it.

His father, Max, was a clever but argumentative man whose family, it was said, had raised horses in the Ukraine. From there he had made his way to London, where he briefly trained to become a rabbi, before moving on to Canada and, from there, for no apparent reason, to Lima. It was in this former oil town, on November 29, 1917, that Lubinsky was born.

For a short period, the family prospered. Lubinsky's father, an Orthodox Jew, went into the shoe business. He was good at his trade, although he tended to argue with customers. Year after year he put money in the bank. There were six children, and their proudest possession was a pony. Lubinsky's mother, Jennie, who had been born in Budapest, would reward the children with rides if they applied themselves at school. Prayers were said every morning and night and before meals; Lubinsky understood scarcely a word.

The prayers brought scant solace when, in 1929, Jennie died of pneumonia. Soon after, the onset of the Depression destroyed Max Lubinsky's shoe business; his contrariness was now envenomed by a lifelong bitterness. The house had to be sold, the pony, too. Lubinsky's bar mitzvah the following year was memorable for its bleakness. The family moved from place to place in the Lima area, eking out an existence. They knew poverty and its unspoken adjunct, humiliation. The three older children left home. Lubinsky went to school hungry. His younger sister cooked for them all, often having to conjure something from produce bought for a quarter.

Lying about his age, Lubinsky joined the Civilian Conservation Corps in the mid-1930s. He was just sixteen but claimed to be a year older. There was little or no employment available, but the "Three Cs," as it was known, created work for young men. He went to Idaho to fight a forest fire and to California, where he fought a brush fire. He helped build a log fence around Yellowstone National Park; he built roads; he laid bricks. Whatever pay he received, and it was meager, was sent to his father.

The year the war broke out in Europe, 1939, Lubinsky found a job as a stock boy at a Montgomery Ward farm store in Lima. He was good at remembering where things were, was conscientious and honest. These qualities were remarked upon, and he soon worked his way up to assistant manager, before being appointed manager of a store in Hillsdale, Michigan. For the first time, he had money in his pocket, perhaps even a future, enough of one, anyway, to propose to his childhood sweetheart, Clara Griffin. They wed in 1940. Lubinsky got a draft deferral by going to work for Ohio Steel, and in 1942 the Lubinskys' son Terry was born. But this tranquil domestic life in a Midwest now delivered from the Depression came to an end the next year.

Lubinsky trained at Camp Shelby in Hattiesburg, Mississippi, with the New York 69th Infantry, and in May 1944 was sent to England as a replacement soldier. Being short, he wondered how he would fare if it came to fighting the Nazis with bayonets at close quarters. But he was muscular and strong-willed; his gaze was unflinching, and he tended to earn respect. Having a young family, he found, gave him a sense of steady motivation, one he had first learned in overcoming penury, that some of the younger, more privileged, more imposing men lacked.

Soon after arrival in England, he was summoned to a camp of the 82nd Airborne Division. Weighed down with bandoliers, rifles, hand grenades, and ammunition belts, he was told he would soon go into Normandy with glider troops. "My stomach was clear down to my feet," Lubinsky said.

But a benign doctor, intent on saving as many men as he could, held him back at the last minute for urgent dental treatment. "At the time," Lubinsky remarked, "I had perfect teeth." Later, in France, he would see many of the ill-fated gliders hanging from trees.

By then, he was a private in the 28th Infantry Division, and had landed in France on D-day plus ten: June 16, 1944. As Lubinsky waded ashore, it seemed to him that the water was still red with the blood of the 29th Infantry Division. He looked up and there was a wall in front of him. How the first guys in ever made it up that cliff alive, he did not know. But he did know one thing: if that was possible, anything was, even survival. Thanks to those who had come before him, there were ropes hanging down and footholds dug out of the cliff.

From that day, he was on the line, through the terror of Normandy under mortar fire, on through Paris where he saw the Eiffel Tower and rejoicing crowds on the Champs-Élysées, and out eastward toward Belgium. Lubinsky was "scared every second of every minute of every hour of every day. I never thought I would see the next minute."

Some men were born hunters. He was not. The first time he saw a dead body, he threw up. The nights were hell, sleeping with a grenade next to you, not knowing when another grenade might come in and blow you to pieces. He woke to dawns that were hazy, the mist pregnant with menace, the bushes too thick, the fields too fertile, the air damp. A lot of the villages and towns were bombed to pieces. People were dying by the hundreds, by the thousands, in a cultivated and civilized place. The roads were old. The long lines of mature plane trees beside them told you that. He hated those trees. Each one of them might hide a German sniper, and often did. He did not feel brave; he simply learned to fire without thinking. Guys dropped around him, guts opened up, faces smashed. He saw veterans crack suddenly, squealing from shell shock, and he tried to efface that ugliness from his mind. There were two choices only: to take it or to go berserk. Lubinsky took it, asking only that he be spared a slow death. To his surprise, he kept hearing the bullets zipping past, a good sign, because he knew that when you are hit, you do not hear the bullet. Or so they said.

As a communications man, Lubinsky had to string wire up from the switchboard to the line companies and then farther on to the outlying observation posts, from which air corps officers and line officers would direct bombing raids and artillery fire. Sometimes the Germans would tap the phone lines and get a good fix on where he was, and then the mortars came uncomfortably close.

They never came closer than in the Hürtgen Forest on the Belgian-German border in November 1944. He was up a tree with his clamps, hanging on as he tried to string some wire, his legs around the trunk. A shell smashed into the tree, and Lubinsky could feel the heat of it surge right up through his genitals. He was afraid to look down, afraid to feel down there.

"Schwarz," Lubinsky called to his buddy below him, "is there a hole in me?"

The answer was a reassuring negative. When he did eventually look down, Lubinsky found a good chunk of iron in the tree right below his testicles. "Oh boy," he said. "That was hot."

For week after week, the Germans held off the American forces in the Hürtgen with mortars and machine-gun and rifle fire. The fear instilled by the gloomy forest was insidious, Lubinsky found, worse even than the terror of house-to-house fighting in the western German city of Aachen. There Lubinsky had met another Jewish GI, a crazed soldier, or so it seemed to him then, who talked about Nazi atrocities against European Jews. Lubinsky had heard something back in Ohio of German synagogues being burned by the Nazis, but he had never heard such detailed accounts. He noted that the Jewish soldier took no German prisoners.

Within a month of the Battle of the Hürtgen Forest, Lubinsky was himself a prisoner of the Germans, captured on December 18, at the Battle of the Bulge. The Germans fooled the American generals, fooled everyone. The Bulge was a sucker punch. Lubinsky, like thousands of other GIs, took it on the chin. He was moving back from an observation post in the region of Clervaux, Luxembourg, when shrapnel from a mortar hit him in the leg. Lubinsky was so shocked he scarcely felt the wound, as he crawled back to the switchboard. An ambulance took off without him, and he was left there with a buddy, Shorty, as the German tanks moved in. Out of the corner of his eye he saw the switchboard blown up, Shorty with it, and then a grenade coming in, and he thought, Well, this is it, here I go, hope it's quick.

"I was sure I'd been killed," Lubinsky said. "But it was a concussion grenade, and I came around a few hours later feeling dizzy."

He staggered down to Clervaux, where he was taken prisoner and offered wine and bread by a Wehrmacht officer. An American soldier was lying on a table dying, the blood flowing steadily out of him like paint from a tube being squeezed. Even after the encounter in Aachen, Lubinsky had not given a great deal of thought to his Jewishness, or to how it might affect him in Hitler's Europe. In this he resembled most other Jewish GIs. They were American soldiers, period. They had rights, under the Geneva Conventions and other rules of war.

Those illusions were swept away at Stalag IX-B, when the order came around that Jews should step out of their barracks and that anyone throwing away an *H* dog tag would be shot. "The German commandant and the guards said that. They came around to each barracks to say that," Lubinsky recalled. "We were all scared. A lot tried to hide. I figured I was born a Jew, I'll die a Jew. Might as well die a Jew. No reason to die anything else."

So it was that he was segregated from other prisoners and eventually brought to Berga. But he did not want to die in the tunnels. When SS guards inspected work in the shafts and taunted him for

being a "dirty Jew," Lubinsky felt a surge of restorative hatred, like a
second wind in a marathon. He saw other Americans giving up,
withdrawing from the world, their skin turning slightly greenish,
their eyes losing focus, and he vowed not to drift away because his little son would never forgive him. At the age of twenty-seven, Lubinsky was, among the Americans, something of a veteran, and he felt
that his age, experience, and family gave him an advantage over boys
who were twenty or younger and seemed to abandon hope, and the
adrenaline spur of hatred, more easily.

Sometimes, standing at the mouth of his tunnel, Lubinsky
watched the other, larger group of prisoners in striped uniforms he
had seen on his first day of work. He now knew that they were
housed in a concentration camp in the town. Many were teenagers,
and they seemed to work mainly laying railroad track, or dumping
rocks in the river, or on night shifts that began when his ended.
These captives were so reduced to skin and bone as to appear almost
translucent. He wondered who they were, what had happened to
them in German hands. They seemed to speak no English; their
expressions were blank. Lubinsky and other American prisoners
began calling them "the zombies."

The first clue to the zombies' identity came when one of them
approached a fellow Jewish American, Private Milton Stolon of the
106th Infantry Division. A Polish Jew, he addressed Stolon in Yiddish. Perhaps, Lubinsky reflected, even the worst stories he had
heard of Nazi treatment of European Jews were but a pale reflection
of the truth.

Hauer tried to ignore the pain. As the SS guards herded the Auschwitz survivors westward toward Germany, his spine, weakened by
beating, ached and his left foot went numb. His father told him that
he would have preferred a fiery death in the Jawischowitz infirmary
to the agony of this forced march to Buchenwald. Hauer put his
father's bony arm around his shoulder and helped him forward. To
quench their thirst there was only snow. Their two loaves of bread
were quickly frozen solid.

It was Janek, Hauer's Polish block leader, who kept them moving
forward. He went back and forth along the line of prisoners offering
encouragement. But some could take the punishment no longer and

collapsed. Every few minutes, shots rang out as the SS dragged the fallen into a roadside ditch and put a bullet through their heads. The bedraggled Jews left a trail of corpses as their footprint, dark little blotches in the snow.

Night came but brought no comfort or warmth. The survivors were ordered to stop in open country at the margins of a dead forest of sinister stumps, seemingly decimated by artillery. The European continent was dying. Nothing could now stop its descent into rubble. Hauer and his father wrapped themselves in their blankets and pressed their bodies together. But the cold still cut like a knife. Hauer slept fitfully, wondering how close the Russians were, these men who had come from so far and would not now stop.

Explosions woke them. For the first time, Hauer saw fear in the eyes of the SS men as they scurried about screaming at the prisoners to get up and move. Those who did not awaken fast enough were shot dead. From the highway, Hauer looked back at a landscape of death, the huddled corpses scattered in the snow among the tree stumps, watched by crows perched on desiccated, leafless branches. Ponds scattered in the woods were covered in blue-gray ice. The bodies were slight, crumpled things that seemed to bear little relation to the human form, and the snow had already begun to gather them into its blanket. Artillery boomed in the leaden distance as the column of prisoners, now much reduced, began to trudge down the road. The shots of the German executioners that had punctuated the march on the first day now rang out more regularly. The sound seemed unremarkable. This was death in a minor key.

About six hours later, the Germans ordered a pause. Hauer laid out a blanket in the snow and prepared to sit down with his father and Baruch Schreiber. But at that moment, Weber, the SS guard, approached.

"We will rest here for thirty minutes," he said. "Do not sit down. If you sit down, you will fall asleep and freeze. You will never be able to get up."

But Hauer's father had already slumped on the blanket and fallen asleep. When the time came to move, Hauer shook him; his father stirred but refused to move.

"Leave me here, my child," David Hauer said. "Let me sleep. I had such a beautiful dream. I was home with Mother. It is so good to dream, I want to dream some more."

"Father, I cannot leave you. They will shoot you. We will be free in a short time, and then we will see Mother, not in a dream but in reality."

"My son, believe me, I am too tired and I prefer to dream. I am just a burden to you at this stage. Without me hanging on you, I believe you have a chance. But I am going to die anyway. Here I can sleep, and I do not care if they shoot me."

Weber was close by, waiting for them to move. "Your father is right," he said. "He will not make it, and you can hardly move yourself. You must leave him."

There was a logic to everything, Hauer thought, once you made the Nazis' initial pact with the devil—a logic to infanticide, as when the SS man tried to explain the murder of Lea Wertheim's baby as the means of saving her; a logic to patricide, as Weber now sought to make clear that the only way for Hauer to save himself was, in effect, to kill his father. But from his two dead friends, Katz and Yankele, Hauer had learned the trap of such insidious but craven logic, served up by those whose souls are already compromised. Perhaps Weber was indeed an agonizing German. Perhaps he had, as he said, been subjected to intolerable pressure in his hometown before opting to join the SS. Still, he had served the SS. He had played his little part in Hitler's design. He had been brave enough, with defeat near, to speak out to Hauer and to offer him food, but Weber was not a brave man. He was a murderer with a conscience.

Hauer grabbed his father and, with Schreiber's help, tried to hoist him to his feet. But David Hauer resisted. Another SS man approached with a pistol, ready to put an end to the struggle. With what little force he had left, Hauer slapped his father, who went limp. He and Schreiber dragged David into the line.

That night, the column reached the railroad station. Only the help of other prisoners enabled Hauer to bring his father to this point: four of them carried what was left of David Hauer the last several miles. He weighed no more than ninety pounds, Hauer reckoned, but still the effort was enormous.

The Germans announced that the train to Buchenwald would leave the next morning and that prisoners would be permitted to sleep in the storage depot of the station. This prompted a stampede. Everyone sensed that another night in the open would kill them. But the prospects inside the depot did not seem much better. Hauer watched prisoners clawing their way on top of one another and was reminded of worms in a fisherman's bucket. These had been human beings. Now they formed a writhing heap of skin and bones, piled layer upon layer, and those at the bottom did not even have the strength to utter a sound before they suffocated.

Hauer and Schreiber, with no alternative, began climbing over the mass of bodies, dragging David as they ascended. At last, Hauer felt something metallic in the darkness: the roof of a railroad passenger car. On it they slept. In the morning, the night's toll became apparent: hundreds of prisoners were dead, crushed at the bottom of the pile.

The survivors were ordered to seat themselves atop open wagons filled with coal. Hauer wondered if the coal came from his mine and what had become of the Polish foreman, Kowalsky, who had given him hope. His thoughts strayed to Emerich and Benji and his mother and Edith. Where were they? The war tossed people this way and that like petals in the wind. He had to outlast the gusts—even the final furious ones—and find his mother.

Climbing up onto the wagons required an enormous effort. One man slipped, broke a leg, and was shot dead by the SS. The Germans boarded the only two passenger cars, one behind the locomotive and the other at the back of the train. They were sheltered from the piercing wind. Hauer dug a hole in the coal, big enough for his father and Schreiber and himself, and put a blanket over them. He managed to shatter what was left of his frozen bread with a piece of coal and force his father to eat.

They slept. The train rattled forward. Night came. Hauer had no idea how much time passed. Just before the German border, Janek jumped off the train, bidding them farewell and good luck. Hauer hoped the Pole, who had done much to keep him alive, would find his wife and children. In moments of wakening, he listened for the sounds of war, the sounds of the Russians approaching. But he heard nothing. What he did hear, very faintly, was the sound of his father's heartbeat as he put his ear to David's chest. By the time the train pulled into Buchenwald, no more than three hundred of the approximately three thousand prisoners who had left Jawischowitz were still alive.

Once more, at the entrance to the camp, Hauer saw the words ARBEIT MACHT FREI. He could not believe that once upon a time, in early summer, those same words had seemed encouraging. The barbed-wire fences, the guard towers, and the SS with dogs were by now so well known to him that he hardly paid attention. The camp seethed with people in various stages of a familiar degradation and despair.

He and Schreiber carried David into a large room, where they were ordered to undress, keeping only their belts. Hauer undressed his father and helped him into a second room with showerheads, just like the ones he had first seen at Auschwitz seven months earlier. From them, with a hiss, spurted warm water.

Hauer gently soaped his father, who opened his eyes and cried. There was nothing left of him, no more than a shell. David Hauer could not speak, and he could not stand unsupported. When an SS officer came in to inspect them, Hauer had little illusion about what would happen. The prisoners were duly separated into two groups, one still able to stand and so, presumably, to work; the other too weak to do anything. David Hauer was taken away as part of the second group.

At Berga, sixty miles from Buchenwald, Shapiro could not get used to the hangings. They took place in the *Appellplatz* of the concentration camp. The bodies, emaciated in their striped uniforms, were left there as warnings to the other inmates. Sometimes there were several of them suspended from a robust crossbeam. He felt the same tension as when, fighting his way across France with the 28th Infantry Division a few months earlier, he saw a shell hit a foxhole some distance away. Before he got to the point of impact, he knew there would be body parts all over the place. He knew that, as a medic, he would have to sift through them. But it was always hard to look, as it was now at these dangling men.

In general, he saw them in the early morning as the white beam of the camp searchlights gave way to a pale dawn. Shapiro would cast a furtive glance at the gallows, anxious not to draw the attention of the SS troopers whose cruelty was often on display. Growing up in the Bronx, he had been shown photographs of a lynching in the South and had wondered at the smiling faces of the white murderers. But he had never seen a hanging.

Shapiro was at a loss. He had plunged into some netherworld where hangings were public and terrified adolescents with yellow triangles on their sleeves were made to stand at attention in the frigid air before being beaten with batons or rifle butts, but he could not say what this hell was, how it had been constituted, why it existed. Without knowing it, he had entered the universe of the Holocaust.

As a medic, one of nine in the group of 350 American prisoners, Shapiro had been selected on arrival at Berga for the food detail. He had to wake before daybreak and steer a large hay wagon loaded with fifty-gallon containers down the hill from the cluster of four American barracks to the concentration camp. It was here, as he waited for the food to be doled out, that Shapiro would see the hanging men, their heads lolling to the side, limbs stiff from some combination of rigor mortis and cold.

Steering the wagon was not easy. A long pole was attached to the front axle. Two men gripped the pole, in the position normally taken by horses, two held the cart from behind, and four others walked on either side. The chief difficulty on the downhill leg was preventing the vats from tumbling off and the whole contraption from careening out of control. When the large camp gates swung open, they maneuvered the cart toward the kitchen, to the left of the entrance.

Scores of prisoners in their ragged, pajama-like attire scurried around. Many looked very young, no more than teenagers. Appearing busy seemed important. They did not so much look at him as through him. Some hollowness forged in suffering had possessed them; it resided in their eyes, permeated their bodies, inhabited each feeble gesture. Sometimes the prisoners seemed as insubstantial as ghosts. The SS guards, their insignia gleaming, loomed large and heavy beside them, German shepherds straining on leashes at their sides. The guards patted the animals to quiet them.

Shapiro shivered. He did not ask questions. He collected the food, twice a day, morning and evening. The vessels were filled with the same food the concentration-camp prisoners consumed: a vile liquid masquerading as coffee, turnip-filled soup devoid of real sustenance, an occasional piece of cheese or sausage, and loaves of dark bread that had to be split among four men in the first weeks, later among five.

On one occasion he watched what appeared to be a gruesome pantomime: a young prisoner removing his hat, bowing to an SS man, trying to answer a question, failing to do so correctly, and being beaten. The grim ritual was repeated again and again, beginning with the hat and ending with the wielding of the truncheon. On another occasion he saw a boy being beaten with a crop by an SS guard for inadvertently splashing the German's boots with mud as he ran past. Who were these people? That many were Hungarian Jews, that the Jews of Europe had long been collected and eliminated in such camps by the Germans, that the Nazi death camps in Poland had been overrun by the Russians and the survivors herded westward into places like Berga in Germany—none of this was known to Shapiro.

Eight weeks of imprisonment since his capture at the Battle of the Bulge had eroded his will to the point where his only remaining idea was survival. Asking questions could compromise that quest. He remembered his bright letters home on arrival at the first prison camp at Bad Orb, his requests for pancake flour and packets of hot chocolate and Kraft cheese. To think that he had believed he would receive them.

"The gallows was just part of the landscape of the concentration camp," Shapiro said. "Sometimes it was one person, sometimes five. I don't know what the punishment was for."

The road back up the hill with the loaded wagon was hard. The women of Berga, their husbands off at the front, gazed at the Americans in silence. He smelled the woods, a resinous whiff of freedom that taunted him. The German guards would not allow them to pause. Shapiro's whole body ached. But he soon realized that his hardships were mild compared with those of most of the other GIs, who, like Lubinsky, had been sent to work in the tunnels being mined in the hills on the far side of the Elster River.

Shapiro was spared tunnel duty because his Red Cross card identified him as a medic. When he was not on the food detail, he worked in an improvised dispensary set up in one of the barracks. It was, however, a dispensary with virtually no medicine because the Germans refused to provide any. In sworn testimony given on May 29, 1945, in London, Private Stephen J. Schweitzer of the 106th Infantry Division said: "Only the men who were so sick that they could not walk were put in the dispensary. The sick men who could still walk were made to work." A German speaker, Schweitzer demanded that medicine be provided, but his pleas were dismissed.

Decisions on medical attention, as on all matters relating to the Americans, were made principally by Sergeant Erwin Metz of National Guard Battalion 621, headquartered about thirty miles away. He took over in mid-March from a Sergeant Kunz, who had overseen the GIs. His chief mission appears to have been to enforce a tougher discipline after several escapes.

From testimony provided soon after the war ended and from the recollections of several survivors, it seems that Metz, then fifty-two, was a man of vindictive cruelty. He was educated only to the sixth grade and had begun his career as a bank official. But his professional life had been anything but smooth. In 1927 he was convicted of embezzlement. This was followed by further convictions, for fraud in 1933 and 1936. In all, Metz had served close to two years in prison for these crimes. On the eve of the war, he had a job as a manager in a starch factory.

It is in the nature of the social upheaval engineered by Hitler and often of war itself to thrust the mediocre into positions of authority, where they can play out every previously frustrated fantasy. War is also opportunity. Metz's bearing was military and his manner cutting. He had gold crowns on his upper front teeth, a curiously high-pitched voice, a ruddy complexion, pale blue eyes. He wore rimless spectacles and a couple of large gold rings on each hand. On his chest he sported a dagger-and-wreath bronze medal and a Russian campaign ribbon. The best gauge of a man's fitness to work, Metz believed, was the state of his tongue.

Private Leon E. Trachtman of the 100th Infantry Division said of Metz: "Oh, he just bullied me and pushed me and slapped me once or twice. One thing I can say. Metz fancied himself as sort of a doctor. When the fellows went on sick call, he would examine them by asking them to stick out their tongues. He would say, 'Healthy tongue. Go to work.' Many fellows who were forced to work like that repeatedly did die eventually."

One of the victims was Private Arthur S. Rosen, who died in March 1945, a few weeks after arrival at Berga. Rosen pleaded not to go to work in the tunnels because he was sick, but Metz examined his tongue and pronounced it "a wonderful tongue, clean as a whistle." Two days later Rosen was found to have double pneumonia and quickly died. Metz was unmoved.

He supervised about two dozen guards and reported to Captain Ludwig Merz, aged fifty-seven, of the same National Guard Battalion 621. Merz visited the American camp on a regular basis, reviewing the situation with Metz at least twenty times. But ultimate control of the camp system within which the Americans now found themselves lay with the SS and Lieutenant Willy Hack, who was under intense pressure to complete the underground jet-fuel production facility at Berga by October 1. Prisoners—Americans, Hungarian

Jews, Russians, Slovakians, Italians, and others—were to be driven relentlessly to this end, even as Hitler's armies disintegrated on the western and eastern fronts. Metz interpreted this requirement with unyielding ardor. He was ruthless in pushing Americans into the tunnels, even when they could scarcely hold themselves upright.

Private David Goldin of the 79th Division kept a diary of his captivity on a single scrap of paper. Entries were necessarily brief. Goldin, at thirty-four, was the oldest of the American prisoners and had a wife and son back in Virginia. On February 14, the day after arriving at Berga, he noted: "Valentine's Day and thinking of you all at home and missing you."

Two days later, after the first experience of work on a drill in the tunnels, Goldin wrote: "Didn't want to go back to work, but was forced to." On February 19, his fifth day in the shaft, he suffered a bad accident: "Got hit by a large rock falling from the ceiling on top of my head and was knocked unconscious."

In testimony given to American war-crimes investigators in France, Goldin said he was unconscious for four hours and "didn't receive any medical attention from the Germans." An American prisoner had some sulfa that was quickly applied and may have saved him from infection. The injury was serious; Goldin bled heavily. Yet his diary records that he returned to work on March 1, nine days after he was struck by the rock.

Private David Young of the 28th Infantry Division, who had been severely beaten with a shovel by a German guard while working in a tunnel on February 20, died at Berga in the third week of March, soon after Metz took over from Kunz. Strikingly similar accounts of his death were given by Private Irving Pastor of the 106th Infantry Division, Private Stanley B. Cohen, a college student from Brooklyn, New York, who served in the 422nd Infantry, and Trachtman. Common to all their testimony given to war-crimes investigators was the information that Young was lying on his bed in a state of near collapse when Metz, rebuffing the pleas of Young's colleagues, had him hauled out of bed and made to stand. Young fell to the floor, some say because Metz struck him and then threw a bucket of cold water over him, the coup de grâce that killed him.

"Metz pulled Young from his berth and Young fell to the floor," Pastor said. "Metz pulled him up by the collar, and I saw Metz strike Young a light blow in the face, disbelieving Young's tale of being sick. Young fell to the floor again, and thereupon Metz went to a nearby bucket, picked it up, and dumped cold water on Young to revive him." About fifteen minutes later, Pastor recalled, Young died.

Cohen also witnessed Young's death. He gave this description of it on June 1, 1945: "I called the *Kommandoführer* in and told him Young was sick and in no condition to go to work. He ordered Young pulled out of bed. I emphasized that Young was in no condition to leave his bed, that he was not, strictly speaking, conscious. He reiterated his order and I called for two medics to help Young out of bed. He commanded Young to stick out his tongue. Young collapsed on the floor. This *Unteroffizier* Metz took a bucket of cold water and splashed it over Young. Young flickered his eyelashes and gave no other indication of his consciousness."

Metz then gave permission for Young to miss his shift and ordered that he be left on the floor until he regained consciousness. Cohen placed Young in the care of an American medic named Tony Acevedo, from the 70th Infantry Division.

"Ten minutes later," Cohen told the investigators, "Tony came in and reported Young dead."

The splashing of freezing water on exhausted American prisoners was a method widely favored by Metz. Kurt Seifert, a German guard who worked under Metz, was asked by American investigators on June 17, 1945, whether he had ever seen Americans carried from the tunnels to the barracks because of exhaustion. "Yes," Seifert replied, "I saw that practically every day, especially during the first part of my stay there. When one fell down coming to or coming from work, Metz ordered a helmet full of water, cold water, thrown on the man to see whether he was really out or only feigning."

Shapiro and Acevedo worked together. Acevedo was twenty, a Mexican American who had been in Durango, Mexico, when he volunteered for the army in 1943. There was little these two young medics could do as Metz drove the Americans to their deaths. Occasionally, the very sick were examined by a German doctor, but Metz was always present and treatment was, with few exceptions, superficial or nonexistent.

In the dispensary, Shapiro had ample opportunity to monitor the rapidly deteriorating condition of those who were working in the tunnels. Fungal infections in damp areas such as the crotch and armpit became common. Teeth got loose from lack of nourishment. Fecal matter accumulated in underwear. Coughing, diarrhea, bruising, infected cuts, dysentery, diphtheria, and pneumonia spread. Every cut or abrasion from the sharp slate rock became infected. Each illness was aggravated by lack of food, lack of heat, lack of medicine, and lack of appropriate care.

For Shapiro, the worsening plight of his fellow captives could be measured by the volume of the hacking coughs that punctuated the night and the heavy clatter of army boots as men stricken with diarrhea raced to the wooden receptacle that served as the nighttime latrine. Men chewed pieces of wood or charcoal, if they could find any, to try to stanch the diarrhea. Lice kept everyone awake. Men removed some of their clothes to try to kill the bugs. To kill one could give satisfaction, actually providing a moment of pleasure. But the itching never eased. Socks and undershirts stuck to wounds, growing together to the point where the clothing could be excised only with a knife. At least there were no mirrors to provide a daily portrait of degradation.

The fights over portions of bread were another measure of the American prisoners' growing desperation. It did not matter that the bread tasted of sawdust—they still argued. The person cutting the bread had the last choice of a piece, a system that was supposed to ensure that a loaf was cut fairly into four or five equal segments, but it failed to stop the bickering over who got what. Rituals with the bread became more elaborate. Shapiro watched men break their pieces in half, then in half again, then in half again, so that the bread would appear to last longer as it was eaten in nibbles, and he saw men licking their fingers to pick up crumbs from the filthy floor; he saw men trying to toast pieces of bread no larger than a thimble by holding them close to a flickering fire at the camp, before the Germans stopped the making of any fires because they feared Allied bombing raids at night.

Hunger broke every bond. Self-preservation took over, some base instinct, until that, too, evaporated. People who die of hunger and thirst die in silence. When you were sleeping next to a man and could not feel warmth from him anymore, you knew. Shapiro woke up next to a dead man once and pushed the memory so far back he could never remember the soldier's name. Either you strangled the memory or it strangled you. In the trenches, bleeding to death, they said, "Mama, Mama, Mama." They wailed like babies to the stars. Not here. They had been buddies. Now Shapiro was not sure what they were, these ragged American boys raging over crumbs, chewing wood, eating snow, coughing blood, slipping away in the night without a word.

Mordecai Hauer found himself housed in one of several wooden blocks at Buchenwald that had clearly been added in haste to the redbrick buildings that once constituted the camp. With the Nazi killing centers in Poland gone, overrun by the advancing Russian troops, the prisoners from the disbanded death camps poured into concentration camps in the Reich. Those who could still stand provided a new labor supply for the Reich's strained war industry.

The blocks had the merit of being warm, and the food, while meager, seemed sufficient after the death march. There were no lice. For days Hauer drifted in and out of sleep, thinking of very little. His strength slowly returned. One day, he learned from another prisoner that his group was to be placed in the *Transport Schwalbe*. The phrase meant nothing to him.

As he grew stronger, Hauer also grew more restless. He wanted to know his father's fate. His assumptions were based on the *Muselmann* selection at Jawischowitz: those not strong enough to work were gassed. But he heard rumors that the weakest survivors of the death march had not been killed. Rather, they had been placed in "quarantine" in a block a few hundred yards from his.

He devised a plan. He volunteered to collect food from the kitchen, which was closer to the so-called quarantine block in a section of the camp that was cordoned off from the rest. The food—thin soup, bread, and ersatz coffee—was delivered between one and two in the afternoon. Six volunteers wheeled a large pushcart into the kitchen and loaded the heavy cauldrons onto it.

As they approached the kitchen, Hauer told the other volunteers he had an errand to run and would be back in a few minutes. He walked fast. The gate to the quarantine unit was closed but not locked and a sign warned EINTRITT VERBOTEN—"Entrance Forbidden." Hauer entered.

The stench of the block almost made him turn back immediately. In bed after bed, untended prisoners were dead or dying. Useless now to the Germans, they had been left to die. A terrible sound of wheezing and gasping filled the room along with the foul breath of shriveled figures who clung, despite themselves, to life. Dying can be hard work, Hauer reflected. Its embrace approaches and recedes, a hand proffered and withdrawn. He walked briskly down a narrow aisle, looking to the left and right for his father, whom he found at last, unconscious and struggling to breathe, in a bed at the end of the room.

"Father, Father," Hauer said.

David Hauer, the emptied being that still bore that name, did not hear him.

Hauer, his heart numb, kissed his father's bloodless lips, kissed his forehead, kissed his hand, and left. He had done what he could. The long struggle was over. The last thing his father had given him, on the march, was a spoon, a small silver spoon, for which he said he no longer had any use. Hauer had no idea how his father had hidden the little spoon that he now raised to his lips.

When he reached the kitchen, the vessels of soup were being loaded onto the cart. One of the volunteers whispered that Hauer's absence had been noted. At that moment, an SS man appeared at the kitchen door.

"Here is the bird that flew the cage," he said. "Where have you been?"

"Officer, I went to see my dying father. I wanted to see him a last time before our transport leaves this camp. We were separated on arrival here—"

"How touching. But you left your group without permission, and unless I am wrong, your father is in the quarantine unit to which entry is barred."

"Yes, sir, but—"

The officer ordered Hauer to report to him in the kitchen when he had finished loading the food. Once the cart was rolling, Hauer did so. The SS man made him stand and wait for an hour. Finally, he addressed Hauer: "Anyone else in my place would send you into the quarantine unit, which means certain death. But I am not a cruel man. I will find some other means to teach you that a prisoner must obey discipline."

Hauer pleaded to be allowed to return to his block, but the German rose, motioning Hauer to follow him. He opened a door leading from the kitchen into a refrigeration room with slabs of red meat hanging from hooks on the walls.

"I am sure that a couple of hours in here will not kill you," the SS man said. "In fact, this may do you good. You certainly picked up some germs in the quarantine block, and the cold will destroy them. I will come and get you out later."

With that, he shoved Hauer into the large, icy, concrete-floored chamber and slammed the door. Hauer started pacing the room, lit by a single lightbulb on the ceiling, in a bid to keep his blood circulating. But the cold was insistent; he grew steadily weaker. His teeth chattered and his body shook. Once again the pain in his spine became unbearable. He fell to the floor, and a terrible desire for sleep washed over him. The sensation was pleasurable and brought with it visions of his mother and of Ilona and of Sharon and of lying on the grass of the spa hill hear Goncz watching the bright rims of the clouds as they approached the sun, brightest of all as they were about to cover the sun and cast the world into shadow. How bright were the clouds and the new leaves, so light, and how the fields of wheat shimmered and how the air was sweet, and Ilona's skin so pale and the scarlet of her lips . . .

Hauer shook himself from his reverie. To dream was to die, and he had to live. He had to raise himself from this icy concrete floor that would take his life. He gazed at the hooks, the hooks from which meat hung. He looked at the marbled flesh, the layers of fat, the knuckles of white bone. Could he not suspend his own flesh from these hooks and so get off the freezing floor? He tore off his belt and fastened the buckle on the last hole. He crawled along the floor to the wall and, pushing against it, raised himself to his feet. He put both his arms through the loop and attached it to the hook. With an immense effort, he hoisted himself to a point where his body hung from the belt, the tips of his shoes just touching the floor. Then he passed out.

It was the smell of alcohol that brought Hauer around. He did not know how much time had passed. The SS man was pouring schnapps into his mouth. A colleague was massaging his chest. The two Germans were talking to each other.

"Imagine me, sitting with a beer, when I remember that I left him in the freezer after I went off duty at four. I ran all the way to get him. I guess I didn't want the kid on my conscience."

"When I saw you running, I didn't know what was up. First time I've seen you run to save a Jew."

Hauer felt dizzy from the alcohol and drifted into sleep. When he awoke, he was back in his block. For the remaining time that he was at Buchenwald, the SS man who had almost frozen him to death brought him chocolate, extra rations of bread, and good soup from the German kitchen. By the time he boarded the train for Berga in February 1945, Hauer had been fattened for labor by another murderer with a troubled conscience, another Nazi with a wife and children who no doubt loved him as a good husband and a good father, another German who had allowed himself to run with the raging beast that, Hauer now believed, resided somewhere in every human being.

When the 350 Americans arrived in Berga, they had little idea where they were. If anything, they hoped for and had been led to expect an improvement on Stalag IX-B. So it took time to understand that they had entered a world where the German aim was to work them to death. This, for a young American in Europe, unaware of the extent, ferocity, or even the very existence of the Holocaust, amounted to a realization of almost unfathomable enormity.

But by the last week of February, some of the Americans had begun to understand that they were now slaves of the Nazis, just like the starved, pajama-clad figures working in and around the tunnels, the men they called the zombies or the political prisoners. The February 21 diary entry of Edward Gorinac—"They treat us like slaves. We are even on slave rations like the Jews and political prisoners"— demonstrates the beginnings of this awareness.

Milton Stolon, who had trained at Camp Upton on Long Island, spoke enough German to understand the guards. He was twenty-one and had been drafted the month after his wife gave birth. "My crew was at tunnel number ten," he said. "The holes were spaced about a half-meter apart; they were drilled to a depth of a meter and then packed with dynamite, and then they exploded. The tunnel would fill with rock dust. In coal mining, you spit up black, but here you'd be spitting your lungs out. Bloody. The rock dust would rip them apart. The German guards did not care if they killed you or not. One beat me with a rubber hose. He hit me in the neck. Tried to hit me in the private parts until I fell. Stepped on my hands. Every day he beat me. The purpose was to kill you, but to get as much out of you before they killed you."

After weeks of this treatment, Stolon collapsed. The Germans laid him on the rocks beside the river. Two guards walked by, and one of them asked about the prone body. "Don't worry," said the other, "it's just another American Jew dying." Stolon, hearing this exchange, was livid. "I got so pissed off that I got up and went back to work," he recalled.

Gerald Daub worked with a jackhammer. "Sometimes the foreman put a board against my back," he recalled, "and leaned his weight against mine. I would try to get it askew a little in the hope that the drill would break, to slow down production. When a bit broke, you got a little time off. We would drill a series of holes in the face of the shaft, and then the foreman would put dynamite in the holes and connect it to a wire, and we would all leave the shaft. As soon as the rock was blown, we reentered and it was totally filled with stone dust. We walked into a cloud, we looked like stone statues."

In an attempt to grasp his situation, and its place in the war, Morton Brooks would talk to some of the European concentration-camp prisoners. He was working in the tunnels, drilling, swallowing dust, taking blows from pickax handles and rubber hoses whenever the whim took the German guards, getting weaker every day. In a makeshift latrine near the river, he would run into the Europeans. One or two spoke a little English. They told him they were Jews and gave accounts of the progress of Allied forces, accounts that were encouraging but impossible to verify. Brooks felt nervous talking to them. He hesitated to make any connection between his own Jewishness, theirs, and the shared fate that had befallen them. "That there was a holocaust going on, that this was a work-to-death program, and that *you*, an American soldier, were in it with the Jews of Europe, these were things that in the midst of a crazy, mixed-up war were impossible to comprehend," he said.

What was incontrovertible, by mid-March, was that the Americans were beginning to die in significant numbers. Most died in the night. Shapiro found himself gazing around the barracks trying to identify who among the young men would not awaken the next day. They were withdrawn, silent, their skin taut, their mouths open, and they made no attempt to remove the black dust and fecal matter that clung to them. They dragged themselves to work in the tunnel, they came back, they ate, they fell asleep, and in the morning they were gone.

Private Walter Rogers died on March 9; Shapiro was on the burial detail. A combination of pneumonia and exhaustion appeared to have taken Rogers, who had been forced to work when he could scarcely stand. His body was loaded onto a cart and taken across town

A view of Berga in the 1950s. A quaint East German village concealing memories of horror. *(Courtesy of Wolfgang Fritz)*

The one surviving wooden barracks where American prisoners were held at Berga in 1945. *(Charles Guggenheim/Guggenheim Productions)*

Above: Berga was already swept up in the Nazi movement in 1933, the year Hitler came to power. Here, volunteers assemble with a swastika banner, ready to do manual labor for the Führer. Their devotion is displayed between the two drums in the front row: I SERVE. *(Courtesy of Sabine Richter)*

Opposite page above: The textile factory once owned by the Jewish Englander family, who fled Berga during Hitler's rule. The plant was revived after the war by East German Communist authorities but is now abandoned. *(Charles Guggenheim/Guggenheim Productions)*

Opposite page below: Thousands of Americans who were captured at the Battle of the Bulge were taken to Stalag IX-B, near Frankfurt. Conditions were bad. But for the 350 GIs selected to go from here to Berga, they were to get much worse. *(Courtesy of R. W. Peterson)*

Left: The American prisoners, cold and hungry and unwashed, slept two to a bed in Berga on these three-tiered bunks with straw mattresses. *(National Archives and Records Administration)*

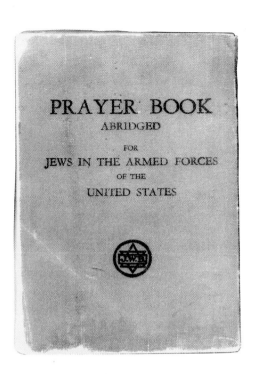

Jews accounted for about 3 percent of the American armed forces during World War II. They wore *H* (for Hebrew) dog tags and carried this prayer book. Of those selected to go to Berga, more than 20 percent were Jews. *(Courtesy of Leo Schlocker)*

Below: American infantrymen in trenches in France at the time of the Battle of the Bulge. This sudden counter-thrust by Nazi forces, Hitler's last big gamble on the western front, took Allied forces by surprise. *(National Archives and Records Administration)*

Hans Kasten, the proud German American who was the chief American "man of confidence," or chosen representative, at Stalag IX-B and, before his daring escape, at Berga. He was outraged by German demands that he help in the segregation of Jewish American soldiers. *(Courtesy of Hans Kasten)*

Tony Acevedo, the Mexican American medic whose diary of captivity in the slave labor camp at Berga provided a record of the steadily growing list of American dead.
(Courtesy of Anthony Acevedo)

Sanford Lubinsky, with his son, Terry, and mother-in-law. Memories of Terry and hatred of the Germans sustained Lubinsky during his imprisonment at Berga.
(Courtesy of Sanford Lubinsky)

William Shapiro, the medic from the Bronx, who was terrified by the hangings of European Jews at Berga. Like the other American prisoners, Shapiro took decades to understand that he had been swept into the whirlwind of the Holocaust. *(Courtesy of William Shapiro)*

Morton Goldstein, a GI killed at Berga. A German-speaker of great charm, Goldstein was shot after an attempted escape. The circumstances of the killing were bitterly disputed at a postwar trial of German commanders of the camp. *(Courtesy of the Goldstein family)*

Left: Joe Littell (right), flanked by a solider of the 106th Division, Don Young. Littell had been schooled partly in Germany but had never imagined the barbarism that would engulf the country under Hitler. He escaped from Berga with Hans Kasten and Ernst Sinner. *(Courtesy of Joseph Littell)*

Gerald Daub (right) with Bob Rudnick, a Brooklyn friend who was also imprisoned in Berga. Daub had heard before the war, from a German Jewish refugee, of the oppression of Jews by Hitler but did not imagine he himself would face such persecution. *(Courtesy of Gerald Daub)*

Below: Mordecai Hauer (right), the young Jew from Hungary who survived Auschwitz and Buchenwald and then found himself working as a slave laborer with American GIs at Berga. He is flanked by his wife, Masha, and brother Benjamin. *(Courtesy of Mordecai Hauer)*

Above: German commanders compiled a list of the 350 American prisoners deported to Berga. The first names on the list read: Slotkin, Feinberg, Philosoph, Salkain, Black, Swack, Goldstein, Ascher, Silberstein. Nearly all of the first eighty names are recognizably Jewish. (*National Archives and Records Administration*)

A typed American list of the Berga prisoners compiled after the war. It is notable that the list was initially considered "confidential" and was classified. (*National Archives and Records Administration*)

The bluff on the banks of the Elster River, near Berga. It was in this hill that American prisoners were put to work as slave laborers, boring tunnels that were to lead to an underground synthetic-fuel facility. *(National Archives and Records Administration)*

Machinery inside one of the tunnels. The Americans worked with no protective clothing or gloves as they held heavy drills against the rock face and loaded rock into small carts. Explosions sent fine shards of slate dust into their lungs and cuts quickly became infected. *(National Archives and Records Administration)*

Conditions inside and outside the tunnels where the GIs slaved were appalling. Heavy lengths of rail track had to be carried. Anyone who showed signs of weakness was beaten. *(Sketch by Anthony Acevedo)*

Americans at the entrance to one of the tunnels after the liberation of the Berga camp in 1945. Later the area was ceded to the Soviet army. The fact that Berga was in Russian-occupied East Germany helped ensure that many of its secrets were not revealed. *(National Archives and Records Administration)*

Beginning early in March 1945, three weeks after their arrival at Berga, the American prisoners began dying. Tony Acevedo kept a grim record of the deaths in his diary. The right-hand page records the killing of Morton Goldstein. *(Courtesy of Anthony Acevedo)*

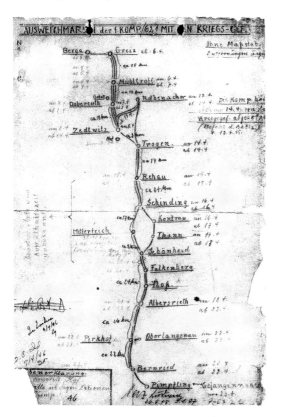

Left: The route of the march from Berga in April 1945 that left close to fifty GIs dead. They were herded onward to their deaths by their Nazi tormentors even in the last days of Hitler's Reich. *(National Archives and Records Administration)*

Above: A sketch by Tony Acevedo of conditions on the death march. Those too weak to walk were laid out on wagons pushed and dragged by other prisoners. Some suffocated on the wagons. *(Courtesy of Anthony Acevedo)*

As the Allies closed in, the Nazis pushed European prisoners out onto death marches like that endured by the Americans. Those too weak to move were summarily shot at several locations. Here is a scene from the Braunlage Forest. *(National Archives and Records Administration)*

Survivors of Berga were emaciated and close to death by the time of their liberation between April 20 and April 23, 1945. Here is one group of survivors. From front to rear: Winfield Rosenberg, Paul D. Capps, James Watkins, Joseph Giugno, Alvin Abrams. *(National Archives and Records Administration)*

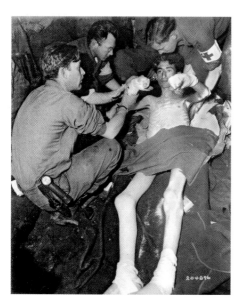

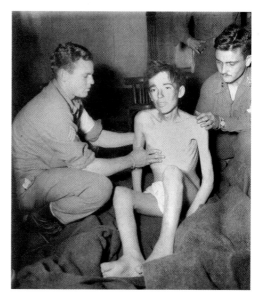

Private Alvin Abrams, age twenty-two, of Philadelphia, was close to death after being starved and forced to work in murderous conditions at Berga. His unseeing eyes were typical of those who had been subject to the Nazi program of "death through work." *(National Archives and Records Administration)*

Private James Watkins, age twenty, of Oakland, California, survived the death march from Berga. By the time they were liberated by American forces, the Berga prisoners did not have the strength to move. *(National Archives and Records Administration)*

American corpses on the road south from Berga, disinterred at Topen on June 11, 1945. As the exhausted prisoners walked, the death rate accelerated. *(National Archives and Records Administration)*

Eight more corpses, disinterred on June 13, 1945, at Heinersburg, near Kreis Rehau, lying in a field by the side of a forest. An American soldier examines them. *(National Archives and Records Administration)*

A war-crimes investigating team was sent to Berga in May 1945. Here they exhume the body of an American soldier who died during the death march. *(National Archives and Records Administration)*

Berga civilians exhuming the bodies of prisoners who died at Berga. These include American and Russian slave laborers. In and around the tunnels, Americans and European Jewish survivors of Auschwitz labored in the same devastating conditions. *(National Archives and Records Administration)*

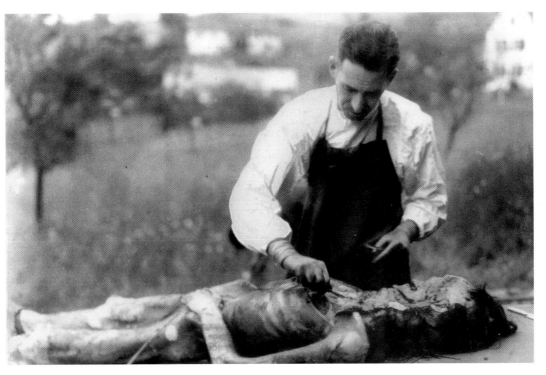

An American pathologist, Major Herman Bolker, examines the body of an American prisoner who died at Berga. The autopsy was performed on June 3, 1945. (*National Archives and Records Administration*)

An American war-crimes investigator in May or June 1945, standing over the grave of an American soldier who died at the Berga camp. The gravestone says John Simcox, but on the prisoner list he appears as John Sincox. Exhumed bodies revealed the extent of malnutrition and infection. (*National Archives and Records Administration*)

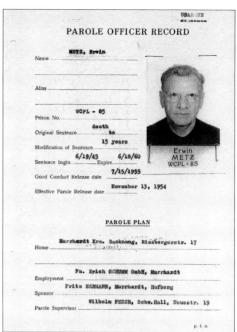

Willy Hack, the SS commander of the Berga camp. He delighted in tormenting the Americans, particularly Hans Kasten. Hack slipped away at war's end but was captured in East Germany and hung by the Communist authorities in 1952. *(Bundesarchiv)*

Erwin Metz, the German National Guard sergeant whose vindictive cruelty drove many of the Americans imprisoned at Berga to their deaths. Condemned to death at a war-crimes trial in 1946, he had his sentence commuted and was released on parole eight years later. *(National Archives and Records Administration)*

In June 1945, American authorities pressed Berga authorities to hold a memorial service for the dead American soldiers. The mayor appeared with a wreath. Murderous anti-Semitism quickly gave way to a display of the Star of David, as if the killing had been a foolish mistake. *(National Archives and Records Administration)*

to a plot just outside the town cemetery. It was a warmer day, and snow fell from the pines with a whoosh. The women of Berga, some holding small children, watched them pass in silence with their grim load. It was not easy to dig a grave in the hard ground.

Soon after the end of the war, Major Herman Bolker, a doctor in the U.S. Army Medical Corps and a member of an American war-crimes investigating team, visited the grave site. There, on June 1 and 2, 1945, he found twenty-two American bodies, including that of Rogers. He described them as follows: "The general appearance of all the bodies was that of malnutrition to various degrees. It was severe in some, estimated weights being 100 pounds in one body, 110 in another, and 65 in another, while three were noted to weigh about 125 pounds. Six bodies were autopsied, recognizable evidence of pneumonia was found in three. In those bodies on which drawers were found, considerable fecal matter was present. The causes of death in all these bodies were judged to be a combination of factors, chief among which were extreme malnutrition incident to intestinal infection."

On June 7 Bolker questioned Dr. Rudolf Miethe, a German physician, in Berga. Miethe was the doctor called in to examine some of the worst cases of illness among the Americans at the camp. He said he had noted twelve cases of pneumonia, three of diphtheria, ten of probable pulmonary tuberculosis that could not be verified because nobody was x-rayed, and several cases of malnutrition.

"The whole situation of my treating the sick prisoners at the camp was very unsatisfactory to me, and I was unhappy about my inability to alter conditions there," Miethe said under oath. "It was my opinion that these prisoners who were badly undernourished should not have been put to physical labor of the type they were made to do but the SS at the camp made them do so. Therefore many of the prisoners became sick and some of them died."

This amounted to a clear statement that the Germans had killed the Americans by forcing them to work when they were not physi-cally able to do so. They did so not in some remote place, but in the midst of a small German town. Ernest Kinoy, from the 106th Divi-sion, was selected one day to go down to the concentration camp, get some supplies, and drag them back up the hill. He found himself standing in a yard as a Nazi sergeant beat a young prisoner. Across the street stood three or four German women with baby carriages. "The guard would scream at this thirteen-year-old kid, call him to attention, and beat him," Kinoy said. "And you could see these three or four ladies from town standing there sort of continuing their discussion, looking across watching this guy beat up this kid. And I've always found that significant as a symbol in terms of what the German public did and did not know about what was going on. These ladies did not even turn away."

Acevedo, who had trained briefly as a medical technician in Springfield, Missouri, before being thrown into the conflict in eastern France in December 1944 and captured there on January 6, 1945, watched the dying and, in a diary, noted the details. A slim, pale green volume started on March 1, the diary records the admission of sick American soldiers to the makeshift dispensary and Acevedo's rough diagnosis. It is a chilling chronicle of the accelerating death rate among Americans at Berga.

Among those GIs whose death Acevedo recorded in March and early April 1945 were Fred Haughton ("Cardiac"), Seymour Millstone ("Pneumonia"), Julius Schultz ("Grippe"), Arthur S. Rosen ("Pneumonia"), Arthur Arndt ("Strep Throat"), John Sincox ("Dysentry" [sic]), Clifford Stevens ("Dysentry" [sic]), Richard Humphrey ("Malnutrition"), Howard Goldberg ("Malnutrition"), Wiley T. Scruggs ("Malnutrition"), Robert Horton ("Malnutrition"), Stanley Rubenstein ("Grippe"), and Alfred Johnson, Jr. ("Jaundice").

The Germans set out to destroy the Americans' will. Stanley Cohen watched Private Jerome C. Cantor, whom he described as "a slow-thinking, methodical person," being repeatedly beaten with rubber hoses by the Germans because they were dissatisfied with his work rate. Cantor "came back beaten up day after day." He tried to work faster but only cut himself more; the cuts became infected. Cantor's arm became hugely swollen, but still he was forced to work. On March 29, Cantor died. Four days later, on April 2, Acevedo noted simply: "Deaths are increasing in great number. Men forced to work in the mine whether they are ill or not."

Private Charles H. Clark of the 422nd Infantry died that day. He had been severely beaten by the Germans in tunnel 17 a few days earlier, a beating witnessed by Private Paul Van Horne of the 106th Infantry Division. Clark was not feeling well and asked the German overseer to be allowed to stop work. Shortly afterward, he slipped away, returning at the end of the shift, between ten and eleven o'clock at night. When Clark reappeared, the Germans in the tunnel set upon him and beat him for about twenty minutes.

"After they stopped, Clark was in a semiconscious condition," Van Horne said. "His eyes were swollen shut, and his face was completely deformed."

Van Horne and some other Americans carried Clark back to the barracks. He was in dire need of medical attention but received none. The following afternoon he was forced to return to work. A foot infection was worsening and Clark was in no condition to function in the tunnels, but Metz insisted that he go out. Private Norman Martin of the 106th Division saw Metz examine the infection, which Martin described as gangrenous. Metz, Martin recalled, "said it was just an infection and would be all right in a short time." But in a short time, Clark was dead. His body, like that of other Americans, was left outside the barracks for a couple of days.

Morton Goldstein's corpse lay there for several days, with bullet wounds in it. Shapiro had come to know Goldstein at Stalag IX-B, where he was a raucous, dominant personality in his reversible white army-issue parka designed to provide camouflage in the snow. "He ran the craps games; he was like the croupier, and people would congregate with him," Shapiro said. A member of the 106th Infantry Division, he had just come overseas when he was captured by the Germans.

Goldstein, a young man brimming with self-confidence, bridled at the conditions at Berga and, as a good German speaker, was confident that he could escape and avoid recapture. He had begun to plot his getaway as soon as he arrived. One day he volunteered to accompany Shapiro on the afternoon food detail, taking the hay wagon down to the concentration camp to be loaded with supplies. On the way back up the hill in the gathering darkness, he took off into the woods, evading the guards.

Anny Neusser, a twenty-eight-year-old German housekeeper, found Goldstein two days later, at about noon on March 19. She was on her bicycle when she saw him lying by the side of the road. He had been shot in the right rear of the head; the black curly hair around the wound was burned, she noted. It was clear to her that he was an American because of his leather army boots with thick soles and what she called "a fur-lined coat with a cape." She immediately informed Walter Zschaeck, the mayor of the nearest village, Wildetaube. Zschaeck was shocked: the American was clearly the same man who had been delivered to his house during the night and taken away that morning by Metz.

Goldstein had been turned over to Zschaeck at about three in the morning by the two Volkssturm men who had captured him. There was no jail in the village. The mayor took Goldstein into his kitchen and offered him what was left of his supper: sauerkraut, bread, and coffee.

"He was very helpful and wanted to help us," Zschaeck said of Goldstein. "He started the fire for us and would hardly sit down. He also had eight little potatoes in his pocket and roasted them in the fire. My wife made a sandwich and put it in his pocket."

The two men chatted. Goldstein told the mayor he had been in the army only eleven months. He talked about conditions in the prison camp and why he had tried to escape. The conversation went on for several hours. It was not until about nine in the morning that Metz, who was furious, arrived to reclaim Goldstein.

"What, you're making yourself comfortable here?" Metz bellowed. "I'll fix you." He ordered Goldstein to stand at attention facing the wall.

In testimony provided to American investigators on June 3, 1945, Zschaeck said that Metz had made clear that he planned to kill Goldstein. "When he got ready to go he went over to the prisoner and said to him that he was going to march back and he would beat him up and would shoot him while the other Americans watched," the mayor recalled. "He said that you are starting out on your death march. The American was standing there shivering."

Metz then left with Goldstein and, on the road back to Berga, shot and killed him. "He was shot in the back of the head and the lower back," Miethe, the German physician who examined the corpse, said.

In what precise circumstances the shots were fired is not clear. Metz claimed that Goldstein had tried to escape, that he shouted "Halt" three times, then shot him. The fact that both bullets remained lodged in his body suggests that Metz fired from a distance. But Acevedo, who examined the body, said Goldstein was shot with wooden bullets designed to splinter and lodge in the body. In a diary entry of March 20, Acevedo wrote of Goldstein: "He was shot while attempting to re-escape. So they say, but actually was recaptured and shot thru the head." If indeed Goldstein tried to escape, as Metz claimed, it is strange that the corpse was found by Anny Neusser immediately adjacent to the road.

The very fact that Metz himself, rather than one of the guards working for him, went to collect Goldstein is striking. It is known that he left Berga in a foul temper. This was observed by another guard, Kurt Seifert, who also testified, "There was a story circulating among the guards that Metz had boasted in Wildetaube that Goldstein would not get back to camp alive."

Zschaeck's testimony supports the view that Metz planned to execute Goldstein as an example to the other prisoners, several of whom had also tried to escape. Stanley B. Cohen was told by a guard who was friendly to the Americans that an eleven-year-old boy had witnessed Metz's execution of Goldstein "in cold blood."

Certainly, Metz did all he could to display the corpse as a warning. He ordered other American prisoners to collect Goldstein's body, which was brought to the prison camp on a cart and placed outside a barracks, where it remained for three days. His bloody clothes were hung on a fence to underscore the admonishment. As punishment, Americans were made to strip down to their underwear and run outside in the snow in bare feet.

Otto Rittermann, a German guard who worked under Metz, saw Goldstein's body and, during the twenty-four days he served at Berga, an estimated twenty other American corpses lying beside the barracks. Asked by American investigators on June 4, 1945, why the Americans had died, Rittermann said: "They were sick because of the poor food and the lack of air in the tunnels and effects of blasting in the tunnels and the extremely heavy work."

He was also asked how often Metz beat the American prisoners. "Practically every day," he replied.

"With what did he beat them?"

"With his hand or with a stick that he would pick up."

"Was Metz responsible for feeding the prisoners?"

"Yes, he was. He would say whether there were to be five or six men to a loaf of bread or more or less."

"Were the prisoners underfed?"

"They were underfed."

Mordecai Hauer, better fed than he had been for a long time, left Buchenwald in February 1945, at about the same time the Americans arrived at Berga. He was loaded into another boxcar, but conditions were not as bad as those he had known. It was a mild day, with the snow glittering in the sun, and he was allowed by the SS guard to sit at the open door of the boxcar with his feet dangling outside. After a journey of about two hours, the train stopped at a station in the middle of a small town. A sign said BERGA AN DER ELSTER; the station clock read noon.

The prisoners, many of them Hungarian Jews, were lined up outside the station by the SS. Hauer prepared himself for yet another long march into some new inflection of horror. But in fact the prisoners marched for all of two minutes. This, for a survivor of Auschwitz, Jawischowitz, and Buchenwald, amounted to a wonderful surprise. It was equally extraordinary to see the inmates of the camp staring at him with their hands resting on the barbed-wire fence. So, Hauer thought, the fence is not electrified. The camp, in all, had the appearance of an improvised affair, a converted factory of some sort, far less menacing than those from which he had come. It appeared to Hauer that it held about a thousand prisoners.

These prisoners came from all over Europe. After the European Jews who arrived in Berga in November 1944 had been deemed *arbeitsunfähig*—unfit for labor—the Germans brought in several hundred Soviet prisoners of war as well as smaller numbers of Italians, French, Dutch, and Slovaks. The 350 Americans incarcerated nearby were the last to arrive.

Despite Hauer's first impression, conditions in the camp were terrible. Every morning at five-thirty the so-called death commando assembled. It consisted of prisoners, themselves reduced to skeletal form, who had to roll two-wheeled carts stacked with naked corpses covered only with rags through the town to a mass grave in the hills.

Marianna Schmidt, then a nineteen-year-old working in a dentist's office, would watch the grim procession. "The dead were brought on wheelbarrows, their bodies resting on planks," she recalled. "They were half covered, but often there was a limb, a foot, or a hand sticking out. They were all tossed in the mass grave." Gertrud Pecher, then seventeen, said the prisoners wheeling the cart would "raise their hands to their mouths in a desperate signal that they wanted to eat."

During the four and a half months that the camp existed, 314 prisoners died, a rate of more than two a day; their mass grave was the so-called Jewish cemetery. This was some distance from the town cemetery, next to which the American dead were buried.

Lieutenant Bruno Dombeck, the SS man who directed the camp

under Hack, and the chief guard, Randi Schimmel, were both known for their brutality. Dombeck liked to boast that he was the proud owner of a lampshade and a book jacket made from human skin. Prisoners were regularly beaten and kicked for offenses like trying to steal a potato from the kitchen. Women living near the camp often heard screams as prisoners were hit with shovels. Roll calls in the *Appellplatz* were endless. In the same assembly area, those who tried to escape were hanged, as Shapiro witnessed.

For Hauer, however, after all he had been through, the Berga camp amounted to hell in a minor key. To be in a town, even as a prisoner behind barbed wire, was reassuring. Hauer could see passenger trains going through Berga a couple of times a day. Women and children passed along the street. There were trucks and horse-drawn carts, and the surrounding, undulating countryside was pleasant. The food was terrible, but perhaps a little better than at Jawischowitz, and the everyday cruelty of the SS seemed to him less relentless. When local women slipped turnips, potatoes, or apples to the prisoners, the guards sometimes turned a blind eye.

Hauer stumbled on three old Hungarian friends from the town of Miskolc who had been lucky enough to work on a farm near Auschwitz in relatively mild conditions. He was housed in their block. In all, Hauer felt his life had improved, especially when he discovered that the tunnels where he would work were no more than five minutes' walk from the camp. And although the purpose of digging the tunnels was not clear, it seemed to Hauer they could only signify one thing: the Germans' factories were being heavily bombed by the Allies and the Nazis were in urgent need of underground facilities. That amounted to another indication that the war might soon be over.

So it was that an eighteen-year-old Hungarian Jew from Budapest and young American GIs from Ohio, New York, New Jersey, Wisconsin, and California found themselves in the same little outpost of the Holocaust in the dying weeks of Hitler's war and saw and felt different things because of what they had experienced before. To the Americans, the concentration camp where Hauer was now a prisoner was a place of unspeakable horror peopled by eerie shadows of human beings whose reduction to the state of emaciated somnambulists was a terrifying mystery, a puzzle only gradually unraveled as their own treatment at the hands of the Nazis opened their eyes to the extent of German barbarism. To Hauer—who had known the

Nazi roundup of the Jews in Goncz, the deceptions of Eichmann, the selections of Mengele, the wholesale dispatches of Jews to the gas chamber, the nocturnal marches to the mine, the hanging of Katz, the shooting of Yankele, the death of his father, the disappearance of his mother and siblings, the mass burning of prisoners, the death march and its executions, and finally near-death by freezing in a room-sized refrigerator hung with red meat—to this young European, the Berga concentration camp was something *better* than he had known. In these divergent visions, perhaps, lurked something deeper that presaged the years ahead. On the one hand, there was American ignorance, but also the naïveté of a country with a belief in itself and its power to do good, a nation with enough innocence still to be appalled by horror; on the other, European knowledge, a knowledge carried in the bones and so terrible as to be indelible, an awareness of a kind of collective suicide, a consciousness of having plumbed such depths that faith seems implausible, ambition misguided, power treacherous, and healing elusive.

Hauer was assigned to tunnel 7 in the hills on the far side of the Elster River. His work group was divided by German foremen into several units: one did the drilling and dynamiting, a second broke the bigger rocks with sledgehammers, a third loaded the stones onto the V-shaped wagon, and a fourth emptied the loads into the river. It was the prisoners in striped uniforms doing the latter tasks that Lubinsky had seen on his way to the tunnels for the first time.

The hardest work, by far, was that of the first two groups, because it was done inside the tunnels. On the occasions when Hauer was assigned to the drill or the sledgehammer, he found it was far tougher work even than in the mine at Jawischowitz. The slate dust got in his eyes and lungs; he would sometimes come out spitting blood. But fortunately, unlike many of the Americans, he was not inside the tunnels very often.

About a week after his arrival at Berga, Hauer was working on the banks of the Elster when he saw a group of about fifty men in green uniforms being marched across the river, accompanied by guards. About half of them were assigned to work inside the tunnels, and two came to work in tunnel 7. Hauer soon overheard them speaking in a language he had not heard before but assumed to be English.

"*Sprechen Sie Deutsch?*" he asked—"Do you speak German?"

"No Deutsch," said one of the soldiers. Hauer noticed the whiteness of the man's teeth.

"You England?"

"No. America."

Hauer was amazed. America! To him, it was a faraway country, the land of cowboys and ranchers and sheriffs and the Niagara Falls and big stores and huge factories and towering buildings and Hollywood motion pictures full of song and dance and the victory of love over every obstacle. It had peopled his imagination as a child, a power at once vast and mysterious. He had felt drawn to it, but at the same time it had seemed unattainable, a place of dreams. Yet here in a provincial German town were Americans working as slave laborers for the Nazis.

During the brief lunch break, Hauer sat with the Americans. He noticed that their jackets had zippers rather than buttons; he also noted that their shoes were made of leather. Many of the European prisoners were shoeless and had to make do with wrapping their feet in rags. When one of the American prisoners unzipped his jacket to get something, Hauer glimpsed a small, gold Star of David hung on a chain around his neck.

"*Du Ivri?*" he asked, using a Hebrew word for a Jew.

"*Ivri?*"

Hauer tried again. "*Du Yid?*"

"*Yid! Ich Yid!*" the American exclaimed, pointing to the star. "*Du Yid?*"

Hauer indicated that he was. He gestured to the concentration-camp prisoners around him to convey the idea that most of them were also Jews. At this, he noted an expression of shock on the American's face.

At first the Americans appeared to Hauer to be in better shape than the concentration-camp prisoners. They had overcoats and field jackets, their skin was healthier, their general condition stronger. No newspapers were stuffed into their uniforms for warmth. Several wore watches with elastic straps; one offered him a stick of delicious chewing gum. Occasionally, they tried to talk, and Hauer found the Americans to be open and friendly.

But with the passing of the days, the Americans spoke less, they dragged their feet as they walked, they looked increasingly sick, and sometimes they collapsed. It was not only their perceptions of Berga that were affected by past experience; it was also their ability to survive it. What fire does not destroy, it hardens. Hauer and the other European Jews who had come this far had been hardened. But the Americans, even as their numbers dwindled rapidly, had further to go in their descent into the inferno.

CHAPTER SEVEN

Weasels in a Hole

S LIEUTENANT Willy Hack examined the name on the dog tags just handed to him and drummed his fingers on the desk. "Johann Carl Friedrich Kasten," he said, enunciating each word with the solemn resonance of a bell tolling, "you are a traitor to the German nation."

Kasten had been hearing this kind of thing ever since his capture. Hitler's officials could not grasp the fact that an American with a name so conspicuously German would feel no loyalty to the Thousand-Year Reich, preferring to swear his allegiance to the flag of the United States, an upstart power of no pedigree. They were enraged that a man so evidently an Aryan—the fine blue eyes, upright bearing, and strong chin testified to that—should declare himself an American, a creature of the New World, where Jews ran Hollywood and much else besides. Kasten's view of his identity amounted to an unacceptable insult to the Führer.

"You know, Kasten," Hack continued, leaning back in his oversized brown leather chair, "there is only one thing worse than a Jew. Are you aware of what that is?"

Kasten was silent, a silence that exuded contempt. He had come to Hack's office, accompanied by Joe Littell and Ernst Sinner, to protest the working conditions at Berga. The lack of food and overcrowding at Stalag IX-B had been debilitating, but it quickly became clear to Kasten that there was no comparison between the two camps. At the first, American prisoners milled around during the day. At the second, they toiled until their strength gave out.

"I will tell you who is worse than a Jew," Hack continued. "It is a German like yourself who betrays his country."

But to the three Americans in the room, Germany had betrayed itself. They all had links to the country through family or prewar visits. For Littell, these were finally severed when he saw the American prisoners emerging from the Berga tunnels. He felt a surge of rage, a last unraveling of the bond that had once drawn him to the country. He, Kasten, and Sinner had been spared mining duties because of their positions as intermediaries between the German authorities and the other prisoners. They were given other tasks, like carrying wood. But the agony of the tunnels was conveyed to Littell by the men covered head to foot in black dust who staggered out of the shafts, rubbing their eyes, squinting at the snow-covered hills. In many cases they were too exhausted to speak; their expressions said enough.

Hack, however, saw no reason to change his policy at the Berga complex. His agreement to meet with Kasten had been grudging; his response to complaints from him that putting prisoners of war to work without paying them or adequately feeding them constituted a violation of the Geneva Conventions was scathing. "Your men were brought to Berga to work," Hack said. "That is what they will do: work."

Kasten warned that there would be consequences for Hack once the war was over, and it would be over soon enough, as the Allied planes passing overhead from time to time and the bombs illuminating the night suggested. But Hack, who had a major industrial project to oversee, was blind to the looming demise of the Reich and in no mood to accommodate an insolent German American about whom he had already been warned by the authorities at Stalag IX-B. Turning to Littell, he asked, "Are you Jewish?"

"No, I am a Christian," Littell said. "I am a follower of Jesus Christ, and Jesus was a Jew."

Hack snapped at Littell, telling him to leave Jesus out of the conversation, and inquired of Sinner whether *he* was a Jew. Sinner, opting for prudence over truth, said he was not. With that, the meeting was ended. It was clear enough that Hack believed the majority of the Americans to be Jews.

Kasten had never been one to acquiesce to situations he found intolerable, much less to situations that seemed to threaten his life. When he understood that he could do nothing to effect change through negotiation at Berga, he began to plot escape, sabotage, or some act of insurrection. As a first step, he asked men working in the tunnels to steal dynamite. By the end of February he had amassed six sticks and blasting caps. He had no idea what he might do with them, but at least he was assured that if he went, he would go with a bang.

At the beginning of March a conversation with Hack led him to conclude that escape was his only option. The zealous young SS commander informed Kasten that he had acquired two new dogs of exceptional ferocity and swiftness, trained to kill, with jaws like clamps. What would be more amusing, Hack suggested, than testing the dogs the next day by letting Kasten loose and having the dogs pursue him?

Kasten liked a challenge, but this amounted to a death sentence. That evening, he told Littell and Sinner he planned to escape. They made clear that they wanted to join him, but Kasten urged them to reconsider: the risks were enormous, and Hack's venom was not directed at them. But Littell was by now convinced that the only hope for the prisoners at Berga was to reach the American lines and make the barbaric conditions in the tunnels known to commanders in a position to do something about the abuses. He insisted and at last Kasten relented; they would all go.

The rectangular American prison camp was well guarded but by no means as formidable as the camp Katz had confronted in making his escape through the barrel in Poland. There were spotlights at the four corners, and guards regularly patrolled the barbed-wire fence. But the fence was not electrified, the lighting was uneven, and the controls on the Americans' whereabouts less strict.

Because one of the two barracks at the rear of the camp was built on a slight slope, there was a small space beneath its front end. Here the three men hid in the early evening, awaiting their moment. They saw a guard pass and lock their barracks door for the night. Kasten had the sticks of dynamite in his pocket and thought to himself: If I get shot, we're all fish bait. But even that prospect was better than being chewed alive by a pair of Hack's dogs.

The guard walked back and forth along the perimeter before reaching the side fence through which Kasten, Littell, and Sinner had decided to make their escape. This section was less well lit because the downward beams from the lights on that side were defective. Apart from the dynamite, they had amassed half a loaf of bread, razor blades, sixty reichsmarks, and matches—hardly an impressive horde, but enough, they hoped, to see them through to the approaching American lines.

They made their move as the guard, his collar raised high against the freezing night, turned along the back fence. Passing first under a wire fence beyond which the Germans had orders to shoot any prisoner, they advanced about ten feet and confronted the barbed wire. Sinner was the first man out as Littell and Kasten pulled the wire far enough apart for him to wriggle through. For once, their loss of weight was advantageous. Littell followed. But as Kasten tried to maneuver through the wire, the guard returned. They all froze. The German, passing only a few feet from them, seemed stunned by the cold and walked on. At that moment, an air-raid siren sounded and the whole camp was plunged into darkness.

"Run!" Kasten said. They did, into the dark forest, as guards emerged sleepily from their barracks.

The three men traveled mainly at night. They snipped off the brass buttons from their overcoats because they bore the emblem of the American eagle, and they cut off their telltale epaulets. They fed themselves on beets stacked by farmers for cattle. The sugar was energizing. They avoided the main roads, until a snowfall partially covered their olive jackets and made them less distinguishable from everyone else. When they met passersby, they were prompt with greetings of "*Heil Hitler,*" a salutation Littell had already practiced as a junior high school student in Germany six years earlier, and Kasten during his German sojourn of 1936.

In villages, Germans could be seen dragging suitcases and bags, apparently fleeing towns bombed by the Allies. The tide had turned; America would inherit the world. But the three soldiers had to endure long enough to see that day. They set their course chiefly by the stars, heading west, determined to reach the advancing American army.

There was a cohesion to a seasoned combat unit, a silent communication of the spirit. However appalling the conditions, however many men fell, bonds that were sacred held fast. Your own life became part of the collective life of the company, inextricable from it, inconceivable without it, and so you became your brother's keeper, and he yours. A mystical connection formed. It was as strong as that between mother and child, and life was simplified even as the loss of it became a routine matter. War was not without its redeeming grace.

So it was devastating to see the bonds erode in captivity at Berga,

the collective life fragment, and the codes of companionship sup-
planted by the devices of weasels in a hole. Kasten, Littell, and Sinner took off on March 2. The dying began soon after, and the
disintegration. Starvation does strange things. It brings out the fem-
inine glands, pushes the timbre of the voice up a pitch, makes hair
silkier. An intended punch becomes a feeble slap. It does terrible
things, too. Hunger in the night will drive a man to anything.

Private Donald Hildenbrand watched with alarm as things
broke down, people became unglued. He and his comrades had been
captured at a time when the war was supposed to be almost over and
been fed ever since on rumors and indications that Hitler's over-
throw was near. But the war dragged on; Metz still did his dirty work;
a drill or a section of railroad track still had to be lifted every day and
more rock shards inhaled. Frustration mounted.

Hildenbrand had a mathematical turn of mind. The calculation
he now made was not difficult. The diet for him and his comrades
provided a daily intake of perhaps eight hundred calories. The
energy they expended, however they tried to dither, was at least two
thousand. What was left after a while was less than zero. But Hildenbrand was not going to make it easy for the Germans to annihilate
him. At the age of twenty, he was sure of that. His life had given him
a certain toughness. When he was four, his father had died; at the age
of twelve he found himself packed off to a boarding school near Bal-
timore that admitted on scholarships a quota of poor children who
had lost a parent. You had to work there to get whatever you needed.
Nobody was going to help you take care of yourself.

He had been a long-distance runner at school, acquiring discipline along with knowledge. Giving up was a death sentence. You
had to believe you had a chance of making it because death's angel
slipped in quietly, whispering that there was no way out, coaxing you
into her embrace. You had to resist her. Those who did not, who
withdrew, who despaired, did not wake up in the morning.

The war had already taken him to North Africa in 1943, then
back to the United States in a detachment guarding German prisoners, and finally into France through the southern port of Marseilles
on October 20, 1944. He knew how easy it was to flip or abandon
hope; his own squad leader had lost it at one point, crawling to the
rear, saying he couldn't take it any longer.

As he trudged each day to the tunnel, Hildenbrand repeated a
mantra: *I'm going to make it out of this damn hole. I'm not going to let*

it get to me. It may get to me. But I'm not going to help it. I'm going to do every damn thing I can to stay alive. If it gets to me, I'm going to fight it.

Forget civilization, forget the Geneva Conventions, forget all that. They had pampered those German prisoners he had taken back to America, but there was no point thinking about that now. The veneer of the civilized world was very thin. One of the first things he saw after he was captured near Rimling, France, on January 8, 1945, was a group of American airmen hung from lampposts in Frankfurt, lynched and strung up there, grotesque as gargoyles. The image stayed with him, made him shudder.

What he needed now was food, in the middle of the day, in the tunnels, when his bones ached and the cuts on his lips burned. So Hildenbrand saved a small piece of his bread from the night before, with a great effort of will, because he wanted to elude the fate the Germans had prepared for him.

"But I wasn't able to keep the bread," Hildenbrand recalled. "I tried repeatedly, but somebody would always find it and steal it. I finally quit because it didn't seem to matter where I put the thing, somebody would get it, and that happened eight or ten times or more. In the end I could not figure any place to hide it and I just put it in my mouth."

Hildenbrand had seen GIs cutting the rings from the fingers of dead Germans and taking other valuables. That was bad, but not as disconcerting as trying to absorb the fact that fellow prisoners, fellow Americans, were stealing from him. He had a pair of army-issue gloves stolen. Nothing was more valuable in the tunnels. They disappeared in the night. So he fashioned protection for his hands from the wool lining of a sleeping bag. Prisoners cut off the ends of the bags to wear them under their coats, and sometimes pieces were left lying around. Nobody would help him anymore. That was now clear. He had to husband the scraps.

Any article could be traded for food or cigarettes, the most coveted items in the camp. John W. Reifenrath had managed to hang on to a watch given to him as a high school graduation present. During the day, he carried it in his pocket; when he slept, he hung it on a nail in the wall beside his top bunk. One night, a fellow GI climbed onto the bunk and stole the watch. A few days later, as the weather grew warmer, Reifenrath took off his sweater and hung it outside the tunnel in which he was working. That, too, was stolen.

Everyone had a breaking point. Sidney Lipson smashed rocks with a sledgehammer. He bent down and tossed the pieces into the small carts and pushed the carts out of the tunnel, and sometimes they would come off the little rail track. Then he and others would try to heave the cart back. The Germans were always suspicious that the Americans were trying to sabotage the operation, and they were ferocious in the beatings they gave with truncheons when a cart was derailed or slipped into the river. Sometimes the prisoners did give the carts a nudge. They did what they could to delay the Germans, but Lipson often felt he could not last another day. What was the lowest form of life? An amoeba, a single cell—he had learned about that back in Boston. He felt he was less than an amoeba. What an idea! A bunch of Jewish boys raised in cities trying to operate pneumatic drills! Miners for the Reich! He became delirious sometimes, imagining his helmet filled to the brim with scrambled eggs and bacon. He did not think of women, did not even think of his parents, he thought of that.

When the man next to him in bed died, a Jew from New York, Lipson took the little cache of food he found beside the corpse. The man was dead anyway. But Lipson didn't feel good about what he did.

Another infantryman, Leo Zaccaria of the 28th Infantry Division, said: "Self-preservation takes over and you do some bad things. You bicker and you steal. It's hard to have good friends under conditions of life and death because survival is the only thing you have in mind. I did not think I was a good person. I beat up people if things were not right. I was an ugly beast."

David Goldin was afraid to take his uniform off because he was convinced somebody would steal it. When he received bread, he ate it in nibbles, to prolong the pleasure. "If I kept any bread, I would put it in my pocket," he said. "And my hand would never come out of my pocket, because if it did, someone would have the bread."

Days blurred into one another. The prisoners of war were cut off. Around them were only death and the lunacy that caused it. The whole enterprise was crazed, a massive underground project to serve a Führer who now spent most of his own time underground in Berlin as the whole edifice of his twelve-year-old imperium imploded. The tunnels were to converge on a single large chamber. When the American prisoners were about two hundred feet in, some of the tunnels began to turn to the left, others to the right. The Germans wanted higher ceilings at this point. But it was clear to everyone that whatever it was they were building at the likely cost of their lives would never be completed. German obedience drove the tunnels deeper despite the mounting evidence that the whole undertaking was spectacularly pointless. Awareness of that absurdity was no help to the Americans.

"It was written down," said Ernest Kinoy. "The project was written down in some plan so the Germans kept it up and there wasn't a chance in the world that it would be completed in time to do anything. We knew that, the Germans knew that, and still we had to keep digging."

In the distance artillery could sometimes be heard, faint but distinct. The Allied bombing runs at night became more frequent; air-raid sirens punctuated the night. Reifenrath was approached by a German major who had worked in Philadelphia before the war and who spoke good English and reminisced fondly about his time in the United States. War's bitter logic was fraying to reveal the human beings beneath the uniforms, but not fast enough to stop the killing of Americans in the construction of a subterranean labyrinth leading nowhere.

Despite the evidence, and no matter what they had been told, it was not easy to believe that the war would soon end and this agony with it. The fighting dragged on, their strength drained away. On March 21, Tony Acevedo wrote in his diary: "More planes came over today. Their bombs were dropped not very far from here." But he added: "Another one of our boys is pretty low today, he is not expected to live till night." The daily dying dashed fleeting hopes.

So, too, did the sight of the concentration-camp prisoners collapsing. Many had strange wooden clogs on their feet. When there were sections of track to be laid, these prisoners were put to work carrying them. Eight or ten of them would carry a single piece, tottering along. If the strength of one prisoner gave out, the whole little column would collapse, like a house of cards going down. The SS would move in and beat the feeble creatures huddled on the ground.

Stephen J. Schweitzer, who became the leader of the Americans soon after Kasten escaped, watched an SS guard in the concentration camp beat to death a young man he judged to be sixteen. The killing seemed to have all the significance to the German of swatting a fly. The prisoner had failed to remove his hat and come to attention as the guard passed. He was then smashed to the ground with a long-handled shovel and kicked with heavy boots. "I heard the boy scream and saw that his head was crushed and the brain matter was oozing out into the ground," Schweitzer testified on June 1, 1945. "This happened within ten feet of where I was standing at the time."

With each week, it became clearer that the Germans wanted to reduce the Americans to the same level as this European victim. It was the last shred of human dignity they sought to destroy, as Janek, the Pole at Jawischowitz who helped Mordecai Hauer, knew well.

To make animals of them: that was Nazi policy. Gerald Daub saw this clearly. "I never did anything but march from the barracks to my mine shaft and back from the mine shaft to the barracks," Daub said. "I worked with a jackhammer, vibrating violently all the time. When the dynamite blew up, and rocks fell to the ground, we all started to pick up the rock and put it in these little carts and we would push the carts like donkeys and empty the rock into the stream. Like donkeys. That was it: drilling into the black face, connecting it up, blowing it up, picking up the rock again. I was made a slave; I am not proud of that."

At night Daub did not dare take his boots off for fear they would be stolen. A pair of boots could be traded for a chunk of bread or several ersatz cigarettes. If the boots went, socks might go, too. They were also worth something. He slept pressed against a fellow prisoner and old acquaintance, Robert Rudnick, who had attended the same kindergarten in Brooklyn. They had an agreement: each tapped the other when he wanted to change the side he was sleeping on, and they turned in unison. When Daub wanted to save bread, he would tuck it into his shirt. There was no way anyone could steal that bread, pressed between his chest and Rudnick's back. But every time he tried this method, the bread disappeared. Like Hildenbrand, Daub gave up; there was nothing to do with the bread but eat it at once.

Of such silent admissions and compromises were the American prisoners' lives composed. Shame accumulated, in different forms. It was shameful to watch the murder of concentration-camp prisoners and do nothing. But what could they do? They could not avoid seeing the killing and assuming the terrible responsibility of witnesses, yet they were powerless to stop the infliction of pain. That burden became theirs, forever. It was shameful, somehow, to see others like you die, American boys not yet twenty years old, and inevitable to wonder why *they* were gone and not you in their place. That shame lingered, too. It was shameful to steal, but a pitiless instinct possessed some of them, an urge more powerful than desire, a clinging to life even at the expense of others. That shame could hardly be avowed, so terrible was it, and it festered.

After two days of moving across country, sleeping in woods, Kasten, Littell, and Sinner were hungry and cold. At nightfall they reached the little town of Goschwitz, about twenty miles from Berga. Several uneventful encounters with Germans on country roads had emboldened them to the point where they felt the risk of seeking a room in a small inn was minimal. Their German was excellent, and Germany, by now, was a nation awash in bedraggled vagrants not unlike themselves.

The first inn they encountered was full of people, smoky and noisy, with enough beer swilling around for the travails of war to be briefly forgotten. Kasten found the innkeeper and asked if he might have a room.

"Are you crazy?" the man shot back. "We have people sleeping in the corridors thanks to the American and British bombing." He suggested Kasten try another inn up the street.

Accommodation was not available there, either, so the three men found a table at the back of a crowded, dark room and ordered bread, sausage, and beer. The inn was warm, a wonderful feeling. They had no real desire to drink alcohol, but not ordering beer in a *Bierstube* would have made them look conspicuous. That they did not want, especially when they noticed that a German air force officer was seated at an adjacent table with a gun on his belt. But when the waiter arrived with their order, Littell blundered in his attempt to blend in with the crowd.

German grammar is treacherous territory, reserving a multitude of cases, genders, and inflections with which to trap the foreigner. Trying to be convivial, Littell ventured that the beer was welcome because he had a "terrific thirst," but he got his genders mixed up, thinking the German word for "thirst" (*Durst*) was neuter rather than masculine. This gaffe aroused the curiosity of the officer, who began to eye them suspiciously.

"Let's get out of here," Littell whispered.

The officer accosted them near the door, demanding to see their papers.

Kasten looked down at him with contempt and declared: "We

have no obligation to show you our papers. Call the police if you wish."

This bravado provoked a change of tone. "I hear you are looking for a room," the officer said. "I know the innkeeper down the road. Perhaps I can help you."

They walked back to the first inn with the officer a few feet behind them. Kasten was wondering what he could do with his dynamite. He would have to take it out, stick a cap in it, light it, and throw it. All four of them would probably be blown up. That did not seem like a good solution.

Once they were inside, the officer again asked, in a loud voice, for their papers. Kasten repeated his show of defiance, and this time, two elderly policemen soon appeared, dressed rather comically in long green coats with shiny black helmets. Less comical were their rifles and the way these were pointed at them when a further request for their papers produced the candid response that they did not have any.

"No papers?" the two policemen shouted in unison. "What is this? Hands up!"

When a search revealed the sticks of dynamite in Kasten's pocket, the scene took on a Keystone Kops quality. "*Sprengstoff!*"— "Dynamite!" one of the policemen yelled, setting off a stampede for cover in the cozy little inn. The policeman holding the dynamite rushed outside, his hands trembling; his colleague kept his rifle very unsteadily trained on the three Americans. Within minutes, however, the burlesque gave way to more serious business: the Gestapo arrived, bundled Kasten into one car, Littell and Sinner into another, and sped off in the direction of the local Gestapo headquarters in Gera, about fifteen miles northwest of Berga.

Littell was the first of them summoned for interrogation. He was ushered into a large room dominated by a picture of Hitler, who stared down at him from behind the face of a thin German officer with a tight little moustache and a pince-nez that appeared to Littell to have been provided by central casting.

"So, are you spies, or are you commandos sent in behind our lines to disrupt communication?" the German asked.

"No. We are prisoners from Berga. We have escaped and we are trying to get back to American lines."

"Nonsense," said the officer. "Why, then, are you carrying dynamite?"

That, Littell had to admit, was not a bad question—one, he also had to admit, to which he did not have a ready answer. The fact was that Kasten kept his own counsel.

Kasten was the next to be questioned. The first thing the Germans did was to strip him naked and search everything. What, they wanted to know, had he intended to do with the dynamite? He was a prisoner of war, Kasten responded, and had no obligation to provide any information beyond his name, rank, and serial number. "You will pay for this defiance," the German officer said.

They were taken down to three freezing cells. As the jailer locked Littell in for the night, he said: "You know, of course, that you will be shot at dawn."

The remark did not encourage sleep. Early the next morning, a breakfast tray was brought to Littell's cell. A reprieve, he wondered, or a last concession before the executioner's bullet? Littell decided the Germans were too practical to feed a man they were about to shoot.

Lieutenant Hack, accompanied by a couple of guards, was waiting for them. When they were hauled upstairs and lined up against a wall in the Gestapo chief's room, the Berga commander was there to identify the three escapees.

"They are the ones," he said, pacing slowly back and forth, his polished boots resounding against the wooden floor.

The first blow was delivered to Kasten's face. Then Hack's boot went into his groin. Hack grabbed a rifle from one of his guards and drove the butt into Kasten's chest. Down Kasten went to the floor. Hack hauled him up, and the officer with the pince-nez went at him with a smashing blow to one cheek that sent Kasten's head swiveling to one side before a blow on the other cheek drove it back the other way. Kasten kept his chin up, and to Littell, the message was clear enough: You can get me, and you can get my two buddies, but you can't get the Americans; they are on their way.

Littell and Sinner had to haul Kasten, semiconscious, back down the stairs to their cells. Before they went, Hack conferred with the officer and said: "We have decided that all three of you will be shot."

An hour later they were dragged out of their cells again, fearing the worst. But the death sentence pronounced by Hack had not won the approval of the German officer and local Gestapo chief, who ordered that they be taken to Stalag IX-C at Bad Sulza and held in solitary confinement.

A German lieutenant and a noncommissioned officer accompanied the Americans. They were shackled together, Kasten tottering in the middle, and marched toward the railroad station through the quaint cobblestoned streets of Gera—criminals in chains in a medieval setting. It was a harrowing passage. They were taken for airmen who had been shot down, and the rage of the locals turned on them.

"Dresden! Dresden! Dresden!" people shouted. Others yelled *"Amerikanische Unmenschen!"*—"American beasts."

A couple of big men came bounding toward them, pointing their fingers, accusing them of killing thousands of women and children in the firebombing that had coincided with their arrival at Berga. They knew nothing of the bombing of Dresden other than that it had illuminated the sky and killed the family of one of the Berga guards. The Germans wanted to lynch the Americans, but the guards persuaded them that Kasten, Littell, and Sinner were not airmen. Women spat at them, old men threw manure, children made faces.

The train provided a brief haven. It took them to Weimar. From there, they were transported by car to Stalag IX-C, a camp not far from Buchenwald that was used mainly to hold British, French, and Russian prisoners of war. They were taken immediately to the solitary-confinement barracks and thrust into three cells so small that by standing in the middle and swaying a little you could touch all four walls. A glimmer of light entered through a tiny, high window; the bed consisted of hard wooden slats. At night Kasten watched the mice. He felt the urge to catch one and eat it.

A couple of weeks later, another group of Berga prisoners arrived at the Weimar railway station on their way to Stalag IX-C. There were about a dozen of them in all, including four medics and several critically ill American prisoners lying on a makeshift cart on the platform, too weakened to walk.

The mission to deliver these men to a hospital at the camp was a grim one. But for William Shapiro, one of the medics, the journey was also a relief. The sight of German civilians and soldiers waiting for trains provided a welcome glimpse of something resembling normal life. His spirits, after more than a month at Berga, were lifted by contact with the outside world and by the bread and sausage provided by a German guard during the journey.

Dr. Miethe had authorized the transport of the sick, but only after the American dead at the camp had begun to pile up, and too late to save at least two of the prisoners, Edward Gorinac and George Snyder. A British sergeant major greeted Shapiro at the camp, taking him and the other medics to be showered and deloused, while the sick were rushed to the hospital. Shapiro and the other medics did not see them again.

The camp had guard towers and electrified fences, but the atmosphere contrasted with Berga. British prisoners could be seen strolling around an open field. To Shapiro, they appeared clean and well fed. The shower he was directed to take was his first in three months.

"The soap and hot water caused my open, infected lice bites to burn and itch," Shapiro wrote more than four decades later. "I had bites and sores all over my body. I remember scrubbing and scrubbing to stop the itching and burning."

Shapiro was given an American Red Cross parcel, whose rich contents amazed him: powdered milk, a can of hashlike meat, crackers, a chocolate candy, soap, vitamin tablets, toilet paper, and enough cigarettes to barter for much other food. The horde was as good as, or better than, the one he had once hoped to receive from his parents. The British said that the camp had a large stock of such Red Cross parcels, whose distribution to prisoners of war was supposed to be automatic.

Incensed by this information, Shapiro explained that not far away, more than three hundred American prisoners were starving at Berga. Apparently as surprised to hear this as Shapiro had been by the package, the British sergeant major said he would press the Germans to send a truckload of Red Cross parcels to Berga at once.

Littell, in his tiny, cold, solitary-confinement cell at Stalag IX-C, was also aware of the Red Cross packages. He had heard the whoops of jubilation a day earlier that had accompanied the arrival of six thousand of them, delivered by French Red Cross trucks. Information on this cargo—four thousand French parcels and two thousand American—had been provided to him by the German guard who brought him his meager daily diet of bread and thin soup.

Short and stout, the guard had become more communicative and amenable as word spread of the rapid American advance eastward across Germany. He introduced himself as Werner Quint. Clearly hedging his bets, he gave Littell some books, including *A Tree Grows in Brooklyn* by Betty Smith. They had been sent by the leader of the British prisoners. To be able to feed the mind, Littell found, offset a little of the desire to feed an empty stomach.

Soon after the delivery of the Red Cross packages, the British man of confidence was allowed to visit Kasten, Littell, and Sinner to make sure that the three American prisoners in solitary confinement also received their parcels. Kasten took the opportunity to inform the British of the suffering of the Americans at Berga. "Please use your influence to make sure that the Berga prisoners get some of these parcels as fast as possible," Kasten said. The British officer promised to do whatever he could.

It appears that the British were informed more or less simultaneously by Shapiro and Kasten of the existence of the Berga camp, although each of the American prisoners was unaware that the other was at Stalag IX-C. Indeed, it was generally believed in Berga that Kasten, Littell, and Sinner had been killed by the Germans shortly after their escape on March 2. What is certain is that the effect of the pleas of the two men was immediate.

On March 21 Acevedo wrote in his diary: "U.S. medics went down to the SS kitchen for our food. On our way back we were surprised to meet a British Red Cross truck with Red Cross packages for our men."

The leader of the British prisoners had been allowed to travel on the truck and assured Kasten and Littell on his return that he had seen at least some of the packages being distributed to elated prisoners at Berga. But Metz appears to have taken possession of almost all the parcels and taunted his starving captives by refusing to distribute them.

On March 23, two days after the arrival of the packages, Acevedo wrote: "Something in the wind. Everything is so quiet. We have not had any air alarms in three days. Perhaps an armistice. But that would be too much to expect. Still the Red Cross packages have not been released. Everyone thinking of the delicious food but most of the boys craving for smokes."

A day later he noted: "Another of our boys died last night from malnutrition. Red Cross packages still remain under lock and key. We hope to get them out soon as possible to stop our men from dying."

On March 25 Metz continued to hold the packages back, insisting that the Americans needed to be clean and orderly before receiving them, a request as realistic in the conditions of Berga as demanding that the men remain dry in a rainstorm. This was an act of sadism notable even by Metz's standards, one that could have no other purpose than to ensure that more Americans died. Cleanliness and the camp were incompatible. Acevedo wrote: "Palm Sunday. No chances of going to a church, but still our prayers are holding everyone up. This day reminded me of the hundreds of people attending mass at the Cathedral in Durango, Mexico. I wish I could be there."

It was only on March 26 that Acevedo was able to write: "Red Cross packages were released to us today and the boys are as happy as kids." The next day, he got together with the other medics and "ate scrambled eggs and sausage from our Red Cross boxes. Boy did we enjoy it."

When Hildenbrand went in to receive his Red Cross parcel from Metz, the German was smoking rifled American cigarettes. "Hildenbrand!" he said between puffs. "That's a fine German name!"

The Red Cross packages arrived in the immediate aftermath of Morton Goldstein's escape and Metz's shooting of him on March 19. The day after Goldstein's escape, another prisoner, George Morabito, got away. His fate was apparently determined by a particularly brutal guard named Hans Grieshammer. Sydney L. Goodman, who kept a diary at Berga, recalled that Morabito's body was brought back "the next day after they had returned Goldstein. Morabito had been shot, too." Both bodies lay in the snow as a warning to other prisoners, along with two or three other dead men who "had died of illness or malnutrition."

It appears that the withholding of the parcels may have been part of the punishment of the Americans for the attempted escapes. Stanley B. Cohen told war-crimes investigators: "When we received the Red Cross packages, one week before Easter, the *Kommandoführer* refused to hand them out and held them over our heads to prevent the men from continuing to attempt to escape. Eight days later, he handed the packages out."

By the time they were distributed, Shapiro was back at Berga. Returning was a shock. He had not realized how strong the stench of the Americans' barracks was. The place reeked of feces and the putrid effluences of the dying. Yet, before his brief interlude at Stalag IX-C, he had smelt nothing. Being so much part of the horror, he had not been able to see its extent. Now he quickly became part of it again. Death was everywhere. You felt its relentless encroachment but had to disassociate yourself from it in order to survive. Feeling requires energy, and Shapiro, even after his break outside the camp, had little or none to spare.

Paul Frenkel, aged fifteen, worked in the Berga concentration-camp kitchen. Deemed too young to work in the tunnels, he peeled potatoes and turnips and helped make the soup that fed the European camp prisoners and the American GIs. It was enviable work: the kitchen was warm, and there were scraps to eat. Every morning the young Hungarian boy filled the large, two-handled kettles with the thin gruel, which was then collected by Shapiro, Acevedo, and the other medics to feed the GIs.

When he first saw the Americans, Frenkel, like his compatriot Mordecai Hauer, was astonished. Here were men in military uniforms, albeit dirty and crumpled, while he wore the yellow triangle of the Jew on his baggy striped prison clothes. "I looked over and there were these figures, these people in uniform, whom I had never seen before," Frenkel recalled. "Some of them had the Red Cross armbands on. They looked proud and upright to me."

The German guards would not allow any contact, but Frenkel soon learned that these prisoners were Americans held in an adjacent little camp. Their presence seemed extraordinary to the boy. His image of the United States had been shaped by the presence in Long Island of three uncles who sent money from time to time to members of the family. The men—brothers of his mother, Ida—had done well. America came to symbolize hope, opportunity, and prosperity.

So the sight of Americans in conditions of misery was disturbing. The notion that the American army was close enough for soldiers to be taken prisoner by the Germans and brought to this piece of hell had never crossed his mind. If anything, Frenkel had thought that liberation might one day come from the Russians. He wondered what the Americans thought of a place where people died every day and lay prone as they fell—in the barracks, on steps, in the *Appellplatz*—before being carted away to an anonymous grave.

Although a mere teenager, Frenkel was already an experienced survivor. When he could, he smuggled some extra soup or a piece of potato to his older brother, Gabriel, nineteen, who had been put to work pushing carts loaded with rock taken from the shafts being mined in the Berga hillside.

The Frenkel boys had been deported to Auschwitz-Birkenau from a small town in eastern Hungary called Hadad (now Hodod in Romania), where their father, Maurice, was the local physician. Their departure in the early summer of 1944 had been delayed slightly because the government tried for some time to keep Jewish doctors from deportation. A large proportion of the Hungarian medical profession was Jewish; the government had feared the effect of losing so many doctors at once. So the Frenkel boys watched as the other Jews in the town of two thousand people—the rabbi, the tailor, the shoemaker, the owner of the bar, about twenty families in all—traipsed out of town in a dismal procession, marshaled by members of the Hungarian gendarmerie. They never returned.

Dr. Frenkel might, at this juncture, have fled with his family. But he was a professional, a respected citizen. He had been sent to Budapest by his deeply religious parents to study to become a rabbi but had used the money to study medicine instead. Progress and emancipation were the values he advocated and represented, and he did not believe his country would turn its back on them. He had fought as an officer in the army of the Austro-Hungarian Empire during World War I. The medals that honored that service were a source of great pride. Had his family not been excepted from the deportation of Jews? Was the war not almost over? Were the Russians not drawing near? Dr. Frenkel did not want to rock the boat. Any other course would be madness. Common sense demanded that they obey instructions and wait out the war. The family would be safe, he was sure of it.

About three weeks after the deportation of the other Hadad Jews, Dr. Frenkel was told he would have to accept a transfer to another provincial town farther east, close to the Romanian border, where he would work as the general practitioner for the region. He left town by horse-drawn carriage, still convinced that no harm would come to the family. Soon his wife and children were obliged to join him. They were then moved again—this time by gendarmes who accompanied them to the train station—and found themselves locked in a brick factory near Sibiu in the far east of Hungary, where other Jews were gathered. The Hungarian government had yielded to Eichmann's insistence that all Jews be sent to their deaths.

The result of the delayed departure was that the train that brought the Frenkel family to the death camp in early June 1944 carried an unusually large proportion of doctors. They took themselves and their status seriously and were shocked to find themselves crammed into cattle cars, abused by the SS, robbed of their rings, watches, and other valuables. Still, they believed they would be spared. As they drew near the camp, the two Frenkel boys were pressed against the single window of the boxcar. They saw prisoners working on the tracks who pointed to the sky, or simulated the slitting of a throat, to communicate the fate that awaited those in the train.

"Did you see those gestures?" Paul Frenkel asked his older brother.

"Yes, but don't tell Mother and Father."

Dr. Frenkel was relieved, on arrival, to see in the midst of the mayhem a man in the white smock of a doctor. "Good," he told his sons, "a colleague."

Assembled in two lines—men to one side, women to the other—the family prepared for the rite of passage into the camp, whose true nature was unknown to them. At the moment of inspection, Dr. Frenkel approached the man in white, Josef Mengele, and told him there were at least twenty-five Hungarian doctors on the train who would like to offer their services in a professional capacity, given the evident physical plight of many at the camp. German barbarism briefly gave way to the German susceptibility to titles: Yes, *Herr Doktor, Herr Kollege,* that seems a reasonable request. So did Dr. Frenkel save himself and several other Hungarian doctors, although their expertise was never put to use by the Nazis, whose interest was not in conserving life but in managing death. The two Frenkel boys were also saved from immediate dispatch to the gas chamber, but their thirty-six-year-old mother, Ida, like Camilla Hauer, disappeared and was never seen again.

Even after being stripped, showered, deloused, dressed in striped uniforms, shaved, and tattooed with their identification numbers, the Hungarian doctors, including Maurice Frenkel, would gather in small groups at the camp and assure one another that nothing would happen to them because the Germans needed their assistance. They were encouraged, also, by news of the D-day landings, which a prisoner had learned about from a scrap of a German newspaper.

The Frenkels did not stay long at Auschwitz. After eight days they were loaded into another boxcar heading west to Buchenwald. From there, they were transported to a camp in the nearby town of Zeitz and put to work rebuilding a bombed factory in which the Germans planned to make synthetic fuel out of peat coal. They unloaded bricks from railcars, filled bomb craters in the road, stacked packages of ball bearings. Their strength ebbed steadily, and Dr. Frenkel—aged forty-eight, like David Hauer—began to crumple.

One day, trains arrived to take the first shipment of fuel. At that moment an air-raid siren sounded, and the two thousand prisoners, many of them Hungarian Jews, were marched back to the camp and treated to an uplifting spectacle: Allied bombs falling on the factory and destroying in five minutes all their work of the past three months. The Frenkels rejoiced silently in the cacophony of bombs and antiaircraft guns. But their joy was tempered somewhat when they saw two planes shot down and the parachutes of Allied airmen open.

A few weeks later several hundred prisoners were selected to be sent back to Buchenwald. Dr. Frenkel was among them; his sons insisted on going with him. They were stripped naked. An SS officer passed down the rows of emaciated prisoners, picking out those now too weak to work, including Dr. Frenkel, deemed to have attained the state of *Muselmann*. The boys, powerless, embraced him; they told one another they would be united back in Hungary at the end of the war. Dr. Frenkel marched away in a line of men, turning as he went to look back at his sons, until a guard ordered him to face forward. The boys only learned much later that their father was sent back to Auschwitz and its gas chambers.

Now alone, the brothers were sent to a new labor camp—Berga. Their names appear as numbers 752 and 753 on a list of 1,100 prisoners transported from Buchenwald to Berga on December 13, 1944.

On Christmas Day the Germans presented each of the prisoners with a cookie they said had been sent by the citizens of Berga. There were other glimmerings of German humanity encountered in the midst of the mass murder. At Zeitz, a woman had come into the factory several times, in an obvious state of panic, and given the Frenkel boys apples she had hidden under her clothes. When she learned that their mother was missing, she tried to comfort Paul Frenkel, who looked very young. But he shook her off. A short time later, a German saw the *U* on their uniforms indicating they were from Hungary (*Ungarn* in German), and whispered that the *U* stood for "*unschuldig,*" or "innocent."

But conditions at Berga were in general punishing. Having been pushed to build a synthetic-fuel factory aboveground in the bombed factory at Zeitz, the brothers now became part of a last-ditch Nazi effort to make such a factory underground.

Soon after their arrival, their group of prisoners was asked to form a line with the younger men at one end. Paul Frenkel thought the boys his age would be taken away and shot. But several were told to report for work in the kitchen—an assignment that saved them—as the others, including Gabriel Frenkel, were taken off to the tunnels.

To Gabriel, who labored beside the tunnels, it was the ramshackle nature of the Berga camp that was most striking after Auschwitz and Buchenwald. Much was familiar—the SS, the dogs, the beatings, the lice everywhere, the crowded barracks filled to the ceiling with bunks—but the whole thing had an improvised air. "It was very makeshift, very primitive, rows of cots in old storehouses," he said.

The other striking thing was the cold. "It was very hard. Many of the people I worked with died next to me. There were many Hungarian Jews, quite a group from Budapest. One was a judge; another a doctor. They were older than I was, of course, and they just . . . they just died."

He saw one younger man sitting in grievous condition beside the barbed-wire fence. Blood was running out of him, perhaps from self-inflicted cuts. He wore the ridiculous prison clothes, some sort of hat contrived from paper on his head, the yellow triangle on his sleeve, and he started to cry as the little puddle of blood beside him grew larger. Guards looked on and did nothing. There was no need to do anything; this death would take care of itself. Gabriel could see that the young Jew knew he was dying, and it was wretched to watch this life simply expend itself on the hard ground, in the icy air, far from home. A life could have all the weight of a mote carried on the air. The man's blood scarcely impinged, even for a moment, on the enveloping grayness. He seemed a clown, a fool, yet all the tragedy of the continent was in him.

The image haunted Gabriel, but he tried to be disciplined about his own survival. By the time he reached Berga, he had learned to conserve energy whenever he could. He worked very hard at trying not to work. This was not easy, because the SS were generally vigilant and brutal, but as the weeks went by, he noted a certain fraying of this discipline, as if some of the Germans were only going through the motions in the knowledge that the war was lost. Some days he was able to remain idle for hours. Still, staying alive remained arduous, and the bowls of soup his brother managed to smuggle to him in the middle of the night provided a critical boost.

If Paul Frenkel, in the kitchen, perceived the Americans as relatively vigorous, Gabriel, beside the tunnels, saw a different picture. "The Americans looked so bad that we felt sorry for them," he said. "They seemed like bewildered children. I guess they did not know where they were and what had happened to them. They were pushing these carts, the typical miners' carts full of stones and clay and dirt. And they were weak; they were being hit with truncheons by the SS standing next to them if they did not push hard enough. We watched them come back from work in the evening. Some of them could not walk, and usually you saw that two of them on each side were carrying the third one."

Some of the discrepancy in the two brothers' view of the Americans may be explained by the fact that the medics like Shapiro whom Paul Frenkel saw at the kitchen did not have to work in the tunnels and so were in better physical shape. Both brothers were struck by the almost dreamlike strangeness of finding American GIs mixed up in Hitler's persecution of the European Jews.

They seemed like visitors from another universe, these increasingly bedraggled GIs. Gabriel gazed at their varying physiognomies. Some looked like Mexicans; others were tall and blond, almost Scandinavian in appearance; still others looked Italian. He was used to the more or less homogeneous appearance of Hungarians. The physical differences led him to wonder what this New World of mingled nations and races might be like. His ability to daydream in captivity had often helped him, taking him to other places far from the misery he inhabited, and now the sight of the Americans afforded him moments of reverie in which towering cities full of large cars loomed in a country of endless expanse.

One day in Buchenwald, Gabriel had been transported with particular intensity. He was in the latrine and looked down to find a scrap of paper in the mud, torn from a glossy German magazine. When he inspected it more closely, he found, of all things, the introductory verses to Goethe's *Faust*. He began to read—his German was good—and was enraptured by the first lines:

Ihr naht euch wieder, schwankende Gestalten,
Die fruh sich einst dem truben Blick gezeigt.
Versuch ich wohl, euch diesmal festzuhalten?

You come back, wavering shapes, out of the past
In which you first appeared to clouded eyes.
Should I attempt this time to hold you fast?

As he read on, the "wavering shapes, out of the past"—the school where he had first studied Goethe, his mother playing the piano and singing with her clear voice, the fields near the village where he roamed, his grandfather saying prayers at the evening meal—came back to him, and all the filth and fury beside him faded, the stench of the latrine replaced by country air, the suffering blanked out like a dream forgotten upon awakening. By the time he reached the last lines,

Was ich besitze, sehe ich wie im Weiten,
Und was verschwand, wird mir zu Wirklichkeiten

What I possess, seems far away to me,
And what is gone becomes reality

Gabriel felt restored to all that he had lost, and he had become convinced that in the miraculous appearance of this scrap of paper lay a sign that he might recover his life, if not all that had been swept away, at least enough of it to make survival worth the fight. He knew that Buchenwald lay close to Weimar and that in Weimar Goethe had written his greatest works. It was unfathomable that beauty and barbarism could reside in such proximity. But those lines in the mud suggested to him that the beauty was indelible, invulnerable even to the boots and bayonets and brutality of the SS.

At Berga that notion stayed with him. The miraculous appearance of the Americans and the gathering sound in the distance of artillery reinforced his confidence that he could outlast the Germans. The sounds were muffled at first. But as Passover 1945 drew near, the boom of cannons and the explosions from intensified Allied bombing grew clearer. So, too, did the growing fear of the Germans that they themselves might now be captured.

In late March, as the Allies closed in on the Germans' last defenses, the surviving Americans at Berga were moved to a new camp, immediately adjacent to the concentration camp where Hauer and the Frenkels were housed. By this time, most of the GIs had lost between thirty and forty pounds. Conditions in the new location were no better, but the walk to the tunnels was shorter and the run to the camp kitchen quicker. At about the same time, most of the Americans stopped having to work inside the tunnels, laboring instead on the banks of the river, where they moved sections of rail and emptied the carts full of stone emerging from the shafts. The work was still hard, but the air was better, and each day the weather grew milder and the rumors of possible liberation more insistent.

Tony Acevedo's diary of the last days at Berga gives a sense of the alternating hope and despair as an end to the captivity seems possible but deaths accumulate:

> **March 28 [1945]:** Russian and American fronts are supposed to be 140 kilometers apart. We are supposed to receive another Red Cross package Easter Sunday. Hope the Germans keep their promise this time.
>
> **March 29:** Holy Thursday. We medics still bringing the chow for our men—3 o'clock in the morning we go for coffee or tea—at 11.00 we march out for soup hoping it will be Potato Soup or Oat meal and at night we go for more coffee and bread is given out and butter (margarine) and marmalade. We pray very constantly for our loved ones back home. No war news today, but the general opinion is that it won't be long.
>
> **March 30:** Good Friday. On this Holy Day our thoughts are all at home and of the dinner Easter Sunday. It is also the feast of Passover for our Jewish comrades and they also think of home and family. From the French and Jewish underground, we receive good news—Americans are 200 kilometers away from here, which means they are moving very fast.
>
> **March 31:** Still more sick men are admitted to our hospital, the most serious are taken and the recovering are sent back to their barracks. Holy Saturday. Lent fast ends at noon today. But does not apply to us. We have been fasting since December 31,

1944. Today we saw the biggest formation of our planes pass over this morning. Looks like they mean business.

April 1: Easter Sunday. Our men don't work today. Red Cross Boxes are given out.

April 2: Two more of our men died today and one last night . . . living in unsanitary conditions, water must be boiled before it is drunk, no latrines. Deaths are increasing in great number. . . .

April 3: Excellent news today. Americans are only 100 kilometers from here. Rumors are that we are to be moved away. . . .

April 4: Very definite that we are moving away from here and on foot. This is not very good for our sick men. . . .

Acevedo's last words written at Berga proved prescient. Although release from the camp was only a day away, release from captivity was not, and the death rate among the Americans, already high, was to increase sharply.

At Stalag IX-C, where Kasten, Littell, and Sinner had been held in cold, dank solitary confinement since early March, the three prisoners also noted the growing German agitation as the Allies advanced. Kasten had been taken out of his cell and beaten several times in the early days, but now the guards, led by Quint, were preparing to change hats. The means by which they sought to evade retribution were not subtle.

One day in early April the three prisoners were invited into a room where a large bowl of rice and raisins sat on a table. The Germans asked them to sign a letter saying they had all been well treated at the prison. "In front of this pile of rice, I would have signed anything," Kasten said.

They did, but using phony serial numbers, and were regaled not only with the rice but with a bottle of *Sekt.* Kasten saved the label from the bottle, making note of the date and where they were.

Littell kept a diary, which he hid in the crook of his back, under his belt. On April 5, sitting in his small cell, he recorded that Quint was "going to pieces" as American armored divisions advanced to within one hundred kilometers. "He's still fearful the Americans will punish him, even kill him, for keeping the three of us in solitary." That day the barracks with the solitary-confinement cells was closed down and the Americans were moved into the sick bay, along with 350 British prisoners who had just arrived after a long death march from Upper Silesia.

On April 6 Littell noted that a German transport column of 150 men had fled to Bavaria, leaving a skeleton guard to surrender the camp to American troops. Two days later he wrote: "They're getting closer, and the [German] Supermen are dazed, scared, shamelessly subservient, and usually stinking drunk, even on guard duty."

The Germans guarding Hauer, the Frenkel brothers, and the other concentration-camp prisoners at Berga were, however, anything but drunk that day. Rumors had spread rapidly through the camp that Allied forces had overrun Buchenwald, and nobody in Hauer's barracks could sleep. The building where the SS slept was a hive of activity. In the early evening, explosions were heard. Hauer thought for a moment that the hour of liberation had come at last. He looked out the window and saw the SS burning papers, just as they had done at Jawischowitz. The explosions gradually died down.

The next day Hauer's disappointment was bitter as his work detail was ordered out to the tunnels as usual. But at about noon the sound of artillery was heard, seemingly just over the ridge where they worked. SS guards came running out and ordered the prisoners back to the camp, where a new complement of SS men, headed by an old officer with an ominously brutal manner, awaited them, ready to march them away yet again.

The prisoners were not allowed back into their barracks. They were given a bowl of soup that had to be consumed immediately and a loaf of bread to take with them on the road. With his memories of the death march from Jawischowitz still vivid and his spine still brittle, Hauer felt a surge of apprehension.

The newly arrived SS commander assembled everyone on the *Appellplatz* for a last time. "The enemy is nearing this town," he said, "but you won't be left here. The war is not over yet. The Führer has promised us victory, and I believe him. He has a secret weapon, more terrible than our enemies have ever known. This weapon will turn the tide in our favor! But even if we should lose, there is nothing in it for you. You should know that I volunteered to serve in the SS because I hate you dirty Jews. We have enough machine guns and ammunition to execute a group ten times larger than you are."

The German paused a moment for his words to sink in before resuming his tirade: "On our march, we will pass through peaceful towns and villages. Anyone caught taking fruit or vegetables will be shot. Even a single stolen potato will bring an automatic death sentence."

CHAPTER EIGHT

The Dying Weeks

THE RIVER IS HIGH, swollen with the melted snow of early spring, the resin-filled air brisk. On north-facing slopes patches of ice linger, but the grip of winter is broken and one or two daisies poke their little yellow-and-white heads through the grass. The road south from Berga, skirting pine forests, hugs the banks of the Elster, and Sanford Lubinsky gazes at the restless water swirling down toward the tunnels that he has now left behind.

It is April 5, 1945. The Americans are embarked on a march to an unknown destination, guarded by twenty-eight aging Germans, mainly from the National and Civilian Guard, under the command of Sergeant Erwin Metz and his superior, Ludwig Merz, who has received the order to move all the Americans, including the very sick, southward. They are being herded away from the Allied advance, but there is no more serious purpose to their movement than there was to the tunneling that has decimated their ranks. The tunnels went nowhere and now there is nowhere to go; the Allied and Soviet noose has closed on the Nazis. Driven by Germans obedient to the last, the Americans are wandering without reason in a Europe in ruins.

Of the 350 young Americans who arrived in Berga a little more than six weeks earlier, two dozen are already dead, another two dozen have been hospitalized, and a handful have escaped. The number forced out onto the road has dwindled to just under 300. With each step their strength ebbs further.

At the front, Lubinsky muses: You are in hell but you fight back. Your gun is inextricable from your being, and you use it with no more thought than you give to breathing. Here you are a nonentity—nothing. The guards prod him forward. The Americans had been trained to walk twenty-five miles in a day with full packs on their backs, but there is not much left of them now. Lubinsky eyes the fields. It is too early in the year for dandelions. What else might he eat? He sees a horse turd and considers trying to extract from it the oats or corn or whatever it is the animal has eaten. By the side of the river, he and another GI manage to trap a toad. Lubinsky pops an eye into his mouth.

There is not enough to eat; that is why they are dying. Metz has handed out a tenth of a loaf of bread and part of a Red Cross package as a ration for the road. Lubinsky wants to conserve some of this but worries about thievery. Men will steal to live.

He has become familiar with death, formed a passing acquaintance with his own. It begins with a falling away, on the inside, and you step far enough outside yourself to perceive that you have become very small. You wonder who you are, what that speck of lost humanity might be. Drifting away then would be easy enough, Lubinsky sees, no more traumatic than succumbing to sleep, but some part of him fights back, summons an image of Clara and Terry waiting for him at home in Ohio, or of Morton Goldstein's corpse lying in the snow. These provide the spur to the love or rage that pulls him through.

The men are soon strung out over several hundred yards. Some have swollen feet and can't get boots on, and they put an arm around the shoulder of a fellow soldier and stumble forward. Some have bleeding mouths from infections; they have difficulty swallowing anything. The weakest, those unable to walk, lie on a horse-drawn cart commandeered by Metz.

The terrain is undulating. Here and there they come upon a little village nestling in a river bend, smoke wafting from the chimneys of the houses gathered around a church, and for a moment the world has all the appearance of being at peace. The villagers stare at the skeletal Americans, intruders on their gabled idylls, and when one woman tries to give Lubinsky an apple, the guards shove her away.

Diarrhea is a constant scourge. Many of the men have to stop periodically, only to be told to move on by a guard. "*Schnell, schnell*"— "Quickly, quickly"—is all they hear. Sometimes an old German rushes out of a house gesticulating at them to go relieve themselves elsewhere. Clearly, Lubinsky muses, these good Germans find the behavior of the American prisoners uncouth.

U.S. Soldiers' Death March, April 5–23, 1945

STALAG IX-C
■ Bad Sulza

BUCHENWALD
■
● Weimar
● Jena
Elster
● Gera

Eastern Front
Soviet troops advancing

GERMANY

Berga ●

April 5
The Americans embark on
a march to an unknown destination.

Greiz ●

American soldiers are lodged in a
school. Four die.

Housed in a castle.
Four American soldiers die.

Mühltroff ●

Mühltroff–Dobareuth:
One soldier dies on march.

Two Americans die.

Dobareuth ●

● Töpen

Czech territory
ceded to
Nazi Germany
at Munich in
1938

Zedtwitz ●

Lodged in a barn for five days.
Eleven GIs die.

Rehau ●

Zedtwitz–Dürenloh:
Eight Americans collapse on
march and are buried along the road.

Dürenloh–Kaiserhammer:
One soldier dies on march.

● Dürenloh

Four GIs die and are
buried at Thierstein.

● Kaiserhammer
Thierstein

Grosslattengrün ●

Lodged in a barn.
Seven soldiers die.

Fuchsmühl ●

Housed in a barn. Four soldiers die.

● Seidlersreuth
● Schönficht

On the way to a hospital, one
GI dies. At least thirty prisoners
later liberated here.

Metz, the Nazi overseer of the
Americans, flees on his bicycle.

Schommersrieth ●

Americans pause
here on April 20.

Western Front
American troops advancing

CZECHOSLOVAKIA
Bohemia and Moravia
annexed by
Nazi Germany in
1939

Rötz ●

April 23
One GI dies here.
A group of 169 American
prisoners is liberated.

0 Kilometers 20
0 Miles 20

● Cham

The Americans carry no water with them, so they pause to drink from the river or a stream; in some villages they are offered water by the women. But Metz is determined to enforce another of his bizarre medical theories: that the consumption of water only aggravates diarrhea. He orders the guards to make sure that the offers of drinking water are rebuffed.

Lubinsky entered the army weighing 165 pounds. He reckons he is less than 100 pounds now. That he is being destroyed, day by day, has become clear to him. The process is systematic. Perhaps the Germans believe this is a cost-effective way to wage a war: extract every last ounce of energy from a prisoner before discarding the corpse. But it seems almost as wasteful as it is barbaric.

He looks at the cart on which the bodies of the ailing are stacked like logs and thinks of Metz with hatred—Metz who has declared, when confronted, that he *is* the Geneva Conventions. Lubinsky works on the idea that, if he is to die, he could take Metz with him, sink his teeth into the German's jugular, or into his testicles, or into an eye, make him scream. He has come to understand fully the sustaining power of hatred.

After walking all day they reach Greiz, about ten miles south of Berga. "The men were pretty well beat up," Acevedo notes in his diary. The Americans are lodged for the night in a school and fed a thin carrot soup and tea. They are provided with straw on which to lie down; they squabble over how much straw each man gets.

That night, in silence, four of them die: Louis E. Young, Vincent L. Lonergan, Charles J. Wilson, and Robert J. Claffy. Two go in the early evening, two in the early morning.

Claffy, of the 106th Infantry Division, was in particularly bad shape when they set out from Berga. He had been beaten in the tunnels a couple of weeks earlier. Private George A. Tabele, also of the 106th, watched as Claffy was knocked off a staging area by a German guard and fell onto the rocks. Injured, he was forced to go on working. The guard was from Aachen; his wife and children had fled the city because of American bombing. "That is why he hated the Americans so much," Tabele said.

Death certificates prepared by a German doctor in Greiz give the causes of death for Young, Wilson, and Claffy as "exhaustion." Lonergan's death is attributed to "exhaustion and heart weakness." A German postmortem examination notes feces in the clothing and extreme weight loss with no sign of external injury.

The Americans are woken the next morning at six. On the way out Lubinsky sees the corpses, stacked beside the school, and the anger inside him increases a notch; he thinks of the furnaces back at the steel mill in Ohio, the red heat of them—his rage is like that. The second day's march begins about two hours later, and Lubinsky wonders if what he feels can get him through the ordeal. They have been cast out on a lonely road; they are falling. The horses have gone in the night. The men will have to push the cart carrying the sick themselves.

Mordecai Hauer is on the move again in a long line of weary prisoners. Once more, as on the march from Jawischowitz toward Buchenwald, he hears the low rumbling of the nearby front. But it is never close enough to bring liberation, never close enough for him to see the flash of the muzzle that will make the Germans run. He tries to block out the sound, the aural equivalent of a cruel mirage. His spine and left leg ache constantly; his whole body seems to rise in revolt at further punishment. Once again, only thoughts of a reunion with his mother give him the strength to push forward. Only the pale sun of a mild spring provides any balm.

The Berga concentration camp has been emptied of its approximately twelve hundred European prisoners three days after the departure of the Americans. In their striped uniforms, most of them are pushed out onto the road and move southward, forming a bedraggled column guarded by SS men whose zeal seems undiminished by impending defeat.

The American and European victims of Nazi persecution find themselves moving in the same general direction, two columns adrift on a continent in flames. The prisoners carry their illusions with them: the young Americans still do not understand the deadly Nazi mechanism that has ensnared them; the Europeans, most of them Jews, do not yet know the extent of their loss, dreaming of their communities as if they still exist, even though they have been erased from the map of the continent. Not quite a year has passed since Hauer and his family were asked to leave their home in Goncz and assemble at the local school, yet it has been time enough for the world of his childhood to be obliterated, time enough for the near death of Jewish life in Hungary and across wide swathes of central Europe.

Hauer's column passes through German villages, to be met by blank stares neither sympathetic nor hostile. On the windows of the village stores, Hauer notes the sign KEIN FLEISCH—"No meat." Many in the column are teenagers, like Paul Frenkel, who hears one German onlooker mutter: *So young and already criminals.* The European prisoners, like the Americans, sleep in barns and in stables, huddling together for warmth. Those who do not awaken fast enough when the shouted order to assemble comes are summarily shot and left where they lie.

When his bread is finished after a couple of days, Hauer becomes an expert on grasses, shrubs, and weeds. He learns which are bitter, which sweet, which tasteless. He scans the fields for beets or turnips that he might grab before the SS guards see him.

A young Hungarian named Sami, no more than fourteen years old, has latched on to him. They met at the Berga camp and sustained each other with stories of what they would do when liberated. "We'll take a car and we'll drive home and everyone will cheer us, and we will eat like kings," Hauer said, earning the wide-eyed admiration of the boy, who sticks close to him on the march, asking him every few hours how close they are to liberation and that triumphant journey home. Hauer likes to think of returning Sami to his family.

On the fourth day of the march, the prisoners stop at noon for the customary half-hour rest. They are in undulating countryside, in the foothills of the mountainous Erzgebirge region. It is getting colder again as they move into the hills. There is a small apple orchard nearby. Sami darts off and returns with a shriveled apple that has evidently lain under the snow for months. He is about to eat it when an SS guard spots him. "Stealing German property?" the guard, a man in his fifties, yells.

The boy is speechless with fear. "It is just a tiny old apple," Hauer says. "Nobody would want it. He could not resist because he is starving."

Deaf to this appeal, the guard grabs Sami and marches him off to the adjacent apple tree. The boy is trembling, pleading incoherently for his life.

"Give me your belt," the guard orders. He takes it and straps the boy to the tree. Then, holding up the puckered apple, not much bigger than a golf ball, he pronounces his verdict: "For the theft of German property, a sentence of death is hereby passed."

Hauer has a sudden vision of his friend Andras, hanging from an apple tree after his suicide in Goncz: tree of temptation, tree of tribulation.

"No!" he screams, too weary now of senseless murder even to consider the risks of protest. "He did not steal the apple from a German, he found it under a patch of snow, a shriveled piece of nothing."

The guard points his pistol from a range of a few feet and blasts a hole in Sami's head. The boy slumps over. The guard hurls the little apple into the distance and strides away. Hauer looks to the gray heavens he now knows to be godless.

Shapiro pushes the wagon of the dying. It is easier, he finds, to push than to pull. The sick grow in number each day; a constant fear is that those lower down in the pile will suffocate. At the bottom of a hill, those pushing pause to see if any of the ailing are able to hobble up the road, lightening a load that also includes the baggage of the German guards. Shapiro had grown used to pushing the food cart up the hill from the concentration camp, but he is weaker now and the burden greater.

The weather is mild at first, a mixed blessing, because sweat exacerbates the itching in the crotch and armpits. Thirst comes quickly, and Shapiro watches with rage and envy as the guards swig water from their flasks. They are not young; the march is taking a toll even on these Germans with full stomachs. Shapiro pauses now and then to help stragglers who are giving up. Because he is a medic, he is permitted to do this. Excrement, he notes, turns green, as the Americans, too, are driven to eat grass, leaves, whatever they find.

They trudge southwest toward Mühltroff, a slightly longer march than the first day, about twelve miles, but the effort seems greater. Why, Shapiro wonders, do the majority of those who die seem to do so not while walking but at night? Nothing in his limited medical experience suggests an answer. Another question presents itself with growing insistence. Will the Germans drive them until they all die? He can see no logic to that, because it would be far easier to shoot them, but he has learned with reluctance that reason has no place in the world he inhabits. There are rumors that the Germans want to use the Americans as hostages to secure the safe passage from Berlin of senior Nazi officials, but such notions seem far-fetched.

At Mühltroff they are housed in a small castle and given tiered bunks with straw mattresses. At least three more of them die that night, without warning or whimper. The Germans haul the corpses out in the morning: Ernest Strada, Frank Fladzinski, Joseph Rhlagar. The death of a fourth GI, Chester Vincent, is recorded in diaries by other Americans, but there is no German record of his corpse. The bodies are taken away in a local ambulance.

Onward the Americans move, due south now, toward the village of Dobareuth, a dozen miles away. What hope they still have comes from the sounds of Allied artillery and bombing that seem close at times, only to fade like an approaching storm that veers away. Private Israel Cohen collapses. In late March he tried to escape from Berga, only to be hauled back and beaten unconscious by Metz. Since then, he has been among the weaker prisoners.

The guards load Cohen onto the cart. "Private Cohen was on the bottom of the cart, and as each man would collapse they would be thrown on top of Cohen," Private Norman Martin recalled. "Toward the end of the day, there were many men piled on top of Cohen. When I saw him he was dead, and from the position he was lying, he must have died from suffocation from all the men being placed on top of him. I say he must have died from suffocation because his face was a picture of agony, and from the position of his body, he looked as if he had been struggling to get air."

Private Marcel Ouimet also observed the death of Cohen. "The guards threw him into a cart and piled bodies on him," he said. "We tried to get the bodies off to prevent him from suffocating, but by the time we did so, he was already dead."

Cohen's body is brought to the little village of Gefell, just north of Dobareuth, on the morning of April 8, along with two other corpses, those of Private John Gaines and Private Clarence Jahr. They have died during the night. A handwritten note from Metz accompanies the three corpses, explaining that because there is no cemetery in Dobareuth, he has been obliged to dispatch the bodies.

To Otto Rittermann, one of the German guards on the march, it is clear why the Americans die in such numbers: "Nothing to eat, weak, sick, exhausted."

Metz provides no explanation of the deaths in his note. Nor does he mention the fact that eleven Americans in his charge have now died in the space of three days. Shapiro, for the first time since his restorative break at Stalag IX-C, begins to contemplate the likelihood of his own demise. When he tries to recall his family in the Bronx, he finds, to his alarm, that his former life seems little more than a blur.

At dusk on April 8, the column of American prisoners straggled into the village of Zedtwitz, about fifty miles south of Berga, where they paused. They had walked just seven miles that day. The Allied bombing was intense, with some fighters sweeping low enough for the pilots to be visible, and Metz clearly felt it was too risky to go farther.

They were housed in a barn, where fights, by now customary, broke out over straw bedding. Everything from the Red Cross packages was now gone. Gerald Daub encountered some potato peels and sour milk in a pig trough and found himself unable to resist eating it. The donkey of the mines, he mused, the pig of the march. But he wanted to live; it was as simple as that. Men whose boots were giving out eyed the GIs who appeared close to death, ready to step into their shoes. If the boots were too big, they would use scraps of cardboard from the Red Cross boxes to pad them.

Over the next five days, ten Americans died: Bernard J. Vogel, Leonard E. Domb, Merle L. Smith, Robert E. Kessler, Joseph A. Land, Jr., Russell W. Johnson, William Maxwell, Charles Wagner, George Burdeski, and Marvin Willis.

Tony Acevedo watched Vogel of the 106th Division go. A mild-mannered young man from a New York Jewish family, Vogel had earlier tried unsuccessfully to escape from Berga, had his rations cut, been doused in cold water, and been put to work cleaning out the latrine, in addition to his duties in the shafts. "He died in my arms, did not have the will to live anymore, just died of a weakness that took him," Acevedo said. "I tried to feed him, tried to talk about the good things waiting for him back in the United States, but he was saying he wanted to go and just slipped away."

Metz was in a foul temper, apparently unmoved by the accelerating death rate. On April 12 he struck Norman Martin in the shoulder blades with the butt of his rifle for no apparent reason and deliberately spilled some soup being served to the prisoners. The reason he gave, Martin testified later, was that the GIs were making too much noise.

Anxious to have the corpses removed, Metz signed three pieces of paper with the names of the dead and had the ten bodies transported to the cemetery in the nearby village of Töpen. Kurt Seifert, one of the German guards, accompanied them. The GIs were buried haphazardly, without coffins, without grave markers, piled one on the other in their soiled underclothing, some with dog tags, some without, withered limbs intertwined, abdomens hollowed out, with no more substance to their corpses than those Hauer saw in a pit as he made his way into the Auschwitz-Birkenau camp.

In this way, a small American mass grave was added to the myriad larger ones dotting Europe after six years of war. Less than two months earlier, these young Americans had arrived at Berga in passably robust condition. Of the efficacy of Hitler's work-to-death program there could be no doubt.

On April 13 the bitter news reached the Americans that President Franklin D. Roosevelt had died the previous day. They were still huddled in the barn at Zedtwitz because, as Seifert later put it, the Germans were unsure what move to make "due to the advance of the American forces." A German officer in the sidecar of a motorcycle approached Shapiro as he stood outside the barn and said, in good English: "Your President Roosevelt died today. It is a terrible day for Germany."

With that, the officer took off and Shapiro began to weep. He had no idea what to make of the German's remark. Only later did he understand that, in defeat, Germany preferred the United States to the Soviet Union. The Americans held a makeshift service for their deceased president. For many of them, aged twenty or less, having known no other president since their boyhood, the sense of loss was overwhelming and all hope that an end to the war was imminent evaporated once more. Some of the German guards taunted them, rejoicing that "America's Jew president is dead." The old canard that the president's real name was Rosenfeld—one first heard by Littell at his German junior high school in 1939—was still making the rounds among the Nazis.

By the morning of April 14, another American, Arthur Arndt, had died. The next day, Metz ordered the American column to begin marching south again. After traveling about fifteen miles, they reached the little village of Durenloh, just south of Rehau, but not before another eight Americans had died. They were buried in improvised graves beside the road. The corpses included those of Leo Wildman, Milton Kornetz, Jim Gilmore, Raymond Deaver, Robert Parkin, Charles Breum, and Edward Cooper.

From Durenloh the procession trudged due south once more. Private Lawrence Osborn dropped dead on the road and was buried in an adjacent wood. His demise brought the number of American dead in the ten days since the march began to thirty-one. Metz prodded the survivors forward still, aided in particular by two guards, Andres Pickart and Hans Grieshammer, who were merciless in beating with the butts of their rifles the Americans who lagged on the road or were slow to get up in the morning. Grieshammer was a drunk with a sadistic streak; his pleasure was the Americans' pain. Rittermann, one of the more sympathetic guards, saw Pickart striking the Americans "every day." Pickart had an incapacitated left arm that kept him out of the army. He could not raise the arm above shoulder level but wielded his right fist with force and regularity.

That evening, after a twelve-mile walk, they reached Kaiserhammer; during the night, three more Americans died. It fell to Max Zippel, the mayor of the adjacent village of Schwarzenhammer, to arrange for their burial. When he arrived to oversee the loading of the bodies onto a cart for transport to the nearby town of Thierstein, he was told that a fourth American had died. But as the four were lifted onto a cart, he noticed that one was still breathing and rushed off to seek a doctor.

Zippel, on his bicycle, caught up with the cart again near Thierstein, finding it accompanied by four German guards and three American prisoners. The priest was already at the cemetery, but attempts to locate a doctor had proved vain. "We began to dig the grave," Zippel said. "Meanwhile we looked after the still living man . . . and observed that signs of life were decreasing. When we had dug the grave about halfway we made the observation that the American had died."

So four bodies were piled in the grave at Thierstein on April 16—those of James E. Cullina, John O. Weller, Arnold Ascher, and Hardy Millsap. A Paternoster was said for the men, the Americans and Germans praying in unison. Later, the three Americans who had gone to Thierstein as part of the burial detail were allowed to remain in the protection of Germans alarmed at the accumulating evidence of the cruelty of Metz and his cohorts. The proximity of the American army had begun to focus the Germans' minds.

From the outset, Metz had offered succinct advice to Seifert and the other guards on the appropriate treatment of the Americans dur-

ing the march: "Beat them if they don't walk." Eleven days after setting out from Berga, thirty-five Americans were no longer walking;
they were buried here and there on a senseless trail.

There was a hush to the forests, so when the bursts of small-arms fire
came in the rear of the column, one after the other, at brief intervals,
the sound was shocking. Hauer and the Frenkel brothers thought for
a moment that Allied forces had at last reached them. But as they
rounded a bend, Paul Frenkel looked back and saw SS men systemat-
ically executing all those who could not keep up, several hundred of
them, killing them like flies. The corpses dotted the roadside, some
lying flat on their backs, some huddled in fetal positions, forming a
trail of death.

All through the day, the firing continued. They were ascending a
steep incline; many fell back and, as soon as they did, were shot.
Snow fell on the bodies. The column of European prisoners had
entered a wintry terrain once more, in mountains near the Czech-
oslovak border. There was no more grass to feed on; the prisoners
turned to eating moss, tree bark, and snow. Hauer felt the last of his
strength evaporating. Like his father on the road from Jawischowitz,
he wanted to drift now into a consoling sleep. At night, soaked and
half dead, the marchers were packed into a wooden barn. Some
instinct pushed Hauer to claw his way to the top of the human pile,
near the rafters, where there was air. He was reminded of the storage
depot at the station on the way to Buchenwald, where so many on
that earlier march had suffocated.

The Germans herding the prisoners seemed increasingly confused. They knew they were in a shrinking pocket between the
American and Russian fronts. Yet they kept killing, eliminating witnesses to what they had done, clinging perhaps to the far-fetched
hope that crimes on such a scale could disappear without trace.

At one point, in a clearing, they rounded up a large group, including the Frenkel brothers; it seemed they were about to execute
them all. But an order to abandon the exercise came from somewhere. Perhaps, Gabriel Frenkel thought, the Germans no longer
had enough ammunition or enough men for such a mass execution.
Yet they killed those in the rear without compunction.

Discipline was starting to fray. Escape seemed possible. But fear
of the Nazis was so deeply instilled by now that the Jews hardly

believed it. They had seen executions for a stolen apple or a couple of pilfered potatoes. So they waited, unsure when to make a move, reluctant to risk anything when remaining invisible to the Germans had for so long been the best insurance of survival.

Because of the weeklong pause in Zedtwitz, the American GIs were now behind the Europeans, despite having left Berga a few days earlier. On April 17 they were forced to march another twenty miles southward from Kaiserhammer to the vicinity of Grosslatengrün, where they paused near a mill called Grapsmühle. On the road, Private Donald Rowe died.

Private Marcel Ouimet witnessed Rowe's death. "On April 17, 1945, we were marching along when suddenly Don Rowe fell from weakness and could not get up," Ouimet recalled. "The American army was close behind our column of prisoners and I guess the Germans did not want the Americans to see him in that condition, so when he fell and could not get up, one of the guards struck him on the forehead with the butt of his rifle, which killed him. The Germans stopped the column and picked a detail of four men to bury the body. I was one of the four. We were given a shovel and taken under guard a short distance off the road, where we buried him."

More than thirty men were laid out on two horse-drawn wagons, too sick to walk. Many of the Americans appeared to be in a trance. At night, in a barn, another seven soldiers died, including Ernesto Zaragoza, George Hanson, Ralph Levitt, William Kelly, Ray Christiansen, and Clarence Vensel. They were buried in makeshift graves, of which there were now forty-three containing American corpses on a meandering path south of Berga. The death rate since the march began was higher than three a day.

Stanley B. Cohen said of the burials along the road: "We would dig a hole and throw the bodies in. We didn't have any coffins, didn't have any way of dealing with the delicacies. We just wanted to make sure that they weren't eaten by the animals in the fields." John Griffin was also on several burial details: "Just all into one hole and that was it. No casket, no nothing."

Sometimes, German authorities wanted to place a cross over the grave, but because Jews and Christians were generally buried together, the Americans tried to resist this. At one churchyard where they were digging a grave, the sexton came out and asked the religion of the dead soldiers.

"We've got Catholics, we've got Protestants, and we've got Jews," said Cohen, who spoke some German.

"Well, you can't bury the Jews in consecrated ground."

Cohen protested, but the sexton insisted they take them all out and dig another grave outside the cemetery.

On April 18 the Americans reached the small town of Seidlers-reuth, where they were lodged in a barn for two nights. By now, they had traveled about a hundred miles from Berga. Many had a greenish look; they muttered indecipherable things. Shapiro's mind was blank; he had become an automaton. He lay in the straw gazing into space. In Seidlersreuth three more soldiers died: Leo Best, Milton Rothman, and Joseph Greene. They were taken for burial to the nearby village of Falkenberg.

As the American army drew closer, German civilians became more responsive to the skeletal state of the prisoners, many of whom now weighed no more than ninety pounds. Milton Stolon passed a farmhouse and heard the sounds of Ruggiero Leoncavallo's opera *Pagliacci*. He saw the owner and said, "*Pagliacci*"; the German was amazed that this emaciated American savage knew something about opera. The farmer gave Stolon a sandwich. Offers of milk, even eggs, became more frequent.

Metz had been told to keep the Americans captive and herd them southward; he would do as he was told. But his task was now arduous. It had become clear to anyone glimpsing the deathly procession that he was killing those in his charge. The mayor of Seidlersreuth was appalled, and Donald Hildenbrand witnessed an angry confrontation in which the mayor told Metz he must take all the GIs to the nearest hospital, but Metz balked. They shouted, Metz insisting that none of the Americans be released, the mayor calling him a barbarian.

After that, Metz appeared to be in shock. His authority had been questioned by a fellow German. In the end, a compromise was reached: at least thirty-one of the GIs—those too weak to walk, who had been traveling on the two horse-drawn carts—were taken to the nearest hospital, at Fuchsmühl, run by a German doctor named George Sperber, a former army captain in the Afrika Korps. The Americans arrived at the hospital on April 19, and Sperber managed to save all but one, Private Robert M. Gray.

On April 20 a diminished American column started to move again. Private Advil Breeding had died, and at least a dozen prisoners had managed to escape in the night with the connivance of some of the guards and local Germans. As they passed through the village of Schönficht, Metz told Seifert and other guards that he wanted to try to locate the GIs who had escaped. He took off on a bicycle and was not seen again by the Americans.

During a fifteen-day march, Metz had presided over the death of almost fifty American soldiers, adding to the two dozen dead at the Berga camp, an attrition rate unknown elsewhere among American prisoners of war on the European continent. Metz was stubborn, stupid, and sadistic, a mediocre man for whom tyranny was opportunity. Applied in the blind service of the Führer, hitched to the apparatus of power, Metz's commonplace traits became those of a mass murderer. There is no evidence that Metz—a man of modest commerce, a provincial German, a family man—ever saw in the suffering and dying around him any reason to reconsider what he viewed, to the last, as his duty: obedience to the Third Reich and its policies of persecution, even when those involved were American prisoners of war. Indeed, the evidence is overwhelming that he took pleasure in pushing agonized young GIs to the point where their strength gave out.

With Metz gone, the death rate declined sharply. "They got more to eat," Seifert, the guard, said. On the night of April 20 they reached the village of Schommersrieth. Here a new group of German guards, from the Civilian Guard rather than the National Guard, took charge of the Americans, and Seifert and other members of his unit returned to Greiz. The column continued to move southward through terrain that was increasingly threatening.

Tony Acevedo noted in his diary: "Day and night it rained. Everyone wet from top to bottom. We march and as we walked along the road you could see men who had been shot through the head. These were political prisoners. Every twenty-five yards, there lay three or four men, men who couldn't make the march, had to drop out, and then were shot."

The Americans had stumbled on the macabre traces of the death march of the European Berga prisoners, the mass killings witnessed by Paul Frenkel. Even after all they had been through, the scene— a landscape of death—made an indelible impression on Shapiro, Lubinsky, Hildenbrand, and the other American prisoners. They had not been in Auschwitz or in any of the other German death camps; they were still unaware that mass murder has been part of Nazi policy, indeed central to it. For the Americans, the corpses on either side of the road seemed to betoken acts outside the range of human behavior encountered even in war, for there had been no battle here, there had been only executions, single bullets blasted from close range through the heads of the victims. Yes, the Americans themselves had been dying in large numbers, but not like this, and it was only now that the enormity of what the GIs had suffered began to assume its full weight in their hearts and minds. They had been blinded by innocence. Their passage into experience, its bitterness and pain, became decisive on this corpse-ridden road, because here they saw for the first time, although they did not yet comprehend it, what exactly they had been part of in the nine weeks since they arrived at Berga. The naked evidence of the Holocaust was before them, and what they saw would never leave them, even when they grasped its place in their own story and the history of the European conflict. It was here that the truth began to come home: they had been sent to Europe to defeat Hitler's Germany, but in captivity they had become soldiers of another war, one without rules, one not fought between armies, one whose essence had been the annihilation of the Jewish population of Europe. As prisoners of that other war, their burden would be great, for this was not a war for which anyone had prepared them. For American military and political authorities to acknowledge what they had been through was also to acknowledge the failure that brought them to this place and this pass.

"It was hellish," said Shapiro. "As we were walking up the hills, we saw there were bodies on either side of the road, and these were Jews who were in kneeling positions, fetal positions, and every one of them had their heads blown off. They were shot from close range through the back of their skulls. We were walking through bone fragments, and the road was wet with blood; there was brain all over the place, and I began to tremble. There were ten here, three there, one there, as we ascended the hill very slowly. None of them faced the road, they all faced away from the road, and they all had gunshots, from a rifle or a pistol. For the Germans, it must have been like stepping on cockroaches. Instead of trees lining the road, there were bodies. In the distance we heard rapid fire, and we knew they were killing prisoners in the woods. That's when I thought I knew I was going to die, and maybe not make it up the hill. There would be some point when I could not go further and somebody would come up and shoot me in the head."

Stephen Schweitzer counted two hundred dead bodies lying by the road. Donald Hildenbrand trudged through the bleak terrain, feeling a terrible rage mounting in him, one he thought himself too weary to summon. "Nothing, nothing, no authority, no force of any kind, could have brought them, or obliged them, to murder all these innocent civilians," Hildenbrand recalled. "That came home to me, and that I could not forgive."

John Reifenrath thought at first that a plane must have accidentally strafed the area, so extensive was the killing. But then somebody picked up a spent cartridge and said it was German. All through the day, he came across bodies, often on both sides of the road. Sometimes he found a piece of brain or skull. Stanley B. Cohen asked one of the German guards why they were shooting the European Jews.

"Oh," the guard responded, "if we leave them here, they may waken, and they'll be on the loose, free to shoot and rape German women."

To Morton Brooks, "it was just plain mass murder. We did not know about the Holocaust, and we had not seen anything like that before. It shook me up, even after all we'd seen, because with Metz there had been individual cases, but not people lined up and killed willy-nilly." Brooks dreamed of tying Metz to a fence and carving him up, but carving him slowly, ensuring that his death was drawn out.

Ahead of him, Sanford Lubinsky heard the shots of the executioners. He felt he was about to black out. Death might be pleasurable indeed. He looked up to the pines, whose dark green mass seemed to block out the sky, their branches swaying in unison. The trees were neatly planted, in straight lines, one after the other, an army of trunks. He felt himself being pulled into that green vortex, but then a voice came from somewhere saying, No, not here, back in the United States, that is the soil to be buried in. And the fury in his heart dragged him back to life and drove him on up the hill, past the bodies strewn before them like roadkill.

Hans Kasten had enough hatred in him to be ready to kill. While his fellow prisoners from Berga trudged southward, he was already armed with several daggers and a couple of pistols, on the loose, at the wheel of a Mercedes, searching for Willy Hack. A slow death was what Kasten had in mind for Hack, the young devotee of Hitler and a Jew-hater who could not comprehend that a man with so German a name as Kasten's would opt to fight against the Reich. Yes, a lingering death would suit Hack, with his slicked-back dark hair and sharp little eyes, the butcher of Berga.

Kasten had been liberated along with Littell and Sinner on April 11, when the spearhead of the American 6th Armored Division reached Stalag IX-C. A medical unit found the three Americans—the only ones in the camp—and, alarmed at their emaciated state, immediately arranged for a jeep to take them to Weimar and, from there, to an American army hospital in France. Littell was more dazed than joyous about his freedom.

When the jeep came for them, however, Kasten was nowhere to be found. Littell and Sinner spent several hours searching for him, to no avail. The camp was a mess, with a lot of the French prisoners drunk on brandy, reeling or even dying from its effect on empty stomachs, and Kasten had disappeared. He had, in fact, already taken off by himself, determined to mete out his own justice.

"The first thing I did was take down the Nazi flag that was flying over the camp," Kasten recalled. "Then I went into the town. At the city hall they were accumulating all the weapons that were available, and I collected a whole bunch of beautiful daggers and things like that. And then I liberated a Mercedes-Benz and the tankers filled it with gas and gave me a couple of jerry cans of gas and a big case of rations. And I took off looking for Hack."

Kasten was then a crazed figure, emerging from a long spell of solitary confinement, weighing ninety-eight pounds, his blue eyes gleaming, obsessed with his mission, unhinged by his rage. He had no time for anything else; he did not even say good-bye to Littell and Sinner, and he did not know the fate of the other Americans who had been at Berga and were now on a death march farther south in a Germany still not liberated.

Down country roads, through villages teeming with civilians looking for food from the country's new American rulers, Kasten gunned the Mercedes, seeking out collection camps for German prisoners. At each one, he explained to the American commanding officer that he was looking for a certain SS lieutenant who was a murderer. The officers understood. Down the lines of German prisoners he strode, seeking the smirking face of Hack, a German who, like myriad other Germans, had defiled Germany. Pale faces, tired faces, frightened faces stared at him blankly, the fervor stripped away now, together with the belief in an all-powerful Führer, leaving only fear and the hope of being allowed to shuffle away to an anonymous life.

Hack was nowhere to be found. Exhausted, Kasten collapsed on a bunk in one of the camps, only to be awoken by an American sergeant saying his colonel wanted to see him at once. Kasten went out into a field. "You wanted to see me, Colonel?"

"Yeah. I have something for you."

"What's that?"

The colonel pointed to a young German SS lieutenant, standing in the sun, looking frightened.

"That's not the man I'm looking for," Kasten said.

"So what? He's SS. He's a lieutenant. Take him."

Why not? Kasten told the German to follow him. Accompanied by the American sergeant, they made their way to the basement of a bombed-out house nearby. The German had a watch; Kasten took it. The floor was wet and muddy. "Take off your boots," Kasten barked.

The SS man stood there for a few minutes, barefooted in the muck, and then made the mistake of invoking the Geneva Conventions. Kasten exploded. The sergeant started to unbuckle his pistol. The German was trembling. Perhaps he had a dozen dead Jews on his conscience and did not deserve to live. But this was not the man Kasten had come to kill; he told the sergeant to cool it.

"Put on your boots and get out of here, or we'll be obliged to make sure you never mention the Geneva Conventions again," Kasten said. The SS man stared at him, incredulous, uncomprehending. He grabbed his boots and rushed out of the building.

Kasten moved on from camp to camp in a state of gathering exhaustion and delirium. Some old instinct led him to the Black Forest resort of Baden-Baden, where he used to go before the war with German relatives. At the Aster Hotel he pulled up in his "liberated" Mercedes and, planting a stack of money acquired on his travels atop the reception desk, demanded the best room in the house. This was hastily arranged.

He fell onto the bed and passed out for two days. That might have been the end of Kasten, but a Polish woman tending the room became concerned and called the local American military authorities. Two sergeants appeared.

"What can we do for you?" one said.

Kasten handed them the keys to the Mercedes, told them they could do what they wished with it, but he needed help. His head was pounding. An ambulance soon appeared and took him to a nearby camp with a clinic, where he was treated for severe malnutrition and exhaustion. Other American survivors of prison camps were there, waiting to be flown out to the big American hospital at Camp Lucky Strike, near Le Havre.

One day Kasten returned from the clinic and found that his two duffel bags full of "souvenirs" picked up after his liberation had been stolen. That pushed him over the edge. With a pistol in each hand, he stormed into a room where the Americans were gathered and started firing through the ceiling and floor. "The first son of a bitch I see with any of my stuff is going to be a dead son of a bitch!" he roared. Within a short time, everything was returned.

It was not possible for the others to comprehend Kasten's delirious rage. Littell could understand it, but he was elsewhere, at an American military hospital in Commercy, about 125 miles west of Paris. On his way out of Stalag IX-C in the jeep, Littell had passed a turnoff in the road with a sign to Buchenwald. The camp's liberation by the United States Third Army revealed the horror of the crematoria and the agony of the more than eighty thousand surviving inmates. It was from the fringes of this Nazi netherworld that they had emerged, but to explain where they had been and what they had seen was not easy.

It is bright outside, spring sunshine, shafts of light slanting through gaps in the rafters of the barn. They don't know where they are. All that the skeletal American prisoners know is that they are sprawled in the hay, again, and that not far away, in the German countryside, assuming this is still Germany, tank shells are exploding.

The previous night they were fed hot, cooked potatoes, a rare treat, but on this morning of April 23, 1945, Private Jack Bornkind from Detroit appears close to death. His mouth quivers slightly, but he will not eat and he is beyond words. His skin is gray-green. Gerald Daub and his two closest friends, Robert Rudnick and Joseph Marks (then Markowitz), are trying to save him.

Discipline on the march has eroded, and, since the departure of Metz, the balance of power has shifted. The Germans are visibly scared. Civilians invite the prisoners into their homes and want to feed them in exchange for letters saying they have helped the Americans, letters they hope will provide their passport to security under what seems to be coming: American rule of Germany.

Daub and Rudnick make an improvised stretcher from an overcoat hitched to two pieces of wood, place Bornkind on the stretcher, and tell one of the guards they want to take him outside for some air. The guard grunts. The German is still obeying orders, but he has given up the struggle.

There are now only 169 Americans left in this main group of prisoners. The single march has become several. During a strafing of the road a couple of days earlier, chaos erupted, with guards and Americans alike taking off into the woods and a nearby village. Many do not return, finding shelter in German homes or hiding in the dense forest. Among those who escape are Robert Widdicombe and Lawrence Gillette. Some prisoners, including Stanley B. Cohen, are put into trucks, apparently in an attempt to rush them farther southward or into Czechoslovakia.

But Daub, Rudnick, and Marks remain in the column. Perhaps, they feel now, as they carry another dying man out into the sunlight, they missed an opportunity to escape. On the day of the strafing, they had found themselves in the home of a German woman with a French girl working for her. Hidden in a cellar, they were fed an apple cake—heavenly—and hoped to remain there, but the woman eventually deemed the risks too high. Still, Daub did agree to write a letter commending her for the help given, a letter portraying her as a good German.

Next to the barn is a small hut, and they carry Bornkind inside. A goose egg is lying there, and they prop Bornkind up and try to get him to suck on the egg. His mouth continues to quiver, but he will not suck. Rudnick himself is also close to death, breathing unevenly.

As they struggle to save their fellow GI, the sounds of battle draw nearer. A distant rumbling, the dull boom of artillery, and the occasional crack of small-arms fire have accompanied them almost since the march began eighteen days earlier. But now it seems they are encircled.

Daub looks out of the hut and sees a tank coming over a rise opposite him. It has a white star on it. He looks again. It is an American Sherman tank with a Red Cross jeep just behind it. He starts to wave his arms. The tank's cannon is pointing directly at him. To die in friendly fire at this juncture would, he feels, be unreasonably cruel.

Inside the barn, the German guards are screaming: *"Raus! Raus!"* They want the Americans to keep marching! But the Americans balk; they know the game is up just as they know that any last vestige of their strength is gone.

Tony Acevedo's last diary entry in captivity, on April 23, tells of a German pointing a pistol at the prisoners and trying to get them to budge: "For a while, our men wouldn't move, until all of a sudden we heard the tanks coming. The guards started taking off . . . everybody was yelling in the barn 'till one German guard came up to us and gave himself up, saying that we were free."

Shapiro staggers out. He sees the big white star on the Sherman tank. It is very bright, too bright. The glare seems vicious, and people are running back and forth, screaming and waving. *Who are these skeletal figures in American uniforms?* Somebody fires a shell in the direction of the barn, and everyone hits the ground. Shapiro gets to his feet, staring straight ahead, tottering, and a jeep pulls up. From it comes an American voice: "Climb in, soldier."

Three words, a new universe. The sun is warm. Bleary-eyed, Shapiro looks to the sky. Where am I? he wonders. His liberator hands him a chocolate bar, a ration. It is familiar but strange, an object from another world. He ate hundreds of them while in combat in northern France, a long time ago, before his passage through hell. He cannot get the wrapping off. Helplessly, he fumbles with the chocolate until at last one of the Americans on the jeep opens it for him. "There you go."

That American voice again, steady and warm. Three simple words in English, spoken softly, not shouted. It has been a long time since he has heard a voice like that, one that comforts rather than castigates.

He is starving but can scarcely eat. He is free but can scarcely smile. He is a young man but scarcely more than a lost child. Who are you? his liberator asks. Where have you been? The shoulder patch on his jacket tells the members of the 11th Armored Division who have freed him that Shapiro comes from the 28th Infantry Division. But he seems unrecognizable, to them, to himself.

Daub stumbles forward toward the Red Cross vehicle. "We have a very sick man," he says. "Here, inside the hut."

The medic jumps down. He looks at Daub and says, "We've been looking for you guys." Farther north, other Berga prisoners have al-

ready been found over the previous three days and have informed
Patton's Third Army of the column of Americans.

The medic goes into the hut, emerging a few minutes later to
declare: "The guy is dead. I'm very sorry."

Bornkind is the forty-ninth and last American to perish on an
eighteen-day death march that has taken them more than 125 miles
south from Berga.

Daub goes back, takes a last look at his friend, removes the high
school graduation ring from his finger, and slips it into his pocket.

Donald Hildenbrand has also emerged from the barn waving.
Some rations are thrown in his direction. He bends to pick them up
and collapses. He cannot move, cannot gather up the rations; the
determination to survive that has been driving him on evaporates,
and at the very moment of liberation, he finds himself empty. Half
his body weight has disappeared in the space of nine weeks, and now
there is nothing left. At last, a field ambulance picks him up.

The first thing Sanford Lubinsky sees when he emerges from the
barn is a blue field with white stars. The field is in the upper left corner of the Stars and Stripes. It's a beauty, he thinks, that flag, a beautiful thing. Tanks and half-tracks are coming up the road and firing
away, over his head, with their fifty-calibers. The troops give him
candy, some cigarettes, and a pistol, and everything feels sweet until
the candy makes him sick.

Most of the Americans are loaded into field ambulances or jeeps.
They drive toward the town of Cham. Lubinsky has a cigarette in
each hand, candy in his mouth, and his pistol loaded with four bullets. White flags hang from bombed-out buildings and white cotton-
ball clouds glide across the blue sky. Occasionally, a shot rings out
from some pocket of resistance. In the town, they are delivered to
what appears to be a Catholic hospital run by nuns.

The question keeps returning: Where have you been? They are,
without exception, strange figures: skeletal, covered in lice and fes-
tering wounds, and scarcely able to keep food down. It is from a distant shore that they come, and that strange land on the far bank of
the Styx is unknown to their saviors, who try to be helpful. Kerosene
and disinfecting powder are given to them to clear out the lice eggs;
nurses extract socks and other clothes from open sores.

The Berga survivors are stripped and showered and laid on
stretchers. The next day, April 24, army photographers arrive to take
pictures.

"We want evidence of your mistreatment," one of the photographers says. But it is not clear how, when, where, or to what purpose this evidence will be used.

The Americans were freed just one week before Hitler took his life in the bunker in Berlin, with Soviet troops already in the Tiergarten and at Potsdamer Platz. Before his suicide, the Führer produced a final political testament in which he wrote: "Centuries will pass, but the ruins of our cities and monuments will repeatedly kindle hatred for the race ultimately responsible, who have brought everything down upon us: international Jewry and its accomplices."

To the last, Hitler pursued his demon. The statement might have been taken from his first years as a political activist, more than a quarter century earlier. Hatred of the Jews and the determination to drive them from Germany and all of Europe were immutable cornerstones of his actions. As the Führer's word and whim, indeed his very breath, had the force of an order to the last, even when the Thousand-Year Reich lay in ruins and was lost, this murderous doctrine was enough to keep in captivity a group of American GIs perceived by their captors as Jewish, Jew-like, or as troublesome as Jews, until more than 20 percent of them were dead. That, after working as slaves for the Reich, these Americans were herded like cattle to their deaths until seven days before Hitler's decision to take his own life may appear remarkable. But these deaths were not remarkable. Nor were the unmarked graves into which the American corpses were piled. The fate of the GIs was one shared by millions of Europeans, further testimony to the unstinting zeal for obedience that the Führer was able to foster in the hearts and minds of Germans and to exploit until the very eve of his suicide.

For Mordecai Hauer, the agony continues for another two weeks, into early May. The prisoners are pushed eastward toward the Czech town of Manetin, in the last remaining pocket between the Allied forces advancing from the west and the Russians from the east. There civilians block the road, hurling insults at the SS, awed and appalled by the deathly figures in the Germans' charge. The column is not able to pass; the SS guards are obliged to allow the Jews to stay in the town's *Kulturhaus,* or cultural center, where people bring them bread and vegetables.

The prisoners' status is now a murky thing, somewhere between captivity and freedom. Manetin is just over the Reich's redrawn border with Czechoslovakia and still subject to Nazi control. But no objection comes from the SS when prisoners venture from the cultural center to adjacent houses. Hauer is invited into a home, where he learns that the town's population is divided between German-speaking *Volksdeutsche*, or ethnic Germans, and Czechs. The former, who include the mayor, are terrified, because Germany's surrender is now thought to be days, even hours, away.

The couple give Hauer food. "You have suffered enough," says the farmer simply, unable to wrest his eyes from the bones that protrude from Hauer's arms and legs. Hauer himself has not seen a mirror for many months; he has no idea what he looks like. All he has known for as far back as his mind will go is hunger and exhaustion. Even sexual desire is but a vague memory. The impact on this couple of his agonized form begins to provide him with some notion of the extent to which he has withered and shriveled.

Returning to the cultural center, Hauer notices that just above the town, about three hundred yards away, lies the edge of a dense forest. German defeat, he knows, is imminent, but he doubts that this ineluctable fact will prevent the SS commanders from herding the prisoners out of Manetin the next morning. For a long time he has clung to the belief that Katz's decision to escape was noble but foolish and that the best hope for survival lay in somehow outlasting the Germans. But he now knows himself to be in an environment that is largely sympathetic, even if still treacherous, and German will is no longer what it was at Jawischowitz. His mind is made up: he will slip out of the cultural center that night and hide in the nearby woods until Manetin is liberated.

Ever since his arrival in Kassa almost a year earlier, Hauer has been accompanied in his odyssey of death and suffering by Baruch Schreiber, the young man whose father was designated a *Muselmann* at Jawischowitz and went to his death. Schreiber is skeptical. The town is still under German occupation; many people are collaborators; liberation is near.

"We waited this long, why not wait a few more days?" Schreiber says. "Why risk being shot now, when Allied troops will soon disarm the SS?"

Hauer hears his own vain arguments to Katz echoing inside him. For a very long time now he has heard, and been sympathetic to, the case for patience. But his own patience, and his strength, are at an end. He will go no farther than Manetin, come what may. "I have made up my mind," Hauer responds. "But I do not want to involve you. I know we have long dreamed of liberation together. But let each of us act as he thinks fit."

Schreiber, however, refuses to let Hauer go on his own. That night, toward dawn, they slip out of the cultural center, accompanied by three other young Hungarian Jews. Their plan is to hide separately in the forest and then reunite at a designated house in the village after liberation. But as they hurry toward the edge of the forest, lights come on in the *Kulturhaus* and searchlights sweep the terrain. Hauer tries to run, but he is slower than the others, and as he reaches the trees, a bullet slams into his left shinbone. He cries out and falls.

"Is that you?" Schreiber shouts from the forest.

"Yes, but keep running," says Hauer. "I'm right behind you. Run!"

Hauer crawls into the undergrowth. The pain is so intense he has to bite his lip to stop himself from screaming. SS men, shouting and cursing, plunge past him into the forest. He feels he is falling off a cliff, but slowly, like a white sheet, and waiting for him with outstretched arms are Yankele and Katz.

Hours later, he awakens to find himself curled around a tree, on his right side. The pain from his injured left leg is intense. He cannot see the wound, but his pants are soaked in dried blood. All is quiet; sunlight filters through the branches; the ground is damp. Spring is stirring; he can smell its sweetness and sap. How much blood has he lost? He feels hot and feverish. Is the wound infected? He drifts in and out of consciousness, waiting for nightfall so that he can make his way back to the town.

At dusk he starts to crawl. He wants to reach the house where he was given food, but it seems farther away then he remembered. There is no light in the cultural center; the other prisoners have moved on. He tries to get up, but a shooting pain from his foot to his groin topples him. He crawls but has to stop every few meters. An urge to surrender and swoon sweeps over him, as it did in the refrigerated room at Buchenwald. He will never reach the good farmer's house. But somehow he keeps moving, and when he comes to a residence, he knocks once on the door and faints.

A German voice awakens him. *Tetanus injection . . . young man . . . these pills every two hours . . .* Hauer is terrified. But then comes a

Czech voice, followed by assurances from the German that although he is a *Volksdeutscher*, he is first and foremost a doctor and will not denounce the Czechs for harboring a Jew. Before leaving, the doctor says he will return the following evening because he may have to amputate the leg to save the young man's life.

Hauer drifts in and out of consciousness, slowly becoming aware that he is hidden in an attic, squeezed in between small arms, boxes of ammunition, and communications equipment. His hiding place is also the clandestine headquarters of the underground in Manetin. Over the next couple of days he hears radio broadcasts claiming that the German surrender is imminent alternating with German stations claiming that the defeat of the "Anglo-American and Communist puppets of the Jewish conspiracy" remains inevitable. A teenaged girl named Bozena Napranikova, the red-haired daughter of the house, dabs his forehead with cool towels; the German-speaking doctor returns to pronounce the infection under control. But the Napranik family remains fearful to the last that Hauer will be discovered and all of them shot.

The tension in the house only lifts completely on May 7, two weeks after the liberation of the Americans, when American troops enter the town. For two days already, Nazi control of Manetin had evaporated, but the arrival of the Americans causes pandemonium. Cries of "We are free!" echo through the house, and people clamber on the Allied jeeps and tanks. Hauer joins the joyous crowds in the street but has only one question on his mind: Where is Baruch Schreiber?

They had agreed to meet in the house of a grocer befriended by Schreiber; Hauer makes his way there. Why is his friend not on the street celebrating? The grocer will not look him in the eye, says only that Schreiber and the others never appeared. He insists he knows nothing more. Only back at the Napranik house does Hauer learn from Bozena that his friend and the three other Hungarians were all killed in the forest by the SS. To die in this way, just days before liberation, seems almost grotesque and Hauer feels a terrible responsibility.

He has always imagined freedom in association with joy. It was an end to suffering, of course, but it would also lead to a joyous resumption of his former life. The images have filled his mind for weeks: traveling home with young Sami and Baruch Schreiber, singing and swaggering, finding his mother and his sister and his brothers, rediscovering his love for Sharon, or perhaps even Ilona, recovering what he has lost, even without his father; he has imagined countless times the sweetness of his mother's embrace, a comfort unlike any other. But now Sami and Baruch are dead in the war's last senseless spasms, and Hauer's head is filled only with doubt and dread and his eyes with tears and his heart with pain and foreboding. Were they all dead, his family, his friends, the very life he had lived in little Goncz?

Despite the pleas of the Napranik family, and especially a smitten Bozena, that he remain in Manetin, Hauer soon boards a train for Prague, the first step on his journey home. He passes quickly from American-occupied Europe into the Soviet-occupied zone and finds himself in the shattered city of Prague, whose beauty he has heard much about, a beauty now shrouded in desolation. Stray dogs pick their way through pockmarked, rubble-strewn streets, and Soviet soldiers from central Asia bestride the once elegant avenues.

With the help of a cane provided by the German-speaking doctor in Manetin, Hauer staggers into the station waiting room. On the floor is a pile of discarded German military uniforms. Without thinking much, he dons a warm Wehrmacht overcoat that will be useful if he has to sleep in the open. He also takes a rucksack and fills it with the food given to him by the Napraniks. On a bench he falls asleep, awakening in the middle of the day. It is time to move on.

"When is the next train in the direction of Hungary?" he asks a man at an information desk, who eyes him with evident suspicion and fails—or refuses—to understand his German. He makes a sign for Hauer to wait and disappears.

Two Russian soldiers come hurrying back with the man, grab Hauer, and drag him into a small office, where a Russian officer soon appears and, in passable German, introduces himself as the security chief at the railroad station. "Name, rank, unit, and serial number," he says, a pen poised in one hand.

"Hauer, Mordecai. I'm a Jew, a concentration-camp survivor."

The officer's fist crashes down on the desk. "I said name, rank, unit, and serial number."

"But I'm a Jew, not a soldier," Hauer says, his voice trembling. "I was a prisoner in Auschwitz, Buchenwald, and Berga an der Elster. I am limping because I was shot by the SS as I tried to escape a few days ago."

"You think I was born yesterday?" the Russian snaps. "That's about the same story I heard today from three other German Nazis."

"It's not a story!" Hauer shouts, his fear now turning to rage. "Look at this tattooed number on my arm. I came from Auschwitz. I am not a liar!"

The Russian examines the tattoo—A9092—but is unimpressed. "It could be a fake. Many Germans try that trick. Take off your coat, jacket, and shirt. Raise your arms. And hurry!"

Satisfied that Hauer is concealing nothing on his upper body, the Russian leaves the room, returning a few minutes later with a fellow officer.

"What's your name?" says the second Russian, in Yiddish.

"Hauer, Mordecai."

"Where were you born?"

"In a small town in Hungary."

"Your Yiddish sounds strange, more like German."

"I speak better Hebrew."

The Russian pulls out a battered prayer book, opens it at random, and says, "Read."

Hauer immediately recognizes a prayer from the Sabbath morning service and starts to chant quietly, by heart. The Russians are astonished and tell him, enough, he can stop, but Hauer has been swept away by the traditional melody that is part of the life he once had and his voice rises and rises, soaring with a feeling now imbued with all that he has experienced of life and death, stronger and deeper than it has ever been despite his loss of faith, and the prayer fills the room of these soldiers from a dawning Communist empire, one of whom secretly carries an old Jewish prayer book, disarming these Russians who have come so far to defeat Hitler, out of central Asia on a tide of rage, until Hauer chokes on his own tears and is silent.

"This is a Jew," says the Russian Jewish soldier, putting his arms around Hauer. "He is a Jew who speaks the truth."

In Manetin, Paul Frenkel was separated from his older brother when they disagreed on whether to try to escape or not. When Gabriel slipped away, Paul remained with the cornered Germans, who kept turning west toward the Americans, then east toward the Russians, bouncing back and forth like frightened animals between the powers that would soon divide their country and all of Europe.

Paul only emerged from the woods where he had hidden when a German-speaking forester approached him and said: "You can go, the war is over."

But go where? Europe was a madhouse filled with lost humanity, its roads choked with people going back and forth, searching for relatives and places that were dead or battered or unrecognizable. He had no idea whether his brother was alive or where he was, and a long search in Manetin proved fruitless. Like Hauer, he decided that Prague lay on the most direct route home to Hungary. On foot, he set out toward the Czech capital and soon came upon two American soldiers sunning themselves beside the road. It was spring, and the war in Europe was over.

"Papers!" said one of the Americans, eyeing Frenkel suspiciously.

"I'm a Jew, a concentration-camp survivor," Frenkel replied. "I have none."

"Hey, the guy says he has no papers," the soldier said, turning toward his superior.

The American sergeant, a lanky man, looked Frenkel up and down. "Let him go," he said lightly, gesturing down the road. "He looks like he's had a hell of a war. Just let the guy go."

After spending almost a year in the captivity of German officers and soldiers, Frenkel was startled by the body language of this American, so loose and relaxed, yet authoritative. That, he thought to himself, is my country, the end to my journey—America.

The American survivors of Berga were free, but not free of the rage inside them. Leo Zaccaria found a German in a hospital bed in Cham, grabbed him, and threw him on the floor. "That's my bed," he said. "Get out of here."

In a hospital in Reims, France, where he was taken after about a week, Zaccaria found himself being carried around on a stretcher by German prisoners of war put to work as hospital orderlies. He weighed just over ninety pounds. One day he saw some German prisoners in a hut, being fed large bowls of hot, nourishing soup.

"They were serving one thing and another," Zaccaria recalled. "And I busted into the place. And I banged them around, tipped over the food, broke chairs and everything else. Did the windows. You know I was so disgusted with hate. I never had one solid piece of food. And here were these guys fattening up."

He might have killed one of the Germans if he had had the strength. A Catholic chaplain calmed him down, told Zaccaria he should not behave like the very people he hated. That gave him pause. Still, the animal inside him was restive, and later, in a Paris hospital, he grabbed a nurse who had just awakened him and tried to pull her down on the bed. What he was doing, he hardly knew; the rage was beyond his understanding or control. But he thought it wise, after that, to throw away the knife he had been keeping under his pillow.

Sanford Lubinsky had no knife, but he nursed the pistol with four bullets given to him at his liberation. German prisoners of war brought him food. He had his pistol ready and was prepared to kill one of them when a nurse walked in. "Give me that," she said.

After that, the nurses rather than the prisoners brought the food. Lubinsky did not know what to say to anyone. They could not understand his readiness to kill a German. "I wanted to grab a rifle and start firing," Lubinsky said.

When he began to speak of the tunnels, of the blows, of the starvation, of the willpower required to resist death when death is the only escape you are offered, Lubinsky was met by the blank, disbelieving gazes of well-meaning people who knew war, but not the other war that was his; people inclined to nod with sympathy at his tales but think to themselves that so much hardship may induce distortions, delusions, and even delirium.

For all the American survivors of Berga, the journey home to loved ones would now take only days or weeks. But the journey back to the truth of what they lived through in German hands would take decades.

CHAPTER NINE

Orders from Nowhere

B ERGA CONFORMED TO no pattern. The Nazi concentration camps in Europe were for Europeans, not Americans, for European Jews, not American Jews. The leap of credence required to accept the camp's existence and the systematic killing there was large. In many ways, over many years, and for many reasons, that leap was never made. Berga was liberated by Americans, but its memory was held captive.

The facts, however, were soon known. Herschel Auerbach was a member of War Crimes Investigating Team 6822, the first such American unit to comb Germany after the war ended. The team reached Berga on May 30, 1945. Terrible discoveries of Nazi slaughter and abuse had been a daily occurrence. But, as Auerbach observed, it was one thing to uncover the torture of European civilians or an individual American airman, another to find that several hundred captured GIs had been held, starved, and killed in a slave-labor camp identical to the worst centers in Germany for the enactment of Hitler's evil.

"When we got to Berga and it was American soldiers, it became personal," Auerbach said. "What we couldn't understand is American GIs being starved to death, being tortured, being beaten to death simply because they were American GIs. That we couldn't take."

But such outrage stopped at the local level. It never reached the highest echelons of the American military. Attempts to bring those responsible to justice, or even to find out what exactly had happened to loved ones, were continuously frustrated. Bureaucracy and postwar politics belittled and obfuscated the barbarism.

The Gorinac family had been informed of their son Edward's death on April 24, 1945. Six months later, on October 12, Gorinac's brother, Joseph, wrote to the adjutant general of the United States Army with a request for information. He asked to be told where the camp of "Berger Elester" was located and "what disposition of his body was made by the Germans."

By now, from the diary they had received in July 1945, two months after the end of the war in Europe, the family knew of Gorinac's suffering at Berga. The letter concluded: "Even if he is dead, knowing it for a certainty and where he is buried would be some measure of comfort and relief."

But the reply from Major General Edward F. Witsell, the acting adjutant general, was scarcely comforting. In a letter dated October 24, 1945, he wrote: "With reference to your desire to ascertain the location of Berger Elster, it has been learned that there was no German prisoner of war camp by that name. There is, however, a city of Berga which is located on the Elester [sic] River, near Plauen, Germany, South of Gera. Our soldiers who were in Stalag 9B were sent to Berga on a work detail and from the information contained in Private Gorinac's diary, it appears that he was among these prisoners of war."

The letter makes the American government's position at this time clear: *There was no Berga camp, merely a city of that name.* What occurred in that town was a "work detail," where some American prisoners of war had been sent. This despite the fact that Gorinac, who after all was there, had been explicit in his diary, a copy of which is in the files of the Department of the Army: he was at a "Slave Camp" in Berga.

More than two years later, in a letter dated March 11, 1948, Pauline Gorinac McClelland, a sister of the dead soldier, tried again. Her tone was dignified but her exasperation clear: "At this time when other families who have lost sons and brothers overseas and who are having their bodies sent home, we do not feel we are asking too much to have just the information as to the name of the camp, the location of the camp and whether or not my brother was buried or cremated, and if there is a grave. We want to know where his grave is!"

She noted that, from the diary, it was evident that Gorinac was in Stalag IX-B, at Bad Orb, before being transferred to "another camp," where he worked in a "stone mine." Why, she demanded, are there not more details on Gorinac's death? She concluded: "I am asking this information for the sake of my mother who is still alive and who has been brooding over the death of my brother. She is still strong in her belief that he will return as the government has not notified any-one where the body is."

Witsell again replied, in a letter dated April 7, 1948, but could only express the Department of the Army's regret that nothing fur-ther was known about the circumstances of Gorinac's death. In pro forma tones, he wrote: "It is, unfortunately, one of the tragedies of war that some of our men were called upon to make the supreme sac-rifice and their families are denied the comfort that may be derived from a complete report of the circumstances attending the death of their loved ones."

"Tragedy" is a word that may serve as a gloss suggesting some-thing inescapable and unfathomable. But the tragedy of Gorinac's demise was, in fact, no eternal feature of war, as Witsell suggested. His killing was a war crime. It was planned and perpetrated by indi-vidual Germans. The United States War Crimes Branch was aware, at least by the summer of 1945, that a group of American prisoners—a significant proportion of them Jews—had been separated from others at Stalag IX-B and sent by the Germans to work mining tun-nels at Berga. Gorinac died because he was in this group and so found himself working alongside European Jews rounded up as part of the Final Solution.

But Berga quickly fell into the Russian zone after the Allied vic-tory. A hot war became a cold one; political imperatives changed. West Germany was now an ally, East Germany in the enemy camp. As the Identification Branch of the U.S. Army's Memorial Division noted in a communication about Gorinac, dated January 31, 1950, further field investigation was needed in the Russian zone of Ger-many, but the political situation made it "impracticable to conduct the necessary field investigation at this time."

One year later, an American investigation at the Hildburghausen cemetery in East Germany at last resulted in Gorinac's remains being identified. Almost seven years after her son's death, the army informed Anna Gorinac, the soldier's mother, of the successful recov-ery of his remains.

The letter, dated February 19, 1952, expressed appreciation for her patience. "The remains," it noted, "have been casketed and are now being held in an overseas mortuary pending disposition instructions from the next of kin." Edward Gorinac was buried soon afterward in plot C, row 17, grave 11 at the United States Military Cemetery at Neuville-en-Condroz, Belgium. His remains had been found, but the delay and confusion attending the investigation reflected the absence of any urgency in the quest to understand his death or to deliver justice.

Sanford Lubinsky was transferred from Cham to a hospital in Paris, and from there to Crile General Hospital in the Cleveland area. He had been spurred to survive by hatred of the idea of burial in German soil. Thoughts of his wife, Clara, and infant son, Terry, had also sustained him in the darkest hours of Berga and the death march. But his homecoming was bleak.

Terry, aged three, would come to the hospital and push his frail father around in a wheelchair. Lubinsky could scarcely move an eyelid, so weakened was he. He wanted to communicate what he had suffered, make the extent of it clear, put the doctors and military questioners in those tunnels of hell, but lucidity eluded him. It was not just half his body weight that had gone, it was a section of his soul, but he did not know how to say that.

Ohio, that summer of 1945, was as green and placid and unassailable in its American convictions as ever. The boys were home, or on their way, and the war was won. In the orchards, apples ripened. Who was he to cut them open and reveal a tangle of writhing worms? Yet this was the message he carried, of the twisted abomination lurking beneath the surface of things, of the serpent housed in the human heart, and it was not easy to find a listener. Where he had been was too far away, too improbable in its monstrousness, and he had been there with a bunch of other privates, in a small German town on a river that did not figure on Allied wartime maps, a place now being gathered into the Soviet empire.

The Veterans Administration was incredulous. "They would not believe me at the VA in Cleveland," Lubinsky said. "That I had been in a Nazi concentration camp. That I had been in the tunnels. I was not able to talk right. I could not talk right, I was too confused, and I should not have been questioned at that time and in that condition." Like other survivors, Lubinsky was unable to secure compensation for the abuse he had suffered at Berga. His request for 100 percent disability payments was rejected.

Clara believed him from the outset. She knew his story was true. But Lubinsky's aging father and other relatives in Lima wondered how it could be that the Red Cross had told them he was a prisoner of war, being treated like other prisoners of war, when in fact he was a slave laborer in a concentration camp. They found the returning soldier incoherent. It is hard to make sense when you are full of hate. Like jealousy, the hatred consumes you. There is not much room left for coherence. Lubinsky's hatred jabbed at him, a sudden shadow like that cast by a descending aircraft on a sunlit highway.

Slowly, Lubinsky's strength returned. He was able to take Terry in his arms. The warmth of the boy seemed to signal hope. It was time to return home and begin again. America would gather them into its generous embrace. But, said Lubinsky, "even after I got back to our place, I used to carry bread in my pockets, and if I heard a noise outside the house, I would go out with a butcher's knife ready to use it. If I could have got one of those SS guys, *bang!* Yes I would. And I would have been laughing."

Auerbach's War Crimes Investigating Team 6822 was headed by Major Fulton C. Vowell, a World War I veteran. Its task was to find physical evidence of German crimes and, where possible, capture the perpetrators. In Berga, neither of these tasks proved particularly arduous.

Just seven weeks after the departure of the American prisoners, the investigators saw the bunks and straw mattresses where the GIs had fitfully slept, the tunnels where the GIs had slaved, and the cemetery to which servitude at Berga had delivered twenty-two American corpses, or about one every two days. The etiolated bodies were exhumed—eloquent of malnutrition, sickness, abuse, and suffering—and later many more bodies of GIs were found scattered on the route of the death march southward as the investigators retraced it. Vowell could scarcely contain his fury at the wanton killing.

The placidity of the vanquished Germans and their turncoat hypocrisy appalled Auerbach. The horror and homeliness of little Berga seemed impossible to reconcile. A picture of Nazi crimes against the Jews and others, now clearly delineated, was at that time a shifting and often blurry image. Auerbach was unaware of the nature of the extermination camps farther east, and the fact that millions of Jews had died in them. He knew Jews had been driven out of Germany, some into camps, but he did not know of their systematic annihilation. From evidence already gathered through questioning of American survivors of Berga, he and Vowell also knew that a significant proportion of the GIs imprisoned at Berga were Jews. But the connections that would bring together the pieces of this picture had not yet been made, and the Germans' apparent ability to plead ignorance and innocence with equanimity clouded things further.

"Every German blamed everybody including his mother, his grandmother, his grandfather, his brother, his sister, anyone except himself," Auerbach recalled. "Nobody assumed any responsibility for anything. If you interrogated somebody, the attitude was: I didn't do anything, but that fellow over there, he did it, she did it, someone else did it." So can millions die and a nation try to claim it did not know.

When the American bodies were discovered in the Berga cemetery, Vowell determined that there should be a memorial service. The whole town turned out in a display of pious German remorse. A large cross was built and even a large Star of David; both were placed at the cemetery. The mayor appeared; young ladies laid wreaths; everyone expressed regret over the fog of war that had allowed such terrible deeds to occur at such proximity and yet with so little outside knowledge. The Germans, terrified of the Russians, were delighted to be able to place themselves in American hands; they took every opportunity to demonstrate that they wanted to cooperate to clear up any misunderstanding. In many ways, the whole performance was pitiful.

Erwin Metz, dressed in civilian clothes, was at his home in Erkmannsdorf, about fifteen miles from Berga, when Vowell and his team arrested the tormentor of the Americans on June 19, 1945. Vowell, who had already learned much of Metz's cruelty, interrogated him the same day. Metz portrayed himself as an innocent pawn, a man obliged to obey orders who had done what he could to help the Americans.

"What were your duties at Berga?" Vowell asked.

"I was in charge of the guards for the American prisoner-of-war camp there," Metz responded.

"Were you in charge of working the prisoners in the tunnels?"

"No, I had nothing to say about that."

"Were you in charge of feeding the prisoners?"

"No, that was taken care of by others."

"Who had charge of the Red Cross packages?"

"I was in charge of giving out the Red Cross packages and had help from a clerk under me."

"Did you deliver the entire contents of every Red Cross package to the prisoners?"

"Yes."

The lies came tumbling out on each and every point. Vowell now turned to close questioning of Metz about the killing of Morton Goldstein. He established that when Metz set out to pick up Goldstein from the *Bürgermeister,* or mayor, of Wildetaube on the morning of March 19, 1945, he was armed with a pistol and was alone.

"Did you tell the *Bürgermeister* that you were going to take the prisoner back and that it would be his last march, or words to that effect?" Vowell demanded. This was the recollection of the mayor, Zschaeck, who had provided testimony two weeks earlier.

"I did not say that, but I said that prisoners who ran away should be shot on sight and that there was an order to that effect."

Another American officer, Captain Robert G. McCarty, took up the questioning. He established that Metz had been enraged to find Goldstein warming himself by the fire and had made him stand at attention facing the wall. McCarty demanded: "Do you deny that you said to him, 'What, are you making yourself comfortable here? I'll fix you'?"

"I do recall that I said something about being comfortable," Metz replied.

"Did you not also say 'I'll fix you,' or words to that effect?"

"No."

"What time did you depart from the *Bürgermeister*'s house to return the prisoner to camp?"

"About ten or ten-thirty that morning."

"What time did the shooting take place?"

Metz replied: "About three quarters of an hour later."

Under further questioning, Metz said the killing had taken place at a secluded spot a little over a half mile from Berga, when he stopped to talk to "a civilian." He could not remember the name of the civilian, nor where he was going, but did recall *turning his back* on Goldstein while he talked to the man.

"What was the prisoner doing during this conversation?" McCarty asked.

"When I met the man I stopped for a few seconds and turned. The prisoner kept on walking, and when I yelled, 'Halt,' the prisoner jumped into the woods on the right side of the road."

Metz claimed that Goldstein was thirty meters from him, that he told him to slow down, that he then shouted "Halt" three times, before firing two shots that hit Goldstein in the back and in the head. Contradicting himself in his testimony, he said that Goldstein "jumped" into the woods at the first cry of "Halt," but also that he "laid about thirty meters from the road" when killed. Anny Neusser, the housekeeper who found Goldstein, said his corpse was adjacent to the road.

Asked if the civilian had seen the shooting, Metz said he must have heard it. Yet he also said they were talking immediately before the killing. Metz added that, after the shooting, "the civilian walked away" and said nothing.

Vowell took up the questioning. "How much experience have you had with weapons?"

Metz said he was not experienced and never had a weapon until he was drafted into the Wehrmacht in January 1944.

"How much experience have you had with shooting pistols?"

"I had no pistol training at all."

"How many times did you shoot the pistol you carried?"

"I had never fired it before. That was the first time I fired it."

And yet, Vowell inquired, he had been able to hit a running man in the head at a range of at least thirty meters as he plunged into the woods?

"Yes," Metz declared. "I am a good shot at rifle shooting on the range."

Metz argued that, in killing Goldstein, he was merely obeying his superiors' orders to shoot escaping prisoners. His assiduous devotion to orders was evident throughout his interrogation, not least when attention turned to the death march. Dozens of GIs died, he conceded. Asked why, he said they were weak. Vowell demanded to know if Metz had denied water to men with diarrhea. Metz said he had because that was the order from "the doctor."

"Did you ever get medical care for them?" Vowell asked.

"No," Metz said.

"Did you ever take any of them to the hospital?"

"No."

"Why?"

"Because there was no hospital."

"Were you in Greiz?"

"Yes."

"Isn't there a hospital at Greiz?"

"Yes, there is."

"Why didn't you take them to the hospital?"

"Because I did not have an order."

"You knew they were dying, didn't you?"

"No."

"They did die, didn't they?"

"Yes."

"Do you have to have an order to put a dying man in hospital?"

"Yes."

When Gerald Daub returned to New York in the summer of 1945, he refused to talk about his experiences at Berga except with his old Brooklyn school friend Bob Rudnick, who had shared a bed with him there. Daub told himself there was no time to dwell on what had happened when he was in Nazi hands because, as he put it, he had "to catch up on what my life ought to be." The GI Bill of Rights, signed by Franklin Roosevelt in 1944, offered returning servicemen wonderful opportunities to get a college education. Daub attended the Pratt Institute and studied to be an architect. He pressed forward, the better to repress the past.

What would he tell his parents and his sister? To have been a prisoner of war was no badge of honor; it was shameful. "It wasn't a good experience, and I didn't want to reexperience it," Daub said. He had stepped over dead bodies to collect his ration of bread, he had eaten from a pig trough, he had returned but many had not. To make sense of all this was not easy, especially because the government and the military appeared to have no particular interest in his experience. He had, it seemed, lived some terrible aberration—something like a case of mistaken identity—and it was best forgotten.

But the experience was real. Tangible proof of that lay in the gold high school graduation ring he had removed from the finger of Jack Bornkind just before his death on the day they were liberated. Daub recalled trying in vain to feed him the goose's egg, a golden gift that came too late. He shuddered. He would fondle the ring in his pocket, a kind of talisman. He had to return the ring to Bornkind's family. In a Detroit phone book, he found the address. Bornkind, he learned, had a sister who lived in New York. Having described how he came to have the ring, he gave it to her. But he never heard back from the Bornkind family. Perhaps they were too grief-stricken. Perhaps they, too, had opted for silence.

Sometimes it was not easy to remain silent. Daub's uncle had a neighbor who was the father of Stanley Rubenstein, one of the men who died. The father desperately wanted to talk to Daub, to know every detail of what had happened. It seemed to Daub that this was a needlessly painful exercise. How could such talk assuage the loss?

He tried to avoid Rubenstein, twice slipping out of his uncle's apartment rather than confronting the bereaved parent. But on a third occasion, he agreed to talk. Why, the father wanted know, had Daub survived and his son not? "He was bigger than you, stronger than you, he should have made it," Rubenstein exclaimed. Daub suggested that perhaps being smaller was an advantage because you needed less food. What he knew but did not say was that survival was above all a question of the mind. When the will broke, the body followed soon enough.

Another Jewish survivor of Berga, Norman Fellman of the 70th Infantry Division, knew this mental chemistry of death intimately. He had been with Bob Gray the day he died on the death march, at Fuchsmühl. "He was talking about dying, he wanted to give up," Fellman said. "And I talked to Gray practically all night, telling him the different reasons why he should hold out. He had brothers. I asked him questions about his family. We talked about his life at home, and he stopped talking and I kept talking and talking. Well, somewhere along that night he died in my lap. The guys who were convinced they were going to die, died. They didn't disappoint themselves."

Soon after the war, Fellman was in the New York area and was contacted by Gray's father, Edwin A. Gray, who lived in New Jersey. He agreed to go over to the Grays' house. It was a painful experience. "They questioned me about details," Fellman recalled. "They got down to each minor detail. Had to know every little detail, couldn't leave it alone. I had to leave. I got up and walked out."

Details: Fellman joined the army weighing 178 pounds and came out of Berga weighing 86. Gray must have weighed less when he died. Fellman could also give lurid details on the German blows in the tunnels. Or the way men were beaten when one of the little carts full of stone toppled over into the river. Or soldiers who starved to death because they traded their tiny ration of food for cigarettes. Or

Gray, on that cart with all the sick and dying men, his head in Fellman's lap, giving up and unable to hear Fellman's entreaties. How do you explain that a young man abandons hope? How do you explain that a starving man would rather smoke than eat?

It was agony to return there in the mind, impossible, it seemed, to explain how death could so quickly overtake so many young Americans. Besides, Fellman had received official encouragement to keep quiet.

On April 25, 1945, almost immediately after his liberation, he was made to sign a "Security Certificate for Ex-Prisoners of War." This stated, in its first clause: "Some activities of American prisoners of war within German prison camps must remain secret not only for the duration of the war against the present enemies of the United States but in peacetime as well."

This requirement was justified by the need to protect the interests of American prisoners still in Japanese camps and the interests of prisoners in the event of future wars. But for Fellman, this oath he signed meant, in effect, that his country did not want him to talk about Berga. He didn't really understand this, but he set the question aside. For a time after the war he focused on his job in his father's footwear business. Then came marriage and a family. Sometimes, he found himself exploding into an unreasonable rage provoked by some little thing one of his three daughters had done. He was reluctant to look for the roots of that rage.

Later, the link between the anger and Berga became clear, the cost of all he had repressed. He would look again at the odd oath he had signed. The best explanation he could find was that his story and that of other Berga captives would be an acute embarrassment to West Germany, a postwar ally of central importance to the United States. "Keeping us quiet was expedient given the desire not to embarrass the German government," Fellman said. "It was the same reason avowed Nazis who were also skilled scientists were brought over here: we needed them. So somewhere in the American government, they decided to deny our existence."

On July 13, 1945, Vowell submitted his report on war crimes at Berga to the Seventh Army command. It was a detailed account, based on close inspection of conditions at the camp and on the questioning of Metz, German guards, witnesses in the town, and various German officials who had encountered the Americans during the death march.

At times, with Metz, the work had been exasperating. "When Metz was interrogated, he stood at attention," Auerbach recalled. "And he barked at you: *Jawohl, Jawohl, Jawohl.* He was very arrogant. And Vowell got very angry because Metz refused to admit what he had done to the Americans. So Vowell threw him down the stairs and cracked his head open. Fortunately we had a doctor, Bolker, who took care of him." More than seventy Americans had died. Vowell was beside himself.

Vowell, Auerbach said, ordered a couple of his men to make the German run around on all fours and bark. They did. If he barked, they figured, let him crawl.

Metz kept repeating that he only obeyed orders and did what he could, whenever he could, to improve conditions for the Americans. But every other witness, including the German guards who worked with Metz, contradicted him. They dwelt on his apparently sadistic pleasure in inflicting pain on the GIs.

In his report, Vowell concluded, "Erwin Metz is guilty of the murder of Goldstein, an American prisoner of war, on March 19, 1945, in violation of Article II, Geneva Prisoner of War Convention." He was also, Vowell said, guilty of "beating American prisoners of war" during the death march, forcing them to march more than twenty kilometers a day, failing to provide sufficient food or adequate clothing to the American prisoners, and illegally obtaining American cigarettes.

Metz and Hack were, in addition, guilty of "permitting American prisoners of war to be utilized for strenuous, unhealthy work" in dusty tunnels. As for Ludwig Merz, Metz's immediate superior, he was guilty of failing to provide sufficient food and forcing the GIs to march distances that, in their diminished state, killed them.

Auerbach's own conclusion amounted to a kind of epiphany. He had gone to Europe knowing of Hitler's persecution of European Jews, but not of the plan to exterminate them. He learned of that as he went through postwar Germany. And in Berga he discovered that, "as far as the Germans were concerned, they did not treat American Jews any differently from European Jews."

The Vowell report was reviewed by Lieutenant Colonel Paul T. Rigby, the chief of the War Crimes Branch, and he pronounced it "as thorough as the circumstances permitted," "complete," and "sound." It was submitted three months before Witsell, the acting adjutant general, told the Gorinac family there was no camp at Berga.

As this suggests, investigation of Berga and prosecution of the crimes there slowed and slid into vagueness once the Vowell report was submitted. Of course, the Allies were initially focused on the major Nazi war criminals whose trial at Nuremberg began in November 1945. The whole issue of the extent to which Nazis should be tried and purged in postwar Germany was a controversial one. Metz and Merz were not Göring or Speer. Still, they had driven dozens of Americans to their deaths by sucking them into the apparatus of the Holocaust. The case was unique; it appeared to demand vigorous attention. But it languished.

By early 1946, Charles Vogel, a New York lawyer, had become frustrated by the inquiry. He was the uncle of Bernard Vogel, who had died on the death march. Vogel embarked on an energetic attempt to gather testimony from Berga survivors and provide it to the judge advocate general in Washington.

His efforts were at first viewed as helpful by the War Crimes Branch, but friction soon developed as Vogel demanded swift justice. The responses to Vogel from surviving GIs were full and sympathetic. Dozens of them offered to testify against Metz and Merz at trial if so requested. Such a request was never made.

In a letter to the judge advocate general dated March 25, 1946, Vogel made clear that he was already in touch with many Berga survivors. "When one has become conversant with the facts," he noted, "it should not take much time to interview each survivor, obtain his story, find out what details may be missing from what is already known, and put it in an affidavit for the use of your office."

A reply from the Civil Affairs Division of the War Department, dated May 8, 1946, thanked Vogel for the letter and said, "This office is endeavoring to identify all the individuals who were responsible for the crimes against the 350 American prisoners of war who worked at the Berga mine. Any information which helps in their identification will be most valuable."

Encouraged, Vogel set to work. One of the letters to him over the summer of 1946 came from Winfield Rosenberg of the 106th Division. He wrote: "I saw your nephew die. There was not much to him, as we did not get much to eat and he got less than everybody else.

Your nephew tried to escape and got recaptured. They made him work after we got done working in the mines. He had extra details and less food than we got, which wasn't much."

Naturally, such information spurred Vogel to press harder. But military investigators were becoming concerned. On May 17, 1946, Lieutenant Joseph S. Smith of the Security and Intelligence Division was dispatched to Vogel's New York office to examine the lawyer's papers. Vogel first wanted assurance that the statements would be used to bolster the investigation and would not disappear into the Washington bureaucracy. By late May, the military was getting impatient. A letter to Vogel from David Marcus, the chief of the War Crimes Branch, said that his "transferring all of the papers and information" to the government at once would be the wisest course.

A month later, tensions had risen further. Another intelligence agent visited Vogel's office and concluded, in a memorandum dated June 25, 1946, that "Vogel appears to have some idiotic fixation on the question of releasing the original records and leads to some ninety plus witnesses whom he has located regarding the Berga POW Camp. He denied my request to authorize his secretary to turn over the records to me."

After receiving written assurances from Marcus, Vogel did send the testimony he had gathered to the War Crimes Branch in early July, requesting at the same time "a copy of topographical maps of small scale showing the sectors from Berga to Cham." On July 3, 1946, Marcus thanked Vogel but said he was unable to obtain any such maps. Just how a serious investigation of the crimes at Berga and later on the death march could be conducted without a detailed map of the area is unclear.

What is apparent is that, by July 1946, the military had in its possession not only the detailed report from Berga compiled by Vowell but also testimony from at least seventy survivors that had been gathered by Vogel. Such testimony supplemented the information available from the military's own questioning of Berga survivors soon after their liberation. The case could scarcely have been more complete.

But the outrage that spurred Vogel and Vowell and inhabited the relatives of the dead appears never to have infected the military's higher investigating authorities.

Among the letters sent to Vogel during the summer of 1946 was one from Laura M. Ryan, the mother of William Kelly, another GI who did not survive Berga. She described how she had heard from others imprisoned there how Kelly was "continually beaten and also starved." The Germans responsible, she said, "should be starved and beaten in the same way until they are dead."

For several days after his liberation, William Shapiro felt he was in a "twilight zone before death." A soldier debriefed him on his experiences at Berga, but he was too weak to be of much use to the man. In early May he was flown to England and taken to a hospital near Bedford. There he learned of the Nazi surrender on May 8, 1945, and, two days later, received a Purple Heart in recognition of his service. The spring weather was mild, with big, bright cumulus clouds racing across the English sky; Shapiro took long walks. The treatment was good, and he began to regain some of the sixty pounds lost at Berga. On June 15 he was flown to the United States, landing at Mitchell Field, New York.

His brother, Dave, lived nearby, in Forest Hills. But Shapiro had forgotten that he needed to look in the Queens section of the phone book for the number. Only with the help of a Red Cross worker was he able to find it and speak to his sister-in-law. He felt like a child obliged to learn to walk anew.

Soon his parents, accompanied by his girlfriend, Betty, were at the front gate; Shapiro staggered toward them. He was thin but no longer skeletal, and the joy of the reunion was overwhelming. Driving to the Bronx, his hand in Betty's, the nineteen-year-old medic felt himself suspended in a strange limbo. Happiness and warmth enveloped him, but the gallows of the concentration camp and the ordinary bustle of busy Pelham Parkway seemed impossible to place together on a single planet, let alone reconcile in a single mind.

It was a happy summer. America felt bountiful. After a couple of days in Halloran Hospital, Shapiro was granted a seventy-five-day furlough. His courtship with Betty moved into high gear. There were parties and outings and, in August, the wild celebrations of the Japanese surrender. Shortly before that, Shapiro had bought Betty an engagement ring. Their thoughts were of the future: medical studies, a home, eventually a family. The war was the past. On October 2 Shapiro was discharged from the army after two years. He sent a cable to his parents: CALL ME MISTER.

Shapiro was a serious young man. He entered college in 1946 and then, in 1948, began the medical studies that would turn that "Mister" to "Doctor" and lead to a successful career as an obstetrician.

He was cautious with money, prudent in his practice, ever vigilant. Berga sat somewhere in the back of his mind, but even as he learned more about the Holocaust and the Nazi crimes, Shapiro erected a wall of defense that prevented him from linking his own experience fully to the mass murder of European Jews. One vision in particular haunted him: that of the bodies of the European concentration-camp prisoners scattered on the road south of Berga with bullets through their heads. When he saw insects flattened on a windshield, he would think of them. Sometimes a headache would follow. It would grow into a migraine. His skull throbbed. He wondered what went on in the German mind. The killers of those prisoners on the road no doubt sat now with their families in quaint homes enjoying hearty meals and embracing their children. Where inside them had they put the crime? Had they simply rolled it up like a rug and tucked it somewhere? Did they feel remorse or seek forgiveness? These questions did not haunt him every day, but sometimes they came at him like a sudden squall. Then he felt lost.

The nightmares did not begin immediately, but they proved inescapable and repetitive. Always he was running from the Germans, and always they caught him. He felt small. Harsh cries assailed him. Nobody could hear his own. His assailants had clubs. He told Betty what he could, but could not go on repeating the same story.

As time went on, Shapiro would get dressed quietly and leave after one of the nightmares. Betty would always tell their three children he had a patient in labor. Shapiro would call the answering service at his practice and say he would be taking calls, even when it was his partner's turn to be on duty. The partner would come in at six-thirty in the morning and ask what the hell Shapiro was doing there. Shapiro would say he couldn't sleep, but he never said why.

Shapiro didn't want sympathy; he was not that kind of man. A lot of emotion tended to trouble him. Occasionally, someone would ask him about the war and he would try to begin an account of his experiences. The words seemed inadequate, unrelated to the vivid visions in his head, and as he spoke all he could hear was something faint and feeble, like the last of an echo swallowed in a wooded valley. It was not surprising that the attention of those listening seemed to wander.

Before the war, his immigrant parents had done all they could to make a break between life in Europe, which had been threatening, and the possibilities of America, which were great. The menace of his parents' memories had become real to Shapiro in Europe; they had nearly taken his life. Back in the womb of America, he reverted to the model in which he had been raised. What went on over there was best forgotten. He took no interest in the fate of Metz.

The trial of Metz and Merz, who had been captured near the Czech border on April 23, 1945, opened on September 3, 1946, in Dachau. The former Nazi concentration camp had been converted into War Crimes Enclosure Number 1, for the housing of German prisoners awaiting trial. In the grounds stood the notorious "Hanging Tree," not a gallows but a large tree with a horizontal branch from which, as a punishment, prisoners of the Nazis had been suspended by their arms, with their feet dangling just above the ground. The blackened chimney stack of the crematorium was a reminder of how such treatment of prisoners often ended.

In the camp itself, a host of ghoulish experiments had been carried out on inmates, including immersion in ice water for hours (to test the effects of freezing), confinement in a low-pressure chamber (to mimic the effect of high-altitude flying and determine the limits of human endurance), and the injection of extracts from mosquitoes to induce malaria (so that the efficacy of various drugs could be reviewed). In short, it was not an inappropriate place for the Berga trial.

Unlike conventional judicial procedures, the Dachau trials were conducted as military tribunals, with American military officers acting for the prosecution and the defense. The onus was on the accused to prove innocence, not on the prosecution to establish guilt. The first trial held there, between November 15 and December 13, 1945, was that of the commandant of Dachau, Martin Weiss, and thirty-nine others. All were found guilty, and thirty-six of them sentenced to death. Five of the death sentences were later commuted to prison terms. Just prior to the trial of Metz and Merz, seventy-three SS soldiers had stood trial for the Malmédy massacre, the shooting of more than eighty defenseless American prisoners of war in early 1945 that had alarmed young GIs such as Daub who were captured at about the same time and ended up in Berga. Forty-two of the defendants were sentenced to hang, but the sentences were later commuted and by 1956 all the accused were free.

Metz faced three charges: the deliberate and wrongful killing of an unknown prisoner; the beating and assaulting of unarmed prisoners of war; and the deliberate mistreatment of American prisoners by "failing to provide adequate food, adequate medical care and adequate clothing; said failure resulting in the death of several unknown members of the United States Army." Merz, fifty-nine, a teacher by profession, was accused only of the last charge. The failure to mention Goldstein by name in the first charge and the reference in the third to nameless American victims, although many of the names of the dead were known, gives some sense of the holes in the prosecution's case.

Despite the work of Vogel, the affidavits of only twelve former prisoners were used by the prosecution. None of the Berga survivors was present at the trial. The evidence presented therefore lacked the immediacy of direct testimony.

Throughout the trial, Metz strove to portray himself as a victim of circumstance, a benign man thrown into a job he did not want, trying wherever he could to ease the situation of the GIs, eating as badly or less well than they did, maneuvering to get them relieved of the work in the tunnels, searching far and wide but in vain for doctors during the death march, succumbing at the last to depression because he had not been able to do more for his American "comrades." It was quite a performance. "I cared for the prisoners of war in a fatherly manner and did everything in my power to lighten the work and living conditions of the prisoners," he declared, adding that his conscience was clear.

The prosecution hammered at Metz to get him to concede that his cruelty had led to the death of dozens of Americans under his charge over a period of a few weeks. But Metz responded like an automaton. Any link between his own behavior and the daily demise of young GIs was rebuffed.

"Look, Metz, can't you look at a man and tell when he is starving to death?" the prosecuting attorney demanded a few weeks into the trial.

"Nobody starved to death," Metz said.

"Was anyone worked to death?"

"No, nobody was worked to death, either."

"Was anyone beaten to death?"

"No."

"How do you say these men died?"

"It was the usual procedure," Metz said. "If somebody was ill his condition deteriorated and as a final result the man died."

The killing, in other words, was a normal event, as ineluctable as the sunset, the result of a series of circumstances with an inexorable logic that no lowly soldier like Metz could influence or modify one way or another. In this attitude, admitting of no personal responsibility, and of no imperative of humanity or sentiment that might outweigh an order, the colossal German abdication that made the Final Solution possible was evident.

The questioning continued: "Metz, you and Captain Merz and everybody else knew that anybody that worked in that tunnel was going to die, didn't you?"

"You couldn't say exactly that they were going to die because of that work; that depends on the state of health and the physical condition of every individual."

"Every man that worked in that tunnel developed a cough, didn't he?"

"Well, you couldn't say exactly that all of them developed a cough but the majority of them had a cough due to the dust in the tunnels."

The responses are meticulous. Nothing can be said "exactly" in Metz's world because it is an extremely slippery place. His replies suggest a punctilious mind, one that dissects but will not make connections, perhaps because the whole picture is so damning. Details deflect emotion; Metz was manic about detail. Confronted by the accusation that he would inspect sick prisoners' tongues and then send the men out to work, he conceded that once he did see the tongue of a GI, but not to examine it, merely to "take a look," because he was "interested in the coat of the tongue."

On every incident of cruelty cited by the prisoners, Metz offered a denial. No, he did not inspect Young's tongue. No, he did not throw cold water on Young or anybody else. No, he did not drive sick men back into the tunnels. No, he did not beat men during the march. In short, Metz argued, "I never mistreated anybody."

Metz said he acted throughout his time at Berga "in accordance with the instructions of Captain Merz, the service instructions of Captain Merz." But Merz insisted that he, too, was not in a position to change anything.

"Why didn't you order these men out of the tunnels?" Merz was asked. "You were the commanding officer of the guards, weren't you?"

"I cannot order them out," Merz said. "That can only be done by the employer in connection with the employment office, or whatever way there is, I don't know."

"Your company guards took these men to the tunnels each day, did they not?"

"Yes."

"And you could have ordered them not to take them to work, couldn't you?"

"That would have been sabotage of the work and I could have been immediately charged with committing sabotage."

The ultimate employer at Berga, of course, was the SS, whose project it was to build an underground fuel factory. Beyond Hack were his superiors, all the way up to Himmler. The passing of responsibility could go on almost without end.

Merz said, under questioning, that he protested to Hack about the work conditions of the GIs, but "Hack always treated me somewhat arrogantly and did not want interference in this matter." Still, Merz claimed that the Americans were relieved of tunnel duty during their last days at Berga as a result of his efforts.

Prosecution lawyers at the trial largely ignored the question of how the Nazi selection of the 350 prisoners for Berga was made, or how the fact that the first 80 GIs had been chosen for slave labor because they were Jewish might have affected the general treatment of the men.

Yet Allied investigations at Bad Orb had already made clear a year earlier that a Nazi selection involving a quest to find Jews took place. For example, on July 25, 1945, the War Crimes Branch had questioned Sergeant Howard P. Gossett "in the matter of segregation and unknown disposition of eighty American Jewish prisoners of war at Stalag IX-B." Gossett said that eighty American Jewish prisoners had indeed been separated and later removed from the camp. The same month, Private Wesley Clayton Schmoke, another Bad Orb prisoner, said, "When the American prisoners arrived at Bad Orb, the Jewish prisoners were separated from the Gentile prisoners and kept in a separate barracks." They were later taken away, he said, to an unknown destination rumored to be a salt mine.

At the trial, the only exchange on this question of the Jewish selection for Berga came on October 10, 1946, when a prosecution lawyer asked Metz if there "was segregation of the Americans according to race."

"I heard that was done by Kunz," Metz replied, referring to his predecessor.

"What was done by Kunz? Please explain."

"Kunz allegedly billeted the Jewish prisoners of war, because they so desired it, in separate rooms."

Metz, having made the outrageous suggestion that American Jews were housed together because they wanted to be, insisted that he had allowed the Americans to move into whatever barracks they wished. But he did concede that after Kasten's escape, the selection of Stanley Cohen as the next American man of confidence had been rejected by the German authorities because Cohen was a Jew. Cohen had told investigators on June 1, 1945, more than a year before the trial, that at Berga "the Jewish boys were segregated into one barracks. There were eighty Jewish boys who started out from Bad Orb, Germany."

The omission of this issue at the trial appears grave. It would have brought into focus the Nazi view of the Americans, which was that they should be annihilated through work, just like the European Jewish prisoners at Berga who worked every day in the same tunnels. By establishing that the selection was driven in the first instance by the desire to identify American Jews, the prosecution could have drawn a direct connection between the GIs taken to Berga and the mass murder of the Holocaust. The killing would then have ceased to be seen as the regrettable result of omissions or, at worst, isolated acts of cruelty by Metz and Merz. It would have become clear that the deaths were the premeditated result of a systematic plan, as inevitable in their way as the deaths of Hauer's family at Auschwitz.

When questioning turned to the death march, both Metz and Merz portrayed themselves as the men trying hardest to save the Americans, despite the fact that close to fifty died in the space of fifteen days. Merz said he protested to his superiors when told that the sick had to be taken on the march; he even suggested he was so disturbed by the order that he wanted to disobey it and deposit all the sick Americans at once in the nearest hospital. But he did not explain why he had failed to do so at the first stop in Greiz.

During an interrogation by an American officer prior to the trial, Merz had been asked who was responsible for the deaths on the march. "I think the order for the march was responsible," Merz said. Disembodied and sacred, the order was the refuge of every last German who had sold his soul.

Like Metz, Merz danced to every order, real or imagined. What would he do if there was a man with a severe case of pneumonia being herded into the tunnels to work? "I could request Hack to release that man," Merz said. But Hack would not do that because of the orders he was under. In the end, it seemed, only Hitler bore any responsibility because it was from him ultimately that every Nazi order stemmed.

Merz was also asked during the interrogation how many Americans had died on the death march, which he accompanied until its last day, April 23, 1945. "Ten or eleven," he replied, about one fifth of the actual number. In his way, Merz was as much in denial as Metz. He said that he did not know of "a single case" where the Geneva Conventions had been infringed during the Americans' time at Berga.

"Were the Americans fed sufficiently?" an American officer demanded.

"Yes," Merz said, "I looked after that thoroughly."

He added that he did not understand why he had to drive the Americans away from the lines but had been given a clue by a superior, who said to him, "Every American soldier is something precious in the hands of the Führer when it comes to peace negotiations with America." It seems possible that Hitler's fantasies of a negotiated settlement persisted to the last days in the bunker.

Metz also asked the court to believe that he wanted, in his heart, to help the dying GIs. "When we stopped in certain towns, I myself would look for a doctor as far as that was possible for me, but otherwise that is up to the company, it is up to the company to provide a doctor."

He had never wanted to take the sick in the first place: "Captain Merz repeated the order to me but I made an objection as to the transportation of the sick and I told him that I could not take the sick people along and then he again explained the order to me."

Asked if it was true that GIs died all along the route taken, Metz replied that this was not the case.

"In what way is it not true?" the prosecutor asked.

"Because nobody died along the route. All the people who died died in their quarters almost exclusively."

Even by Metz's standards, this claim was preposterous.

The trial meandered along for six weeks. At times the arguments of the defense took on an almost grotesque character. Defense lawyers tried, for example, to make much of the fact that only twelve of the Americans had been "sufficiently disturbed about their experiences to dictate to anyone their recollection." This, of course, was not true, although the testimony of only twelve had been presented at trial.

Excluding the dead (wrongly numbered at fifty-nine), the defense argued: "The vote, by count, is approximately 279 to 12 against the thought that what happened at Berga was a crime or even worthy of complaint." The defense lawyer, warming to his theme, continued: "Through their very silence, the overwhelming majority of 279 seems to remark to the 12, 'What the devil are you talking about? We went through all that, too, and we can't understand what the devil you are growling about. Sure it was rough, but that is the way war is.' "

The defense also pointed out that none of the twelve was before the court and so there had been no chance to test anyone's "ability to say with exactness what he is trying to say or if he really has anything worth saying." In fact, of course, such a presence might have brought home the reality of the American suffering and the German crimes that caused it. The failure to call surviving GIs amounts to a staggering omission.

Not to be outdone by his lawyers, Metz presented the shooting of Goldstein as his agonizing obligation, despite the warm feelings he had for the prisoner. Metz wanted the court to believe that, as they walked up the road, surrounded by the beauty of the woods, the two men exchanged intimate confidences only minutes before the shooting. "What we talked about was that he said he would like to be in a place like this rather than in Berga. I said that I myself would wish that for him and his comrades from my heart."

Metz then repeated the story of his three cries of "Halt" before his decision to fire. "As he did not stop then, it was clear to me that it was an escape. For that reason I had to act and use my service weapon and shoot at the prisoner of war." His account gained some support from the testimony of two doctors who had examined the body and said the bullets must have been fired from a distance because they lodged in the corpse, which, Metz conceded, was then left outside at the American barracks for three days.

At the moment he found Goldstein dead, Metz said, he was grief-stricken. "I felt very sorry for him just as if it had been a close friend of mine. I thought of his young years and that he soon could have returned to his homeland."

Joe Littell came home in late June 1945, sailing by Liberty ship from Le Havre to New York. At Fort Dix, New Jersey, he was told that because his weight had dropped to 132 pounds from 180 during his captivity, he would be assigned two months of rest in Asheville, North Carolina. He thought about Berga during that summer, of course, but somehow the fact that it was an exceptional experience did not register on him.

"My family and friends and later my colleagues at college thought that maybe I was overfatigued or hallucinating or had embellished the experience when I talked about Berga," Littell recalled. "My story tended to provoke knowing nods."

When he was drafted, Littell was eighteen. Most of the boys thrown into the infantry from the Army Specialized Training Program were about that age. They were not students of the Geneva Conventions; they had little or no leadership experience and no idea to what extent the experience of Berga was an anomaly. Because nobody in the government or the military encouraged them to believe it was, these young men brought a screen down on the horror.

"We had no idea that this should be anything other than something to forget," Littell said. "Perhaps if it had been a bunch of staff sergeants or first lieutenants in Berga, things would have been different."

As it was, none of the survivors thought about making a fuss. Nobody went to seek out representatives in Congress or the Senate to tell them what had happened. Nobody went to the press with a detailed story. For the government and military, Littell believes, the whole affair was initially an embarrassment. Had it been widely known that 350 Americans were held in a Nazi slave-labor camp, with an attrition rate of more than 20 percent, questions would have been asked—about failures of intelligence and the failure to try to rescue them sooner. "Berga just got tucked away," Littell said. "It was shuffled down to the lower part of the stack, in part because it would have cast an aspersion on some part of the government."

Before his discharge from the army on September 1, 1945, Littell received a Purple Heart. But like many other survivors of Berga, he received no compensation or disability benefits. He threw himself into his work at a publishing company and took no interest in the fate of Metz or Merz. He was afraid of failing. The notion of failure terrified him. All his energy was needed for his career and later his family. His mind was on the next day's meeting. Sometimes he felt tired mentally, but his response was to push himself harder. Even when he went to the Frankfurt Book Fair, a regular occurrence as his career progressed, he never went to Bad Orb, although it was little more than a half-hour drive away.

When he thought of Berga, he sometimes felt guilty that his knowledge of German had kept him out of the tunnels. But another memory outweighed that of Berga. It was of the young German he had shot in the Ardennes before his capture. Littell kept seeing the soldier, no more than sixteen, plunging toward him and then falling into the snow after he pulled the trigger. It was so easy to end a life; it took almost nothing, like shutting a door or flicking a switch. The boy, he felt, had looked at him, with a grimace or, it sometimes seemed to him, a hopeless smile.

Metz made his last appeal to the court on the afternoon of October 15, 1946. He began by asking the tribunal to bear in mind the economic conditions in Germany at the end of the war. He said he felt remorse over the number of dead, but insisted, "In my manner of leading the detail I followed a saying by Beethoven: 'Brother is working for Brother. When he can help he does it gladly.' "

Once again, he tried to explain his actions in killing Goldstein. "Hate is unknown to me and I do not know any hate or enmity in the regrettable death of Goldstein. It was not deliberate or willful on my part. I did like Goldstein very much. I gave him a special position of trust and I had no reason to be angry with him. When I was forced to act it was my soldierly duty and if I had not done it I would have been put before a military court myself."

In conclusion, Metz, the man of duty, the follower to the letter of orders, the archetypal German of the Third Reich, declared: "I have only hatred for war and National Socialism. I hate the war and the consequences of war, the cruelty that derives from war. I ask the Court to consider the facts, to consider my personal limitations as a sergeant, and to consider that I did the best that it was possible for me to do under the circumstances."

Merz then spoke, placing the blame on his unnamed superiors who made it impossible for him to save the Americans. "My hands were bound tightly by existing regulations," he said, "and the chaotic circumstances of the last months of the war. I must state that I had the feeling, and this feeling is becoming greater to me all the time, that my superior authority left me holding the bag."

The court adjourned for two hours. Then the presiding officer, Colonel Raymond Conder, told Metz to stand. "Accused Metz," he declared, "the court in closed session, at least two thirds of the members present at the time the vote was taken concurring in each finding of guilty, sentences you to death by hanging at such time and place as higher authority may direct."

Merz then stood and was also sentenced to death by hanging at a time and a place to be determined by higher authority.

Despite the shortcomings of the prosecution's case, it appeared that two of the Germans responsible for killing at least seventy-three American prisoners of war in the space of nine weeks would receive the severest punishment. But higher American authorities were to decide otherwise.

The thorough elimination of the Nazi creed and its adherents from German life, and the punishment of war criminals, had been embraced by the Allies as a policy at Potsdam in July and August 1945. But as the Western powers became more preoccupied with the developing cold war, and as German lobbies raised growing opposition to the execution of large numbers of Nazis, the commitment to denazification faded. Building a German future became more important, in many instances, than punishing a German past.

Kenneth Royall, the secretary of the army appointed in 1947, made little secret of his belief that the rapid reindustrialization of West Germany, now on the front line of the conflict with the Soviet Union, should be a priority and that denazification should not stand in its way. Increasingly, American policy adopted this paradigm. As Churchill put it in 1948, Allied policy should now be "to draw the sponge across the crimes and horrors of the past—hard as that may be—and look for the sake of all our salvation, toward the future. There can be no revival of Europe without the active and loyal aid of all the German tribes."

When Konrad Adenauer became the first chancellor of the Federal Republic of Germany in 1949, his willingness to place former Nazis in senior positions was symbolized by his appointment as state secretary of Hans Globke, the man who had written the commentary on Hitler's Nuremberg racial laws. No serious objection to this appointment was raised by the Allies.

It was against this backdrop that the appeals of Metz and Merz against their death sentences made their way through the review process. Statements were collected from various German guards at Berga saying that the two men had done all they could, in adverse conditions, to ease the lot of the GIs. In a statement dated October 29, 1946, Metz's wife, Martha, portrayed her husband, once again, as a misunderstood man whose deepest desire had been to help the Americans.

When Metz came home after the death march, she said, he was not well. "The thing that stands out in my mind most as I think about my husband's attitude when he came back from this long march was his depression," she stated. "The main thing was that he was depressed and angry because he had not been given an order to put all the Americans on the big wagons."

Seldom, it seems, has a man been so put out and so paralyzed by the absence of the orders he felt he needed to do—anything at all. Even putting a man on a cart required an order.

Martha Metz concluded by saying that some of the Americans had told Metz, in broken German, that he was a *"guter Soldat."* This touched her husband—really it did. "He was proud of the praise that the American prisoners of war gave him on this occasion."

Two former prisoners, Milton Stolon and Paul Arthur Van Horne, did provide post-trial statements that were advanced by defense lawyers in support of the appeals. The material the lawyers used was highly selective. Stolon had given a forthright view of Metz shortly after his liberation, on June 1, 1945. He told investigators that Metz "was directly responsible for every one of the deaths in the camp due to negligence. If we asked him to call a doctor, he'd say the doctor wasn't available at the time. If the men were sick, he'd pull them out of bed and send them to work."

After the trial, Stolon was more measured. He said the lack of food in the camp could not be blamed on Metz, but he went on to speak of Metz's brutality, his beating of prisoners, and his enthusiasm for interpreting orders in the harshest way possible. He concluded by saying that Metz and Merz should get six months in the tunnels under the same conditions; then they would see how long they survived under such duress. As for Van Horne's recollections, they were confused and contradictory.

The appeals slowly made their way through the American military bureaucracy, and on January 29, 1948, the War Crimes Review Board recommended that Metz's death sentence be commuted to twenty years imprisonment, from October 15, 1946, and Merz's to five years from the same date. The board said that the trial court had committed "numerous errors" and that the first charge against Metz—that of murdering Goldstein—was not sustainable. "A ballistic expert stated that the bullets found in the body were fired from a distance greater than fifty feet," it said. "The Board therefore concludes that there is a reasonable doubt that the killing was unlawful."

It seems possible that in considering the sentencing of Metz and Merz, the review board may have been sensitive to the revelation of irregularities influencing the verdicts arrived at in the Malmédy massacre trial. The conduct of the Dachau prosecution in the Malmédy case, including coercion of suspects by interrogators, may have sensitized the board to the possibility of prejudice against the accused leading to unduly severe sentencing. But of course the cases were quite distinct.

A couple of weeks later, General Lucius D. Clay, the United States military governor in Germany and the man with ultimate authority over the fate of the two men, commuted Metz's sentence to life imprisonment and Merz's, as recommended, to five years. Later, in a letter to an outraged Dr. Jacob Cantor, the father of Jerome Cantor, one of the dead GIs at Berga, Clay attempted to explain his decision: "In this case, unfortunately, all of the persons responsible for the conditions at the camp had not been apprehended and were not before the court. As to Merz, there was little evidence connecting him directly with any atrocities and there was considerable evidence to the effect that he did the utmost within his power to ameliorate conditions for the American prisoners. I considered five years imprisonment for Merz to be an adequate sentence."

Clay continued: "The evidence showed that Metz was a sergeant in charge of the work details of the camp and was guilty of much brutality. The only evidence in the record, however, connecting him with the killing of an American involved an escape incident. There was direct conflict in the evidence as to whether the victim was actually trying to escape or whether he was summarily killed. Considering the evidence on the Record of Trial as a whole, I considered the ends of justice were met."

In fact, of course, that evidence had been limited by the absence from the courtroom of any of the survivors whose accounts might have made clear that the Goldstein incident, while important, paled in the light of the annihilation in short order of more than seventy other Americans under Metz's charge.

Dr. Cantor continued to push for the death sentences to be upheld. In an open letter called "This Is the Evidence, American People," he set out all he had discovered about Berga. He argued that, given the number of American deaths, "there cannot be the minutest vestige of doubt regarding the legality and justice of the death sentences for both of them."

In conclusion, Cantor said that at the trial "the War Crimes Commission did not present a single survivor, GI or civilian as witness, although any number of GI survivors requested—nay, begged—for the opportunity of confronting their malefactors and giving their testimony against these monsters. These heroic dead and the survivors of this horror are owed justice—full justice. In this case that can only mean one thing. The guilt of Merz and Metz can be expiated only—and in small part—by their hanging as war criminals."

Cantor was not the only bereaved parent to be deeply troubled by the reduction of the sentences. In a letter of protest that reached Secretary Royall, Edwin Gray, the father of Bob Gray, wrote:

Neither Mrs. Gray nor myself have any desire to be vindictive. If Bob had died in combat, we would have accepted our loss as thousands of other parents have done. But now we carry with us always the thought that he was brutally murdered as a defenseless prisoner. Someone who apparently had no interest whatsoever in all those fine young men who gave their lives in this war has decided that this sentence of the Trial Court was unduly harsh and, as they express it, that Metz was only an "agent" carrying out the orders of his superiors. We have two younger sons who served in both France and Germany. As a family, we believe that we have the right to protest as strongly as we can against the unfeeling injustice of both this action on the part of the Commission and its approval by the Army.

Attached was a statement from a fellow GI, Norman Martin, describing how "Bob Gray could not walk as he dragged behind. Metz beat him badly. That was Metz's tactics. He beat the sick and the lame and they died."

On October 21, 1948, Royall replied in a letter replete with legalese. The reduction of the sentences, he wrote, arose "as part of the procedure common to all such cases as well as to other military cases where the final reviewing authority, after reviewing the trial record for legal sufficiency, concludes that the record does not contain evidence sufficient to warrant the sentences imposed. Nor does there appear to be any foundation in fact for Mr. Gray's fear that the defendant Metz is about to be freed since he is, as indicated above, serving a sentence of life imprisonment."

For good measure, Royall added some numbers. "Statistical reports submitted by the European Command show 1,672 tried under its jurisdiction, of whom 1,416 were found guilty and 256 were acquitted. Thereafter, on review, 1,090 of the 1,416 sentences were approved as originally adjudged, 69 sentences were disapproved and 255 sentences were reduced. One defendant died in prison and another was extradited to Polish authorities before their cases were reviewed."

Three months earlier, on June 11, 1948, the War Department had summed up its capitulation in a letter to Vogel. Edward H. Young, the chief of the War Crimes Branch, said the sentences had been commuted "based on the facts that the accused were underlings, that the defendant, Metz, though guilty of a generally cruel course of conduct toward prisoners, was not directly responsible for the death of any prisoners except one who was killed during the course of an attempt to escape, and that the defendant, Merz, did many things to ameliorate conditions under which the prisoners lived." Just what these improvements were was not specified.

Vogel replied that this information came as "a surprise and a shock," given the evidence he had amassed of systematic mistreatment leading to the deaths of scores of GIs. But his was almost a lone voice. At the end of 1948, a petition protesting the commuting of the sentences was sent to President Truman, signed by several of the survivors and their families, but it appears to have made scant impression.

Within three years, Merz was free. In the same year, Metz's sentence was commuted again to fifteen years. Two of the members of the court that had condemned him to death, Lieutenant Colonel Lewis Sorley and Lieutenant Colonel Edward Walker, had concluded that the "confused conditions" in Germany at the time the GIs were imprisoned at Berga "limited the ability" of Metz "to alleviate the hardships of American prisoners of war who were then in the custody of the accused."

They argued that the absence of any American witnesses during the trial made it impossible for "the court to accord the proper weight to their different testimonies, to test their various credibilities, and to ascertain the exactness of their knowledge surrounding the facts about which they testified in their affidavits." Once again, the absence of American survivors from the courtroom was used in defense of Metz and Merz, when several of these survivors had wanted nothing more than to be there to bolster the prosecution's case.

Metz remained in prison for another three years. Then, in 1954, he was released on parole, despite the fact that it was discovered that, on an earlier application for clemency, he had lied about his three previous convictions for fraud and embezzlement. His behavior after his release was described as exemplary, and on September 6, 1955, he was conditionally discharged. Finally, on May 2, 1957, his sentence was formally reduced to the time already served. In the end, Metz served a nine-year prison sentence, roughly a year for every eight Americans killed under his charge.

This was no more than the logical end to a saga of evasion and paper-shuffling. The bewilderment of the returning young soldiers, the quickly dawning politics of the cold war, the embarrassment of the government and the military over Berga, the disappearance of the little town into the Soviet sector, and the failure to bring survivors into court to tell the whole story had all contributed to the fact that, within nine years of the death march, Metz and Merz were free men. So, too, did the fact that the war-crimes investigation into the segregation of eighty Jews at Bad Orb—one inextricable from the Berga inquiry—never went anywhere. No German was ever tried in connection with these events, which led directly to the Berga killing.

Royall had tried to reassure the Gray family that Metz would remain in prison for life. But events showed that his words were worth about as much as the various official communications to the Gorinac family. American authorities persistently tried to push off issues in the hope that with time they would be forgotten.

History is written by the victors. But the minds of the victors quickly turn to the new worlds they have inherited through force of arms. It is these worlds they want to shape, these struggles they want to engage. With their minds so focused, the past easily becomes just another weapon to manipulate in the cause.

SS Lieutenant Willy Hack was conspicuously absent from the Dachau trial. The commander of the Berga camp and the nemesis of Kasten and Littell slipped away at the end of the war, eluding the Allies and Kasten's attempts to effect a summary execution of the man who had tormented him. But Hack was spotted by a former Berga prisoner in the East German town of Zwickau in 1947. The SS man was paying a visit to an old girlfriend. He was arrested by the Communist East German authorities and sentenced to death in 1949. His appeal went to the superior court in Dresden; a retrial was held in Zwickau in 1951. This resulted, once again, in a death sentence for Hack, handed down on April 23, 1951. He was hanged on July 26, 1952, in Dresden.

The cold war was many things, not least a great moral battle. It pitted the free and open societies of the West against the closed and oppressive systems of the Soviet bloc. But wars, even cold ones, are ugly, and the moral equations of America's great struggle with the Soviet Union were never quite as simple and satisfying as they might seem. The world was an extravagant chessboard of surrogates. Western interests sometimes dictated the enlistment of thugs in the service of values that were supposed to bear no relation to thuggery. Compromises were made; history was molded to serve each side's struggle; truth was elusive.

But truth will out in the end. In this instance, at least, it seems that justice for the crimes of Berga was better served in the Soviet sector of Germany than in the American. This small detail of the cold war, long overlooked, amounts to a stain on America's conscience. For it was young Americans who gave their lives at Berga and on the winding roads south of there, youths from Ohio and California and New York sucked, on the basis of a vile Nazi selection, into a world they could not comprehend, a horror they could not fathom, a system of annihilation that lay beyond the realm of their training, their knowledge, or their still brittle, and now forever darkened, imaginations.

Epilogue

THE SEVENTEEN SHAFTS of death are set back about fifty feet from the Elster River, their mouths supported against the hillside by blocks of stone and brickwork. Each of them, with the exception of tunnel 14, is sealed today. As the door is opened, I shudder inwardly as I feel the frigid air on my face. It comes from afar, this cold. Long forgotten, still abandoned, the tunnels seem to hold some secret for which I searched in Germany, some key to the puzzle of this most troubled of nations.

The holes drilled by American soldiers are still visible in some places in the black slate walls. The suffering of these prisoners seems close at hand. But the concerns of André Matzke, the official with the German Naturschutzbehörde, or Nature Protection Authority, who has agreed, exceptionally, to open the tunnel, are rather different. They center on bats.

An endangered species of bat now chooses to hibernate in the seventeen tunnels. Intruders disturb them. The Nature Protection Authority, active here as all over Germany, wants to prevent such disturbances. Matzke wants all the tunnels sealed, including the one we are in, leaving only narrow vents through which bats will be able to pass.

"Every animal," Matzke says, "is needed for the ecosystem." He is an earnest young man with a light beard, and his concerns are genuine. Their historical irony seems to escape him.

Attempts to break into the tunnels have increased of late because rumors about them are multiplying. Perhaps the most outlandish is that the Amber Room, looted by the Nazis from a Russian palace in 1941 and since lost, is concealed within them. Made by German master craftsmen, the jewel-encrusted amber paneling was given to

Peter the Great by King Frederick William I of Prussia in 1716; later it covered the walls of a large room at Catherine the Great's palace in Tsarskoye Selo, near St. Petersburg.

When, soon after the start of the ill-fated Russian campaign, the Nazis took the area in 1941, they dismantled the room piece by piece and took its contents to Königsberg in the German Reich (now Kaliningrad Oblast in Russia). There it was stored in the city castle. But in 1945, Allied bombing forced another transfer westward to a still unknown destination. Some German historians and businessmen, apparently acting on the basis that the treasure appears to have reached nearby Weimar, are convinced that the Berga tunnels hold the treasure. They have demanded access.

Klaus-Werner Jonas, the mayor of Berga, is disinclined to grant it. Making the tunnels safe would be costly—they are believed to be unstable—and he does not even have the funds to repair the façade of his city hall. In short, he has other problems. The entire region of Berga is depressed. Attempts to develop a tourist industry featuring picturesque walks or bicycle rides along the Elster have yet to yield results. New industries have stayed away since German unification. One of the few modern additions to Berga has been a number of power-generating windmills on the surrounding hills. These gyrating white intruders are solitary beasts, rather in the spirit of the fragmented and individualistic new Germany that brought them.

Jonas has little to say about the Americans held in Berga. After the war, the official story of the Berga camp and tunnels was that European prisoners from Buchenwald labored and were tortured in them. The mayor, who was born in the western part of Germany, only learned of the American presence when two survivors visited him after unification in 1990. He then searched for further information in city archives. "But we found nothing here," said Jonas. "And today, of course, people have different concerns; they want to know if they have a future."

Germany wants to look forward. It wants above all to be "normal." But in almost every German family there is a locked drawer, a place where some secret is kept. Confessions of an abrupt intimacy punctuated my stay in Germany: a young woman saying she loathed her beautiful blue eyes, usually concealed behind tinted glasses, because they recalled her father, who had been a concentration-camp commander; a drunken man telling his daughter of his shame at having, at the age of ten, denounced a spy during the war and then seen the man summarily executed; a troubled avowal that a child's birthday, April 20, was also that of Hitler ("I suppose somebody has to be born then"); a proffered family picture of a Wehrmacht officer whose family insists he acted honorably, despite the swastika on the uniform, because he knew nothing of the Final Solution and little of the activities of the SS ("What can I say? He was a good father to me")—things hidden, half-avowed, finally blurted out in tearful catharsis.

As I listened to the mayor, it occurred to me that perhaps Berga was a paradigm of all this. The camp, the tunnels, the chambers of death, so buffeted by Europe's twentieth-century storms, yet now so lost and unacknowledged in the silence of the German woods: these, too, were closed drawers from which occasionally a troubled whispering filtered. Liberated by the American army in 1945, later taken over by Soviet troops, the tunnels had been explored as spooky recesses by children in the postwar years, then sealed, only to come to life again at the cold war's end as possible repositories of wartime Nazi treasure, as the nexus of a bitter German-American story that it suited few people to tell or remember while West Germany stood as an ally on the front line of Europe's division, and, finally, as a nature reserve for bats. In short, this is a shifting story, as restless as these hills' long shadows in the eddying waters of the Elster. But the corpses were real. They had demanded answers.

If there were so many corpses so near the end of the war, when all was already lost, when the entire Berga project had no hope of completion, when Hitler was already confined to his bunker, when the Reich was in ruins, it could only be because Germans like Hack, Merz, and Metz went on obeying orders rather than listening to anything that might resemble the vestige of a human conscience.

Befehl ist Befehl—an order is an order—is still a phrase heard often enough in Germany. Sometimes the expression is used to justify an action; more often it is invoked as a dismissive illustration of the way things were in the past, but no longer are in the new Germany of bear hugs and Prosecco and benign policemen in green uniforms. Yet the German zeal for rules and regulations is still real enough to stir intermittent questions about what state of mind prompts in a citizen the need or desire to be a personal enforcer, rather than a mere follower, of laws and bylaws.

So, in the spring of 2000, on the fifty-fifth anniversary of the

German surrender to the Allies, the honoring by Germany of a man who disobeyed orders during World War II seemed a remarkable event. The country, very late in the day, decided to rename a military base after a soldier in Hitler's army who refused to do what he was told, saved hundreds of Jews, and was executed by the Nazis for his acts. This salute to disobedience was particularly significant because the base had previously been named in honor of an army general, Gunther Rudel, who, although never linked to any atrocities in his military actions during World War II, had served as an "honorary judge" of the People's Courts of the Third Reich, vehicles for Hitler's brutality.

In place of the general's name went that of Anton Schmid, a lowly army sergeant whose conscience was moved by the suffering of Jews in the Vilnius ghetto. Born in Vienna and drafted into the German army after the *Anschluss* of 1938, Schmid found himself stationed near Vilnius in the fall of 1941. The Germans had entered Lithuania not long before. There he witnessed the herding of Jews into two ghettos and the shooting of thousands of them in nearby Ponary.

Schmid described his horror at the sight of this mass murder of Jews almost three years before Eichmann went to work in Hungary. In a letter to his wife, he lamented that children were "beaten on the way" and confided: "You know how it is with my soft heart. I could not think and had to help them." Schmid hid 250 Jews, saving them all. Over a period of months, he supplied matériel and forged papers to the Jewish underground.

Arrested in January 1942 and summarily tried before a Nazi military court on February 25, Schmid was executed on April 13, 1942.

Watched by earnest and red-faced German army recruits, Rudolf Scharping, then the German defense minister, presided at the ceremony honoring Schmid. He told the sergeant's story and declared: "We are not free to choose our history, but we can choose the examples we take from that history. Too many bowed to the threats and temptations of the dictator, and too few found the strength to resist. But Sergeant Anton Schmid did resist."

Why was Schmid almost alone in such an act of conscience? In more than a half century since the war, no such action by a soldier had previously been honored because none had come to light. Millions of Germans must have known that what they were doing, or allowing to happen, was wrong, worse than wrong: vile, unconscionable, despicable. It must have occurred to them to try to stop the mass murder. But almost every one of them, after whatever internal debate occurred, acting out of fear, or opportunism, or convenience, or anger, sided with complicity, active or passive.

This harsh fact, it sometimes seemed to me, had never been entirely absorbed or acknowledged in Germany. The people responsible for the mass murder had done a vanishing act and were now blotted out from family histories, absent from conversation, shunted into a realm of silence. Germans learned dutifully about the Third Reich and its leaders; school groups trooped off to concentration camps; memorials to the Jews were debated and built; official contrition was de rigueur. But the moral decisions of individual Germans, those that carried out, permitted, ignored, or condoned the killings, the grandparents, great-uncles, or fathers of the generations running Germany today, seemed to have been lost in a blur. Memories did surface, but not often, not unprovoked, and seldom without the prodding of an outsider.

Perhaps unhappy memories always tend to be suppressed. But there was something deeper at work. Many Germans, it seemed, clung to the notion that Nazi atrocities were not the work of the army—in other words, of the institution representing the broadest swathe of the population—but of Hitler's elite SS and fanatical death squads. This belief, like other similar ones, reserved opprobrium for a small group of Germans and granted others the blessing of ignorance. Whatever truth was contained in this conviction—the Wehrmacht was indeed not the SS—was overshadowed by the larger lie it condoned.

When the Wehrmacht general's name was stripped from the base to make way for that of Schmid, a former commander, Baron Hans von Falkenhausen, refused to attend the ceremony. He protested: "In two wars, General Rudel served the Fatherland in outstanding ways." An exhibition at the time, "The German Army and Genocide," was bitterly contested because it sought to illustrate how completely the Wehrmacht was a tool of the Nazis, even if the access of ordinary soldiers to Hitler's designs was limited. Falkenhausen was far from alone; the notion that ordinary people knew and nodded, or knew and looked away, is still contested.

Schmid, a sergeant like Metz, did not look away or take refuge in the sacred imperative of orders. His decision led quickly to his death. But his action did not disappear into oblivion. As Hannah Arendt has observed, "Under conditions of terror, most people will comply but some will not." She continues, "Humanly speaking, no more is required, and no more can reasonably be asked, for this planet to remain a fit place for human habitation."

Today, the German army stresses the importance of *innere Führung,* or inner direction, by which it means the moral compass necessary to determine when an order is barbaric and as such unacceptable. It takes Schmid as an example.

As for Schmid himself, he needed no instruction in the functioning of such a compass. He knew when to disobey. In his last letter to his wife, he wrote: "I am today so peaceful that I can hardly believe it, but our dear God wanted to make me strong. I hope that He will make you as strong as I am." He concluded: "I merely behaved as a human being." It was the absence of such human beings in any significant numbers, even in the last four months of Hitler's crumbling rule, that made Berga possible.

Mordecai Hauer came back to Goncz in the early summer of 1945 to discover a town of ghosts. He had returned full of illusions: that his mother and siblings would be there, that many of his Jewish friends would also limp home, that life would somehow resume where it had been interrupted a little more than a year earlier. But he found only a great emptiness. His mother, his lovely and indestructible mother, was nowhere to be found. Of his brothers and sister there was no trace. How could a beauty as overwhelming as his mother's, a vitality so irrepressible, be effaced? Hauer grappled with this question, unable to tame it with reason. He had no photograph of Camilla. Her image eluded him sometimes and sometimes came to him with a terrible vividness. He could touch her in such moments; he could feel her cool touch on his cheeks. Such visions filled sleepless nights. The only consolation lay in alcohol. Often enough, Hauer drank himself into a stupor.

His house had been taken over by the ascendant Communist Party, whose presence was announced by a big sign. Slogans urged workers of the world to unite. All the goods from the family store, once a center of village life, had disappeared. Even the shelves were gone. The big room had become a makeshift meeting hall filled with rows of folding chairs, adorned with party posters, mainly of Stalin, now the Georgian inheritor of a central European empire. From the family living room almost everything had vanished, including the Persian rug that had been his mother's pride. But Hauer cared nothing for the looted possessions. What was gone was life itself, the one he had lived, in all its ho-hum and precious ordinariness.

He wandered down the main street with its one-story homes stretching back into a maze of inner courtyards overgrown with wildflowers, half-collapsed trellises, and weeds. Cats slithered here and there; scrawny dogs lay asleep in the sun. In a daze he banged on the doors of houses that once belonged to Jewish families: Hamburger, Fried, Kornweitz, Reiss. There was no reply. They had vanished, as completely as Hauer's own family, gone up in smoke. All was familiar. Nothing was. These houses now seemed no more than props for a drama on which the curtain had fallen. Hauer felt he might nudge them and they would topple over and shrieks of laughter would rise from the surrounding hills.

When Hauer called at Dr. Grossman's house, one of the finer Goncz residences, he was surprised to find the door opened by a policeman, Veres, whose anti-Semitic rants and arrogance had made him a much hated figure in the Hauer family. Now Veres was all smiles and bonhomie. He welcomed Hauer with open arms, assured him that he was only "taking care" of the house until Grossman's return, and asked his wife to prepare some food to celebrate this unexpected homecoming. Only a handful of Jews had returned, Veres said casually, a dozen at most, and they all seemed to be working for the Communist Party. They were filled with hatred for some reason, the policeman continued, especially against honorable people like himself who had only served Hungary dutifully. "You know, Mordecai, how I worked to help your family, to save them from fines, to arrange things for them," he concluded. "I know that you will vouch for me, if ever there is a need." Hauer rose and left in disgust.

There was nothing for him here. The new faith, communism, held no appeal. As a Jew, he had learned, he would always be vulnerable. At best, in good times, if such times ever came again, someone would pat him on the back and call him a good Jew and a good Hungarian patriot. But if the tide turned, if jobs disappeared, if anger boiled, Hauer was sure he would again be the target of the ire of all those waiting to loot goods and rugs and rings and gold. A few of the Jews who had come home tried to persuade him that he had a future in the new Hungary. But Hauer did not believe that. The only thing that made him stay was the obstinate belief that his mother might one day appear. He felt a deep despair, alleviated only by word that his younger brother Benji had returned and was housed in an orphanage in Miskolc. Hauer set out to find him.

He rode a train through a familiar undulating landscape, taking him to the town where he had kissed the lovely Ilona one spring day not so long ago. But now the train connected towns inhabited by people with a strange amnesia surrounded by the emptied homes of phantoms. He had been told in Goncz that Ilona had married into a prominent family in the region. He wondered how she was, if she had married for love, and remembered her gentle but electrifying touch on the train from Budapest.

Benji looked surprisingly vigorous. Now aged sixteen, he had been in the orphanage for several weeks. Hauer urged him to leave and return to Goncz to await their mother's return, but Benji would have none of it. "Mordecai," he said, "don't you understand that Mother is dead?"

"Who told you that?"

"Nobody, but how can you be so naïve? We saw where she went in Auschwitz."

"Don't say that again," said Hauer. "Not everyone who went to the left was killed. I am sure the Germans put her to work."

Benji turned away in disgust. He had his own plans. Arrangements had been made for a Jewish family in Detroit to adopt him. He told his brother that as soon as he was eighteen, he would enlist in the American army. Hauer thought of the soldiers he had briefly known in Berga, and the visions of an all-powerful country that even those men had inspired.

"Germany is dead," said Benji. "Europe is dead. Perhaps one day I will come back in a beautiful American uniform and you will be proud of me."

The brothers parted the next morning. Hauer felt lonelier than ever. He decided to go to Encs, Sharon's hometown, in the hope that the last girl he had loved was still alive. But she had been killed by the Nazis. Sharon's sister told Hauer that, in the last weeks of her life, she had talked of their brief romance. "I knew there was something between you at Kassa," she said, "but I never suspected she loved you so much. She told me to tell you that she would have been proud to be your wife."

There was nothing left for Hauer but to gather up his things in Goncz and leave. As a first step, he decided, he would go to Budapest to inquire with the Red Cross if there had been word of his family. In his despair, he thought of his two friends, Katz and Yankele. At the last, Katz had cried, "*Am Yisrael Chai*"—"The people of Israel shall live." Faced with a final choice between a curse and a blessing, he had chosen a blessing. Yankele, even in the worst moments, had predicted, correctly, that the Jewish people would survive Hitler and that to do so they did not have to hate.

The dog was in every man, a beast that could be unleashed. That, at least, was Hauer's conclusion. Man was a divided being. In the right circumstances, with enough encouragement, the dogs would rampage. He recalled how in the camps, on a bright day, he might sit in the sun and feel happy for a moment as he crushed the lice that crawled all over him. Killing them was some measure of revenge on a living thing actually weaker than him. The pleasure was ephemeral. But in everybody there lurked some potential to find contentment in another's pain. In Germany, all constraint had been cast off, the beasts had run wild. The Germans now had to live with that knowledge. Even as a Jew who had lost almost all his family, Hauer felt himself better off than a German who had to live with that burden.

He could not hate the Germans. Hatred brought nothing, only destruction, an endless spiral downward. Understanding alone could tame the dogs. It was toward understanding that he must strive, even if it was painful, even if a quicker relief and release lay in a less patient course.

Zealotry chases out understanding, substitutes fervor for reflection, quashes the need for thought. No Nazi obeyed with greater zeal than Adolf Eichmann, the man who delivered the Hauers and millions of other Jews to their fate. What drove him? Gabriel Bach was a leading prosecutor at the 1961 trial of Eichmann. He tried as hard as anyone to answer this question.

Bach was born in Germany in 1927. For a short time, after the Nazis came to power in 1933, he attended the Theodore Herzl school in Adolf Hitler Square in Berlin. Even now, Bach remembers every result from the 1936 Berlin Olympics. He would emerge from school and sit on the yellow benches for Jews and sing Zionist songs, a small act of defiance that brought some satisfaction as he gazed at the graffiti-smeared Jewish stores. In 1938, when he was eleven, the

Bach family managed to assemble the papers needed to leave Germany. They escaped by train to the Netherlands. Eventually, they reached Palestine.

It was not always easy for Bach to maintain his composure during the Eichmann case. At one point, he had been reading the book by Rudolf Höss, the last commander at Auschwitz. Höss confessed in the book that on some days as many as one thousand Jewish children were killed, and some begged on their knees to be saved. Then, Höss wrote, his own knees sometimes went wobbly. But later, after talking to Eichmann, Höss felt ashamed of his weakness because Eichmann asked him: "How can you kill the parents when you do not kill those who will potentially avenge these deaths, those who will re-create the race?"

Eichmann, the coordinator of the death factories, knew the power of memory. So he was determined to eradicate it. Bach, a symbol of Eichmann's ultimate failure, had to sit at the same table as the Jews' chief executioner and be calm. To this end, he sought to understand the Nazi mind.

Bach tried to be cool in his analysis, but once, during the trial itself, he lost control. A witness was testifying about his arrival at Auschwitz with his family. "The wife and daughter were shoved to the left," Bach said, "and he was shoved to the right with his son. The SS man hesitated about what to do with the thirteen-year-old boy, but then sent him to the left, too, to be gassed. And then the witness said his little daughter happened to be wearing a bright red coat that day and as his family was consumed in the gray, condemned crowds, being kicked and beaten by the camp guards, that little dot of red, getting ever smaller, that diminishing red dot, was the point at which his family disappeared from his life."

Bach was silent again. The disappearing red dot hovered in the air. Eventually he continued: "It so happened that I had just bought my own little daughter a red coat, and this story cut my throat. I could not utter a sound. My heart was thumping. I was silent for at least three minutes."

Bach recovered his composure to help make the case that sent Eichmann to the gallows of the Jewish state. He has managed a reconciliation of sorts with today's Germany. But certain things remain a mystery to him. The frustrations on which Hitler played, the hypnotic power of his propaganda, the intoxication of absolute power, the dominion of fear: the role of all of this in cementing Nazi power was clear enough to Bach. However, as he went through the archives of the Nazi ministries he found correspondence that baffled him.

For example, he stumbled on a letter from the director general of Hitler's health ministry, a doctor, an educated man. The letter, addressed to the minister, concerned a "milk bank"—a store of milk from women who had too much. The official had discovered that a woman who was one quarter Jewish had donated some milk, and he wrote that his first thought had been to arrange a "show trial" for the woman to demonstrate her crime. But then, on reflection, he had decided that this would have a demoralizing effect on Aryan mothers who might think that their children were contaminated. This, from a doctor, Bach found flabbergasting.

He had also found a letter from an engineer protesting the difficulties for German drivers seated in carbon monoxide gas vans, the precursors of the gas chambers that eventually brought production-line killing to Auschwitz and elsewhere. The driver, the engineer complained, had to listen to the screams of the Jewish victims in the back, screams that gradually grew softer. This was inhuman treatment for the drivers. In response, the engineer had invented a soundproof barrier that could be placed in the vans; he appealed for its immediate installation. This focus on the suffering of the tormentor rather than the tormented was unfathomable to Bach.

But what, he wondered, was the soundproof barrier in Eichmann's mind? At the outset, being an "expert on Jewish affairs" was simply a means for Eichmann to further his career. The mass murder of the innocent from 1942 onward, however, required some wall against madness.

Eichmann's insulation, it seemed to Bach, was to become more fanatical than his superiors in his determination to rid the world of Jewish biological material. With sufficient focus on the objective, the human beings who stood in the way of it became mere abstractions. Even as German generals on the eastern front clamored for more matériel to fight the war, Eichmann managed through subterfuge to keep his trains to the death camps running from Hungary. More Jews were killed as more critical battles were lost to the Soviet army. No matter! If the trains with their condemned loads stopped, Eichmann's statistics would be skewed, his targets would be unmet. He would fail in his job, his appointed task, his duty! This, to an archetypal bureaucrat, was unthinkable, just as it was unthinkable to Metz and Merz to halt the march south that took dozens of GIs to their pointless deaths.

Eichmann's target, at least in this stage of the construction of the Thousand-Year Reich, was the Jews of Europe. American GIs, even the Jews among them, had no place in his obsessions. But without some sense of the blind zeal that was his—and not only his—it seems impossible to understand the fate of Shapiro, Daub, Lubinsky, and others who ended up in Berga.

Bach did not go back to Germany for three decades after the war. When he arrived, he went for a walk in a Berlin park with his wife. On each balcony of the nearby apartment buildings geraniums flowered in window boxes; his wife remarked on how beautiful they were. But what Bach perceived in the arrangements was a fastidious German precision that made him shudder and stirred a memory.

When his uncle, Robert Bach, had been hauled off to Buchenwald by the Nazis after *Kristallnacht* in 1938, he had been made to pay a train fare to the camp. On arrival, he was told to remove his wedding ring. When he said he could not, the Nazi guards arrived with an ax. He then managed to prize it off. The ring was taken.

A few days later, his wife was summoned by the Gestapo. She thought she might be arrested, too, but was anxious enough about her husband's fate to comply with the summons. A Nazi official explained that her husband had been taken to a work camp and had paid twenty reichsmarks for the train fare. But the cost, he noted, was 18.90 reichsmarks. He was therefore eager to give her the change of 1.10 reichsmarks. Otherwise it would be impossible to enter her husband's transport in his register in an appropriate way. There was, of course, no mention of the ring. So it is that refuge in the punctilious can mask the temperament of brutes. So it is that the bureaucrat of death seeks some skewed solace.

As Gabriel Bach looked up again at the red flowers above the Berlin streets, he saw, in place of the geraniums, the sea of red swastika flags that adorned those same buildings in the 1930s, unfurling in unison, declaring Germany to be what for centuries it was not: united, cohesive, strong, and one.

William Shapiro has similar visions that intrude on the placidity of his retirement: of men hanging from gallows, of a dead American soldier whose name he cannot remember beside him in bed, of gaunt faces covered in slate dust. For him, too, there are disappearing red dots that hover in the air; there are red flags that unfurl unbidden.

The specters from the life of Private Shapiro are strange intruders on the golf courses of Florida, where the only flags are set in the middle of putting greens.

For the surviving GIs of Berga, understanding took a half century. During that time, almost without exception, they repressed what they had lived. Their story interested nobody; the records of the various government investigations into the camp were classified, some of them for at least three decades. The men were dispersed—Kasten in the Philippines after a business career in Asia, Littell in California, Shapiro and Daub in the New York area, Lubinsky in Ohio and then Florida. They had bills to pay, children to raise, careers to pursue. Americans are taught not to dwell on the past, especially a hellish past. They pushed forward.

All that they had held back only became clear to Shapiro in 1997. At a reunion of prisoners of war from Stalag IX-B, Tony Acevedo showed him the Red Cross armband he had worn in combat. It is a sepia-colored piece of cloth, about two feet wide, with a red cross at its center. During their time at Berga, Acevedo had asked his fellow medics to sign the armband. There, in the top left corner, was Shapiro's signature, along with his New York address. The sight of his name provoked an uncontrolled sobbing.

He had been there. It was as simple as that. He had been in the places where his nightmares took him. These were not dreams. They were his past. That past had taken him, an American Jew, into the midst of Hitler's assault on European Jews. Another 349 Americans, of all faiths, had been there with him. Many had not returned. They had been destroyed, just as the families of European Jews like the Hauers and the Frenkels had been largely annihilated.

Shapiro was a Holocaust survivor. Those few words seemed hard to accept. For decades, they had proved impossible even to contemplate in a country that would scarcely avow the existence of Berga. But he had to accept what he was, had to be aware of the place from which he had returned, or he would never tame his demons. The armband was his talisman. It gave him a new power. To live unaware is to accept a half life. It was late in the day to acknowledge this, but Shapiro was ready.

In different ways, through different confrontations and epiphanies, many of the Berga survivors came in their seventies to a new avowal and acceptance of the violent storm that took them when they were nineteen or twenty or a little more. Changes in the world helped them. The cold war was over, and with it went various imperatives—of secrecy, of distortion, of silence. Germany was unified and eager to try to expiate the last of its guilt so as to live at last as a normal country, undivided and at peace, at the center of a whole European continent.

America—in a kind of reckoning, a thirsting, perhaps, for a time of moral certainty—was looking again and with new interest at its "greatest generation," boys just out of school who went to fight for the freedom of Europe and the world, those who scaled the Normandy cliffs and battled for each bloodied square foot of Pacific islands, raisers of the flag on remote rocks that became bulwarks of the struggle against tyranny. All of this helped to summon Berga from the subconscious.

Very late in the day, the German government offered compensation to the survivors of Berga. William R. Marks, a Washington lawyer, represented dozens of them in negotiations with Germany that gathered pace in 1997. The State Department got involved. The amounts paid varied. In the cases of Daub and Shapiro, they were in the region of ninety thousand dollars. The process of confronting the truth had taken a little more than fifty years.

A small additional payment came later. On April 23, 2002, Shapiro received a letter from the Conference on Jewish Material Claims Against Germany. It began: "We are pleased to inform you that you are approved for payment under the Claims Conference Program for Former Slave and Forced Laborers in accordance with the Foundation 'Remembrance, Responsibility and the Future.' "

More than a half century after the death sentences of Metz and Merz were commuted, almost a half century after Metz walked free, Germany had admitted that Shapiro and others like him were American slaves, men only living to be worked to death for the Nazi Reich, a mission that Metz and Merz dutifully accomplished. In those words lay also an admission of the gross injustice done in the postwar years. It was cause enough for anger and for outrage.

But Lubinsky, who also received compensation, had outlived his hatred. He had watched his beloved wife die a few years earlier. What he took away from that was the conviction that he did not want to see life and light and intelligence going out of anyone's eyes. Life was too precious a gift, the living of it, even in pain, an honor. He quit hating. The Germans had needed a fall guy for their plight. They had found it in the Jew. Never would they atone for the shame of what they had done. But what Lubinsky wanted to do now was to love. Without love, he had concluded, there is no life. Back there, in Berga, he had found energy in hatred. Goldstein's corpse in the snow: the memory of it had kept him going. He would not end up that way. The hatred had seen him through, brought him back to his America. But in love, he now knew, lay a greater energy, the greatest of all, a force unquenchable, life itself.

A winding road brought Mordecai Hauer to the United States. In Budapest he discovered that his sister, Edith, had also survived and was in a displaced-persons camp at Bergen-Belsen. Hauer made his way northward into Austria. Eventually he was reunited with her in Germany. His increasingly crazed search for his mother gathered pace. He went from camp to camp, filled with the displaced of Europe, looking for Camilla, driven by a frenzy of love, much as Kasten had gone from camp to camp looking for Hack, driven by a frenzy of hatred. The search was in vain, but among the refugees he did find his future wife, Masha, a Polish refugee who, like Hauer, had lost much of her family.

Together they moved to Israel in 1948. Hauer knew that he wanted to be with his own people. He was happy, happier than he had ever been, or so it seemed to him, working on a kibbutz. He labored in the fields, drove a tractor, felt the sun on his back, came home hungry, and there was food. The couple's first two children were born. But his travails were not over. Four years after Hauer reached Israel, he drove a tractor over a mine and was blown up. His spine was broken. Doctors took him to a military hospital and put him in a body cast. He could not move. He lay there, going over the strange violence of his life.

Salvation arrived in the form of an American orthopedic surgeon, Leo Mayer, who was visiting Israel. He told Hauer he need not be paralyzed. Through Mayer's intervention, Hauer was transported to New York. The doctor took bone from his hip and performed a spinal fusion. Recovery and rehabilitation took a year, but, as the doctor had promised, Hauer walked again. By that time, his wife and children had joined him. Masha's mother was also in America. They decided to stay.

It was 1953. His younger brother Benji had already given his life for the United States. As he had promised, Benji joined the army as soon as he could and was dispatched to fight in the Korean War. His last letter to Hauer said he had not really intended to become a warrior, had not expected that there would be another war so soon. "But," the letter concluded, "I swore allegiance and I'll keep my end of the bargain."

Benji was killed soon after on the front line. The armed forces wanted to bury him at Arlington. But Hauer preferred to have his little brother near him in New York, in a Jewish cemetery, where he could go from time to time and kiss the headstone. He could not do that for his mother or his father or little Emerich, who never returned. As for Edith, she made her life in Israel.

Hauer taught himself English, put himself through college, and became a teacher. His children thrived. Sometimes he would talk to them about the Holocaust, but not often. The Auschwitz tattoo was still on his arm—A9092—and his loss there indelible, but he had no hatred in him.

One thought, however, still gnawed at him: that he had no photograph, not a single image, of his beloved mother. When the cold war ended and Hungary joined the West, he placed an advertisement in a local paper in Goncz, offering two hundred dollars to anyone who had a photograph of Camilla Hauer. He corresponded with the mayor, implored him to ask everyone. Some time later, he received a letter from a painter in Goncz who told him that he had been secretly in love with Camilla all his life. Hauer thought the man might have a painting of his mother. This was enough to prompt him to return to Goncz for the first time in fifty years.

The little town had hardly changed. It seemed, if anything, to have faded, the life and gloss sucked from it, replaced by the lingering, rancid whiff of a now discredited Communist rule. The white Protestant church and the ocher Catholic church still rose on either side of the river, which had been large in his memory but was really no more than a stream. The churches, in a wave of post-Communist enthusiasm, were now being refurbished. The synagogue, of course, was gone, sold and turned into a private house. In the end, only about a dozen Jews had returned from the war.

His house, its plaster peeling, its stuccowork undone, its paint faded, was still there, stripped now of its Communist slogans, but he did not have the heart to go in. What would he say? What lies and discomfort would he be subjected to? He had learned to let go. It is important to let go sometimes. People spend their lives and their energy clinging to memories that are useless. Hauer had seen too much suffering to allow himself to wallow. He looked up to the surrounding hills, as verdant as ever, the places of his youthful musings and dreams. He had not expected to live the life he had lived. He had thought he could plan an existence at once sweet and stable. But it is the journey that counts, not the destination, and his had been rich despite its pain. He knew so many people who had never dared to live.

Opposite his house a granite memorial had been erected to the victims of World War II. More than one hundred names were listed, the dead of Goncz: Laszlo Dudas, Istvan Fayger, Sardon Danyi, the list went on and on. It suddenly struck Hauer that none of the Jews from Goncz, none of the more than 150 Jewish dead from this little town, including his own parents and little brother, were on the list. "Learn to love our country from what happened to us," an inscription said. But that country, Hungary, clearly did not also belong to its wartime Jewish citizens who died.

Then, half hidden by a wreath, Hauer saw at the bottom of the memorial a small additional inscription. It said: "We remember our 168 Jewish patriots who became martyrs in the inferno of World War II." But these Hungarian citizens had no name. They belonged to a different category, one made up of anonymous bodies, people stripped of identity. Hauer shuddered.

The Jews as individuals had been forgotten. Their fate had been passed over. They had no names. But he knew the names. As he looked again at the main street, he imagined them in their houses: Lang, Horowitz, Schwarz, Reiss. Nobody spoke now of their existence.

Hauer found the painter, an old man now, but he had no photograph and no painting of the beautiful Camilla. At last, after more than fifty years, Hauer accepted that she would have to live in his imagination alone.

Only one Jew was still in Goncz, Imre Reisman, and he had converted to Christianity. His house was filled with photographs of relatives killed in Auschwitz, young people innocent of the fact they would soon be dead. They smiled. They waved. They held hands. It seemed to Hauer that Reisman had lost his mind. In such a place, with such memories, any other outcome would have been surprising.

He learned that the Jewish cemetery was now abandoned. Nobody had been buried there for three decades. He made his way up the hill toward it. The sounds of the village gave way to those of sparrows chirping, dogs barking, and wood being chopped. As he reached higher ground, he could see vineyards stretching away into the distance. The land was rich, the history bad. A bell chimed atop one of the churches—he could not tell which—and it seemed to Hauer a sound full of hypocrisy, proclaiming a peace that was false because it was built on lies.

The cemetery had fallen into ruin. The municipality saw no reason to spend anything on it. The most valuable headstones had been removed by looters. Those that were left tilted at all angles, overgrown with moss, their Hebrew inscriptions almost illegible. A few names could be made out: Lazar Feinstein, Hermanne Roth, Roza Goldmann. At least they had died here, in peace, before the Nazi whirlwind came. Hauer looked up. Beside the closest farm, a man rhythmically chopped wood, his ax rising and falling, cleaving the crisp air. The farmer had a house to keep warm, children to look after; the tide swept on. The abandonment here seemed to Hauer a thing of desperate sadness, eloquent of every ineffaceable European wound, and his only wish was to be gone, from the town, from the country, and from the whole European continent of forgotten graves and tunnels.

In the Bavarian village of Demmelsdorf, the synagogue, built in 1758, was burned down during World War II. Later it was replaced by a firehouse. There was no further use for a synagogue; all the Jews were gone. No plaque commemorates its existence, but just outside town there is one recalling the Jews deported during the period of Hitler's rule: Jakob Berg, Clara Berg, Emil Heimann, Paula Heimann, Hannelore Heimann, and all the others. As Anselm Kiefer, the German painter, once said of his compatriots: "They amputated themselves. They took half of German culture and killed it."

If this culture is recalled at all in Demmelsdorf and the surrounding area, it is due largely to the work of Jozef Molschmann, a man with a deep interest in Jewish history who has raised money for the study of the disappeared community. For his pains, he recently received a Christmas card with three swastikas on it. "You Jewish dog," it said. "You should be slaughtered with your family."

Most of the Jews who lived in this area were cattle dealers and peddlers. Many left during the nineteenth century in the first waves of German emigration to the United States. Among those who left, and so avoided the Holocaust, were Solomon and Deborah Stix. They made their way to the Cincinnati area. Later, their son Louis helped found a successful wholesale clothing company.

Among their descendants was Charles Guggenheim, who, on the eve of the war, joined the 106th Division as a young soldier out of the Army Specialized Training Program. Many infantrymen from that division were captured at the Battle of the Bulge and later ended up at Stalag IX-B and in Berga. Guggenheim avoided this fate because a foot infection prevented him, at the last moment, from going to Europe. But the story obsessed him for a half century. He would imagine his name on the list of Berga prisoners. He could recite the names: Slotkin, Feinberg, Philosoph, Salkain, Black, Swack, Goldstein, Ascher, Silberstein. Guggenheim seemed to fit right in. So he devoted the last years of his life as a documentary filmmaker to tracking down survivors in order to tell their story.

History does not move in a straight line. It loops around in strange circles of varying dimensions, and somewhere in these patterns lurks an often elusive truth. Patience is needed, and perseverance, and a stubborn passion, to detect what may quickly be hidden by the giddying frenzy of human activity. Germany lost a part of itself in this Bavarian village, at Berga, and in countless other little places. It lost names that seem to be part of the German language itself, names like Bernstein and Auerbach—and Guggenheim. But the Germans who remained, like the Hungarians of Goncz, have little incentive to dwell on this void. It may take an American, returning with a perverse obsession 150 years after his German Jewish family left, to start digging. As Guggenheim once said, "This was the first time Americans who spoke as I did, who looked as I did, who grew up in the same country I did, were part of something that I never comprehended as being close to me."

The countryside above Demmelsdorf is rich and fertile. On a summer's day, marigolds and primroses bloom. The meadows are full of poppies. Insects buzz around the flowering shrubs. Molschmann leads the way up the hillside to a cemetery hidden in the woods, the now unused and semi-abandoned Jewish cemetery. As in Goncz, the headstones lurch this way and that, as if inclining themselves to fate. They are covered in moss. The grass is waist-high. Nobody comes here. Why should they?

It is cool in the woods. The breeze seems to whisper sad stories, tales of lives abruptly upended, ordinary people uprooted, violence descending from nowhere. Death does not efface life; it merely transports the spirit to the air. The whispering here is no different from that carried by the cold air in the now sealed and bat-infested Berga tunnels. Sometimes the sound grows a little louder, and the wind, gathering itself, rustles the leaves in the trees above the graves; it moves out across the fields where the grass shimmers in the sun, and on down the abundant Bavarian valley. The German countryside is tranquil now. All is in order.

A sign outside the forgotten cemetery says: IT IS RECOMMENDED TO THE COMMUNITY TO PROTECT THE CEMETERY. ANYONE WHO DESECRATES IT WILL BE RIGOROUSLY PURSUED.

NOTES

This book is based primarily on interviews with survivors of Berga. From their accounts, provided to me and to Charles Guggenheim, the late documentary film-maker, I have attempted to re-create the experience of the prisoners in the camp as they lived it. Memory is imperfect and much time has passed. On some issues, notably the precise nature of the selection of prisoners for Berga, accounts diverge in significant respects. When this is the case, it is made clear.

Fortunately, there is also a voluminous record of the Berga camp at the National Archives and Records Administration (NARA), Military History Department. This consists of several thousand pages contained in more than a dozen files. A detailed picture of the camp emerges from the trial record of the two camp commanders directly responsible for the suffering of the Americans, Erwin Metz and Ludwig Merz. Transcripts of American interrogations and cross-examinations of the two men are contained in these records, making it possible to use the actual words of these men when confronted by their captors and in court.

It is a strange fact of the history of Berga that the obscurity that long shrouded it had nothing to do with an absence of documentary records. The investigation of the camp by an American war-crimes team in 1945 was thorough. Statements were taken from many survivors. But these records were initially classified, and postwar politics helped forge a kind of collective amnesia.

In examining the injustices suffered by the survivors of Berga after 1945—the belittlement of the camp (and occasional denial of its existence), the passing over in silence of its cruelty, and the failure to prosecute vigorously—I have relied largely on the documentary record. In part, the NARA files speak for themselves. But I also had access to a voluminous correspondence that began in 1946 between Bernard Vogel, a New York lawyer whose nephew was killed in Berga, and war-crimes investigators. Mr. Vogel was frustrated by what he saw as a singular failure of American justice, one that allowed the Germans responsible for the killing at Berga to walk away from prison as free men within a decade of the war's end.

The story of Berga has emerged piecemeal over the past twenty years, beginning in 1983 with an article by Ray Weiss in the Fort Myers *News-Press,* based on an interview with Bernie Melnick and other Berga survivors. Guggenheim was helped in his research by the pioneering work on Berga of Mack C. O'Quinn, Jr. Associations of survivors became more active in the 1990s; Pete House was among those who encouraged them to record their memories. Mitchell G. Bard's book *Forgotten Victims: The Abandonment of Americans in Hitler's Camps* is devoted in part to Berga.

This book is a journalistic narrative of historical events. My goal has been to render those events through the lives of the people who lived them. I have sought the literature of fact that lies within the facts of history. I have taken liberties in my choice of form, such as the occasional use of the present tense, that would no doubt be eschewed by historians but that I believe to be justified in the interests of the narrative.

Where quotes appear in direct speech, they are drawn from records of interrogations or cross-questioning at trial, from transcripts of postwar debriefings of GIs, from the memory of at least one of the participants, or from the unpublished postwar memoir of Mordecai Hauer, the Hungarian Jew who, like hundreds of his compatriots, ended up in Berga alongside the Americans.

I became fascinated by the strange intersection in the Berga concentration camp of European Jewry and American GIs. My aim was to explain the incomprehension that marked this meeting by tracing the unlikely paths that brought these prisoners from different worlds together. One such path was that of Hauer. I could not have evoked the details of his odyssey without the unpublished chronicle of his war years that he made available to me. I am satisfied that this memoir represents an acute observer's faithful recollection of the appalling events that engulfed his family. Those events involved encounters with Adolf Eichmann and Josef Mengele. Hauer set down the words of these two Nazis as he heard them. Nevertheless, he was obliged to do so from memory some time after the event, and so, in these two instances, I have rendered the Germans' words in italics rather than in quotes.

CHAPTER ONE: THE DEVIL QUOTES SCRIPTURE

4   "My arms were coming down": Author's interview with Sanford Lubinsky, July 27, 2002, Casselberry, Florida.

6   Lieutenant Willy Hack: Many details of Hack's activity can be found in *Diplomarbeit* by Heike Kegel, written in May 1990, in the archive at Buchenwald.

6   The first prisoners destined to work: Kegel, *Diplomarbeit.*

6   84,500 prisoners: *Buchenwald: A Tour of the Memorial Site* (Weimar, 1993).

8   Of those 350 men, more than 20 percent would die: One of the prisoners, Anthony (Tony) C. Acevedo, kept a list of the dead. His list includes 67 names but is incomplete. The best estimate is 73, based on American records, the postwar official American investigation of Berga, and German records. Of these, 22 died in Berga; 2 at Stalag IX-C, where they had been transported for hospital treatment; and the rest on the death march. See also Mitchell G. Bard, *Forgotten Victims: The Abandonment of Americans in Hitler's Camps* (Boulder: Westview Press, 1994).

9 German production of airplane fuel: Albert Speer, Minister for Arms and Ammunition, in a speech on June 22, 1944.

9 The plan called for numerous underground facilities: See Kegel, *Diplomarbeit.*

9 Tens of thousands of Jews: See Raul Hilberg, *The Destruction of the European Jews* (New York: Holmes and Meier, 1985), pp. 252–55.

10 he applied for a marriage permit: The Hack file in the Bundesarchiv, Berlin.

11 Edward Gorinac: "Individual Deceased Personnel File," Department of the Army, provided by William J. Shapiro.

13 ordered to take several acutely ill prisoners: The exact number of acutely ill prisoners taken to Stalag IX-C is unclear. Shapiro recalls accompanying eight men. Another medic, Tony Acevedo, recorded in his diary kept at Berga that six men were sent.

14 "They were right up against the fence": Author's interview with Sidney Lipson, July 29, 2002, Lake Worth, Florida.

16 "How can all those trim little houses": Author's telephone interview with Joe Littell, July 20, 2003. He expresses the same sentiment in Joseph F. Littell, *A Lifetime in Every Moment* (New York: Houghton Mifflin, 1995), p. 155.

16 "The houses . . . look as if you could eat them": Stephen Spender, *European Witness* (New York: Reynal and Hitchcock, 1946), p. 6.

CHAPTER TWO: SUCKER PUNCH

18 Private William J. Shapiro: Author's interviews with William J. Shapiro, July 27, 28, and 29, 2002, Boca Raton, Florida.

21 American newspapers published little about the Holocaust: On the contemporaneous view of the Holocaust, see Peter Novick, *The Holocaust in American Life* (New York: Houghton Mifflin, 1999), pp. 20–21. Novick writes: "But 'the Holocaust,' as we speak of it today, was largely a retrospective construction, something that would not have been recognizable to most people at the time."

24 "A person who has been wounded": Primo Levi, *The Drowned and the Saved* (New York: Vintage Books, 1989), p. 24.

24 Sonny Fox: Charles Guggenheim interview with Sonny Fox, October 4, 1999, transcript.

27 Edwin Cornell: Charles Guggenheim interview with Edwin Cornell, July 18, 2000, transcript.

28 Gerald Daub: Author's telephone interview with Gerald Daub, February 2, 2004; Charles Guggenheim interview with Gerald Daub, March 22, 2000, transcript.

32 John W. Reifenrath: John W. Reifenrath's thirty-page story, *An American Slave in Nazi Germany,* written in 1997, edited and published by Stalag IX-A, IX-B, and XIII-B and Berga am Elster [*sic*] Association, edited by Pete House.

34   For Shapiro, the best of times: Author's interviews with Shapiro, July 27, 28, and 29, 2002.

38   Private Stephen J. Schweitzer: Stephen J. Schweitzer, sworn testimony given in London, May 29, 1945, National Archives and Records Administration.

39   Philip Glaessner: Charles Guggenheim interview with Philip Glaessner, November 17, 1999, transcript.

CHAPTER THREE: THE OBEDIENCE OF CORPSES

40   Mordecai Hauer: Author's interview with Mordecai Hauer, March 30, 2002, New York, and Hauer's unpublished memoir of the war years. Hauer's memoir provided an important source. Many of the details of his wartime odyssey are drawn from this vivid account.

40   In the end no Hungarian proclamation of fealty to Hitler: On Hungary and Hitler, see Joseph Rothschild, *East Central Europe Between the Two World Wars* (Seattle: University of Washington Press, 1974), pp. 137–99.

40   more than 4.3 million European Jews had been killed: Raul Hilberg, *The Destruction of the European Jews* (New York: Holmes and Meier, 1985), gives the figure of 4.3 million Jewish dead by 1943 (p. 339).

42   Adolf Eichmann: See Hannah Arendt, *Eichmann in Jerusalem: A Report on the Banality of Evil* (London: Penguin Books, 1994), pp. 194–202.

58   *"I am Adolf Eichmann"*: The speech is presented here as Hauer recorded it in his unpublished memoir written after the war.

59   Eichmann had been hard at work in Hungary: Described in Arendt, *Eichmann in Jerusalem*, pp. 194–202.

61   "We knew this": Peter Bamm, cited ibid., pp. 231–32.

CHAPTER FOUR: THE SELECTION

67   Joe Littell was limping: Author's telephone interview with Joe Littell, July 20, 2003, and author's interview, February 15, 2004, Fallbrook, California. On Littell's German schooling and his prewar sojourn in Hitler's Germany, see Joseph F. Littell, *A Lifetime in Every Moment* (New York: Houghton Mifflin, 1995), pp. 76–90.

70   His report was alarming: The five-page Red Cross report on Stalag IX-B was declassified in the 1970s; National Archives and Records Administration. The United States War Department report, based largely on interrogations of former prisoners, was given to the author by William J. Shapiro.

71   German prisoner-of-war regulations: These were located by a member of the Provost Marshal General's Office shortly after the end of hostilities in Europe, and were translated by the Liaison and Research Branch of the American Prisoners of War Information Bureau. Made available by William J. Shapiro.

72   Shapiro wrote to his parents: Copies of Shapiro's letters home made available to the author.

73 Arthur J. Homer gave the following account: Testimony of Arthur J. Homer, National Archives and Records Administration.

74 As Glaessner put it: Testimony of Philip Glaessner, National Archives and Records Administration.

75 Johann Carl Friedrich Kasten: Author's telephone interviews with Hans Kasten, July 20 and 21, 2003, and Charles Guggenheim interview with Kasten, June 4, 2000, transcript.

82 Goodman wrote: Goodman diary, made available to the author by his family.

82 "An American officer came in": Goodman interview, *Detroit Free Press*, December 8, 1985.

82 Morton Brooks: Author's interview with Morton Brooks, July 29, 2001, Boynton Beach, Florida.

83 Gerald Daub: Author's telephone interview with Gerald Daub, February 2, 2004.

83 Sonny Fox also dates the selection process: Charles Guggenheim interview with Sonny Fox, October 4, 1999, transcript.

83 Edwin Cornell: Charles Guggenheim interview with Edwin Cornell, July 18, 2000, transcript.

85 Stephen J. Schweitzer: Sworn testimony given by Stephen J. Schweitzer on May 29, 1945, in London to American war-crimes investigators, National Archives and Records Administration.

85 "They dragged us all out in the snow": Charles Guggenheim interview with John Griffin, July 14, 1999, transcript.

85 "It seemed to me": Author's telephone interview with Donald Hildenbrand, February 4, 2004. Hildenbrand's unpublished "WWII Memoir of a GI from E/397," written in February 1999, relates his war experiences. Charles Guggenheim interviews with Donald Hildenbrand, October 5, 1999, and June 3, 2000, transcripts.

86 "I was politically aware": Charles Guggenheim interview with Ernest Kinoy, July 12, 1999, transcript.

86 Jack Goldstein: Charles Guggenheim interview with Jack Goldstein, March 10, 1999, transcript.

87 "I figured in the end": Author's telephone interview with David Barlow, July 28, 2003.

87 Peter Iosso: Charles Guggenheim interview with Peter Iosso, March 23, 2000, transcript.

88 "refused to single out Jews for segregation": See p. 3 of the U.S. War Department report, in the "Religion" section.

88 "sent to a work detachment in the Leipzig area": Ibid., described in the "Work" section.

89 Edward Charles Mayer: Testimony given to war-crimes investigators, Conshohocken, Pennsylvania, May 24, 1945, National Archives and Records Administration.

89 "I was working in the American personnel office": Arthur A. Boucher wrote to the Vogel law firm from Niagara Falls, N.Y. Boucher said he was

only removed at the last minute from the list of prisoners destined for Berga. He concluded, "Hoping justice will be made." The letter was sent in response to the postwar investigation of Bernard Vogel, a New York lawyer whose nephew died on the death march from Berga. It was provided to Charles Guggenheim, who sent it on to the author.

90   "Just as the men had been placed in the cars": Author's interviews with Joe Littell, July 20, 2003, and February 15, 2004.

91   "Some of the people were from families": Charles Guggenheim interview with Ernest Kinoy, July 12, 1999, transcript.

92   Winter's goal: Author's interview with Joachim Winter, August 2001, Bad Orb.

CHAPTER FIVE: PRAYER BOOK AND SWORD

93   Mordecai Hauer: The account of Hauer's Auschwitz and Jawischowitz experiences is based entirely on the author's interview with Hauer, March 30, 2002, and on Hauer's unpublished memoir.

94   *"We will now process"*: Josef Mengele's words, as recalled by Mordecai Hauer in his memoir.

105 "Common to all Lagers": Primo Levi, *The Drowned and the Saved* (New York: Vintage Books, 1989), p. 98.

CHAPTER SIX: WALKING SHADOWS

125 As Sanford M. Lubinsky: Sanford Lubinsky's recollections in this chapter based on author's interview with Lubinsky, July 27, 2002, Casselberry, Florida.

125 The barracks closest to the gate: On segregation of Jewish GIs at Berga, see John W. Reifenrath, *An American Slave in Nazi Germany*, edited and published by Stalag IX-A, IX-B, and XIII-B and Berga am Elster [*sic*] Association, p. 20. He wrote: "The first group to work was from the barracks nearest to the gate. This barracks included all those of Jewish faith." See also Charles Guggenheim interview with Hans Kasten, June 4, 2000: "When we went to Berga one of the buildings was, they were all Jewish boys and the one I was in, there weren't any Jewish." Stanley Cohen, a captured GI, also spoke of this segregation in testimony to war-crimes investigators at Camp Lucky Strike, France, June 1, 1945. "Yes," Cohen testified, "the Jewish boys were segregated into one barracks. There were eighty Jewish boys who started out from Bad Orb, Germany." National Archives and Records Administration.

125 lit up the night sky: Joe Littell describes the night sky lighting up over Dresden in his interview with Charles Guggenheim, October 6, 1999.

133 he addressed Stolon in Yiddish: Charles Guggenheim interviews with Milton Stolon, March 8, 2000, and July 1, 2000, transcripts.

133 Hauer tried to ignore the pain: Moredecai Hauer's recollections in this

chapter are from the author's interview with Hauer, March 30, 2002, and from Hauer's unpublished memoir.

137 Shapiro could not get used to the hangings: William Shapiro's recollections in this chapter are from the author's interviews with Shapiro, July 27, 28, and 29, 2002, Boca Raton, Florida; from Shapiro's unpublished war memoir "My Awakening," written in 1998; and from Charles Guggenheim interviews with Shapiro, March 16, 2000, and July 1, 2000, transcripts.

140 a man of vindictive cruelty: The portrait of Sergeant Erwin Metz comes from numerous prisoners and from the war-crimes testimony of Stephen J. Schweitzer (London, May 29, 1945), Marcel Ouimet (Lake Placid, N.Y., August 8, 1945), Leon C. Trachtman (Paris, June 11, 1945), Norman Martin (Paris, May 5, 1945, and Halloran General Hospital, Willow Brook, N.Y., November 13, 1945), and other American prisoners. Two German guards at Berga—Kurt Seifert (Bad Dürrenberg, Germany, June 17, 1945) and Otto Rittermann (Berga, June 4, 1945)—also provided accounts of Metz's harsh treatment of the American prisoners. The record of his previous convictions appears in his appeal for early release in 1954. National Archives and Records Administration.

140 "a wonderful tongue": On Rosen's death, testimony of Stanley Cohen.

141 Private David Goldin: David Goldin's diary, made available to the author; author's interview with David Goldin, July 29, 2001, Deerfield Beach, Florida; and Goldin testimony to war-crimes investigators, May 31, 1945, at Camp Lucky Strike, France, National Archives and Records Administration.

141 Private David Young: Cohen testimony; Trachtman testimony; and testimony of Irving Pastor (Falmouth, Massachusetts, October 3, 1945), National Archives and Records Administration. Trachtman said of Young's death: "Metz, our Commando leader, after we pleaded with him to leave Young in bed, dragged him out and made him stand at attention. He repeatedly slapped and punched him until Young collapsed. At this point Metz dashed cold water in his face and ordered us to put him back in bed. A few minutes later, Young died."

142 Kurt Seifert: Seifert testimony to American war-crimes investigators, Bad Dürrenberg, June 17, 1945, National Archives and Records Administration.

142 Shapiro and Acevedo worked together: Tony Acevedo's diary, made available to the author; author's telephone interview with Acevedo, January 26, 2004; and Charles Guggenheim interviews with Acevedo, October 6, 1999, and June 3, 2000, transcripts.

148 Morton Brooks: Author's interview with Morton Brooks, July 29, 2002, Boynton Beach, Florida.

149 "The general appearance of all the bodies": Dr. Herman Bolker, testimony to war-crimes investigators, Bad Dürrenberg, Germany, June 18, 1945, National Archives and Records Administration.

149 "The whole situation": Dr. Rudolf Miethe, testimony to war-crimes investigators at Berga, June 7, 1945, National Archives and Records Administration.

149 Ernest Kinoy: Charles Guggenheim interview with Ernest Kinoy, July 12, 1999, transcript.

150 Acevedo, who had trained briefly as a medical technician: Acevedo diary, provided to author.

150 Stanley Cohen watched: Stanley Cohen testimony to war-crimes investigators at Camp Lucky Strike, France, June 1, 1945, National Archives and Records Administration.

150 Private Paul Van Horne: Paul Van Horne, testimony to war-crimes investigators, Crestline, Ohio, August 3, 1945, National Archives and Records Administration.

151 Private Norman Martin: Norman Martin, testimony to war-crimes investigators, National Archives and Records Administration.

151 Morton Goldstein's corpse: Testimony of Anny Neusser to war-crimes investigators, Tschirma, Germany, June 4, 1945, and of Walter Zschaeck, Berga, June 3, 1945, National Archives and Records Administration; Acevedo diary entry, March 20, 1945.

153 Otto Rittermann: Otto Rittermann testimony given to American war-crimes investigators in Berga, National Archives and Records Administration.

154 Marianna Schmidt: Author's interview with Marianna Schmidt in Berga, August 8, 2001.

154 Gertrud Pecher: Author's interview with Gertrud Pecher in Berga, August 8, 2001.

154 Lieutenant Bruno Dombeck . . . and the chief guard, Randi Schimmel: Heike Kegel, *Diplomarbeit*, May 1990, unpublished.

CHAPTER SEVEN: WEASELS IN A HOLE

159 SS Lieutenant Willy Hack: The account of the escape of Kasten, Littell, and Sinner is based on the author's telephone interviews with Hans Kasten, July 20 and 21, 2003, and Charles Guggenheim interview with Kasten, June 4, 2000, transcript; author's telephone interview with Littell, July 20, 2003, and interview on February 15, 2004, in Fallbrook, California. See also Joseph F. Littell, *A Lifetime in Every Moment* (New York: Houghton Mifflin, 1995).

163 Private Donald Hildenbrand: Hildenbrand's recollections in this chapter are based on the author's telephone interview with Hildenbrand, February 4, 2004, and interviews by Charles Guggenheim, October 5, 1999, and June 3, 2000, transcripts.

164 John W. Reifenrath: John W. Reifenrath, *An American Slave in Nazi Germany*, written in 1997, edited by Pete House, published by Stalag IX-A, IX-B, XIII-B and Berga am Elster [*sic*] Association.

165 Sidney Lipson: Author's interview with Sidney Lipson, July 29, 2002, Lake Worth, Florida.

165 Leo Zaccaria: Charles Guggenheim interviews with Leo Zaccaria, July 14, 1999, and January 7, 2001, transcripts.

165 David Goldin: Author's interview with David Goldin, July 29, 2001, Deer-field Beach, Florida.

166 "It was written down": Charles Guggenheim interview with Ernest Kinoy, July 12, 1999, transcript.

166 "More planes came over today": Acevedo diary, made available to author.

166 Stephen J. Schweitzer: Sworn testimony given by Stephen J. Schweitzer, May 29, 1945, London, to American war-crimes investigators, p. 8, National Archives and Records Administration.

167 Gerald Daub: Charles Guggenheim interview with Gerald Daub, March 22, 2000, transcript.

171 But for William Shapiro: Author's interviews with William J. Shapiro, July 27, 28, and 29, 2002, Boca Raton, Florida.

174 Sydney L. Goodman: Goodman diary, made available to the author by his family.

174 Stanley B. Cohen: Stanley B. Cohen, testimony to war-crimes investigators at Camp Lucky Strike, France, June 1, 1945, National Archives and Records Administration.

175 Paul Frenkel: Author's telephone interview with Paul Frenkel, February 6, 2004.

176 his older brother, Gabriel: Author's telephone interviews with Gabriel Frenkel, February 10 and 24, 2004.

177 Josef Mengele: The encounter with Mengele was recalled by both Frenkel brothers.

178 numbers 752 and 753: List of prisoners on the December 13, 1944, transport from Buchenwald to Berga provided by Paul Frenkel.

179 To Gabriel, who labored beside the tunnels: Author's telephone interviews with Gabriel Frenkel, February 10 and 24, 2004.

CHAPTER EIGHT: THE DYING WEEKS

186 Sanford Lubinsky gazes at the restless water: Sanford Lubinsky's recollec-tions in this chapter are based on the author's interview with Lubinsky, July 27, 2002, Casselberry, Florida.

189 That night, in silence: On June 9, 1945, as part of Major Fulton C. Vowell's American investigation of war crimes at Berga, Major Herman Bolker of the U.S. Army Medical Corps retraced the steps of the death march, village by village, grave by grave. He was questioned on June 18, 1945, at Bad Dürrenberg, Germany. His testimony provides critical details of the march, including the precise locations of deaths and, in several cases, their causes. National Archives and Records Administration.

189 Private George A. Tabele: Sworn testimony provided by George A. Tabele to American war-crimes investigators at Villejuif, France, June 2, 1945, National Archives and Records Administration.

190 Mordecai Hauer is on the move again: The account of the death march of the Europeans is based on the author's interview with Mordecai Hauer,

March 30, 2002; Hauer's unpublished memoir of his war experiences; and the author's interviews with Paul Frenkel (February 6, 2004) and Gabriel Frenkel (February 10 and 24, 2004).

193   The death of a fourth GI, Chester Vincent: The death of Chester Vincent was recorded in the diaries of Tony Acevedo (number 26 on list) and Sydney L. Goodman (number 28 on list), but his name does not appear on the list compiled by Bolker when he retraced the course of the march and met with German officials in the various towns and villages.

193   Private Israel Cohen collapses: For Cohen's death, see Norman Martin testimony to war-crimes investigators, November 13, 1945, Halloran General Hospital, Willow Brook, N.Y.; also sworn statement of Marcel R. Ouimet, April 22, 1945, at Marktredwitz, Germany; both in National Archives and Records Administration.

193   "Nothing to eat": Otto Rittermann testimony provided to war-crimes investigators, June 4, 1945, at Berga, National Archives and Records Administration.

194   Tony Acevedo watched Vogel: Author's telephone interview with Tony Acevedo, January 26, 2004.

194   On April 12 he struck Norman Martin: Norman Martin testimony to war-crimes investigators, May 5, 1945, in Paris, National Archives and Records Administration.

194   had the ten bodies transported to the cemetery: Kurt Seifert testimony to war-crimes investigators, June 17, 1945, at Bad Dürrenberg, Germany, National Archives and Records Administration.

195   On April 13 the bitter news: Author's interviews with William J. Shapiro, July 27, 28, and 29, Boca Raton, Florida.

196   Andres Pickart and Hans Grieshammer: The behavior of Pickart and Grieshammer is described in Seifert's testimony.

196   "We began to dig the grave": See Max Zippel sworn statement to American war-crimes investigators, June 12, 1945, Kaiserhammer, Germany, National Archives and Records Administration.

197   "Beat them if they don't walk": See Seifert's testimony, National Archives and Records Administration: "He [Grieshammer] hit him at least ten times and Metz was standing alongside and made no protest. Metz then turned to me and several of my companions and said, 'Beat them if they don't walk.' "

198   "On April 17, 1945, we were marching": Marcel R. Ouimet testimony taken by war-crimes investigators at Lake Placid Club, Essex County, N.Y., August 8, 1945, National Archives and Records Administration.

198   Stanley B. Cohen: Charles Guggenheim interview with Stanley B. Cohen, November 3, 1999, transcript.

198   John Griffin: Charles Guggenheim interview with John Griffin, July 14, 1999, transcript.

199   Milton Stolon: Charles Guggenheim interviews with Milton Stolon, March 8, 2000, and July 1, 2000, transcripts.

199   Donald Hildenbrand witnessed an angry confrontation: Author's telephone interview with Donald Hildenbrand, February 4, 2004.

199   at least thirty-one of the GIs: Bolker testimony and Seifert testimony. Gray's death described by Norman Fellman in telephone interview with the author, June 19, 2004.

200   He took off on a bicycle: Seifert testimony.

200   The Americans had stumbled on the macabre traces: The dead European Jews scattered on either side of the road were described in author's interviews with several survivors, including William J. Shapiro, July 27, 28, 29, 2002; Donald Hildenbrand, February 4, 2004; and Morton Brooks, July 29, 2002.

202   Stephen Schweitzer: Sworn testimony given by Stephen J. Schweitzer on May 29, 1945, in London to American war-crimes investigators, National Archives and Records Administration.

202   John Reifenrath: John W. Reifenrath, *An American Slave in Nazi Germany*, written in 1997, edited by Pete House, published by Stalag IX-A, IX-B, and XIII-B and Berga am Elster [*sic*] Association.

202   Hans Kasten: Hans Kasten's liberation and escapades were described in the author's telephone interviews with Kasten, July 20 and 21, 2003, and in Charles Guggenheim interview with Kasten, June 4, 2000, transcript. Joseph Littell describes his liberation in his memoir, *A Lifetime in Every Moment* (New York: Houghton Mifflin, 1995); in the author's telephone interview with Littell, July 20, 2003; and in the author's interview at Littell's home in Fallbrook, California, February 15, 2004.

205   Gerald Daub and his two closest friends: Author's telephone interview with Gerald Daub, March 4, 2004.

208   Bornkind is the forty-ninth and last American to perish: In a letter to war-crimes investigators, dated September 30, 1945, Sydney Goodman, who kept a diary, provided a list of the deaths at Berga and on the march. He described Bornkind as dying "five minutes before we were liberated by the 11th Armored Div." His list of the dead includes 69 names, the last of which is Bornkind. But the list omits deaths, including that of Gray, recorded by other sources, and the best estimate is that at least 73 Americans died.

209   To the last, Hitler pursued his demon: Hitler's final testament described in Joachim C. Fest, *Hitler* (London: Weidenfeld and Nicolson, 1974), p. 746.

215   Leo Zaccaria: Charles Guggenheim interviews with Leo Zaccaria, July 14, 1999, and January 7, 2001, transcripts.

CHAPTER NINE: ORDERS FROM NOWHERE

217   Herschel Auerbach: Charles Guggenheim interview with Herschel Auerbach, October 1, 1999, transcript.

217   The Gorinac family had been informed: Information on Edward Gorinac from his "Individual Deceased Personnel File," Department of the Army, provided by William J. Shapiro.

219   The United States War Crimes Branch: In addition to the army and the navy, the Office of the Judge Advocate General also had organizations investigating and processing war crimes worldwide. The War Crimes Branch had parallel organizations at its Washington headquarters and in overseas theaters of operations, including Europe, the Mediterranean, and the Pacific. War-crimes investigations were also undertaken by the United Nations. Here, the U.S. investigation operated out of the Office of the Chief of Counsel for War Crimes, sometimes referred to as the War Crimes Office for short.

220   Sanford Lubinsky: Author's interview with Sanford Lubinsky, July 27, 2002, Casselberry, Florida.

222   memorial service: Charles Guggenheim interview with Herschel Auerbach, October 1, 1999, transcript. A photograph was taken of the Star of David and the cross at the ceremony.

222   "What were your duties at Berga?": Metz interrogation in trial record of Erwin Metz and Ludwig Merz, National Archives and Records Administration.

225   When Gerald Daub returned to New York: Author's telephone interview with Gerald Daub, February 2, 2004.

226   Norman Fellman: Author's telephone interview with Norman Fellman, June 19, 2004. A copy of the oath Fellman signed was provided by Grace Guggenheim.

227   Vowell submitted his report on war crimes: The Vowell Report; trial record of Metz and Merz, National Archives and Records Administration.

229   "When one has become conversant with the facts": Copy of Vogel letter provided by Grace Guggenheim.

231   "twilight zone before death": Author's interview with William J. Shapiro, July 27, 2002.

233   The trial of Metz and Merz: The account of the trial is based chiefly on the trial record of Metz and Merz, which includes a voluminous written and photographic record of their capture, subsequent interrogations, the trial, and the long aftermath in which the two men sought and obtained clemency; National Archives and Records Administration.

236   Sergeant Howard P. Gossett: Testimony given to war-crimes investigators at Miami Beach, Florida, July 25, 1945.

236   Private Wesley Clayton Schmoke: Testimony given to an American special agent at Pittsburgh, Pennsylvania, July 23, 1945.

240   Joe Littell came home: Author's interview with Joseph Littell, February 15, 2004, Fallbrook, California.

242   The thorough elimination of the Nazi creed: Background on the changing American attitude to denazification and approach to the war-crimes trials from Tom Bower, *Blind Eye to Murder: Britain, America and the Purging of Nazi Germany—a Pledge Betrayed* (London: André Deutsch, 1981); Bower cites Royall's attitude on p. 311. The Churchill speech is from October 28, 1948, quoted by Bower.

243 Hans Globke: See Jan-Werner Muller, *Another Country: German Intellectuals, Unification, and Identity* (New Haven, Conn.: Yale University Press, 2000), p. 78.

243 "The thing that stands out in my mind most": Trial record of Metz and Merz, National Archives and Records Administration.

243 Stolon had given a forthright view of Metz: Milton Stolon statement to investigators, June 1, 1945, at Camp Lucky Strike, France, National Archives and Records Administration.

244 "In this case, unfortunately": Cantor correspondence and Clay's reply provided by Grace Guggenheim.

245 "Neither Mrs. Gray nor myself": Gray correspondence provided by Grace Guggenheim.

248 SS Lieutenant Willy Hack: From Heike Kegel, *Diplomarbeit*, May 1990, in the archive at Buchenwald.

EPILOGUE

250 André Matzke: Author's interview with André Matzke, August 8, 2001, Berga.

251 Klaus-Werner Jonas: Author's interview with Klaus-Werner Jonas, August 7, 2001, Berga.

255 "Under conditions of terror": Hannah Arendt, *Eichmann in Jerusalem: A Report on the Banality of Evil* (London: Penguin Books, 1994), p. 233.

255 Mordecai Hauer came back to Goncz: Author's interview with Mordecai Hauer, March 30, 2002, and Hauer's unpublished memoir.

258 Bach was born in Germany: Author's interview with Gabriel Bach, February 2001, Jerusalem.

263 "We are pleased to inform you": A copy of Shapiro's letter was made available to the author.

267 Jozef Molschmann: Author's interview with Jozef Molschmann, June 8, 2002, Demmelsdorf, Germany.

THE BERGA PRISONERS

The following is an approximate list of American prisoners held at Berga. The names of the seventy-three dead are italicized.

This list cannot be regarded as definitive. It represents a best effort, using all available sources, to establish who was at Berga and who among the prisoners died. The two main sources are a German list written out by hand at the time the prisoners were moved from Stalag IX-B to Berga, and a typed American list later made from it and initially classified as confidential after the war. The main problem is that the German list is smudged, often unclear, and written by at least four Germans—the scripts vary—who are struggling with American names. The American copying this list had problems doing so; several question marks on his roster reflect the difficulties of his task. A few question marks already appeared on the German list. I have retained them wherever some doubt remains. In the few cases where a name is completely illegible, I have used an initial.

The list here is based on several sources, including Anthony Acevedo's accounting of the dead, a list of the dead compiled by Sydney Goodman, the war account of John Reifenrath, and other material. My goal was to correct names on the two lists where possible, and to ensure all known dead were included. The chief source is the original German list, whose partly Gothic and partly Latin scripts were clearly misread in several places by the American copying it.

There are anomalies of numbering on both lists that are rectified here. There were 350 prisoners sent to Berga. Arthur A. Boucher, working in the American personnel office at Stalag IX-B in February 1945, wrote in 1946 that he had received "travel orders for the 350 men." So it proved to be.

1. Slotkin, Edward
2. Feinberg, William
3. Philosoph, Benjamin
4. Salkain, Samuel
5. Black, Samuel
6. Swack, Myron
7. *Goldstein, Morton*
8. *Ascher, Arnold*
9. Silberstein, Harold
10. *Domb, Leonard*
11. Pastor, Irving
12. Levine, Henry
13. *Snyder, George*
14. Leinberg, M.
15. Kinoy, Ernest
16. *Rothman, Milton*

17. *Rosen, Arthur*
18. Cohen, Stanley (09/29/25)
19. Feldman, Alfred
20. *Cohen, Israel*
21. Schulman, Morris
22. Gerenday, George
23. *Vogel, Bernard*
24. Hoffman, Bernard
25. Rosenberg, Winfield
26. Blains, Araul
27. Goldstein, Jack
28. Boseman, Samuel
29. Shapiro, William
30. Silverman, Morton
31. Kessel, Frank
32. Rosenberg, Aaron
33. Abrams, Alvin
34. *Wagner, Charles*
35. Fahrer, Samuel
36. Gritz, Marvin
37. Martin, Norman
38. *Goldberg, Howard*
39. Zimand, Gerald
40. Goodman, Sydney
41. Stolon, Milton
42. Dantowitz, Philip
43. Diamant, Alexander
44. Melnick, Bernard
45. Benjamin, Max
46. *Wildman, Leo*
47. Sweet, Alvin
48. *Schultz, Julius*
49. *Cantor, Jerome*
50. Markowitz, Joseph
51. Caplan, Bernard
52. *Kornetz, Milton*
53. Becker, Max
54. Fridman, Arthur
55. Lubinsky, Sanford
56. Levkow, Harry
57. Steckler, Daniel
58. Reyner, Alan
59. *Kessler, Robert*
60. Lipson, Sidney
61. Sedrish, Murray
62. Cohen, Stanley (07/26/25)
63. Daub, Gerald
64. Rudnick, Robert
65. Cohen, Seymour
66. Morrison, Julius
67. Trachtman, Leon
68. Fellman, Norman
69. Adler, Arnold
70. Linet, Harry
71. Filler, Milton
72. Weissberg, Alexander
73. Goldin, David
74. Brimberg, Morton
75. *Rubenstein, Stanley*
76. *Millstone, Seymour*
77. *Bornkind, Jack*
78. Van Horne, Paul
79. Jerome, Albert
80. *Humphrey, Richard*
81. Bikultouss ?, Edward
82. Dove, Alwin
83. Abeel, Lavern
84. Combador, Angelo
85. Sullivan, Robert
86. *Gilmore, Jim*
87. Christensen, James
88. Iosso, Peter
89. *Clark, Charles*
90. Juvato, William
91. Camarda, Vincent
92. Littell, Joseph
93. Newman, Frank
94. *Hanson, George*
95. Suter, Leroy
96. Marolla, Edward
97. *Scruggs, Wiley*
98. Ballard, John
99. Wells, Karl
100. Spagnola, Richard
101. *Morabito, Charles*
102. *Deaver, Raymond*
103. Edgar, Joseph
104. Bustamante, Asabel
105. Zaccaria, Leo
106. Sohol, Steve

107. Ford, James
108. Magliocco, Joseph
109. Zamora, Juan
110. Sniegocki, Chester
111. Zebrowski, Thomas
112. Sinner, Ernest
113. Enriquez, Francisco
114. *Knierth, Jessie*
115. *Sincox, John*
116. Geyer, Ellie
117. Tillton, G.
118. Horton, Robert
119. Babcock, Wright
120. *Anchorstar, Gustav*
121. Dougherty, James
122. *Breum, Charles*
123. Marck, Cheaira ?
124. Dubois, Johnny
125. *Cooper, Edward*
126. *Young, Louis*
127. Abbott, Henry
128. Muehlenback, Clyde
129. Milton, Ellsworth
130. Porter, Harry
131. Bunch, David
132. Hanion, Karl
133. Gabriel, Joseph
134. Kay, Raymond
135. Mento, William
136. *Vincent, Chester*
137. Michaels, James
138. Roper, Edward
139. *Johnson, Alfred*
140. Howell, Elbert
141. Stuart, Arthur
142. Madoals ?, Edward
143. Magruder, Henry
144. Lee, Edgar
145. Mop ?, W.
146. Hanley, Christian
147. Nagel, Eugene
148. Eaton, Floyd
149. Grindale, Ernest
150. Varnalda, Desmond
151. Ofzourts ?, George

152. Hall, Wendell ?
153. Corning ?, William
154. Hale, Harry
155. Heron, Joseph
156. *Gorinac, Edward*
157. Selby, Edward
158. Bibber, Albert
159. Martinez, Ruvan ?
160. Hoovide, John
161. Boon, Charles
162. Coodam ?, Wallace ?
163. Stapley, Franklin
164. Paston, Mercer
165. Green, Edward
166. Doliogg ?, Richards
167. Madigan, William
168. Adams, John
169. Carter, George
170. *Haughton, Fred*
171. Madeb, Juan
172. *Land, Joseph A., Jr.*
173. Harrington, Charles
174. *Fladzinski, Frank*
175. Claffy, George
176. Leon, Homer
177. Miller, Leo
178. Branson, John
179. Mycos ?, Carl
180. Ouimet, Marcel
181. Katumaris, Costa
182. Kanz, Harold
183. Eckenfeld, Harold
184. Watkins, James
185. Schweitzer, Stephen
186. *Weller, John*
187. *Lahn, Harry*
188. Gillette, Lawrence
189. Stone, Ray
190. *Best, Leo*
191. Czaray, Stanley
192. Drago, Anthony
193. Gillom, Eugene
194. Penn, John
195. Kember, John
196. Drooden ?, George

197. Bobonido, Tonelo
198. Harold, Milton
199. Bowel, William
200. Jenkins, Hayward
201. *Cullina, James*
202. Potts, Albert
203. *Strada, Ernest*
204. Graves, Oliver
205. Wozniak, Walter
206. Minowski, Alexander
207. Stranahan, Norman
208. Gorro ?, Lonnie
209. Phillips, Thomas
210. Bray, Charlie
211. Hunter ?, Charles
212. *Arndt, Arthur*
213. Gorso, Rosario
214. Patrick, Dale
215. Ryan, John
216. Campbell, Everett
217. Puminy, Leroy
218. Porter, Vernon
219. Butler, Robert
220. *Lonergan, Vincent*
221. Reader, Donald
222. *Greene, Joseph*
223. *Willis, Marvin*
224. Lamb, Robert
225. *Rogers, Walter*
226. Cartwright, William
227. *Rowe, Donald*
228. *Stewart, Hamish*
229. *Christiansen, Ray*
230. Lang, William
231. *Millsap, Hardy*
232. Dowell, Samuel
233. Rheoffer ?, Carl
234. Erwin, Walter
235. Farnsworth, Russel
236. Puty ?, Stanley
237. Sloan, Carl
238. Peterson, Harold
239. Davenport, Willy
240. Dambrosia, Albert
241. Williams, Edison

242. Hart, Harold
243. Turner, Charles
244. Want, Martin
245. Hutchison, Samuel
246. *Burdeski, George*
247. Sensel, Harvey
248. *Gaines, John*
249. Widdicombe, Robert
250. *Breeding, Advil*
251. Biby, Charles
252. Cantu, Cesar
253. *Hamilton, James*
254. Quinn, Thomas
255. *Smith, Merle*
256. Fowler, Tommy
257. Moser, Roy
258. Bingham ?, Erwin
259. *Levitt, Ralph*
260. Poore, Fred
261. Hoorwar ?, Edmond
262. Fellows, John
263. Vincent, Edward
264. Rhodes, Russel
265. Miller, William
266. Cortez, Alex
267. McGrath, John
268. Tudman, Gardner ?
269. Carter, Charles
270. Ramsay, John
271. Urwan, Anthony
272. Wood, Joseph
273. Kent, William
274. *Berthiaume, Albert*
275. *Young, David*
276. Tabele, George
277. Martin, Russel
278. Evans, Robert
279. John, Richard
280. Poallo, Emil
281. Rosenfeld, Leo
282. *Rhlagar, Joseph*
283. Healy, Douglas
284. Pugalo, Joseph
285. *Vensel, Clarence*
286. Dondero, Arthur

287. Barron, James
288. Heal ?, James
289. *Maxwell, William*
290. Dalessio, Joseph
291. Reifenrath, John
292. Walker, Robert
293. Jinston, Jacob
294. Gusso, Robert
295. Ballinger, John '
296. Connors, John
297. Kerchner, Jessi
298. *Claffy, Robert*
299. *Zaragoza, Orazio*
300. Friend, Raymond
301. *Jahr, Clarence*
302. Gray, David
303. Courts, Effie
304. Willifort, Clifford
305. Masiel, Juan
306. Gonzalez, Andrew
307. *Stephens, Clifford*
308. Cram, Louis
309. Frederickson, Paul
310. Crawford, Otis
311. Guigno, Joseph
312. *Kelly, William*
313. Fish ?, Barney ?
314. Mareillon, Joseph
315. Griffin, John
316. *Wilson, Charles*
317. Thomson, Grant ?
318. Capps, Paul

319. Hildenbrand, Donald
320. Penton, Oscar
321. Acevedo, Anthony
322. Lane, Robert
323. Anderlich, Raleigh
324. Hobart, Harrison
325. Rosso, Joseph
326. Bean, John
327. Frew, Robert
328. Dodson, William
329. *Schmeiser, Fredrich*
330. *Parkin, Robert*
331. Cook, Arlie
332. *Johnson, Russell W.*
333. Dasher, Alfred
334. Wiggins, George
335. Fuller, Granville
336. Miller, John
337. Cobien, Walter
338. Aquidar, Jesus
339. Mulherin, Daniel
340. Dowdell, Andrew
341. Rabin, Arthur
342. Kulas, Edward
343. Morris, Russell
344. *Gray, Robert*
345. Kitzman, Willfried ?
346. West, Melburn
347. Riley, Thomas
348. *Osborn, Lawrence*
349. Hunt, Howard
350. Kasten, Johann

ACKNOWLEDGMENTS

This book grew out of a chance encounter toward the end of my three-year tour as *New York Times* bureau chief in Berlin. The meeting was with Charles Guggenheim, a documentary filmmaker then researching the largely forgotten story of Berga that I have told here. Charles died in 2002, but not before he had completed his movie *Berga: Soldiers of Another War*, and not before he had convinced me that in the article I had written for the *Times* on the imprisoned GIs lay the germ of something bigger. My debt to Charles is great, for the volumes of research he made available to me, but above all for the inspiration of his quiet humanity and courage. At the Web site www.gpifilm.com, more information may be found on his remarkable film.

To his daughter, Grace, aptly named, I also owe a lot. Her diligence and dedication in pursuing this project went way beyond the call of duty. She and her company, Guggenheim Productions, did the photographic research for the book and provided the photos.

Charles's film was an inspiration, but the book I have written here differs in substantial respects from the movie. In particular, I chose to tell in detail the story of Mordecai Hauer, a Hungarian Jew who ended up in the same camp as the GIs. I am indebted to Mordecai for his generous and unstinting assistance.

The stories of the survivors of Berga lie at the heart of this book. A number of them helped me in sustained ways. They include William Shapiro, Sanford Lubinsky, Joe Littell, Hans Kasten, Gerald Daub, Donald Hildenbrand, Sidney Lipson, Tony Acevedo, Morton Brooks, Norman Fellman, Gabriel Frenkel, Paul Frenkel, and the late David Goldin. I thank each of these remarkable men.

Stephanie Akin did research in Buchenwald, Berga, Greiz, Bad Orb, and elsewhere. Her contribution to this book is deep and substantial, and she has my enduring gratitude.

I would like to thank Ali Oshinsky, who worked closely with Grace and Charles on the Berga movie. Her research was of critical assistance. Victor Homola in the Berlin Bureau of *The New York Times* was always efficient, always helpful. Selma Kalousek cleared up some important details relating to Czech history. Sabine Richter in Berga provided fine hospitality and welcome assistance. Nicola

Letzke and Haidi Kuhn Segal checked the German. Conversations with Fritz Stern and Charles Maier informed my understanding of Germany. A warm salute, also, to my many friends on the Foreign Desk of *The New York Times* and elsewhere at the paper.

In Jon Segal, my editor, and Amanda Urban, my agent, I am blessed to have two of the most remarkable professionals in publishing.

It is the lot of an author's family to be patient. The patience shown by mine has been of an unreasonable generosity. I thank my children—Jessica, Daniel, Blaise, and Adele. I thank my uncle and my sister and my father. I blow a tender kiss to my late mother. To my wife, Frida, goes the last word. She sustained me, despite everything, through everything, an act of love.

INDEX

Acevedo, Tony, 262
    at Berga/Elster camp, 142, 150, 152,
        166, 173, 174, 182–3
    death march of April 1945, 189, 194,
        200, 207
Adenauer, Konrad, 243
Amber Room, 250–1
American Slave in Nazi Germany, An
        (Reifenrath), 32–4
Andras, 45–6
Arendt, Hannah, 254–5
Army Specialized Training Program
        (ASTP), 24, 27, 29
Arndt, Arthur, 150, 195
Arrow Cross movement, 46
Ascher, Arnold, 196
Auerbach, Herschel, 217, 221, 222, 228
Auschwitz-Birkenau camp, 9, 59, 60,
        176, 177
    Hauer's stay at, 93–8
    transport of prisoners to, 64, 66

Bach, Gabriel, 258–61
Bach, Robert, 261
Bad Orb, Germany, 67
Bamm, Peter, 61
Barcsai, 54–5
Barlow, David, 87, 88
bats, 250

Battle of the Bulge, 7, 24–6, 27–8,
        29–33, 34–5, 68–9, 76–7, 132
Becker, Sharon, 58, 62, 63, 64, 257
Berg, Jakob and Clara, 267
Berga (town), 4–6, 16–17, 251
Berga/Elster camp
    administrators of, 6, 10, 140
    Amber Room rumor regarding,
        250–1
    American forces' arrival at, 217
    arrivals of prisoners, 125, 153–4
    beatings of prisoners, 138–9, 147–8,
        149–50, 151, 153, 165, 166–7, 189
    concentration-camp prisoners for,
        9–10
    construction of, 6
    contacts between American and
        European prisoners, 14–15, 148,
        156–8, 175, 180
    daily life at, 11–13
    deaths of prisoners, 3–4, 7, 8, 13–14,
        140, 141–2, 148–51, 154, 172, 179
    dehumanization of prisoners, 167–8
    differing perspectives of American
        and European prisoners, 155–6,
        157–8
    escape and recapture of Kasten
        group, 160–2, 168–71
    executions of prisoners attempting
        escape, 151–3, 174
    facilities for prisoners, 14, 125
    food detail, 138, 139

Berga/Elster camp *(continued)*
   food shortage, 143–4, 153
   German civilians' awareness of
      camp conditions, 7, 150, 154
   hangings of prisoners, 137, 138, 139
   health problems of prisoners, 142–3
   kitchen work, 175, 179
   last days at, 182–3
   map of, 128
   mass graves, 154
   medical attention for prisoners, 139,
      141, 149
   memorial service held at, 222
   Metz/Merz trial testimony about,
      234–6, 237
   Metz's cruel treatment of prisoners,
      139–40, 141–2, 151, 153, 173–4
   postwar uses, 15
   protests by prisoners, 159–60
   Red Cross packages for prisoners,
      172, 173–4
   selection of Americans for, 9–10, 32,
      80–1, 85–6, 87–90
   status today, 3, 14, 15, 250–2
   struggle for survival at, 162–5,
      179–80
   transfer of sick prisoners from, 171–2
   transport of prisoners to, 81, 90–1
   tunnel construction program, 3–4, 6,
      7, 125, 126–7, 132–3, 140–1, 147,
      148, 156, 160, 165–6, 179, 180, 182,
      250–1
   see also death march of April 1945;
      U.S. postwar activities regarding
      Berga
Bertha, 95
Best, Leo, 199
Binet, Mordecai, 41
Bloch brothers, 105–6
Bolker, Maj. Herman, 149, 228
Bornkind, Jack, 205, 206, 208, 225–6
Boucher, Arthur A., 89
Brabag Zeitz company, 9
Braun, Martin, 42

Breeding, Advil, 200
Breum, Charles, 195
British prisoners, 172, 173
Brooks, Morton, 82–3, 148, 202
Buchenwald camp, 6, 9, 123, 178,
      180–1, 184, 205
   Hauer's stay at, 136–7, 144–7
Buchmuller, Werner, 70
Burdeski, George, 194

Cantor, Dr. Jacob, 244, 245
Cantor, Jerome C., 150, 244
capture of American soldiers, 24–6,
      27–8, 29–33, 34–6, 68–9, 76–7,
      132
Christiansen, Ray, 198
Churchill, Winston, 242–3
Claffy, Robert J., 189
Clark, Charles H., 150–1
Clay, Gen. Lucius D., 244–5
Cohen, Israel, 193
Cohen, Stanley B., 141, 142, 150, 153,
      174, 198, 199, 202, 206, 237
cold war, 242–3, 248
compensation for survivors of Berga,
      220, 241, 263
Conder, Col. Raymond, 242
Conference on Jewish Material Claims
      Against Germany, 263
Cooper, Edward, 195
Cornell, Edwin, 27–8, 83–5, 86
Cullina, James E., 196

Dachau camp, 233
Danyi, Sardon, 266
Daub, Gerald
   at Berga/Elster camp, 148, 167
   capture of, 29–32

death march of April 1945, 194, 205,
206, 207, 208
postwar life, 225–6, 262, 263
prewar life, 28–9
at Stalag IX-B camp, 83
death, experience of, 187
death march of April 1945, 8
American prisoners, 186–90, 192–7,
198–202, 205–9
burials of dead prisoners, 194–5, 196,
198–9
deaths of prisoners, 189, 193, 194,
195, 196, 198, 199, 200, 208
escapes by prisoners, 200, 206,
210–12
European prisoners, 190–2, 197–8,
209–10, 214–15
executions of prisoners, 191–2, 197,
200–2, 212
German civilians' reaction to, 199,
205–6, 209, 210
hospitalization of prisoners, 199
liberation of prisoners by American
forces, 206–9
map of, 188
Metz/Merz trial testimony about,
224–5, 237–9
Metz's departure, 200
onset of, 184–5
Deaver, Raymond, 195
Demmelsdorf, Germany, 267–9
Domb, Leonard E., 194
Dombeck, Lt. Bruno, 154–5
Dresden, bombing of, 125, 171
Dudas, Laszlo, 266

Eichmann, Adolf, 42, 53
Hungarian Jews, deportation of,
59–60
Kassa inmates, address to, 58–9
trial of, 258–9

zeal for Jewish extermination
program, 260–1
Englander family, 5, 16–17
Erdos, 42
Esser, Maj. Fritz, 69–70, 90

Falkenhausen, Baron Hans von, 254
Faust (Goethe), 180–1
Fayger, Istvan, 266
Feinstein, Lazar, 267
Fellman, Norman, 226–7
Final Solution, *see* Jewish
extermination program
Fladzinski, Frank, 193
Fox, Sonny, 24–7, 83
Frankfurter, 64
Frenkel, Gabriel, 176, 177–81, 197,
214
Frenkel, Ida, 175, 177
Frenkel, Dr. Maurice, 176–7, 178
Frenkel, Paul, 175–9, 180, 191, 197,
214–15
Fried, Tibi, 54

Gaines, John, 193
Geilenberg, Edmund, 8–9
German prisoners in U.S.,
interrogation of, 68
Germany
compensation for survivors of Berga,
263
dealing with Nazi past, 23–4, 91–2,
251–5, 267–9
denazification program, 242–3
paradox of, 16–17
see also Nazi Germany
GI Bill of Rights, 225
Gillette, Lawrence, 206

Gilmore, Jim, 195
Glaessner, Philip, 39, 74–5
Globke, Hans, 243
Goethe, J. W. von, 180–1
Goldberg, Howard, 150
Goldin, David, 141, 165
Goldmann, Roza, 267
Goldstein, Jack, 86–7
Goldstein, Morton, 73
    execution of, 151–3, 223–4, 239–40,
        241, 244
Goncz, Hungary, 43, 255–6, 265–7
    roundup of Jews, 52–6
Goodman, Karen, 81
Goodman, Sydney L., 81–2, 174
Gorinac, Edward, 11–14, 147, 172
    family's search for remains of,
        217–20
Gossett, Sgt. Howard P., 236
Gray, Edwin A., 226, 245–6
Gray, Robert M., 199, 226–7, 245–6
Greene, Joseph, 199
Grieshammer, Hans, 174, 196
Griffin, John, 85, 87, 198
Grossman, Dr., 43, 44, 45
Guggenheim, Charles, 268

Hack, SS Lt. Willy, 81, 161, 228
    administration of Berga/Elster
        camp, 6, 10, 140
    background, 10
    capture and execution, 248
    Kasten's hunt for, 202–4
    marriage problem, 10–11
    Metz/Merz trial and, 236, 238
    protests by prisoners, rejection of,
        159–60
    recapture of Berga escapees, 170
Hamburger, Ferko, 54
Hans, 119
Hanson, George, 198

Hauer, Benji, 49, 50, 51, 94, 95, 96,
    97–8, 107, 257, 265
Hauer, Camilla, 41, 44, 49, 50, 51, 94,
    95, 98, 101, 255, 256–7, 264, 265,
    266
Hauer, David, 41, 43, 45, 101
    at Auschwitz-Birkenau camp, 94, 95,
        96, 97–8
    at Buchenwald camp, 136–7, 145
    death of, 145
    at Jawischowitz camp, 99, 104, 105,
        107–8, 112, 113–14, 115, 120, 122,
        123
    at Kassa detention center, 57
    march and train transport to
        Buchenwald camp, 133–6
    Passover with family in 1944, 50
    roundup of Jews of Goncz, 52–6
    transport to Auschwitz, 64
Hauer, Edith, 49, 51, 95, 264, 265
Hauer, Emerich, 49, 50, 51, 94, 95, 96,
    97–8, 107, 110, 113, 122, 123, 265
Hauer, Masha, 264, 265
Hauer, Mordecai
    air-raid shelter construction,
        112–13
    American prisoners, contacts with,
        156–8
    at Auschwitz-Birkenau camp,
        93–8
    beating and hanging of hometown
        friend, 45–6
    beatings of, 114–15
    at Berga/Elster camp, 153–8,
        184–5
    at Buchenwald camp, 136–7, 144–7
    care for father in camps, 98, 99, 104,
        105, 107–8, 113–14, 134–6, 145
    death march of April 1945, 184–5,
        190–2, 197, 209–10
    dreams of, 51–2, 66, 146
    escape from Germans, 210–12
    escape to Palestine opportunity,
        61–2

family life, 41–2, 43–4

German occupation of Hungary, 40–1, 42

head injury, 108–9

at Jawischowitz camp, 98–124

Jewish identity, 41

journey home after liberation, 213

journey home from occupied Budapest, 42–3, 46–9

at Kassa detention center, 56–9, 61–4

Katz's escape attempt and subsequent execution, 111–12, 114–20

kindness of some Germans, 109–10, 113–14

liberation by American forces, 212–13

march and train transport to Buchenwald camp, 133–6

"marriage" of, 63, 257

mining work, 102–3, 108–9

Passover with family in 1944, 49–51

personal qualities, 41, 44–5, 48

postwar life, 255–8, 264–7

refrigeration room imprisonment, 145–6

religious faith, 100–2, 106, 109, 120–1, 122, 192, 214

return to Hungary late in life, 265–7

roundup of Jews of Goncz, 52–6

Russians' detention of, 213–14

sexual initiation, 44

spinal injury, 264

"time on his side" realization, 110–11, 155

transport to Auschwitz, 64, 66

tunnel construction work, 156

wounding of, 211–12

Yankele's execution, 121–2

Haughton, Fred, 150

Heimann family, 267

Hildenbrand, Donald
   at Berga/Elster camp, 163–4, 174
   death march of April 1945, 199, 200, 202, 208
   selection for Berga, 85–6, 90

Himmler, Heinrich, 9, 29, 60, 68

Hitler, Adolf, 5, 8, 9, 24, 40, 59–60, 70, 238, 252, 259
   Jewish extermination program, dedication to, 209
   Kasten's meeting with, 75

Holocaust, *see* Jewish extermination program

Homer, Arthur J., 73–4

Horthy, Adm. Miklós, 60

Horton, Robert, 150

Höss, Rudolf, 60, 259

Hubel, Edeltraut, 91

Humphrey, Richard, 150

Hunter, Howard, 30, 31

Hürtgen Forest, Battle of, 20, 86, 131

Ilona, 47–50, 257

Iosso, Peter, 87

Jahr, Clarence, 193

Janek, 99–100, 104, 113, 115, 121, 123, 133, 136

Jawischowitz camp, 98–124
   air-raid shelter construction, 112–13
   arrival of prisoners, 98–100
   daily routine, 100
   evacuation of, 122–4
   inspections of prisoners, 104–5
   Katz's escape attempt and subsequent execution, 111–12, 114–20

Jawischowitz camp *(continued)*
  kindnesses toward prisoners, 109–10, 113–14
  mining operation, 102–3, 108–9
  Muselmann (prisoner close to death) designations, 105–6, 119–20
  religious disputes among prisoners, 101–2, 106–7
  violence toward prisoners, 103–4, 115
  Yankele's execution, 121–2
Jewish extermination program, 21, 23–4, 28–9, 40, 190
  American soldiers' understanding of, 201–2, 205
  Auschwitz-Birkenau camp, 93–8
  Buchenwald camp, 136–7, 144–7
  deportation of Hungarian Jews, 59–60, 176–7
  German civilians' failure to protest against, 61
  German government's determination regarding, 60–1
  Germans' general complicity in, 253–5
  Goncz memorial to Jewish dead, 266
  Hitler's dedication to, 209
  roundup of Jews of Goncz, 52–6
  Schmid's resistance to, 252–3, 254–5
  segregation of American Jewish prisoners, 71–2, 73–5, 79–85, 86–90, 132, 236–7, 247
  zealotry's role in, 258–61
  see also Berga/Elster camp; death march of April 1945; Jawischowitz camp
Jewish Theological Seminary and Teachers' Institute (Budapest), 41
Johnson, Alfred, Jr., 150
Johnson, Russell W., 194
Jonas, Klaus-Werner, 251
Juhasz, 52

Kahn, Siegfried, 29
Kardos family, 54, 56, 64, 66
Kassa detention center, 56–9, 61–4
Kasten, Johann "Hans"
  at Berga/Elster camp, 159–60
  capture of, 77
  escape from Berga and subsequent recapture, 160–2, 168–71
  Hitler, meeting with, 75
  hospitalization of, 204–5
  hunt for Hack, 202–4
  liberation of, 203
  military experiences prior to capture, 76–7
  postwar life, 262
  prewar life, 75–6
  at Stalag IX-B camp, 74, 75, 77–80, 87
  at Stalag IX-C camp, 171, 173, 183
  transport to Berga/Elster camp, 90
Katz, Israel, 102, 104, 106–7, 258
  escape attempt and subsequent execution, 111–12, 114–22
Kelly, William, 198, 230–1
Kessler, Robert E., 194
Kiefer, Anselm, 267
Kinoy, Ernest, 86, 90, 91, 149–50, 166
Kornetz, Milton, 195
Kornweitz, Bela, 54
Kowalsky, 102, 103, 108, 109, 111, 136
Kruly, Misha, 55
Kummen, Theresia, 91
Kunz, Sgt., 139, 237
Kupchinski, John, 76–7

Laczko, Father, 56
Land, Joseph A., Jr., 194
Leoncavallo, Ruggiero, 199
Levi, Primo, 24, 105
Levitt, Ralph, 198
Lipson, Sidney, 14–15, 165

Littell, Joe, 16
    at Berga/Elster camp, 159–60, 161
    escape from Berga and subsequent
        recapture, 161–2, 168–71
    German prisoners in U.S.,
        interrogation of, 68
    liberation of, 203, 205
    military experiences prior to
        capture, 68–9
    postwar life, 240–1, 262
    prewar life, 68, 69
    at Stalag IX-B camp, 67, 70, 71, 78,
        79, 80, 87
    at Stalag IX-C camp, 171, 172–3,
        183–4
    transport to Berga/Elster camp, 90
Littell, Nancy, 69–70
Lonergan, Vincent L., 189
Lubinsky, Clara Griffin, 130, 220
Lubinsky, Jennie, 129
Lubinsky, Max, 129
Lubinsky, Sanford M., 39
    at Berga/Elster camp, 4, 125, 126–7,
        132–3, 156
    capture of, 132
    death march of April 1945, 186–7,
        189, 190, 200, 202, 208
    hospitalization following liberation,
        216
    military experiences prior to
        capture, 130–2
    postwar life, 220–1, 262, 263–4
    prewar life, 127, 129–30
    at Stalag IX-B camp, 132
Lubinsky, Terry, 130, 220, 221
Lucius, 54, 56

Malmédy massacre, 233–4, 244
march and train transport to
    Buchenwald camp, 133–6
march of April 1945, *see* death march
    of April 1945

Marcus, David, 230
Margit, 44, 45, 46, 49, 51, 55
Marks, Joseph, 205, 206
Marks, William R., 263
Martin, Norman, 151, 193, 194, 246
Mathis, 103, 104, 106, 107, 115, 121
Matzke, André, 250
Maxwell, William, 194
Mayer, Edward Charles, 89
Mayer, Leo, 264
McCarty, Capt. Robert G., 223–4
McClelland, Pauline Gorinac,
    218–19
Mengele, Dr. Josef, 94–5, 177
Merz, Capt. Ludwig
    administration of Berga/Elster
        camp, 140
    death march of April 1945, 186,
        237–8
    see also trial of Metz and Merz
Metz, Sgt. Erwin, 193, 202
    cruel treatment of Berga prisoners,
        139–40, 141–2, 151, 153, 173–4
    death march of April 1945, 186, 187,
        189, 193, 194, 195, 196–7, 199,
        200, 224–5, 238–9
    Goldstein's execution, 152–3, 223–4,
        239–40, 241, 244
    prewar life, 140
    stupidity and sadism of, 200
    see also trial of Metz and Merz
Metz, Martha, 243
Miethe, Dr. Rudolf, 149, 152, 172
Millsap, Hardy, 196
Millstone, Seymour, 150
Molschmann, Jozef, 267–9
Morabito, George, 174
Muselmann (prisoner close to death)
    designations, 105–6, 119–20

Nagel, 12
Napranikova, Bozena, 212, 213

Nazi Germany
  Hungary, occupation of, 40–1, 42
  synthetic-fuel production program,
    8–9
  see also Jewish extermination
    program; *specific camps*
Neusser, Anny, 151, 152, 224

Osborn, Lawrence, 196
Ouimet, Marcel, 193, 198

Pagliacci (Leoncavallo), 199
Parkin, Robert, 195
Pastor, Irving, 141–2
Pecher, Gertrud, 154
Pickart, Andres, 196

Quint, Werner, 172–3, 183–4

rage of former prisoners, 215–16
Reifenrath, John W., 32–4, 164, 166,
    202
Reisman, Imre, 266–7
Reiss, Jeno, 54
religious disputes among prisoners,
    101–2, 106–7
Rhlagar, Joseph, 193
Richter, Sabine, 15
Rigby, Lt. Col. Paul T., 228–9
Rittermann, Otto, 153, 193, 196
Rogers, Walter, 148–9
Rona, Dr., 43, 44

Roosevelt, Franklin D., 195, 225
Rosen, Arthur S., 140, 150
Rosenberg, Winfield, 229–30
Roth, Hermanne, 267
Rothman, Milton, 199
Rowe, Donald, 198
Royall, Kenneth, 242, 245, 246,
    247–8
Roys, Fred, 84, 85
Rubenstein, Stanley, 150, 226
Rudel, Gen. Gunther, 253, 254
Rudnick, Robert, 167, 205, 206,
    225
Russian prisoners, 70
Ryan, Laura M., 230–1

Sami, 191–2
Scharping, Rudolf, 253
Scheffel, Marie, 7
Schimmel, Randi, 155
Schmid, Sgt. Anton, 252–3, 254–5
Schmidt, Marianna, 154
Schmoke, Wesley Clayton, 236–7
Schramm, Norbert, 20
Schreiber, Baruch, 105, 134, 135, 136,
    210–11, 212
Schreiber, Samuel, 105
Schultz, Julius, 150
Schwarz, 131
Schweitzer, Stephen J., 38, 85, 139,
    166–7, 202
Scruggs, Wiley T., 150
Seifert, Kurt, 142, 153, 195, 196,
    200
Seltzer, Rabbi Shloime, 46
Shapiro, Betty, 22, 23, 231, 232
Shapiro, Jacob, 20
Shapiro, William J., 38
  at Berga/Elster camp, 137–9, 142–4,
    148, 151, 174–5
  capture of, 35–6

death march of April 1945, 192–4, 195, 199, 200, 201–2, 207
Holocaust survivor status, acknowledgment of, 262
Jewish identity, 21–2, 35
military experiences prior to capture, 18–20, 21–2, 34–5
postwar life, 22–4, 231–3, 261–2, 263
prewar life, 20–1
at Stalag IX-B camp, 72, 73, 74, 83
at Stalag IX-C camp, 171–2
Sieber, Col. Karl-Heinz, 70
Sincox, John, 150
Sinner, Ernst, 78, 90
  at Berga/Elster camp, 159, 160
  escape from Berga and subsequent recapture, 161–2, 168–9, 170–1
  liberation of, 203
  at Stalag IX-C camp, 171, 173, 183
Smith, Betty, 173
Smith, Lt. Joseph S., 230
Smith, Merle L., 194
Snyder, George, 13, 172
Sobibor camp, 9
Sorley, Lt. Col. Lewis, 247
Spender, Stephen, 16
Sperber, George, 199
Stalag IX-A camp, 71, 79
Stalag IX-B camp, 11
  Americans' arrival, 67, 70
  bartering of goods, 87
  deaths of prisoners, 78
  food shortage, 72–3
  killing of guards and subsequent reprisals, 85
  living conditions, 70–1, 78
  Red Cross inspections, 70, 78–9
  Russian prisoners, 70
  segregation of American Jewish prisoners, 71–2, 73–5, 79–85, 86–90, 132, 236–7, 247

  selection of Americans for Berga, 80–1, 85–6, 87–90
  status today, 91–2
  transport of prisoners to, 26–7, 28, 36, 38–9
Stalag IX-C camp, 13, 80, 170, 171–3, 183–4
  liberation of, 203
Steckler, Daniel, 83
Stevens, Clifford, 150
Stix family, 268
Stolon, Milton, 133, 147–8, 199, 243–4
Strada, Ernest, 193
Szálasi, Ferenc, 46

Tabele, George A., 189
Thälmann, Ernst, 15
Trachtman, Leon E., 140, 141
transport of prisoners
  to Auschwitz-Birkenau camp, 64, 66
  to Berga/Elster camp, 81, 90–1
  to Buchenwald camp, 136
  to Stalag IX-B camp, 26–7, 28, 36, 38–9
Treblinka camp, 9
Tree Grows in Brooklyn, A (Smith), 173
trial of Metz and Merz
  charges against defendants, 228, 234
  death march issue, 224–5, 237–9
  defense's case, 239
  Goldstein's execution issue, 223–4, 239–40, 241, 244
  guilty verdicts and death sentences, 242
  location for, 233
  Merz's testimony, 80, 235–6, 237–8, 242

trial of Metz and Merz *(continued)*
  Metz's pretrial interrogation, 222–5,
    228
  Metz's testimony, 234–5, 237,
    238–40, 241–2
  as military tribunal, 233–4
  prison terms served by Metz and
    Merz, 247–8
  prosecution's case, 234, 239
  reduction of death sentences on
    appeal, 243–7
  segregation of American Jewish
    prisoners issue, omission of,
    236–7, 247
Truman, Harry, 247
tunnel construction program, 3–4, 6, 7,
  125, 126–7, 132–3, 140–1, 147, 148,
  156, 160, 165–6, 179, 180, 182,
  250–1

U.S. postwar activities regarding Berga,
  14
  cold war considerations and, 242–3,
    248
  compensation for survivors issue,
    220, 241
  delays in, 228, 229, 240–1
  evidence-gathering for, 208–9,
    221–2
  government's position on Berga's
    status, 218
  memorial service held at Berga,
    222
  report on war crimes, 222–5,
    227–9
  Russian control of Berga area and,
    219
  search for prisoners' remains,
    217–20
  secrecy pledge imposed on survivors,
    227

segregation of American Jewish
    prisoners, investigation regarding,
    73–5, 88, 89
  Vogel investigation, 229–31
  see also trial of Metz and Merz

Van Horne, Paul Arthur, 150, 151, 243,
  244
Vensel, Clarence, 198
Veres, 256
Veterans Administration, 220
Vincent, Chester, 193
Vogel, Bernard J., 73, 89, 194, 229–30
Vogel, Charles, 229–31, 246
Vowell, Maj. Fulton C., 221, 222–3,
  224–5, 227, 228

Wagner, Charles, 194
Walker, Lt. Col. Edward, 247
War Crimes Branch, 73, 219, 228, 229,
  236
War Crimes Investigating Team 6822,
  217, 221
War Crimes Review Board, 244
Weber, Edmund, 109–10, 114, 122, 134,
  135
Weiss, Martin, 233
Weissman, Lasci, 54
Weller, John O., 196
Wertheim, Lea, 54, 66, 93
Widdicombe, Robert, 206
Wildman, Leo, 195
Willis, Marvin, 194
Wilson, Charles J., 189
Winter, Joachim, 92
Witsell, Maj. Gen. Edward F., 218, 219,
  229
Wurffel, 110, 113–14, 115, 123

Yankele, Reb, 101, 104, 106–7, 114, 119, 120–2, 258
   execution of, 121–2
Young, David, 141–2
Young, Edward H., 246
Young, Louis E., 189

Zaccaria, Leo, 165, 215–16
Zaragoza, Ernesto, 198
Zeitz camp, 178–9
Ziegenhain camp, 83, 87
Zippel, Max, 196
Zschaeck, Walter, 151–2, 153, 223

A NOTE ABOUT THE AUTHOR

Roger Cohen was foreign editor of *The New York Times* throughout the aftermath of the September 11, 2001, attacks. He joined the *Times* in 1990, covering the Bosnian war and serving as Paris correspondent and Berlin bureau chief. His prizewinning war coverage in Bosnia formed the basis of his acclaimed book *Hearts Grown Brutal: Sagas of Sarajevo.* During his tenure as foreign editor, *The New York Times* won a Pulitzer Prize for international reporting and two George Polk Awards. He is now the paper's international writer-at-large and a columnist for the *International Herald Tribune.* Mr. Cohen has also worked as a foreign correspondent for *The Wall Street Journal* and Reuters. His work has been recognized several times by the Overseas Press Club. He lives in New York City.

A NOTE ON THE TYPE

This book was set in a typeface called Walbaum. The original cutting of this face was made by Justus Erich Walbaum (1768–1839) in Weimar in 1810. The type was revived by the Monotype Corporation in 1934. Young Walbaum began his artistic career as an apprentice to a maker of cookie molds. How he managed to leave this field and become a successful punch cutter remains a mystery. Although the type that bears his name may be classified as modern, numerous slight irregularities in its cut give this face its humane manner.

COMPOSED BY NORTH MARKET STREET GRAPHICS, LANCASTER, PENNSYLVANIA

PRINTED AND BOUND BY BERRYVILLE GRAPHICS, BERRYVILLE, WEST VIRGINIA

DESIGNED BY ROBERT C. OLSSON

MAPS BY NATASHA PERKEL